An Introduction to Language

An Introduction to Language

Victoria Fromkin
University of California, Los Angeles

Robert Rodman
University of North Carolina, Chapel Hill

Holt, Rinehart and Winston, Inc.
New York, Chicago, San Francisco, Atlanta, Dallas
Montreal, Toronto, London, Sydney

To our spice
Jack and Joanne

Library of Congress Cataloging in Publication Data

Fromkin, Victoria.
  An introduction to language.

   1. Language and languages.   I. Rodman, Robert,
joint author.   II. Title.
P121.F75   410   73–16174

ISBN: 0–03–091995–9

Preface

A revolution in linguistics occurred in 1957 with the appearance of Chomsky's theory of transformational generative grammar. Since that time many textbooks have appeared which deal with language from this point of view. Yet when we searched for an appropriate text to be used in an introductory course for both linguistics and non-linguistics students we were unable to find one. No existing text was broad enough in scope, rich enough in content, and transformationally oriented. This book was designed to fill that need. It is directed toward students of many disciplines because the interest in human language is not limited to linguists.

The book aims to dispel a number of myths about language by dealing with questions such as these: What is language? What do you know when you know a language? Is language unique to man? Why are there many languages? How and why do languages change? Are some languages or dialects superior to others? What is the origin of language? How do children learn languages? Can machines talk? Some of these questions have been discussed for thousands of years. We believe this book is unique in that it discusses both historical and current views of these issues. In addition, it aims to provide more detailed information about the three main components of language—phonetics and phonology, semantics, and syntax—than is ordinarily found in an introductory text. In every section the universals which underlie the diversity of phenomena observed in human language are discussed.

We believe that language is the most unique of man's abilities and also the most complex. We have neither avoided the complexities nor "oversimplified" the concepts. Nonetheless, we have been primarily concerned with basic ideas rather than detailed exposition of the grammar of English or of any other language. The text assumes no previous knowledge on the part of the reader. Every technical term is explained; every new concept is exemplified. "Formalisms" are presented to enlighten, not to overwhelm, the student.

A good introductory text stimulates further investigation by the reader. Therefore, we have included a short bibliography at the end of each chapter.

For the purpose of further elaboration of the points made in each chapter, exercises are provided. These exercises, which range in difficulty from "easy" to "thought-provoking," are conceived to enhance the student's interest in and comprehension of the textual material.

We owe special thanks to the members of the UCLA faculty who have written and rewritten some of the exercises for introductory classes: Professors George Bedell, Peter Ladefoged, Breyne Moskowitz, Paul Schachter, and Sandra Thompson.   We are particularly grateful to Jacquelyn Schachter of the University of Southern California for sharing with us her insightful views on the nature of meaning.

Above all, we are grateful to the hundreds of students who have listened to our lectures, questioned our concepts, completed our assignments, and prodded us to write this book.

V.F.

R.R.

November, 1973

Contents

The ABCs of Language: Writing 280

12

The Gray Matter of Language: Language and the Brain 307

13

Language in the Computer Age 327

1
What Is Language?

When we study human language, we are approaching what some might call the "human essence," the distinctive qualities of mind that are, so far as we know, unique to man.

— NOAM CHOMSKY, *Language and Mind*

Whatever else people may do when they come together — whether they play, fight, make love, or make automobiles — they talk. We live in a world of words. We talk to our friends, our associates, our wives and husbands, our mothers and mothers-in-law; we talk to total strangers and to our adversaries. We talk face to face and over the telephone. And everyone responds to us with more talk. Television and radio further swell this torrent of words. As a result, hardly a moment of our waking lives is free from words. We talk even when there is no one to answer. We talk to our pets. We sometimes talk to ourselves. And we are the only animals that do this — that talk.

The possession of language, more than any other attribute, distinguishes man from other animals. To understand man's humanity one must understand the language that makes him human. According to the philosophy expressed in the myths and religions of many peoples, it is language which is the source of human life and power. To some people of Africa, a newborn child is a *kuntu,* a "thing," not yet a *muntu,* a "person." Only by the act of learning language does the child become a human being.[1] Thus according to this tradition, we all become "human" because we all know at least one language. But what is it that we know? What does it mean to "know" a language?

[1] Massa-Makan, Diabate, "Oral Tradition and Mali Literature," in *The Republic of Mali* (Mali Information Center).

1

LINGUISTIC KNOWLEDGE

When you know a language you are able to produce the sounds which signify certain meanings and understand the meanings of the sounds others produce. You know which sounds are part of the language and which are not and which sound may start a word, end a word, and follow each other. Even in pronouncing a "foreign" word you may (and usually do) substitute an English sound for a non-English sound. How many of you, for example, pronounce the name *Bach* as if it were spelled *bak?* The sound represented by *ch* in German is not an English sound. If you pronounce it as the Germans do, you are using a sound outside of the English sound system.

How do you pronounce the name of the former president of Ghana, the name spelled *Nkrumah?* In your pronunciation do you start this word with the sound represented by the spelling *ng,* as in the word *sing?* This is the way the Ghanaians pronounce it, but we doubt that you would. You probably add a short vowel before the *n* sound, for as a speaker of English, in which no word begins with the *ng* sound, you would not even think of beginning a word that way.

Besides knowing the sounds and sound sequences in your language, you know that certain sound sequences represent different things or "meanings." Language is therefore a system by which sounds and meanings are related. If you didn't know the language, the sounds you heard would mean nothing to you. This is because the relationship between speech sounds and the meanings they represent is, for the most part, **arbitrary.** You have to learn (when you are learning the language) that the sounds represented by the letters *house* stand for the concept

⌂ ; if you know French, this same concept is represented by

maison; if you know Twi, it is represented by *ɔdaŋ*; if you know Russian, by *dom;* if you know Spanish, by *casa.*

Similarly the concept 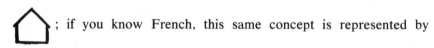 is represented by *hand* in English,

main in French, *nsa* in Twi, and *ruka* in Russian.

The following are words with definite meanings in some different languages. How many of them can you understand?

1. kyinii	4. asubuhi	7. wartawan
2. doakam	5. toowq	8. inaminatu
3. odun	6. bolna	9. yaawa

If you don't know the languages from which these words are taken, you undoubtedly don't know that they mean the following:

1. a large parasol (in a Ghanaian language, Twi)
2. living creature (in an American Indian language, Papago)
3. bridge (in Turkish)
4. morning (in Swahili)
5. is seeing (in a California Indian language, Luiseño)
6. to speak (in a Pakistani language, Urdu)
7. reporter (in Indonesian)
8. teacher (in a Venezuelan Indian language, Warao)
9. right on! (in a Nigerian language, Hausa)

These different words show that the sounds of words are only given meaning by the language in which they occur. The idea that something is called X because it looks like X or called Y because it sounds like Y was satirized by Mark Twain in his book *Eve's Diary:*

> The minute I set eyes on an animal I know what it is. I don't have to reflect a moment; the right name comes out instantly. . . . I seem to know just by the shape of the creature and the way it acts what animal it is. When the dodo came along he [Adam] thought it was a wildcat. . . . But I saved him. . . . I just spoke up in a quite natural way . . . and said "Well, I do declare if there isn't the dodo!"

There is some "sound symbolism" in language. That is, there are words whose pronunciation suggests the meaning. A small group of words in the vocabulary of most languages is "onomatopoeic" — the sounds of the words "imitate" the sounds of "nature." Even here, the sounds differ from one language to another, reflecting the particular sound system of the language. In English we say *cockadoodledoo* and in Russian they say *kukuriku* to represent the rooster's crow.

One also finds particular sound sequences which seem to relate to a particular concept. In English there are many words beginning with *gl*, such as *glare, glint, gleam, glitter, glossy, glaze, glance, glimmer, glimpse, glisten,* all of which have to do with sight. Many rhyming word pairs begin with *h: hoity-toity, harum-scarum, hotsy-totsy, higgledy-piggledy.* But these are a very small part of any language, and *gl* may have nothing to do with "sight" words in another language.

When you know a language you know these *gl* words, the onomatopoeic words, and all the words in the basic vocabulary of the language. You know their sounds and you know their meanings. It's extremely unlikely, of course, that there is any one speaker of English who knows the 450,000 words listed in *Webster's Third International Dictionary.* But even if someone did, and that was all he knew, he would not know English. Imagine trying to learn a foreign language by buying a dictionary and memorizing words. No matter how many words you learned, you would not be able to form the simplest phrases or sentences in the language or understand what was said by a native speaker. No one speaks in isolated words. (Of course you could search in your traveler's dictionary for individual words to find out how to say something like "car—gas—where?" After many tries, a native might understand this question and then point in the direction of a gas station. If he answered you in a sentence, however, it is very possible that you could not even break up what he said into words so that you could look up each word in your dictionary.)

If you know a language you can combine words to form phrases and phrases to form sentences. Unfortunately, you can't buy a dictionary with all the sentences in any language, since no dictionary can list all the *possible* sentences. This is because knowing a language means being able to produce new sentences never spoken before and to understand sentences never heard before. The linguist Noam Chomsky refers to this ability as the "creative aspect" of language. This doesn't mean that you can create great literature, but it does mean you can and do "create" new sentences every time you speak and are able to understand new sentences "created" by others.

Consider, for example, the following sentence:

> Daniel Boone decided to become a pioneer because he dreamed of pigeon-toed giraffes and cross-eyed elephants dancing in pink skirts and green berets on the wind-swept plains of the Midwest.

You might not believe the sentence; you might question its logic; you might even understand it to mean different things; but you can understand the sentence, although it is very doubtful that you have heard or read it before now.

It's obvious, then, that when you know a language you can recognize and produce new sentences. It can't be that all possible sentences are stored in your brain and that when you speak you pull out a sentence which seems to fit the situation, or that when you hear a sentence you match it with some sentence already stored. How can one have in his memory a totally novel sentence never heard before?

The fact that one can't learn a language by memorizing sentences and phrases is demonstrated dramatically for anyone traveling to a foreign country with a phrasebook clutched tightly in his hands. He knows how difficult it is to ask or answer the simplest question by attempting to find just the right phrase. One may find the phrase for "Please bring me some chicken soup" but not for "Do you put artichoke hearts in the chili sauce?" or "I'm allergic to split-pea soup." Even if he could find the right question he would not be able to understand the answer, which would probably not be listed as a phrase in the book.

In fact, it can be shown that simple memorization of all the possible sentences in a language is impossible *in principle*. If for every sentence in the language one can form a longer sentence, then there is no limit on the length of any sentence and no limit on the number of sentences. We can illustrate this by a well-known example in English. When you know the language, you know you can say:

This is the house.

or

This is the house that Jack built.

or

This is the cheese that lay in the house that Jack built.

or

This is the dog that chased the cat that chased the mouse that ate the cheese that lay in the house that Jack built.

And one needn't stop there. How long, then, is the longest sentence? One can also say:

The old man came.

or

The old, old, old, old, old man came.

How many "old's" are too many? Seven? Twenty-three?

We will not deny that the longer these sentences become, the less likely one would be to hear or to say them. A sentence with two hundred and seventy-six occurrences of "old" would be highly unlikely in either speech or writing, even to describe Methuselah. But such a sentence is *theoretically* possible. That is, if you know English, you have the knowledge to add any number of adjectives as modifiers to a noun, as in:

The beautiful, rich, snobbish, stubborn, blond, blue-eyed princess married the hunchbacked, gnarled, lame, dirty old man.

To memorize and store an infinite set of sentences would require an infinite storage capacity. But the brain is finite, and even if it were not we could not store totally novel sentences.

But when you learn a language you must learn something, and that something must be finite. The vocabulary is finite (however large it may be), and that can be stored. If sentences in a language were formed by putting one word after another in any order then one's knowledge of a language could be described simply by a list of words. That this is not the case can be seen by examining the following strings of words:

1 a. John kissed the little old lady who owned the shaggy dog.
   b. Who owned the shaggy dog John kissed the little old lady.
   c. John is difficult to love.
   d. It is difficult to love John.
   e. John is anxious to go.
   f. It is anxious to go John.
   g. John who was a student flunked his exams.
   h. Exams his flunked student a was who John.

If you were asked to put a star or asterisk before the sentences that seemed "funny" or "no good" to you, which ones would you "star"?[2] Our "intuitive" knowledge about what "is" or "is not" a sentence in English convinces us to "star" sentences b, f, and h. Which ones did you "star"?

Would you agree with our judgments about the following sentences?

2 a.   What he did was climb a tree.
  b.   *What he thought was want a sports car.
  c.   Drink your beer and go home!
  d.   *What are you drinking and go home?
  e.   I expect them to arrive a week from next Thursday.
  f.   *I expect a week from next Thursday to arrive them.
  g.   Linus lost his security blanket.
  h.   *Lost Linus security blanket his.

If you "starred" the same sentences we did, then it is clear that all strings of words do not constitute sentences in a language, and our knowledge of the language determines which do and which do not. Therefore, in addition to knowing the words of the language you must know some "rules" to form the sentences and to make the judgments that you made about the examples under sentence groups 1 and 2. These rules must be finite in length and finite in number so they can be stored in our finite brains. Yet they must permit us to form and understand an infinite set of new sentences as was discussed above. How this is possible will be discussed in Chapter 6. It is one of the most interesting properties of human language.

We can say then that a language consists of all the sounds, words, and possible sentences. And when you know a language you know the sounds, the words, and the rules for their combination.

WHAT YOU KNOW AND WHAT YOU DO: LINGUISTIC COMPETENCE AND PERFORMANCE

> *"What's one and one and one and one and one and one and one and one and one and one?"*
> *"I don't know," said Alice. "I lost count."*
> *"She can't do Addition," the Red Queen interrupted.*
>
> —LEWIS CARROLL, *Through the Looking-Glass*

We have mentioned some aspects of a speaker's linguistic knowledge. We said, for example, that our linguistic ability permits us to form longer and longer sentences, illustrating this by showing how we can keep piling

---

[2] It has become customary in presenting sentence examples to use the asterisk before any sentence which speakers reject for one reason or another. We shall use this notation throughout the book.

up adjectives as modifiers of a noun.   We pointed out that this is theoretically, if not practically, possible.   That is, whether one limits the number of adjectives to three, five, or eighteen in speaking, one cannot limit the number of adjectives which one *could* add if one wanted to.   This demonstrates that there is a difference between having the necessary knowledge to produce such sentences and the way we use this knowledge when we are performing linguistically.   It is a difference between what one *knows,* which linguists refer to as one's linguistic **competence,** and how one *uses* this knowledge in actual behavior, which is called linguistic **performance.**

You have the competence to understand or produce an infinitely long sentence.   But when you attempt to use that knowledge – when you perform linguistically – there are physiological and psychological reasons why you cut off the number of adjectives, adverbs, clauses, etc.   You may run out of breath; your audience may leave; you may lose track of what has been said if the sentence is too long; and of course you don't live forever.

In discussing what you know – your linguistic competence – we are not talking about your conscious knowledge.   We learn the rules of the language without anyone teaching them to us and without being aware that we are learning such rules.   That this knowledge is learned is clear from the fact that you use it to speak, to understand, and to make judgments about sentences.

The fact that linguistic competence and performance are not identical and that "knowing" something is not the same as "doing" something is not unique to language knowledge and behavior.   The quote from *Through the Looking-Glass* at the beginning of this section illustrates this difference.   Alice could count up the "ones" if they were written down on paper.   She knew the rules of addition.   She had the competence, but her performance was impeded by the limitations of her short-term memory.

Lewis Carroll was intrigued with the difference between competence and performance in linguistic matters as well, as is shown by the following excerpt from *Alice's Adventures in Wonderland:*

> "I quite agree with you" said the Duchess, "and the moral of that is –
> 'Be what you seem to be' – or, if you'd like it put more simply – 'Never imagine yourself not to be otherwise than what it might appear to others that what you were or might have been was not otherwise than what you had been would have appeared to them to be otherwise.'"
>
> "I think I should understand that better," Alice said very politely, "if I had it written down: but I'm afraid I can't quite follow it as you say it."
>
> "That's nothing to what I could say if I chose," the Duchess replied, in a pleased tone.

The Duchess and Alice were both correct.   The Duchess had the knowledge to go on indefinitely.   Alice had the knowledge to understand, for if the sentence had been written down, Alice could have "worked it out."

To see that this is so, try the following. Combine sentence a with sentence b to form one sentence.

> a. The girl milked the cow.
> b. The cow was brown.

You might have come up with sentence c, d, or e.[3]

> c. The girl milked the cow and the cow was brown.
> d. The girl milked the cow that was brown.
> e. The cow the girl milked was brown.

Now add sentence f.

> f. The boy kissed the girl.

If you used the same "combining rule" as was used to form sentence c, you would get:

> g. The boy kissed the girl and the girl milked the cow and the cow was brown.

If you used the rule which formed sentence d, you would get:

> h. The boy kissed the girl who milked the cow that was brown.

And if you followed the pattern of sentence e, you would get:

> i. The cow the girl the boy kissed milked was brown.

Even when "written down," sentence i is not an easy one to understand. But knowing the rule—and you must know it if you could understand sentence e—you could work out the meaning and even produce such a "crazy" sentence. You have the competence to do so. Sometimes when we use this competence in forming and understanding sentences we get "performance-blocked."

Another example of the difference between competence and performance is illustrated in a quote from the nineteenth-century *Mathematical Gazette* (Vol. 12) attributed to a certain Mrs. La Touche:

> I do hate sums. There is no greater mistake than to call arithmetic an exact science. There are permutations and aberrations discernible to minds entirely noble like mine; subtle variations which it requires a mind like mine to perceive. For instance, if you add a sum from the bottom up, and then again from the top down, the result is always different.

In using our knowlege of the rules of arithmetic we can make mistakes, as did Mrs. La Touche.

In using our knowledge of language in speaking we also make mistakes —slips of the tongue, false starts, spoonerisms, run-on sentences, and so

---

[3] There are, of course, other ways to combine these sentences, for example, *The girl milked the brown cow.* The particular "conjoining rules" illustrated are used to make a specific point.

on. But this doesn't mean that we can't recognize errors – we have the knowledge to do so.

The word "spoonerism" was invented to describe a common type of error made famous by an eminent don of Oxford University. When the Reverend Spooner said "You have hissed my mystery lecture – you have tasted the whole worm" instead of "You have missed my history lecture – you have wasted the whole term," or when he mistakenly called a prominent member of the royal family "queer old dean" instead of "dear old queen," he was making performance errors. He knew what he wanted to say, but his tongue "slipped."

Someone may say, "Well, like, man, I mean – uh – like, you know the – uh – girl like – er – is – you know – going," but that same person would probably not accept that as an "unstarred" sentence of English. His linguistic competence, his knowledge of the language, tells him it isn't proper. His performance could have been the result of a number of factors, mostly nonlinguistic in nature.

If someone is riding a bicycle and falls off, that does not mean he doesn't know how to ride the bicycle. Or if he gets tired in fifteen minutes and stops to rest, it doesn't mean he hasn't the knowledge to ride the bicycle continually for a month, or a year, or forever, if he lived that long. He might not be able to tell you the physical laws he is obeying to maintain his balance, but he knows how to ride the bike. Similarly, you may not be able to state the linguistic "laws" (rules) which account for your knowledge, but these rules make it possible for you to produce and understand an unlimited number of unfamiliar utterances.

A large part of this book will be concerned with discussing just these kinds of rules that you know without knowing that you do. We will be discussing the nature of such rules – the nature of linguistic competence.

WHAT IS A GRAMMAR?

I don't want to talk grammar. I want to talk like a lady.

G. B. SHAW, *Pygmalion*

When you learn a language you learn the sounds used in that language, the basic units of meaning, such as words, and the rules to combine these to form new sentences. The elements and rules constitute the **grammar** of a language. The grammar, then, is what we *know;* it represents our linguistic competence. To understand the nature of language we must understand the nature of this internalized, unconscious set of rules which constitutes the grammar.

Every human being who speaks a language knows the grammar. When a linguist wishes to describe a language he attempts to describe the grammar which exists in the minds of all its speakers. It is this grammar which makes it possible for speakers to talk to and understand one another. To the extent that the linguist's description is a true model of a speaker's linguistic competence, it will be a good or bad description of the language. We call such a model a **descriptive grammar**. It doesn't tell you *how* you should speak. It describes your basic linguistic knowledge; it explains how it is possible for you to speak and understand.

We have used the word *grammar* in two ways: the first in reference to the grammar every speaker has in his brain; the second as the model of this internalized knowledge. We will not differentiate these two meanings, since the linguist's grammar is an attempt at a formal statement (or theory) of a speaker's grammar. That is, when we say in later chapters that there is a rule in the grammar such as: "every sentence has a noun phrase subject and a verb phrase predicate," this is posited as a rule in both the "mental" grammar and the model of it—the linguist's grammar. And, when we say that a sentence is *grammatical* we mean that it is formed in keeping with the rules of both grammars; conversely an *ungrammatical* (starred) sentence deviates in some way from these rules.

The way we are using the word *grammar* differs in another way from its most common meaning. In our sense, the grammar includes everything a speaker knows about his language—the sound system, called **phonology,** the system of meanings, called **semantics,** and the rules of sentence formation, called **syntax.** Many people think of the grammar of a language as referring solely to the syntactic rules. This latter sense is what a student usually means when he talks about his class in "English grammar."

The term *grammar* is used in still another sense. Grammar textbooks may contain what are called **prescriptive** rather than **descriptive** grammars. Their aim is not to explain linguistic knowledge; no one has to teach what is already known. If, however, you want to learn a foreign language in a classroom situation, a prescriptive grammar can be used to tell you explicitly what the grammatical rules of that language are. Such grammars are *teaching* grammars.

In addition, prescriptive grammars of your own language may be used to make explicit what you know about your language, and also to teach you some rules which may not be part of your grammar. The reason for such prescriptive grammars is that every language is made up of *dialects* (which will be discussed in detail in Chapter 10). The rules of the grammars of different dialects may differ somewhat. In your dialect, for example, the advertising slogan "Winston tastes good like a cigarette should" may be a perfectly good grammatical sentence. In the dialect which is usually used for formal discourse this sentence would be starred and *as* would have to be used instead of *like*. The grammar which you may be taught, then, may attempt to "prescribe" what rules to use.

It is important to note that no dialect (and therefore no grammar) is superior to another in a *linguistic* sense. Every grammar is equally complex and logical and capable of producing an infinite set of sentences to express any thought one might wish to express. One grammar, however, may be preferred for nonlinguistic reasons, and is therefore used as the prescriptive grammar. We shall not be primarily interested with such prescriptive grammars in this book. We shall, however, discuss this question further in Chapter 10.

Our aim is more in keeping with that stated in 1784 by the grammarian John Fell in "Essay Towards an English Grammar": "It is certainly the business of a grammarian to find out, and not to make, the laws of a language." This is just what the linguist attempts to do — to find out the laws of a language, and the laws which pertain to *all* languages. Those laws which pertain to all human languages, representing the universal properties of language, constitute what may be called a **universal grammar.** We shall be discussing many of these "laws" in the chapters that follow. Some of these linguistic universals will be concerned with the sound systems of language. Every grammar, for example, includes discrete sound segments, like *p, n,* or *a,* which can all be defined by a finite set of "sound properties." Other phonological universals reveal that every language has both "vowels" and "consonants" and rules which determine the prununication of sentences.

There are also semantic universals which pertain to common semantic properties such as "male," "female," "animate," "human," and "concrete," which are found in all languages.

Finally there are universals of syntax which reveal the ways in which sentences are formed. There is no language, for example, which cannot combine sentences in some way similar to the ways found in English. Every language has a way of forming sentences such as the following:

> Linguistics is an interesting subject.
> I know that linguistics is an interesting subject.
> You know that I know that linguistics is an interesting subject.
> Guinevere knows that you know that I know that linguistics is an interesting subject.

The linguist is also interested in seeing how these universal properties are expressed in particular languages like English, Zulu, Twi, Cherokee, Aztec, Eskimo, Russian, Arabic, etc. That is, linguists are interested in writing descriptive grammars of languages.

The grammar of each language will include (or try to include) everything speakers know about their language. Since all speakers know how to produce sounds and pronounce sentences, one part of the grammar must describe the phonology. We will discuss these questions in Chapters 3 and 4.

Since knowing a language means knowing how to relate sounds and meanings, each grammar must include such semantic knowledge. This will be discussed in Chapter 5.

In addition, every grammar includes a syntactic part which sets forth the rules for sentence formation, the rules that explain how speakers know which sentences are grammatical and which are not, and the rules that explain how sentences are related. The syntactic rules permit the "creativity" we spoke of earlier. The syntactic parts of grammars will be discussed in Chapter 6.

Other topics, such as the language of animals, how languages change, languages of the world and dialects of languages, writing systems, how children learn language, and how computers have influenced linguistic study, will be discussed in the later chapters of the book.

SUMMARY

We are all intimately familiar with at least one language. Yet few of us ever stop to consider what we know when we know a language. There is no book which contains the language English or Russian or Zulu. One can list the words of a language in a dictionary, but not all the possible sentences, and a language consists of these sentences as well as words. Though we can't list all sentences, we can list the rules which a speaker uses to produce and understand an infinite set of "possible" sentences.

These rules comprise the **syntax** of a language. You learn these rules when you learn the language and you also learn the sound system of the language (the **phonology**) and the ways in which sounds and meanings are related (the **semantics**). The sounds and meanings of words are related in an **arbitrary** fashion. That is, if you had never heard the word *syntax* you would not, by its very sounds, know what it meant. Language, then, is a system which relates sounds with meanings, and when you know a language you know this system.

This knowledge (your linguistic **competence**) is different from your behavior (your linguistic **performance**). Even if you woke up one morning and decided to stop talking (as the Trappist monks did after they took a "vow of silence"), you would still have knowledge of your language. This ability or competence underlies linguistic behavior. If you didn't know the language you couldn't speak, but if you know the language you may choose not to speak.

The **grammar** of a language represents speakers' linguistic competence. It includes the basic sounds, words, and rules for the formation, pronunciation, and interpretation of sentences. Linguistic knowledge represented in the grammar is not conscious knowledge. An explicit description of competence is called a **descriptive grammar**. Such a grammar is a model of the "mental" grammar known by every speaker of the language.

It doesn't teach the rules of the language; it describes the rules which are known. A teaching grammar is sometimes called a **prescriptive grammar** and has different aims.

Linguists are scientists who study the general properties of grammars — the universal properties found in all languages — and the specific properties of the grammars of individual languages. In this study they hope to provide a better understanding of the nature of human language.

EXERCISES

1. Part of your knowledge of English includes knowing what sound sequences occur in the language. When new products are put on the market the manufacturers have to think up new names for them, and these names must conform to the allowable sound patterns. Suppose you were hired by a manufacturer of soap products and your job was to name five new products. What names might you come up with? List them.

   We are not interested in the *spelling* of the words but in how they are pronounced. Therefore, describe in any way you can how the words which you list should be pronounced. Suppose for example you named one soap powder *Blick*. You can describe the sounds in any of the following ways:

   1. *bl* as in "blood," *i* as in "pit," *ck* as in "stick"
   2. *bli* as in "bliss," *ck* as in "tick"
   3. *b* as in "boy," *lick* as in "lick"
      and so on.

2. Anyone who knows a language knows what strings of words are grammatical sentences in his language and what strings are "starred" or ungrammatical. Construct five ungrammatical sentences. State, if you can, why you think they are ungrammatical.

3. Below are listed eight English words which are considered to relate sounds and meanings in a less arbitrary fashion than one finds in most words. State why you might be able to figure out what each word means even if you did not know the word previously.

1. ding-dong	5. plop
2. tick-tock	6. cough
3. bang	7. bow-wow
4. zing	8. swish

4. We said that the sounds and meanings of most words are arbitrarily related. This is not necessarily true in all systems of communication, in which the "signs" unambiguously reveal the "meaning."

1. Describe (or draw) five different signs which directly show what they mean. Example: a road sign indicating an S curve.
2. Describe any other communication system which, like language, consists of arbitrary form-meaning symbols. Example: traffic signals where *red* means *stop* and *green* means *go*.

5. State some "rule of grammar" which you have been taught in school but which you do not generally use in producing sentences. For example, you may have been taught that *It's me* is incorrect and that the correct form is *It's I*. But you always use *me* in such sentences. How does this show the difference between descriptive and prescriptive grammars?

6. Suppose you heard someone say *He made a tip of the slung* instead of *He made a slip of the tongue*. How would this reveal a difference between linguistic **competence** and **performance**? Would you expect anyone to err by saying *lpsi of the ngto*? If not, why not?

7. What does the following cartoon reveal about what speakers know about their language?

By permission of John Hart and Field Enterprises, Inc.

References

CHOMSKY, NOAM. *Language and Mind,* enlarged ed. New York: Harcourt, Brace & World, 1972.

CHOMSKY, NOAM. Review of B. F. Skinner's "Verbal Behavior" in J. A. Fodor and J. J. Katz, eds. *The Structure of Language.* Englewood Cliffs, N.J.: Prentice-Hall, 1964.

LANGACKER, RONALD. *Language and Its Structure.* New York: Harcourt, Brace & World, 1968.

LYONS, JOHN. *Noam Chomsky* New York: Viking, 1970.

THOMAS, OWEN, and KINTGEN, EUGENE. *Transformational Grammar and the Teacher of English,* 2nd ed. New York: Holt, Rinehart and Winston, 1974.

2
In the Beginning: Language Origin

*God created the world by a Word, instantaneously, without
toil and pains.*

—The Talmud

The question of how language originated has always fascinated man. All religions and mythologies contain stories of language origin. Philosophers through the ages have argued the question. Scholarly works have been written on the subject. Prizes have been awarded for the "best answer" to this eternally perplexing problem. Theories of divine origin, evolutionary development, and language as the invention of man have all been suggested.

Such widespread speculation is not surprising. Language is man's most unique characteristic. Man's curiosity about himself led to his curiosity about language. Many of the early theories on the origin of language resulted from man's interest in his own origins and his own nature. Since man and language are so closely related, it was believed that if one knew how, when, and where language arose, perhaps one would know how, when, and where man arose.

The difficulties inherent in answering these questions about language are immense. Anthropologists think that man has existed for at least one million years, and perhaps for as long as five or six million years. But the earliest deciphered written records are barely six thousand years old, dating from the writings of the Sumerians of 4000 B.C. These records appear so late in the history of the development of language that they provide no clue at all to the origin of language.

One might conclude that the quest for this knowledge is doomed to failure. The only hard evidence we have about ancient languages is written, but speech precedes writing historically by an enormous period of time, and even today there are thousands of speech communities speaking perfectly "up-to-date" languages which lack writing systems. The language or languages used by our earliest ancestors are irretrievably lost.

For these reasons, scholars in the latter part of the nineteenth century, who were only interested in "hard science," ridiculed, ignored, and even banned discussions of language origin.   In 1886, the Linguistic Society of Paris passed a resolution "outlawing" any papers concerned with this subject.[1]

That such resolutions did not put an end to the interest is clear from the fact that just a few years ago, the linguist John P. Hughes felt compelled to write:

> . . . a word or two should be said in any serious linguistic work to counter the arrant nonsense on this subject which is still circulated in Sunday supplement science features.   According to this pseudo-evolutionary foolishness, based on nothing but rampant imagination, language originated among our caveman ancestors when someone tried to tell the hitherto speechless tribe about the wolf he had killed, and was forced to give an imitation of the wolf . . . or when he hit his thumb with the mallet while sharpening a stone spear, so that *ouch* became the word for "pain" . . . and similar fairy stories.[2]

This view sharply diverges from that put forth two hundred years earlier by Lord Monboddo, the Scottish anthropologist:

> The origin of an art so admirable and so useful as language . . . must be allowed to be a subject, not only of great curiosity, but likewise very important and interesting, if we consider, that it is necessarily connected with an inquiry into the original nature of man, and that primitive state in which he was, before language was invented. . . .[3]

It is not just in Sunday supplements that one finds "pseudo-evolutionary foolishness."   Some of the greatest linguists and philosophers continue to be interested in this question, and speculative theories on language origin have provided valuable insights into the nature and development of language.   For these reasons, the learned scholar Otto Jespersen stated that "linguistic science cannot refrain forever from asking about the whence (and about the whither) of linguistic evolution."

In this chapter, some of the ideas about the origin of language will be examined, both because they may shed light on the nature of language and because there is continuing interest in the subject.

---

[1] *La Société n' admet aucune communication concernant . . . l'origine du langage . . ."* ("The Society does not accept any paper concerning the origin of language . . .") La Société de Linguistique, Section 2, Statuts (1886).

[2] John P. Hughes, *The Science of Language* (New York: Random House, 1969).

[3] James Burnett, Lord Monboddo, *Of the Origin and Progress of Language* (1774).

GOD'S GIFT TO MAN?

> *And out of the ground the Lord God formed every beast of the field, and every fowl of the air; and brought them unto Adam to see what he would call them: and whatsoever Adam called every living creature, that was the name thereof.*
>
> —Genesis, 2:19

According to Judeo-Christian beliefs, God gave Adam the power to name all things. Similar beliefs are found throughout the world. According to the Egyptians, the creator of speech was the god Thoth. According to the Babylonians, the language giver was the god Nabû. According to the Hindus, we owe our unique language ability to a female god; Brahma was the creator of the universe, but language was given to man by his wife, Sarasvati.

The belief in the divine origin of language has continued through the ages. Cotton Mather wrote his M.A. thesis at Harvard on the question, providing a detailed defense in support of this theory. Almost three hundred years later, Lester Grabbe, pointing to the existence in far-removed cultures of stories similar to the Tower of Babel, concluded:

> . . . no acceptable theory has yet been propounded which can satisfactorily answer why man even has the faculty of speech — or language — if there is no Creator. On the other hand, the Genesis account is in complete agreement with all established scientific fact.[4]

Belief in the divine origin of language is closely intertwined with the magical properties man has associated with language and the spoken word. Children in all cultures utter "magic" words like *abracadabra* to ward off evil or bring good luck. Despite the childish jingle "Sticks and stones may break my bones, but names will never hurt me," name-calling is insulting, cause for legal punishment, and feared. In some cultures, when certain words are used, one is required to counter them by "knocking on wood." Language is used to bring down the curses of the gods. Prayers are offered, and thus man converses with his gods in language. According to the Bible, only the true God would respond when called upon; the false idols did not know the "word of God." The anthropologist Bronislaw Malinowski has pointed out that in many cultures, words are used to control events and become sources of power when chanted over and over: "The repetitive statement of certain words is believed to produce the reality stated."

One finds taboo words all over the world. In western societies one

---

[4] Lester Grabbe, "Origin of Languages," *The Plain Truth*, Aug.–Sept. 1970.

is adjured not to "take the Lord's name in vain." In folk tales forbidden names, such as *Rumpelstiltzkin,* can break spells if discovered. Personal names also carry special properties—a Jewish child is not to be named after a living person, and in some cultures it is forbidden to utter the name of someone who has died. In ancient Egypt every person was given two names, one of which was secret. If the secret name was discovered, the discoverer had power over the person. In Athens, in the fifth century B.C., a ventriloquist named Euricles pretended he had a demon in him; special powers were attributed to the ventriloquist's voice. In *The Wasps,* Aristophanes mentions the "sly prophet Euricles" who "hidden in other people's bellies produces much amusement."

The linguist David Crystal reports that someone is attempting to test the idea that the world will end when the billion names of God have been uttered by attaching a prayer wheel to an electronic speech synthesizer.[5]

The belief in the divine origin of language and its magical properties is also manifested by the fact that in many religions only special languages may be used in prayers and rituals. The Hindu priests of the fifth century B.C. believed that the original pronunciations of Vedic Sanskrit had to be used. This led to important linguistic study, since their language had already changed greatly since the hymns of the Vedas had been written. Until recently, only Latin could be used in the Catholic Mass. Among Moslems, the Koran was not to be translated and could be read only in Arabic; and Hebrew continues to be the one language used in the prayers of orthodox Jews throughout the world.

These myths and customs and superstitions do not tell us very much about language. They do tell us about the importance of language to men and the miraculous properties they attach to it. In addition, discussions of the divine origin of language, while not likely to settle the question to the satisfaction of anyone seeking "scientific proof," can provide insights into the nature of human language.

In 1756, a Prussian statistician-clergyman, Johann Peter Suessmilch, delivered a paper before the Prussian Academy in which he reasoned that man could not have invented language without thought, and that thought depends on the prior existence of language. The only escape from the paradox is to presume that God must have given language to man. Suessmilch, unlike other philosophers such as Rousseau (whose ideas will be discussed below), did not view primitive languages as "less developed" or "imperfect." He suggested just the opposite—that all languages are "perfect" and thus the reflection of God's perfection. He cites examples from the European languages, from Semitic languages, and from languages of "primitive" people to prove the perfection of all human language. To oppose the idea that there are primitive languages,

---

[5] David Crystal, *Linguistics* (Middlesex, England: Penguin, 1971).

he noted that the great and abstract ideas of Christianity can be discussed even by the "wretched Greenlanders."

Suessmilch made other sophisticated observations. He pointed out that any child is able to learn perfectly the language of the Hottentots although adults cannot, revealing his awareness of the difference between acquisition of first and second languages. This observation anticipated the current "critical age hypothesis," which states that beyond a certain age a human being is incapable of acquiring a first language. He also pointed out, as did many philosophers of antiquity, that all languages have grammars which are highly regular, for otherwise children would be unable to learn them.

The arguments presented by Suessmilch were based on observations concerning the "universality" of linguistic properties, the relation between psychological and linguistic constraints, and the interdependence of reason and language. He presented powerful arguments, but ones which had less to do with language origin than with language itself.

At the present time there is no way to "prove" or "disprove" the divine-origin theory, just as one cannot argue scientifically for or against the existence of God.

THE FIRST LANGUAGE

Imagine the Lord talking French! Aside from a few odd words in Hebrew, I took it completely for granted that God had never spoken anything but the most dignified English.

—CLARENCE DAY, *Life with Father*

Among the proponents of the divine-origin theory a great interest arose in the language used by God, Adam, and Eve. Men have not always been pessimistic about discovering an answer to this question. For millennia, "scientific" experiments have reportedly been devised to verify particular theories of language origin. In the fifth century B.C. the Greek historian Herodotus reported that the Egyptian Pharaoh Psammetichus (664–610 B.C.) sought to determine the most primitive "natural" language by experimental methods. The monarch was said to have placed two infants in an isolated mountain hut, to be cared for by a servant who was cautioned not to utter a single word in their presence on pain of death. The Pharaoh believed that without any linguistic input the children would develop their own language and would thus reveal the original tongue of man. Patiently the Egyptian waited for the children to became old enough to talk. According to the story, the first word uttered was *bekos*. Scholars were consulted, and it was discovered that *bekos* was the word for "bread" in Phrygian, the language spoken in the province of Phrygia (the northwest corner of modern Turkey). This ancient language, which has long since died out, was thought, on the basis of this "experiment," to be the original language.

Whether James IV of Scotland (1473–1513) had read the works of Herodotus is not known. According to reports he attempted a replication of Psammetichus's experiment, but his attempt yielded different results. The Scottish children matured and "spak very guid Ebrew," providing "scientific evidence" that Hebrew was the language used in the Garden of Eden.

Two hundred years before James's "experiment," the Holy Roman Emperor Frederick II of Hohenstaufen was said to have carried out a similar test, but without any results; the children died before they uttered a single word.

In the seventeenth century, a Swedish scholar, Andreas Kemke, is said to have refuted both views, asserting that God spoke Swedish, Adam Danish, and the serpent French. This view tells us more about the ideology of the scholar than it does about the origin of language. Since he mentions nothing at all about Eve, we are free to assume that she spoke either Phrygian or Hebrew, a most important conclusion since Eve's language would be our "mother tongue."

The legend of Psammetichus shows that the Pharaoh was willing to accept "evidence" even if it was contrary to national interests. It is clear that Kemke's nationalism influenced his views. A German scholar, J. G. Becanus (1518–1572), surpassed Kemke in his chauvinistic zeal. He argued that German must have been the primeval language since the language given by God must have been a perfect language, and since, according to him, German was the most superior language in the world, it had to be the language used by God and by Adam. Becanus carried his arguments farther: German persisted as the perfect language because the early Cimbrians (who were Germans) did not contribute to the building of the Tower of Babel. Later, according to this theory, God caused the Old Testament to be translated from German into Hebrew.

Other proposals were put forth. In 1830 the lexicographer Noah Webster asserted that the "proto-language" must have been Chaldee (Aramaic), the language spoken in Jerusalem during the time of Jesus. In 1887, Joseph Elkins maintained in *The Evolution of the Chinese Language* that "there is no other language which can be more reasonably assumed to be the speech first used in the world's gray morning than can Chinese. . . . Hence, Chinese is regarded . . . as the . . . primeval language."

The belief that all languages originated from a single source is found in Genesis: ". . . the whole earth was of one language, and of one speech." The Tower of Babel story attempts to account for the diversity of languages. In this, and in similar accounts, the "confusion" of languages *preceded* the dispersement of peoples. (According to some Biblical scholars, *Babel* derives from the Hebrew *bilbel,* meaning "confusion"; others say it derives from the name Babylon.) Genesis continues: "Therefore is the name of it called Babel; because the Lord did there confound the language of all the earth: and from thence did the Lord scatter them abroad upon the face of all the earth."

A legend of the Toltecs, given by the native Mexican historian Ixtlilxochitl, also explains the diversity of languages by a similar account: ". . . after men had multiplied, their languages were confused, and not being able to understand each other, they went to different parts of the earth."

A study of the history of languages does indeed show that many languages develop from a single one, as will be discussed in later chapters. But in these attested cases the "confusion" comes *after* the separation of peoples. Any view which maintains a single origin of language must provide some explanation for the number of language *families* which exist. The Bible explains this as an act of God, who at Babel created from one language many, all of which would eventually become individual multi-language families. The monogenetic theory of languages — the single-origin theory — is related to a belief in the monogenetic origin of man. Many scientists today believe, instead, that man arose in many different places on earth. If this is the case, there were many proto-languages, out of which the modern language families developed.

It is clear that we are no farther along today in discovering the original language (or languages) than was Psammetichus when he attempted to use "experimental methods" to answer this question. Any such experiment is bound to fail. For obvious reasons, linguists would not attempt to duplicate such tests — while we may applaud the Pharaoh's motivation we must condemn his lack of humanity. But the misfortunes of life can be as cruel as a Pharaoh. There have been a number of cases of children reared in environments of extreme social isolation. Such reported cases go back at least to the eighteenth century. In 1758, Carl Linnaeus first included *Homo ferus* (wild or feral man) as a subdivision of *Homo sapiens.* According to Linnaeus, a defining characteristic of *Homo ferus* was his lack of speech or observable language of any kind. All the cases in the literature support his view.

The most dramatic cases of children raised in isolation are those described as "wild" or "feral" children, who have reportedly been reared with wild animals or have lived alone in the wilderness. In 1920 two feral children, Amala and Kamala, were found in India, supposedly having been reared with wolves. The most celebrated case, documented in François Truffaut's film *The Wild Child,* is that of Victor, "the wild boy of Aveyron," who was found in 1798. It was ascertained that he had been left in the woods when a very young child and had somehow survived. He was in his early teens when he was discovered. In addition, there are cases of children whose isolation resulted from deliberate efforts to keep them from normal social intercourse. As recently as 1970 a child, called Genie in the scientific reports, was discovered who had been confined to a small room under conditions of physical restraint, and who had received only minimal human contact from the age of eighteen months until almost fourteen years. None of these children, regardless of the cause of isolation, was able to speak or knew any language. Genie is, however, now learning to speak and understand.

Man's unique genetic ability to acquire language is revealed only when the child receives adequate linguistic stimulus. It is true that no one teaches us language, in the sense that we are taught arithmetic or a second language. We learn the language which is used in our environment when we are children. Without exposure to language children do not speak at all — not even Phrygian, or "very guid Ebrew."

Despite the failure of the isolation method and the inability to prove or even test the various theories of language origin, the speculation continues.

MAN'S INVENTION OR THE CRIES OF NATURE?

Language was born in the courting days of mankind; the first utterances of speech I fancy to myself like something between the nightly love lyrics of puss upon the tiles and the melodious love songs of the nightingale.

— OTTO JESPERSEN, *Language, Its Nature, Development and Origin*

The Greeks speculated about everything in the universe. It is therefore not surprising that the earliest surviving linguistic treatise which deals with the origin and nature of language should be Plato's *Cratylus* dialogue. A commonly held view among the classical Greeks was that at some ancient time there was a "legislator" who gave the correct, natural name to everything. Plato, in this dialogue, has Socrates express this idea:

> . . . not every man is able to give a name, but only a maker of names; and this is the legislator, who of all skilled artisans in the world is the rarest . . . only he who looks to the name which each thing by nature has, and is, will be able to express the ideal forms of things in letters [sounds] and syllables.

It was not one of their many gods who named all things, but this wise "legislator." The question of language origin was closely tied to the debate among the Greeks as to whether there is a truth or correctness in "names" regardless of the language, as opposed to the view that words or names for things result merely from an agreement—a convention—between speakers. This debate between the **naturalists** and the **conventionalists** was one of the first major linguistic arguments. In the *Cratylus* dialogue, Socrates analyzes and develops etymologies for the names of Homeric heroes, the Greek gods, mythological figures, the stars, the elements, and even abstract qualities—the proper and common nouns of language. In his attempt to justify the "trueness" or "naturalness" of these names, it is clear that he, at least in part, recognizes the humor in such an approach, for he says that "the heads of the givers of names were going round and round and therefore they imagined the world was going round and round."

In fact, it is clear from a reading of this delightful dialogue that Plato recognized the "arbitrariness" of certain words, and believed that both natural and conventional elements exist in language.

The naturalists argued that there is a natural connection between the forms of language and the essence of things. They pointed to onomatopoeic words—words which are imitative of the sounds they represent—and suggested that these form the basis of language, or at least the core of the basic vocabulary.

The idea that the earliest form of language was imitative or "echoic" was reiterated by many scholars up to recent times. According to this view, a dog, which emits a noise that (supposedly) sounds like "bow-wow" would be designated by the word *bow-wow*. To refute this position one need merely point to the small number of such words in any language and, in addition, to the fact that words alone do not constitute language.

A parallel view states that language at first consisted of emotional ejaculations of pain, fear, surprise, pleasure, anger, etc. This theory—that the earliest manifestations of language were "cries of nature" that man shared with animals—was the view proposed by Jean Jacques Rousseau in the middle of the eighteenth century. Rousseau, a founder of the Romantic movement, became concerned with the nature and origin of language while seeking to understand the nature of the "noble savage." Two of his treatises deal with the origin of language.[6] According to him, both emotive cries and gestures were used by man, but gestures proved to be too inefficient for communicating, and so man invented language. It was out of the natural cries that man "constructed" words.

Rousseau's position was essentially that of the **empiricists,** who held that all knowledge results from the perception of observable data. Thus, the first words were names of individual things and the first sentences were one-word sentences. General and abstract names were invented

---

[6] Jean Jacques Rousseau, "Discourse on the Origin and Foundations of Inequality Among Men" (1755) and "Essay on the Origin of Languages" (published posthumously, 1822).

only later, as were the "different parts of speech" and more complex sentences. Rousseau stated this in the following way: The more limited the knowledge, the more extensive the dictionary. . . . General ideas can come into the mind only with the aid of words, and the understanding grasps them only through propositions.[7]

It is difficult to understand his reasoning. How was man able to acquire the ability for abstract thought through his use of concrete words if he was not, from the very beginning, equipped with special mental abilities? But, according to Rousseau, it is not man's ability to reason which distinguished him from animals (the view held by the earlier French philosopher, Descartes); rather, it is his "will to be free." According to Rousseau, it is this freedom which led man to invent languages. He did not explain how this freedom permitted man to associate certain sounds with certain meanings and to construct a complex system of rules which permitted him to construct new sentences. Rousseau based some of his ideas on the assumption that the first languages used by man were crude and primitive languages "approximately like those which the various savage nations still have today." It is interesting that this man, who spent his life fighting inequality, should espouse such a position. Just one year after Rousseau's treatise, Suessmilch, arguing against Rousseau and in favor of the divine-origin theory, maintained the equality and perfection of all languages.

Almost two hundred years after Rousseau suggested that both the "cries of nature" and gestures formed the basis for language development, Sir Richard Paget argued for an "oral gesture theory":

> Human speech arose out of a generalized unconscious pantomimic gesture language — made by the limbs and features as a whole (including the tongue and lips) — which became specialized in gestures of the organs of articulation, owing to the human hands (and eyes) becoming continuously occupied with the use of tools. The gestures of the organs of articulation were recognized by the hearer because the hearer unconsciously reproduced in his mind the actual gesture which had produced this sound.[8]

It is difficult to know exactly how the tongue and lips and other vocal organs were used as "pantomimic gestures." But it is of interest that there are a number of scholars today who accept a "motor theory of speech perception" which is a sophisticated version of Paget's last statement.

In one short chapter it is impossible to summarize all the ideas which were developed to support man's invention of language. One view sug-

---

[7] Rousseau, "Essay on the Origin of Languages," in P. H. Salus, ed., *On Language: Plato to Von Humboldt* (New York: Holt, Rinehart and Winston, 1969).

[8] Richard Paget, *Human Speech* (New York: Harcourt, Brace, 1930).

gests that language arose out of the rhythmical grunts of men working together. The Soviet aphasiologist A. R. Luria accepted this view in 1970:

> There is every reason to believe that speech originated in productive activity and arose first in the form of abbreviated motions which represented certain work activities and pointing gestures by which men communicated with one another. . . . Only considerably later, as shown by speech paleontology, did verbal speech develop. Only in the course of a very long historical period was the disassociation of sound and gesture accomplished.[9]

One of the more charming views on language origin was suggested by Otto Jespersen. He proposed a theory stating that language derived from song as an expressive rather than a communicative need, with love being the greatest stimulus for language development.

Just as with the theories of divine origin of language, the proposals in support of the idea that man invented language — whether out of the cries of nature, the vocal mimicry of gestures, the songs of love, or the grunts of labor — do not tell us much more than that man is an inventive, imaginative, and intellectual creature.

MAN'S ORIGIN IS LANGUAGE ORIGIN

But language just happened. It happened because language is the most natural outcome in a world of people where babies babble, and mothers babble back — and where the baby also has the potential for metaphor.

— LOUIS CARINI

In 1769, fifteen years after Suessmilch's famous defense of the divine origin of language in opposition to the "invention" theory, the Prussian Academy reopened the discussion. They offered a prize for the best paper on the very same question. Johann Herder, the German philosopher and poet, won the prize with an essay which opposed both views. Herder argued against Rousseau's theory that language developed out of the "cries of nature" which man shared with animals by citing the fundamental differences between human language and the instinctive cries of animals. Herder felt that language and thought are inseparable, and that man must be born with a capacity for both. He agreed with Suessmilch that without reason, language could not have been invented

---

[9] A. R. Luria, *Traumatic Aphasia* (New York: Humanities Press, 1970), p. 80.

by man, but he went further in stating that without reason, Adam could not have been taught language, not even by the Divine Father:

> Parents never teach their children language, without the latter at the same time inventing it themselves. The former only direct their children's attention to the difference between things, by certain verbal signs, and thus do not supply these, but by means of language only facilitate and accelerate for the children the use of reason.[10]

These very insightful remarks foreshadowed the view held by some present-day linguists that no one teaches children the rules of grammar—the children discover them.

Herder's main point was that language ability is innate. One cannot talk of man existing before language. Language is part of man's essential human nature and was therefore neither invented by him nor handed to him as a gift. Herder drew on the universality, or uniformity, of all human languages as an argument to justify a monogenetic theory of man's origin. According to him, we have all descended from the same parents, and all languages therefore descended from one language. He put forth this theory to explain why languages, despite their diversity, have universal common properties. Even though the monogenetic theory is not widely accepted today, the universality of human language is accepted, and can be plausibly explained by Herder's argument that man, by nature, is everywhere the same. Herder accepted the Cartesian *rationalist* position that human languages and animal cries are as different from each other as human thought and animal instinct: "It is not the organization of the mouth which creates language for if a man were dumb all the days of his life, if he reflected, language must lie within his soul."[11]

A more current evolutionary view of language origin has been suggested by the linguist Philip Lieberman. His investigations show that "non-human primates lack the physical apparatus that is necessary to produce the range of human speech."[12] He links the development of language with the evolutionary development of the speech production and perception apparatus. This, of course, would be accompanied by changes in the brain and the nervous system in the direction of greater complexity. This implies that the languages of our human ancestors of millions of years ago may have been syntactically and phonologically simpler than any language known to us today. This still begs the question because the notion "simpler" is left undefined. Speculatively, one may suppose that the primeval language had a smaller phonetic inventory, but beyond this rather uninteresting conclusion we have not yet penetrated.

In linguistic study, as in the study of biological evolution, there appears to be a "missing link." We have no knowledge of man's immediate linguistic ancestors. We know of no creature who might bridge the chasm

---

[10] J. G. Herder, "Essay on the Origin of Language," in Salus, op. cit.

[11] Herder, op. cit.

[12] Philip Lieberman, "Primate Vocalizations and Human Linguistic Ability," *J. Acoustical Soc. Am.* 44:1574–1584.

between the mere animal vocalism of howls, hunger calls, love calls, etc. and the creative system of language which man enjoys.

Certainly one evolutionary step must have resulted in the development of a vocal tract capable of producing the wide variety of sounds utilized by human language, as well as the mechanism for perceiving and distinguishing them. That this step is insufficient to explain the origin of language is evidenced by the existence of mynah birds and parrots, which have this ability. Their imitations, however, are merely patterned repetitions. (See Chapter 7 on animal languages.)

Human language utilizes a fairly small number of sounds which are combined in linear sequence to form words. Each sound is reused many times, as is each word. Suessmilch pointed to this fact as evidence of the "efficiency" and "perfection" of language. Indeed, the discreteness of these basic linguistic elements—these sounds—was noted in the earliest views of language.

Children learn very early in life that the continuous sounds of words like *bad* and *dad* can be "broken up" into discrete segments. In fact, a child that knows these two words may on his own produce the word *dab*, though he has never heard it before. Mynah birds can learn to produce the sounds *bad* and *dad,* but no bird could ever produce the sounds *dab* without actually hearing them.

Perhaps, then, an evolutionary step in the development of language is the acquisition of the ability to "segment" and "order" discrete speech sounds. This ability appears to be centered in just one hemisphere of the human brain. That is, while the brains of all mammals are divided, only the human brain appears to show different specializations for each half. There are anatomical differences between the left and right hemisphere in the human brain which have not been found in other animals. (We shall discuss this topic in more detail in Chapter 12.) What interests us here is the strong evidence that the changes that occurred in the speech-producing and speech-receiving mechanisms of the species were accompanied or preceded by changes in the brain. This leads us to suspect that evolutionary restructuring of the brain has played a significant role in the origin and development of language.

Language was neither invented, nor was it a gift. It was ground out of the evolutionary mill and suffered the tests of survival. These tests were passed, the species "saw that it was good," and so we are blessed with language.

SUMMARY

Man's curiosity about himself and his most unique possession, language, has led to numerous theories about language origin. There is no way, at present, to "prove" or "disprove" these hypotheses, but they are of interest for the light they shed on the nature of human language.

The idea that language was God's gift to man is found in religions throughout the world. The continuing belief in the miraculous powers of language is tied to this notion. The assumption of the divine origin of language stimulated interest in discovering the first primeval language. There are legendary "experiments" in which children have been isolated in the belief that their first words would reveal the original language. Actual cases of socially isolated children, however, show that language develops only when there is sufficient linguistic input. Children will learn the language spoken to them; if they hear no language they will speak none.

Opposing theories suggest that language is the invention of man. The Greeks believed an ancient "legislator" gave the true names to all things. Others have suggested that language developed from "cries of nature," or "early gestures," or onomatopoeic words, or even from songs to express love. We have no better way to test these theories than we have to test the theory of divine origin.

Evolutionary theories oppose both the divine-origin theory and the invention theory. Rather, it is suggested that in the course of evolution man and language originated simultaneously, and that man is innately equipped to learn language. That is, it is language which makes human nature human. Studies of the evolutionary development of both the vocal tract and the brain provide evidence for physiological, anatomic, and "mental" preconditions for language development.

EXERCISES

1. Suppose archeologists discovered an ancient document which they established to be 100,000 years old. Suppose further that the writing on this document was deciphered. How would you argue against the idea that this would tell us what man's earliest language was like?

2. List as many onomatopoeic English words as you can. Are such words sufficient evidence in favor of the "echoic" theory of language origin?

3. Compare the ideas of Rousseau, Herder, and Suessmilch on the origin of language. Note the similarities and the differences. Argue in favor of one of these theories.

4. Invent your own theory of language origin. For example, you might suggest that language arose because extraterrestrial creatures who already had a language possessed the bodies of cavewomen.

5. The naturalists believe that there is a "true" connection between words and what they represent in nature. Had there been debating

societies in ancient Greece, one topic for a debate might have been: "Resolved, that there is a natural true connection between words and what they represent in the world." List some of the points which the *naturalist* team might present; then list some of the points which the *conventionalists* might present. Who do you think would have won the debate, and why?

6. Why do you think there is no substance to the proposal that in the Garden of Eden, God spoke Swedish, Adam Danish, and the serpent French?

7. Assume that Rousseau was correct and that the earliest form of language arose out of the "cries of nature." Invent a language which you think might have been used by our ancient ancestors.

References

CASSIRER, E. *Language and Myth,* trans. Susanne K. Langer. New York: Dover, 1946

CHOMSKY, NOAM. *Cartesian Linguistics.* New York: Harper & Row, 1966.

CHOMSKY, NOAM. *Language and Mind,* enlarged edition, ch. 1. New York: Harcourt Brace Jovanovich, 1972.

HERDER, J. G. "Essay on the Origin of Language," in SALUS, 147–167.

ITARD, J. *The Wild Boy of Aveyron.* New York: Appleton-Century-Crofts, 1962.

JESPERSEN, O. *Language,* ch. XXI. New York: W. W. Norton & Co., reprinted 1964.

JESPERSEN, O. *Language: Its Nature, Development and Origin.* London: Allen and Unwin, 1922.

LIEBERMAN, P. "Primate Vocalizations and Human Linguistic Ability," *J. Acoustical Soc. Am.* 44:1574–1584.

LIEBERMAN, P., and CRELIN, E. S. "On the Speech of Neanderthal Man," *Linguistic Inquiry* 2: 203–222.

NEHRING, A. "Plato and the Theory of Language," *Tradition* 1:13–48.

PAGET, R. *Human Speech.* New York: Harcourt, Brace, 1930.

PLATO. *Cratylus* dialogue. Loeb Classical Library. Cambridge: Harvard University Press, 1962.

ROBINS, R. H. *A Short History of Linguistics.* Bloomington: Indiana University Press, 1967.

ROUSSEAU, JEAN JACQUES. "Essay on the Origin of Languages," in SALUS, 138–147.

SALUS, P. H., ed. *On Language: Plato to Von Humboldt.* New York: Holt, Rinehart and Winston, 1969.

SINGH, J. A. L., and ZINGG, R. M. *Wolf-Children and Feral Man.* Hamden, Conn.: Archon Books, 1966.

THORNDIKE, E. L. "The Origin of Language," *Science* 77: 173–175.

VIERTEL, J. "Concepts of Language Underlying the 18th-Century Controversy About the Origin of Language." Georgetown Monograph 19, 1966, 109–132.

3
The Sounds of
Language: Phonetics

*The voice is articulated by the lips and the tongue. . . . Man
speaks by means of the air which he inhales into his entire
body and particularly into the body cavities. When the air
is expelled through the empty space it produces a sound,
because of the resonances in the skull. The tongue articu-
lates by its strokes; it gathers the air in the throat and
pushes it against the palate and the teeth, thereby giving
the sound a definite shape. If the tongue would not articulate each time, by means of its strokes, man would not speak
clearly and would only be able to produce a few simple
sounds.*

HIPPOCRATES, *De Carnibus,* VIII

When we hear a language that we do not know, it sounds like
gibberish. We don't know where one word ends and another begins.
And even if we did we couldn't say what the sentence means.

In using language to speak or understand, the sounds produced or
heard are related by the language system to certain meanings. Anyone
who knows a language knows what sounds are in the language and how
they are "strung" together and what these different sound sequences
mean. Although the sounds of French or Xhosa or Quechua are uninterpretable to someone who does not speak those languages, and although
there may be some sounds in one language that are not in another, all the
languages of the world together comprise a limited set of sounds.

The study of these speech sounds, utilized by all human languages to
represent meanings, is called **phonetics.** To describe speech sounds one
has to decide what an "individual sound" is and how one sound differs
from another.

This is not as easy as it may seem. You "know" there are three sounds
in the word *cat,* one represented by *c,* one by *a* and one by *t.* Yet, physically the word is just one continuous sound. You can *segment* the one
sound into parts because you know the language. If you heard someone
clearing his throat you would be unable to segment the sounds into a se-

quence of discrete units. When you speak you do not produce one sound, and then another, and then another. If you want to say *cat* you don't utter each sound separately; you move your organs of speech continuously, and you produce a continuous sound.

Despite the fact that the sounds we produce and the sounds we hear and comprehend are continuous signals, everyone who has ever attempted to analyze language has accepted the notion that speech utterances can be segmented into individual pieces. According to an ancient Hindu myth, the god Indra, in response to an appeal made by the other gods, attempted for the first time to break speech up into its separate elements. After he accomplished this feat, according to the myth, the sounds could be regarded as language. Indra thus was the first phonetician.

The early Greeks recognized the continual, ever-changing nature of the speech signal. Perhaps this is why they considered Hermes, the messenger of the gods who was always on the move, to be the god of speech. But the fleeting nature of the continually changing sound did not prevent the Greeks from attempting linguistic analysis. Hermogenes, one of the characters in Plato's *Cratylus* dialogue, asks if language can be analyzed by taking it to pieces, and Socrates answers that there is no better way to proceed.

In this sense music is similar to speech. A person who has not studied music cannot write the sequence of individual notes combined by a violinist into one changing continuous sound. A trained musician, however, finds it a simple task. Every human speaker, without special training, can segment a speech signal; when he learns the language he learns to segment an utterance into its basic discrete elements of sound.

To analyze speech into pieces one cannot start with just the acoustic physical signal, or even with the movements of the vocal organs used to produce speech. Where would the breaks come? The difficulties inherent in such an attempt would be complicated, in addition, because no two speakers ever say the "same thing" identically. In fact, the same speaker never says the "same thing" twice in exactly the same way. Yet speakers understand each other because they know the same language. One's knowledge of a language determines when physically different sounds are judged to be the same.

We have already asserted that language and speech are not identical. Our linguistic knowledge, or competence, imposes a system on the sounds produced and heard.

We are capable of making many sounds which we know instinctively (because we know the language) are not speech sounds in our language. An English speaker can and often does make a clicking sound which writers sometimes represent as *tsk tsk tsk*. But these sounds are not part of the English sound system. They never occur as part of the words of the sentences we produce. In fact, it is very difficult for many English speakers to combine this clicking sound with other sounds as Xhosa speakers do. But a click is a speech sound in Xhosa, Zulu, Sotho, Hottentot, just like the *k* or *t* or *b* in English.

Therefore, what is or is not an individual speech sound depends on the particular language. *Tsk* is a speech sound in Xhosa but not in English; *th* is a sound in English but not in French. But the sound we produce with our mouth closed when we have a tickle in our throats is not a speech sound in *any* language, nor is the sound we produce when we sneeze.

The science of phonetics attempts to describe all the sounds used in language—the sounds that constitute a small but extremely important fraction of the totality of sounds that human beings are capable of producing.

The process by which we use our linguistic knowledge to produce a meaningful utterance is a very complicated one. It can be viewed as a chain of events starting with an "idea" or message in the brain of the speaker and ending with the same message in the brain of the hearer. The message is put into a form that is dictated by the language we are speaking. It must then be transmitted by nerve signals to the organs of speech articulation which produce the different physical sounds heard by the listener.

Speech sounds can be described at any stage in this chain of events. The study of the physical properties of the sounds themselves is called **acoustic phonetics.** The study and description of the shapes of the vocal tract which produce the different sounds is called **articulatory phonetics.** One can also study and describe speech sounds in terms of the nerves and muscles used to produce the different articulatory shapes.

THE PHONETIC ALPHABET

Once a Frenchman who'd promptly said "Oui"
To some ladies who'd asked him if houi
Cared to drink, threw a fit
Upon finding that it
Was a tipple no stronger than toui.

—Anonymous

The one–l lama,
He's a priest.
The two–l llama,
He's a beast.

And I will bet
A silk pajama
There isn't any
Three-l lllama.

— OGDEN NASH[1]

All languages are composed of sounds with different physical properties. So-called "dead" languages are no exception. We have approximate knowledge of the speech sounds produced by speakers of languages such as Sumerian, Sanskrit, and Latin because written records are extant. The written records represent the sounds which were used by speakers.

Alphabetic spelling represents the pronunciations of words. But it is often the case that the sounds of the words in a language are rather unsystematically represented by orthography — that is, by spelling.

Suppose all Earthmen were destroyed by some horrible catastrophe, and years later Martian spacemen exploring Earth discovered some fragments of English writing that included the following sentence:

Did he believe that Caesar could see the people seize the seas?

How would a Martian linguist decide that *e, ie, ae, ee, eo, ei,* and *ea* all represented the same sound? To add to his confusion, he might later stumble across this sentence:

The silly amoeba stole the key to the machine.

English speakers know the pronunciation of these words and know that *y, oe, ey,* and *i* also represent the same sound as the italicized letters in the first sentence. But how could a Martian know this?

This inconsistent spelling system prompted Ambrose Bierce to define *orthography* as "the science of spelling by the eye instead of the ear." When Mark Twain wrote: "They spell it Vinci and pronounce it Vinchy; foreigners always spell better than they pronounce,"[2] he was fully aware that it is not just "foreigners" whose spelling differs from pronunciation.

The discrepancy between spelling and sounds gave rise to a movement of English "spelling reformers." They wanted to revise the alphabet so that one letter would correspond to one sound, and one sound to one letter, thus simplifying spelling. This is a *phonetic* alphabet.

George Bernard Shaw followed in the footsteps of three centuries of spelling reformers in England. In typical Shavian manner he pointed out that we could use the English spelling system to spell *fish* as *ghoti* — the *gh* like the sound in *enough,* the *o* like the sound in *women,* and the *ti* like the sound in *nation.* Shaw was so concerned about English spelling that he included in his will a provision for a new "Proposed British

[1] "The Lama," copyright 1931 by Ogden Nash. From *Verses from 1929 On* by Ogden Nash, by permission of Little, Brown and Co. Also by permission of The Estate of Ogden Nash and J. M. Dent & Sons. This poem originally appeared in *The New Yorker.*

[2] Ambrose Bierce, *The Devil's Dictionary;* Mark Twain, *The Innocents Abroad.*

Alphabet" to be administered by a "Public Trustee" who would have the duty of seeking and publishing a more efficient alphabet.   This alphabet was to have at least forty letters to enable "the said language to be written without indicating single sounds by groups of letters or by diacritical marks."   After Shaw's death in 1950, 450 designs for such an alphabet were submitted from all parts of the globe.   Four alphabets were judged to be equally good, and the £500 prize was divided among their designers.   An "expert" collaborated with these four to produce the alphabet designated in Shaw's will.   Shaw also stipulated in his will that his play *Androcles and the Lion* be published in the new alphabet, with "the original Doctor Johnson's lettering opposite the transliteration page by page and a glossary of the two alphabets."   This version of the play was published in 1962.

This new alphabet was not the first phonetic alphabet.   In 1617, Robert Robinson produced an alphabet which attempted to provide a relationship between "articulation" and the shapes of the letters.   In 1657, Cave Beck produced *A Universal Character,* a publication described on its title page as "The Universal Character by which all the Nations in the World may understand one another's Conceptions, Reading out of one Common Writing their own Mother Tongues."   In 1668, Bishop John Wilkins proposed a similar universal alphabet; and in 1686, Francis Lodwick published "An Essay Towards an Universal Alphabet," which he had worked out and circulated many years before.   Lodwick's aim was to provide an alphabet "which should contain an Enumeration of all such Single Sounds or Letters as are used in any Language. ... All single sounds ought to have single and distinct characters" and no one character shall "have more than one Sound, nor any one Sound be expressed by more than one Character."   Lodwick, like Cave Beck before him and others who followed him, did not use Roman letters.   He designed his own "letters" in such a way that similar sounds were represented by similar symbols.   Even in Shaw's lifetime, the phonetician Henry Sweet, the prototype for Shaw's own Henry Higgins, produced a phonetic alphabet.

If we look at English spelling, it is easy to understand why there has been so much concern about spelling systems.   Different letters may represent a single sound, as shown in the following:

> t*o*   t*oo*   tw*o*   thr*ough*   thr*ew*   cl*ue*   sh*oe*

A single letter may represent different sounds:

> d*a*me   d*a*d   f*a*ther   c*a*ll   vill*a*ge   *A*merica   m*a*ny

A combination of letters may represent a single sound:

> | *sh*oot | *ch*aracter | *Th*omas | *ph*ysics |
> | ei*th*er | d*ea*l | rou*gh* | na*ti*on |
> | c*oa*t | glac*i*al | *th*eater | pl*ai*n |

Some letters have no sound at all in certain words in which they occur:

*m*nemonic	*w*hole	resi*g*n	*gh*ost
*p*terodactyl	*w*rite	hol*e*	corp*s*
*p*sychology	s*w*ord	de*b*t	*g*naw
bou*gh*	lam*b*	i*s*land	*k*nife

Some sounds are not represented in the spelling. In many words the letter *u* represents a *y* sound followed by a *u* sound:

c*u*te	(compare: l*oo*t)
f*u*tile	(compare: f*oo*l)
*u*tility	(compare: *oo*ze)

One letter may represent two sounds; the final *x* in *Xerox* represents a *k* followed by an *s*.

All these discrepancies between spelling and sounds seem to argue in favor of the spelling reformers. One may wonder why they didn't win their struggle. One may also wonder how such a chaotic spelling system arose.

The inventor of printing is a major culprit. When scribes used to write manuscripts they would often write words more or less as they pronounced them. But after the invention of printing, the spelling of words became relatively fixed. The present English spelling system is very much like that used in Shakespeare's time, although pronunciation has changed considerably. Pronunciation changes much more rapidly than spelling. What would we do with all the millions of books printed in English if we attempted to change all the spelling to conform to present pronunciation? Even if these books were reprinted and a law passed requiring all new books to conform to some new system of spelling, it would not be too long before the same problem would occur again.

To illustrate how spelling represents an older pronunciation, consider the words *knight* and *night*. They are pronounced identically today. At one time, the *k* was pronounced in the first word and the *gh* in both. At some point in the history of the English language we stopped pronouncing a *k* when it occurred at the beginning of a word followed by *n*. As for the sound spelled *gh,* it dropped out of the English language completely. It was once pronounced like the last sound in the German word *Bach.*

If the spelling reformers could legislate an end to language change, then maybe their plan would be feasible. But this is impossible. Language is continually changing, and this change, apart from making spelling systems obsolete, also creates different dialects of the same language. An additional problem for the reformers is to determine which dialect the spelling should reflect. Should the same word of British and American English be spelled differently if pronounced differently? If not, how should a word like *schedule* be spelled? The British pronounce it as if it were spelled *shedyule* and the Americans pronounce it as if it were spelled *skedjule* or *skejual*. Such pronunciations lend some credence to Shaw's remark: "England and America are two countries separated by the same language." Even if the spelling reformers decided to spell British and American English differently, what would they do with the American dialects? Should *Cuba* be spelled *Cuber* with a final *r*, as President Kennedy pronounced it, or without the *r*? What about the words *cot* and *caught* or *horse* and *hoarse* or *pin* and *pen*? Some Americans pronounce these pairs identically, and others pronounce them differently.

There are further arguments against the spelling reformers, some of which will be discussed in later chapters. In any case, although English spelling does create some difficulties for children learning to read and write (as well as for many adult "poor spellers"), the system is not quite as chaotic as it appears to be.

But whether or not one wishes to take sides for or against spelling reform in English, it is clear that to describe the sounds of English, or any other language, one cannot depend on the spelling of words. In 1888 the International Phonetic Association (IPA) developed a *phonetic alphabet* which could be used to symbolize the sounds found in all languages. Since many languages use a Roman alphabet like that used in the English writing system, the IPA phonetic symbols are based on the Roman letters. These phonetic symbols have a consistent value, unlike ordinary letters, which may or may not represent the same sounds in the same or different languages.

It is of course impossible to construct any set of symbols which will specify all the minute differences between sounds. Even Shaw recognized this when in his will he directed his Trustee

> to bear in mind that the proposed British Alphabet does not pretend to be exhaustive as it contains only sixteen vowels whereas by infinitesimal movements of the tongue countless different vowels can be produced all of them in use among speakers of English who utter the same vowels no oftener than they make the same fingerprints.

Even if we could specify all the details of different pronunciations, we would not want to. A basic fact about speech is that no two utterances are ever physically the same. That is, if a speaker says "Good morning" on Monday and Tuesday there will be some slight differences in the sounds he produces on the two days. In fact if he says "Good morning" twice in succession on the same day, the two utterances will not be physically identical. If another speaker says "Good morning" the physical sounds (that is, the acoustic signal) produced will differ widely from that produced by the first speaker. Yet all the "Good mornings" are considered to be repetitions of the same utterance.

This is an interesting fact about knowing a language. One knows that some differences in the sounds of an utterance are important, and other differences can be ignored. Even though we never produce or hear exactly the same utterance twice, we know when two utterances are linguistically the same or different. Some properties of the sounds must be more important than others. In describing the sounds of a language, we want to reveal those characteristics that all speakers of a language recognize as important in understanding each other.

A phonetic alphabet should include enough symbols to represent the "crucial" differences. At the same time it should not, and cannot, include all noncrucial differences, since such differences are infinitely varied.

A list of phonetic symbols which can be used to represent all the basic speech sounds of English is given below. The symbols omit many details about the sounds and how they are produced in different words, and in different places in words. These symbols are meant to be used by persons knowing English.

For example, in English the *p* in *pit* and the *p* in *spit* are physically different sounds. In *pit,* the *p* is followed by a puff of air (called *aspiration*). In *spit,* it is not. We will discuss this difference below. The fact that most speakers of English do not even know they produce different sounds represented by *p* is shown by the fact that there is only one symbol for these different sounds.

The list of phonetic symbols for consonants, vowels, and diphthongs provides a number of examples of English words. In all cases the different spellings represent the same sound in the American dialect being described, one which is used by a large number of speakers. Some of these pronunciations may differ from yours, and in a few cases where this is so the examples may be confusing. For example, some speakers of American English pronounce the words *cot* and *caught* identically. In the dialect described here, *cot* and *caught* are pronounced differently, so *cot* is given as an example for the symbol /a/ and *caught* for the symbol /ɔ/. For both dialects, however, speakers pronounce *car* and *cor* differently. If you use the vowel of *car* to say *cot* and the vowel of *core* to say *caught,* you will be "speaking" the dialect that distinguishes the two words.

Consonants

SYMBOLS	EXAMPLES
p	*p*at ta*p* *p*it s*p*it ti*p* hiccou*gh* a*p*ple am*p*le *p*rick *p*laque a*pp*ear
b	*b*at ta*b* am*b*le *b*rick *b*lack bu*bb*le
m	*m*at ta*m* s*m*ack a*m*nesia a*m*ple E*mm*y ca*m*p co*m*b
t	*t*ap pa*t* s*t*ick men*t*or *p*terodactyl scen*t*ing kiss*ed* kick*ed* stuff*ed*

SYMBOLS	EXAMPLES
d	*d*ip ca*d* *d*rip guar*d* sen*d*ing men*d*er love*d* cure*d* robbe*d* batte*d*
n	*n*ap ca*n* *sn*ow *kn*ow *mn*emo*n*ic a*n*y pi*n*t *gn*ostic desig*n* *pn*eumatic sig*n* thi*n*
k	*k*it *c*at *ch*arisma *ch*aracter stic*k* criti*qu*e criti*c* *c*lose me*ch*anic e*x*ceed o*ch*er
g	*g*uard bur*g* ba*g* o*g*re a*g*nostic lon*g*er desi*g*nate Pittsbur*gh*
ŋ	si*ng* lo*ng* thi*n*k fi*ng*er si*ng*er a*n*kle (the sound represented by the *n* in *think* is not produced in the same way as that represented by the *n* in *thin;* say the two words to yourself and notice that the tongue gestures are different)
f	*f*at *f*ish *ph*iloso*ph*y *f*racture *f*lat *ph*logiston co*ff*ee ree*f* cou*gh* com*f*ort
v	*v*at do*v*e ri*v*al gra*v*el an*v*il ra*v*age
s	*s*ap *s*kip *s*nip *ps*ychology pa*ss* pat*s* pack*s* democra*c*y *sc*issors fa*s*ten de*c*eive de*s*cent *s*clero*s*is *ps*eudo rhap*s*ody pea*c*e pota*ss*ium
z	*z*ip ja*zz* ra*z*or pad*s* kisse*s* *x*erox *x*ylophone de*s*ign la*z*y mai*z*e lie*s* phy*s*ics pea*s* magne*s*ium
θ	*th*igh *th*rough wra*th* *th*istle e*th*er wrea*th* *th*ink mo*th* ari*th*metic Me*th*uselah tee*th* Ma*tth*ew
ð	*th*e *th*eir *th*en wrea*th*e la*th*e mo*th*er ei*th*er ra*th*er tee*th*e
š(ʃ)*	*sh*oe *sh*y mu*sh* mar*sh* mi*ss*ion na*t*ion fi*sh* glac*i*al *s*ure deduc*t*ion Ru*ss*ian logic*i*an
ž(ʒ)*	mea*s*ure vi*s*ion a*z*ure rou*g*e (for those who do not pronounce this word with the same ending sound as in *judge*) ca*s*ualty deci*s*ion Carte*s*ian
č(tʃ, tš)]*	*ch*oke *ch*ur*ch* mat*ch* fea*t*ure ri*ch* lun*ch* righ*t*eous consti*t*uent
ǰ(dʒ, dž)*	*j*udge mi*d*get *G*eorge ma*g*istrate *j*ello *g*elatine re*g*ion resi*d*ual
l	*l*eaf fee*l* *l*ock ca*ll* pa*l*ace sing*l*e mi*l*d p*l*ant pu*l*p app*l*aud
r	*r*eef fea*r* *r*ock ca*r* Pa*r*is singe*r* p*r*une ca*r*p fu*r*l c*r*uel
y(j)†	*y*ou *y*es ba*y* pla*y*ing feud
w	*w*itch s*w*im mo*w*ing q*u*een

---

* The symbols /š/, /ž/, /č/, /ǰ/ are those usually used by American linguists and phoneticians; the symbols parenthesized —/ʃ/, /ʒ/, /tʃ/, /dʒ/—are the IPA symbols for these sounds. We will use the American symbols, for the most part, throughout the book.

† The American practice of representing this sound as /y/ creates some problems; /y/ is the IPA symbol to represent a vowel such as is found in the French word *tu*. It will be described below.

SYMBOLS	EXAMPLES
ʍ	*wh*ich *wh*ere *wh*at *wh*ale (only for those dialects that do not pronounce *witch* and *which* the same)
h	*wh*o *h*at re*h*ash *h*ole *wh*ole
ʔ	bo*tt*le glo*tt*al (only for those speakers of the dialect who substitute for the *tt* sound the sound which occurs between the vowels as in *uh-uh*)

Vowels

SYMBOLS	EXAMPLES
i	b*ee*t b*ea*t w*e* s*ee* s*ea* rec*ei*ve k*e*y bel*ie*ve am*oe*ba p*eo*ple C*ae*sar vasel*i*ne ser*e*ne f*ie*nd mon*ey* lil*y*
I	b*i*t cons*i*st *i*njury mal*i*gnant b*i*n b*ee*n
e	b*a*te b*ai*t r*a*y prof*a*ne gr*ea*t *ai*r *eigh*t g*au*ge r*ai*n r*ei*gn th*ey*
ɛ	b*e*t ser*e*nity rec*e*ption s*ay*s g*ue*st d*ea*d s*ai*d
æ	p*a*n *a*ct l*au*gh *a*nger l*a*boratory (American English) comr*a*de r*a*lly
u	b*oo*t wh*o* sew*e*r d*u*ty · thr*ough* p*oo*r t*o* t*oo* tw*o* m*o*ve L*ou*
U	p*u*t f*oo*t b*u*tcher c*ou*ld
ʌ	b*u*t t*ou*gh am*o*ng *o*ven d*oe*s c*o*ver fl*oo*d
o	b*oa*t g*o* b*eau* gr*o*w th*ou*gh t*oe* *ow*n *o*ver mel*o*dious
ɔ	b*ou*ght c*au*ght wr*o*ng st*a*lk c*o*re s*aw* b*a*ll *au*thor *awe*
a	p*o*t f*a*ther p*a*lm c*a*r s*e*rgeant h*o*nor h*o*spital mel*o*dic
ə‡	sof*a* *a*lone princi*pa*l sci*e*nce teleg*ra*ph symph*o*ny ros*e*s diffic*u*lt s*u*ppose mel*o*dy m*e*lodi*ou*s want*e*d kiss*e*s th*e* fath*er* b*i*rd h*er*d w*or*d f*ur*

Diphthongs

SYMBOLS	EXAMPLES
ay	b*i*te s*igh*t b*y* d*ie* d*ye* St*ei*n *ai*sle ch*oi*r l*i*ar *i*sland h*eigh*t s*i*gn
æw	ab*ou*t br*ow*n d*ou*bt c*ow*ard
ɔy	b*oy* d*oi*ly

‡ The vowel italicized in "ros*es*" is phonetically more properly symbolized as /ɨ/ to distinguish it from the italicized vowel in "Ros*a*'s."   There are even finer distinctions which can be made for the unstressed, "reduced" vowels, but these will be ignored for our purposes.   Some linguists symbolize this vowel when it occurs before *r* by the symbol /ʌ/ as in *but*; that is, *bird* would be written as /bʌrd/.

Note: To distinguish between a "long" and "short" vowel, the long vowel can be symbolized as /a:/ or /ā/ and the short vowel as /a/.

Using these symbols, we can now unambiguously represent the pronunciations of words. For example, words spelled with *ou* may have different pronunciations. To distinguish between the symbols representing sounds and the alphabet letters, we put the phonetic symbols between two slashes, as has been done above and as is illustrated by the following:[3]

SPELLING	PRONUNCIATION
though	/ðo/
thought	/θɔt/
tough	/tʌf/
bough	/bæw/
through	/θru/
could	/kʊd/

Notice that only in *tough* do the letters *gh* represent any sound; that is, the sound /f/. Notice also that *ou* represents six different sounds, and *th* two different sounds. The *l* in *could,* like the *gh* in all but one of the words above, is not pronounced at all.

Obviously, the symbols given in the list would not be sufficient to represent the pronunciation of words in all languages. We would need another symbol for the *ch* sound in the German word *Bach* (phonetically this symbol is /x/) and for the French vowel sound in the word *tu* (/y/ or /ü/) and for many other sounds not found in the English sound system.

All of the phonetic symbols represent different sounds. The science of phonetics is concerned with the ways in which these sounds differ, and the ways in which they may be similar.

A phonetic alphabet with symbols like those presented in this chapter is useful in a discussion of the sound patterns of language. We will be using these symbols whenever we wish to refer unambiguously to the sounds of words.

ARTICULATORY PHONETICS

> HIGGINS   *Tired of listening to sounds?*
> PICKERING   *Yes. It's a fearful strain. I rather fancied myself because I can pronounce twenty-four distinct vowel sounds, but your hundred and thirty beat me. I can't hear a bit of difference between most of them.*
> HIGGINS   *Oh, that comes with practice. You hear no*

---

[3] Symbols between slashes represent "broad" phonetic or phonemic symbols as opposed to more detailed phonetic symbols, which are enclosed by brackets, [ ]. This will be discussed further in Chapter 4.

difference at first; but you keep on listening, and presently
you find they're all as different as A from B.

— G. B. SHAW, *Pygmalion*

To understand the nature of language, how it "works," and how children learn it, it is not enough merely to list all the individual sounds and provide a symbol for each one. As noted above, almost three hundred years ago Lodwick wished to devise his alphabet in such a way as to "sort [the sounds] into classes." Thousands of years before Lodwick, the Hindu grammarians classified the sounds of Sanskrit into groups according to the ways they were pronounced.

The ways in which sounds are classified may provide some clues as to how sounds are used in language. Before we examine the properties of speech sounds, let's look at how such sounds are used in a language such as English.

Children who learn English know how to form plural nouns from singular nouns at a very early age — usually by two or three years old. This is before they have learned to write, so they don't know that one adds an *s* to form a plural. In fact this is not what anyone does in speaking, even though in writing that may be the most general rule. Now that we know the difference between spelling and pronunciation, we can state the regular rules that form plurals:

1. Add /s/ after words that end in /p, t, k, θ, f/: caps   cats   sacks   myths   muffs.
2. Add /z/ after words that end in /b, d, g, v, ð, l, r, y, w, m, n, ŋ/ and all vowels: cabs   cads   bags   dives   lathes   mills   cars   boys   cows   cans   rams   things   zoos.
3. Add /əz/ after words that end in /s, z, š, ž, č, ǰ/: buses   causes   bushes   garages   beaches   badges.

Say these words out loud to yourself so you can see that the "plural ending" is either /s/, /z/, or /əz/.

Do children really have to learn the plural rule in this way — by memorizing lists of sounds in each of these classes?

A look at how the past tense of English verbs is normally formed may help us to find some "regularity" in the classes of sounds. The past-tense rules can be stated as follows:

1. Add /t/ after verbs that end in /p, k, θ, f, s, š, č/: reaped   peeked   unearthed   huffed   kissed   wished   pitched.
2. Add /d/ after verbs that end in /b, g, ð, v, z, ž, ǰ, n, m, ŋ, l, r, y, w/ and all vowels: grabbed   hugged   seethed   loved   buzzed   rouged   judged   manned   rammed   longed   killed   cared   tied   bowed   hoed.
3. Add /əd/ after verbs that end in /t, d/: stated   clouded.

If you compare Rule 1 of the "plural formation" and Rule 1 of the "past-tense formation" you will notice that the sounds /p/, /k/, /θ/, /f/ are used in both rules; and if you compare Rule 2 in each formation you will notice that the classes of sounds are almost identical. If the sounds were just listed, but not analyzed, this similarly might be considered accidental. On the other hand, if there are indeed some common properties among the sounds which take an /s/ in the plural and a /t/ in the past tense, and among the sounds that take a /z/ in the plural and a /d/ in the past tense, then a child need not memorize long lists of sounds, but instead may learn just which properties of the classes of sounds distinguish one class from another.

When we analyze the sounds in the different rules we find that the ones that take either an /s/ plural or a /t/ past tense are phonetically "voiceless," and furthermore that /s/ and /t/ are also "voiceless." We also find that the sounds that take a /z/ plural or a /d/ past tense are phonetically "voiced" sounds, and that /z/ and /d/ are also phonetically "voiced."

You don't know *yet* what makes a sound "voiceless" or "voiced," but it is easy to see that there is some method in what first appeared as a lot of madness.

Leaving aside for the moment the classes of sounds that form plurals and pasts by adding /əz/ or /əd/, the rules become much simpler:

1. Add /z/ for the plural and /d/ for the past to a word ending with a voiced sound.
2. Add /s/ for the plural and /t/ for the past to a word ending with a voiceless sound.

Or, more simply, we can say:

3. Add the voiceless sound to a word ending with a voiceless sound and the voiced sound to a word ending with a voiced sound.

By this rule it would appear that we should add a /t/ to a verb ending with a /t/ and a /d/ to a verb ending with a /d/. But then it would be hard to "hear" a difference between a present and a past form of the verb. To test this, try saying the past tense of *state* by adding a /t/ — you would get /stett/. We find it difficult in English to distinguish between a single /t/ and two /t/'s without a vowel in between. That's why we add the little short vowel /ə/ to these verbs. With respect to the plural, /s/, /z/, /š/, /ž/, /č/, /ǰ/ are very similar to /s/ and /z/. In order to distinguish the singulars of words ending with these sounds and their plurals, the little short vowel /ə/ is inserted.

Thus when we analyze sounds according to certain phonetic properties, the individual sounds fall into classes, and these classes are used by speakers to form "rules" of language.

Another example will show how we find the same kinds of classes in very different languages. In English we can change some words into their opposites by adding a prefix. Thus *intolerant* means *not tolerant,* im-

possible means *not possible,* and *incomplete* means *not complete.* The prefix meaning "not" is pronounced /ɪn/ before /t/, /ɪm/ before /p/, and /ɪŋ/ before /k/. (You might not have realized that you pronounce the *n* in *incomplete* as /ŋ/, but most speakers of English do. If you say the word in normal tempo without pausing after the *in* you may notice that your tongue is in the same position as in the final sound of *sing*.)

To form a negative sentence in the Ghanaian language Twi, you add either /n/, /m/, or /ŋ/ before the verb, as shown below:

mɪ pɛ	"I like"	mɪ mpɛ	"I don't like"
mɪ tɪ	"I speak"	mɪ ntɪ	"I don't speak"
mɪ kɔ	"I go"	mɪ ŋkɔ	"I don't go"

Thus in Twi, as in English, you use /n/ before /t/, /m/ before /p/, and /ŋ/ before /k/. This might appear to be just an accident. But when this same "accident" occurs in language after language, there should be some reason.

By understanding how sounds are produced and by classifying them according to their articulatory properties we can provide answers to why we find such similar processes in different languages.

PHONETIC FEATURES

Airstream Mechanisms

The production of any speech sound (or any sound at all) involves the movement of an airstream. Most speech sounds are produced by pushing lung air out of the body through the mouth and sometimes also through the nose. Since lung air is used, these sounds are called **pulmonic** **sounds**; since the air is pushed *out,* they are called **egressive.** The majority of sounds used in languages of the world are thus produced by a **pulmonic egressive** airstream mechanism. All the sounds in English are produced in this manner.

Other airstream mechanisms are used in other languages to produce sounds called **ejectives, implosives,** and **clicks.** Implosives and clicks are **ingressive** sounds because air is sucked in instead of flowing out. Sounds may therefore be classified according to the airstream mechanism used to produce them.

Voiced and Voiceless Sounds

The airstream from the lungs moves up through the trachea or windpipe and through the opening between the vocal cords which is called the **glottis** (see Figure 3.1).

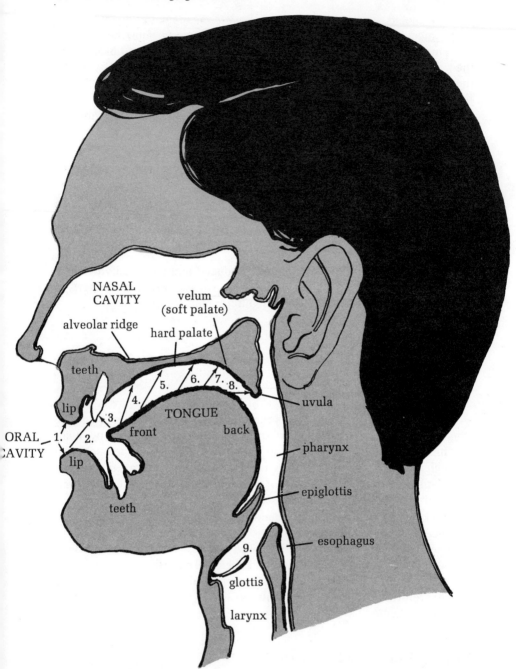

Figure 3.1   The vocal tract.   *Places of articulation:*   *1* bilabial — *2* labiodental — *3* dental or interdental — *4* alveolar — *5* palatoalveolar — *6* palatal — *7* velar — *8* uvular — *9* glottal.

If the vocal cords are apart, the airstream is not obstructed at the glottis and it passes freely into the supraglottal cavities (the parts of the vocal tract above the glottis). The sounds produced in this way are called **voiceless** sounds; /p/, /t/, /k/, and /s/ are voiceless sounds. All the sounds in the /s/-plural class and in the /t/-past-tense class are voiceless sounds.

If the vocal cords are together, the airstream forces its way through and causes them to *vibrate*. Such sounds are called **voiced** sounds. As we have said, all the sounds in the /z/-plural class are voiced sounds; all the sounds in the /d/-past-tense class are voiced sounds; /z/ and /d/ are also voiced sounds. If you put a finger in each ear and say "z-z-z-z-z-z" you can feel the vibrations of the sound as it goes through the vibrating vocal cords. If you now say "s-s-s-s-s" you will not feel these vibrations. When you whisper, you are making *all* the speech sounds voiceless.

Voiced sounds condition the addition of a voiced /z/ or /d/; voiceless sounds condition the addition of a voiceless /s/ or /t/.

The position of the vocal cords during speech permits us to classify speech sounds into two large classes: **voiced** and **voiceless**. We could also call these classes [+ *voiced*] and [− *voiced*]. The only difference between the words *fine* and *vine, pin* and *bin, tin* and *din, seal* and *zeal, cane* and *gain,* is that the first word in each pair starts with a voiceless consonant and the second with a consonant identical in all ways except that it is voiced. The position of the lips and tongue is the same in the two paired words. Only the position of the vocal cords differs in producing /f/ and /v/, /p/ and /b/, /t/ and /d/, /s/ and /z/, /k/ and /g/.

Words may also be distinguished if the *final* sounds differ as to vocal cord position, as in *nap* and *nab, writ* and *rid, rack* and *rag, wreath* and *wreathe, rich* and *ridge.* Again the first words of the pairs end in voiceless sounds, and the second words end in corresponding voiced sounds. Except for voicing, the sounds of each pair are identical.

Sounds must differ from each other in other ways than voicing. That is, /p/, /t/, /k/ are all voiceless, and /b/, /m/, /d/, /n/, /ǰ/, /ŋ/ are all voiced, yet all these sounds are distinct from one another in English. What further differences are there?

Nasal vs. Oral Sounds

If you say *pad, bad,* and *mad* you will notice that the initial sounds are very similar. The /p/, /b/, and /m/ are all produced by closing the lips. /p/ differs from /b/ only because in producing the voiceless /p/ the vocal cords are apart; the glottis is open. /b/ is voiced because the vocal cords are together and vibrating. If you put your hands over your ears and keep your lips together for the /b/ you will feel the hum of the vibrations.   If you do the same and say "m-m-m-m" or *mad* you will see that /m/ is also a voiced sound.   What, then, distinguishes the /m/ from the /b/?

/m/ is a **nasal** sound.   When you produce /m/, air escapes not only through the mouth (when you open your lips) but also through the nose.

In Figure 3.1, notice the part of the roof of the mouth called the **velum.**   It is also called the **soft palate.**   The bony structure of the oral cavity is called the **hard palate.**   You can feel this hard palate with your finger.   You can also feel the section of the palate where the flesh becomes soft and is movable.   At the end of the soft palate or velum is the **uvula,** which you can see in the mirror hanging down if you open your mouth wide and say "aaah."   When the velum is raised all the way to touch the back of the throat, the passage through the nose is cut off.   When the nasal passage is blocked in this way, the air can escape only through the mouth.   Sounds produced this way are called **oral** sounds.   /p/ and /b/ are oral sounds.   When the velum is lowered, air escapes through the nose as well as the mouth.   Sounds produced this way are called **nasal** sounds.   /m/, /n/, and /ŋ/ are the nasal consonants of English.   The diagrams in Figure 3.2 show the position of the lips and the velum when /m/ and /p/ or /b/ are articulated.

The difference between *bad* and *mad, dot* and *not,* is due only to the position of the velum in the first sounds of the words.   In *bad* and *dot* the velum is raised, preventing air from entering the nasal cavity.   /b/ and /d/ are therefore *oral* sounds.   In *mad* and *not* the velum is lowered and air travels through the nose as well as the mouth.   /m/ and /n/ are therefore *nasal* sounds.   Note that /b/, /d/, /m/, and /n/ are all voiced.

Words with final consonants, alike in all other respects, may **contrast** with respect to the oral-nasal distinction.   The final sounds of *rib* and

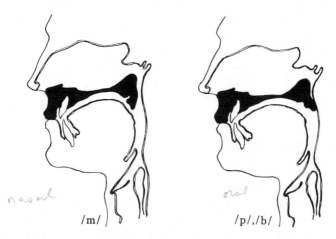

nasal   /m/   oral   /p/,/b/

Figure 3.2 Position of lips and velum for /m/ (lips together, velum down) and /p/, /b/ (lips together, velum up).

rim, mad and *man, dig* and *ding* (the *ng* is the one sound /ŋ/) are identical except the first of each pair is oral, the second is nasal.

These **phonetic features** or **properties** enable us to classify all speech sounds into four classes: voiced, voiceless, nasal, oral. One sound may belong to more than one class, as shown in Table 3.1. We can also classify these sounds by specifying them as + or − for each phonetic property we have discussed:

	/p/	/t/	/k/	/b/	/d/	/g/	/m/	/n/	/ŋ/
Voiced	−	−	−	+	+	+	+	+	+
Nasal	−	−	−	−	−	−	+	+	+

It is easy, by this method, to determine the different classes of speech sounds. All sounds marked [+voiced] are in the class of voiced sounds, all sounds marked [−voiced] are in the class of voiceless sounds, all sounds marked [+nasal] are in the class of nasal sounds, and those marked [−nasal] are in the class of oral sounds.

Table 3.1 Classes of speech sounds

	Oral (−nasal)	*Nasal* (+nasal)
Voiced (+voiced)	/b/, /d/, /g/	/m/, /n/, /ŋ/
Voiceless (−voiced)	/p/, /t/, /k/	All nasal consonants *in English* are voiced

Below we will discuss many other phonetic features. Each feature will determine a class of speech sounds. These classes will be most easily specified by using pluses and minuses, much as we did in the previous paragraph.

Articulatory Modification of Sounds

If /b/, /d/, and /g/ are all voiced non-nasal (oral) sounds, what distinguishes them? We know they are distinct because *brew, drew,* and *grew* and *bash, dash,* and *gash* are different words. There must be other phonetic properties besides those already discussed.

Labials By moving the tongue and lips we are able to change the shape of the oral cavity and in this way produce different sounds. When we produce a /b/, /p/, or /m/, we **articulate** by bringing both lips together. These sounds are therefore called **bilabials**.

We also use our lips to form /f/ and /v/, as in *fine* and *vine*. In this case we articulate by touching the bottom lip to the upper teeth. Hence these sounds are called **labiodental.** The five sounds that comprise the three bilabials /b/ /p/ and /m/ and the two labiodentals /f/ and /v/ are also called **labial.**

Alveolars   When we articulate a /d/, /n/, or /t/ we raise the tip of the tongue to the hard palate right at the point of the bony tooth ridge, called the **alveolar** ridge (see Figure 3.1).   Sounds produced by raising the tongue tip to the alveolar ridge are called **alveolar** sounds.   If you say *two, do, new, Sue, zoo* you will notice that the first sounds in all these words are produced by raising your tongue tip toward the alveolar ridge.   The /t/ and /s/ are voiceless alveolar sounds, and the /d/, /z/, and /n/ are voiced.   Only /n/ is nasal.

Velars   Another group of sounds is produced by raising the back of the tongue to the soft palate or velum.   The sounds ending the words *back, bag,* and *bang* are produced this way and are called **velar** sounds.

Interdentals   To produce the sounds beginning the words *thin* /θ/ and *then* /ð/ you insert the tip of the tongue between the upper and lower teeth.   These are **interdental** sounds.   The /θ/ in *thin* and *ether* is a voiceless interdental, and the /ð/ in *then* and *either* is a voiced interdental.

Palatals (or Alveopalatals)   If you raise the front part of your tongue to a point on the hard palate, just behind the alveolar ridge, you can produce the sounds in the middle of the words *mesher* /mɛšər/ and *measure* /mɛžər/.   The voiceless /š/ and the voiced /ž/ are called **postalveolar** or **palatal** sounds.   In English the voiced /ž/ never begins words, but /š/ is the sound which begins the words *shoe, shut, sure,* and *sugar.*

Manners of Articulation

Stops   We already have a number of distinct phonetic properties permitting many overlapping classes of sounds.   Both /t/ and /s/, for example, are in the class of voiceless oral alveolar sounds.   But what distinguishes the /t/ from the /s/?

Once the airstream enters the oral cavity it may be stopped, it may be partly obstructed, or it may flow freely out of the mouth.   Sounds which are stopped *completely* for a brief period are, not surprisingly, called **stops.**   All other sounds are called **continuants** because the stream of air continues to pass through the mouth opening.   /p/, /b/, /m/, /t/, /d/, /n/, /k/, /g/, /ŋ/ are stops which occur in English.   In the production of nasal stops, the air does continue through the nose, but there is a blockage of the airflow in the oral cavity.   Notice when you produce these sounds that the air is completely blocked either at the lips or where the tongue touches the alveolar ridge or velum.

/b/, /p/, /m/ are bilabial stops.   The airstream is stopped at the mouth by the complete closure of the lips.

/d/, /t/, /n/ are alveolar stops. The airstream is stopped by the tongue making a complete closure with the alveolar ridge.

/g/, /k/, /ŋ/ are velar stops. The airstream is stopped by the back of the tongue making a complete closure with the velum.

In Quechua one finds **uvular** stops as well. These are produced when the back of the tongue is raised and moved backward to form a complete closure with the uvula. The symbol for a voiceless uvular stop is /q/.

Some phoneticians call these stop sounds **plosives** because the airstream after being completely blocked explodes upon the release of the closure.

Aspirated vs. Unaspirated Sounds   When we distinguished above between voiced and voiceless sounds we pointed out that during the production of voiceless sounds the glottis is open and the air passes freely through the opening between the vocal cords. When the following sound is a voiced sound, which it often is, the vocal cords must close.

Voiceless sounds may differ among themselves depending on the "timing" of the vocal cord closure. In English, when we pronounce the word *pit* there is a brief period of voicelessness *immediately after* the stop closure is released. That is, after the lips come apart the vocal cords are still kept open for a very short time. Such sounds are called *aspirated*. When we pronounce the /p/ in *spit,* however, the vocal cords start vibrating as soon as the lips are opened. Such sounds are called *unaspirated*. Similarly, the /t/ in *tick* and the /k/ in *kin* are aspirated voiceless stops, while the /t/ in *stick* and the /k/ in *skin* are unaspirated. If you hold a strip of paper before your lips and say *pit,* the "aspiration" will be shown by the fact that the paper is pushed as if by a breeze. The paper, however, will not move or be pushed when you say *spit.*

In English these two *p* sounds (or *k* or *t* sounds) are not distinguished "linguistically." If you produce an aspirated "p" in *spit,* it will not change the meaning of the word. In Thai the difference between an aspirated and an unaspirated voiceless stop is as important as the difference between a voiced or a voiceless stop. In French all the voiceless sounds are unaspirated. Whether two sounds are considered to be the same or different by speakers of the language depends upon the linguistic system, and not solely on the phonetic properties of the sounds.

Aspirated sounds are usually symbolized with a small raised *h* to distinguish them from unaspirated sounds. This is shown by the following Thai examples:

VOICELESS UNASPIRATED	VOICELESS ASPIRATED	VOICED
pàa "forest"	p^{h}àa "to split"	bàa "shoulder"
tam "to pound"	t^{h}am "to do"	dam "black"
kàt "to bite"	k^{h}àt "to interrupt"	

Fricatives   In the production of some sounds the airstream is not stopped competely but is obstructed from flowing freely. If you put your hand in front of your mouth when you produce an /s/, /z/, /f/, /v/, /θ/, /ð/, /š/, or /ž/, you will feel the air coming out of your mouth. The passage in the mouth through which the air must pass, however, is very narrow, and the narrowness of this passage causes turbulence. The air particles are pushed one against the other, producing *noise* because of the *friction*. Such sounds are called **fricatives**. (You may also hear them referred to as **spirants,** from the Latin word *spirare,* "to blow.")

In the production of the fricatives /f/ and /v/, the friction is created at the lips, where a narrow passage permits the air to escape.

In the production of the fricatives /s/ and /z/, the friction is created at the alveolar ridge.

In the production of the fricatives /š/ and /ž/, the friction or noise is created as the air passes through the narrow opening behind the alveolar ridge.

In the production of /θ/ and /ð/, the friction is created at the opening between the tongue and the teeth.

In modern English we do not have any velar fricatives. Both voiced and voicelss velar fricatives do occur in many languages. Velar fricatives once occurred in English in such words as *right, knight, enough,* and *through.* The spelling *gh* represented this sound. If you raise the back of the tongue to the soft palate as if you were about to produce a /g/ or /k/, but stop just short of touching the velum, you can produce a velar fricative. The voiced velar fricative is symbolized as /γ/, and its voiceless counterpart as /x/. The /x/ is the final sound of the German pronunciation of the name *Bach.*

Affricates Some sounds are produced by a stop closure followed immediately by a slow release of the closure characteristic of a fricative. These sounds are called **affricates**. /č/ and /ǰ/ are such sounds. /č/ occurs as the first and last sound of the word *church* /čərč/; /ǰ/ occurs analogously in *judge* /ǰʌǰ/. Phonetically, an affricate is a sequence of a stop plus a fricative. Thus /č/ is the same as the sound combination /t/ + /š/ and /ǰ/ the same as /d/ + /ž/, as you can see by prolonging the pronunciation of either affricate. This fact can also be perceived by observing that the (natural) pronunciation of the consonants in *white shoes* /waytšuz/ and *why choose* /waycuz/ is usually the same.

Sibilants The fricatives /s/, /z/, /š/, /ž/ and the affricates /č/, and /ǰ/ represent a class of sounds called **sibilants**. When you produce these sounds the friction produces a "hissing" noise. Notice that it is just these "sibilants" which constitute that class of sounds which take an /əz/ in the plural.

Obstruents The non-nasal stops, the fricatives, and the affricates are all called **obstruents** because the airstream is obstructed before its release. Fricatives are continuants as well, because despite the obstruction, the air continues to flow without a total stoppage. Stops and affricates are noncontinuant obstruants because there is complete blockage of the air during the production of these sounds. The closure of a stop is released abruptly, as opposed to the closure of an affricate, which is released gradually, causing friction.

All other sounds are called **sonorants.** The class of sonorants includes the nasal stops, because although the air is blocked in the mouth, it continues to "resonate" and move through the nose.

Liquids   The sounds /l/ and /r/ are also continuants. There is some obstruction of the airstream in the mouth, but not enough to cause friction. These sounds are called **liquids.**

/l/ is a **lateral** sound. The front of the tongue makes contact with the alveolar ridge, but the sides of the tongue are down, permitting the air to escape laterally through the sides.

The /r/ sound is usually formed in English by curling the tip of the tongue back behind the alveolar ridge. Such sounds are called **retroflex** sounds. In some languages the /r/ may be a **trill,** which is produced by the tip of the tongue vibrating against the roof of the mouth. It is possible that in an earlier stage of English the /r/ was a trill. A trilled /r/ occurs in many contemporary languages, such as Spanish. In other languages the /r/ is produced by a single **tap** instead of a series of vibrating taps; or it may even be produced by making the tongue **flap** against the alveolar ridge. This sound can be symbolized as /D/. Some speakers of British English produce a flapped /r/ in words like *very.* It sounds almost like a "very fast" /d/. Most American speakers produce a flap instead of a /t/ or a /d/ in words like *rider* and *writer.* Note the difference in the articulation of *ride* /rayd/ and *rider* /rayDər/, and *write* /rayt/ and *writer* /rayDər/. For many speakers *rider* and *writer* are pronounced identically in regular conversation.

In English, /l/ and /r/ are regularly voiced. When they follow voiceless sounds, as in *please* or *price,* they may be automatically "de-voiced," at least partially. This may be symbolized by a small circle under the symbol, e.g. /r̥/. (The same **diacritic** mark can be used to represent a voiceless nasal—for example, /n̥/.) Many languages of the world have a voiceless /l̥/. Welsh is an example; the name *Lloyd* in Welsh starts with a voiceless /l̥/.

Some languages may lack liquids entirely, or have only a single one. The Cantonese dialect of Chinese has the single liquid /l/. This fact has been the basis for many dialect jokes, in which, for example, *fried rice* is pronounced as *flied lice.* One need but listen to an American trying to speak Chinese, French, or Quechua to know that such humor can be in both directions.

Acoustically (that is, as physical sounds), /l/ and /r/ are very similar, which is why they are grouped together in the class of liquids and why they behave as a single class of sounds in certain circumstances. For example, the only two consonants permitted after an initial /k/, /g/,

/p/, or /b/ in English are the liquids /l/ and /r/. Thus we have *clear* /klir/, *crop,* /krap/ *plate* /plet/, *crate* /kret/, *glad* /glæd/, *grad* /græd/, *bland* /blænd/ and *brand* /brænd/, but nothing beginning */ks . . ./, */kp . . ./, and so on. (Notice that in words like *psychology* the *p* is not pronounced.)

Glides   The sounds /y/ and /w/ are produced with little or no obstruction of the airstream in the mouth.   When occurring in a word they must always be either preceded or followed directly by a vowel.   In articulating /y/ or /w/, the tongue moves rapidly in a gliding fashion either toward or away from a neighboring vowel, hence the term **glide.** Glides are transition sounds, being partly like consonants and partly like vowels, and they are sometimes called **semi-vowels.**

In producing a /y/ glide, the blade of the tongue is raised toward the hard palate, so /y/ is called a **palatal** glide.   The tongue is in a position almost identical to that assumed in producing the /i/ sound as in the word *beat.*   In pronouncing *you* /yu/ the tongue moves rapidly over the /y/ to the /u/.

The /w/ glide is produced by both raising the back of the tongue toward the velum and simultaneously rounding the lips.   It is thus a **labiovelar** glide.   In the dialect of English where speakers have different pronunciations for *which* /ʍɪč/ and *witch* /wɪč/, the labiovelar glide in the first word is the voiceless /ʍ/, and in the second word it is the voiced /w/.   The position of the tongue and the lips when one produces a /w/ is very similar to the positions for the production of a /u/, but the /w/ is a glide because the tongue moves quickly to the vowel which follows.

To produce the consonant /h/ which starts words such as *house, who,* and *hair,* the glottis is open as in the production of voiceless sounds.   No other modification of the airstream mechanism occurs in the mouth.   In fact, the tongue and lips are usually in the position for the production of the following vowel as the airstream passes through the open glottis. The air or noise produced at the glottis is heard as /h/, and for this reason /h/ is often classified as a **voiceless glottal fricative.**   The /h/ is also classified as a glide by some linguists.

If the air is stopped completely at the glottis by tightly closed vocal cords, the sound produced is that which occurs in some dialects in place of the *tt* in words such as *bottle.*   If you ever heard a New Yorker say this word you know what a **glottal stop** symbolized as /ʔ/ sounds like. If you say "ah-ah-ah-ah," one right after the other, but do not sustain the vowel sound, you will be producing glottal stops between the vowels. The /ʔ/ is considered either in the class of glides or the class of stops.

In Table 3.2, each consonant given in the chart of phonetic symbols is specified by its phonetic features.   Note that it is not necessary to include both the features "voiced" and "voiceless" or "oral" and "nasal" since any consonant marked [−voiced] must be "voiceless" and any consonant

Table 3.2 Phonetic feature specification of consonants

Phonetic Segments

Phonetic Features	p	b	m	t	d	n	k	g	ŋ	f	v	s	z	θ	ð	š	ž	č	ǰ	l	r	w	ʍ	y	h	ʔ
Voiced	−	+	+	−	+	+	−	+	+	−	+	−	+	−	+	−	+	−	+	+	+	+	−	+	−	−
Nasal	−	−	+	−	−	+	−	−	+	−	−	−	−	−	−	−	−	−	−	−	−	−	−	−	−	−
Stop	+	+	+	+	+	+	+	+	+	−	−	−	−	−	−	−	−	+	+	−	−	−	−	−	−	+
Affricate	−	−	−	−	−	−	−	−	−	−	−	−	−	−	−	−	−	+	+	−	−	−	−	−	−	−
Liquid	−	−	−	−	−	−	−	−	−	−	−	−	−	−	−	−	−	−	−	+	+	−	−	−	−	−
Glide	−	−	−	−	−	−	−	−	−	−	−	−	−	−	−	−	−	−	−	−	−	+	+	+	+	+
Sibilant	−	−	−	−	−	−	−	−	−	−	−	+	+	−	−	+	+	+	+	−	−	−	−	−	−	−
Labial	+	+	+	−	−	−	−	−	−	+	+	−	−	−	−	−	−	−	−	−	−	+	+	−	−	−
Alveolar	−	−	−	+	+	+	−	−	−	−	−	+	+	−	−	−	−	−	−	+	−	−	−	−	−	−
Interdental	−	−	−	−	−	−	−	−	−	−	−	−	−	+	+	−	−	−	−	−	−	−	−	−	−	−
Velar	−	−	−	−	−	−	+	+	+	−	−	−	−	−	−	−	−	−	−	−	−	+	+	−	−	−
Glottal	−	−	−	−	−	−	−	−	−	−	−	−	−	−	−	−	−	−	−	−	−	−	−	−	+	+
Palatal	−	−	−	−	−	−	−	−	−	−	−	−	−	−	−	+	+	+	+	−	−	−	−	+	−	−

marked [−nasal] must be "oral." There are other features which can be used to group these consonants into larger more inclusive classes. For example, the labial, alveolar, and postalveolar sounds are all articulated at the front of the mouth, while the velar and glottal sounds are produced at the back. One could also use the feature "back" and divide these sounds into the two classes [+back] and [−back].

Using a "feature" specification of this kind, one can easily group all the sounds into all the classes of which they are members; all sounds marked + for a certain feature belong in one class (for example, [+stop] sounds), and all those marked − for a certain feature belong in another class (for example, [−stop] sounds or continuants).

Vowels

In every language of the world, speech sounds can be divided into two major classes — **consonants** and **vowels**. Consonants, as a class, are those sounds which are produced by obstructing the flow of air as it travels through the mouth. Vowels are produced with no oral obstruction whatsoever. Speakers usually know "intuitively" which sounds are vowels and which are consonants. This is because vowels constitute the "main core" of syllables and can be produced alone. We have already seen that some sounds do not fall easily into one of these two classes. Glides, for example, are like vowels in that there is little oral obstruction, but they are also like consonants in that their duration is very short and they always occur either before or after a vowel.

Liquids are like consonants in some ways and vowels in others. Because they are produced with obstructions in the oral cavity they are like consonants. But acoustically they have "resonances" like vowels.

To show the way all the sounds we have discussed group themselves into overlapping classes, we can use the two features **vocalic** and **consonantal** and mark each segment as being either plus or minus for each feature, as in Table 3.3. By such a system, consonants and vowels are distinct classes; they do not share any feature. Glides, however, are like consonants in that they are in the class of [−vocalic] segments, but they are like vowels in that they are in the class of [−consonantal] segments. Similarly, liquids are in the [+consonantal] class with consonants and the [+vocalic] class with vowels. In languages of the world we find this to be a helpful classification because it is true that glides and liquids can function like either consonants or vowels in certain contexts.

The quality of vowels is determined by the particular configuration of the vocal tract. Different parts of the tongue may be raised or lowered. The lips may be spread or pursed. The passage through which the air travels, however, is never so narrow as to obstruct free flow of the airstream.

Table 3.3   Vocalic and consonantal groupings

	Classes			
Features	*Consonants*	*Vowels*	*Glides*	*Liquids*
Consonantal	+	−	−	+
Vocalic	−	+	−	+

Vowel sounds carry pitch and loudness; you can sing vowels. They may be long or short. Vowels can "stand alone" — they can be produced without any consonants before or after them. One can say the /i/ of *beat,* the /ɪ/ of *bit,* or the /u/ of *boot,* for example, without the initial /b/ or the final /t/. But you can't really produce a /b/ or a /t/ without some kind of vowel attached.

There have been many different schemes used for describing vowel sounds. They may be described by articulatory features, as we have classified consonants. Many beginning students of phonetics find this method more difficult to apply to vowel articulations than to consonant articulations. When you make a /t/ you feel your tongue touch the alveolar ridge. When you make a /p/ you can feel your two lips come together or you can watch the lips move in a mirror. Since vowels are produced without any articulators touching or even coming very close together, it is often difficult to figure out just what is going on. One of the authors of this book almost gave up as a linguist and phonetician at the beginning of her graduate work because she couldn't understand what was meant by "front," "back," "high," and "low" vowels.

But these terms do have meaning. If you watched an x-ray movie of someone talking you would understand why vowels have traditionally been classified according to three questions:

1. How high is the tongue?
2. What part of the tongue is involved, i.e. what part is raised? What part lowered?
3. What is the position of the lips?

There are other distinguishing features, such as length, nasalization, and tenseness, which we will discuss below.

The three diagrams in Figure 3.3 show that in the production of /i/ and /u/ the tongue is very *high* in the mouth. But in /i/ it is the *front* part of the tongue which is raised and in /u/ it is the *back* part of the tongue. In /a/ the *back* of the tongue is *lowered.*

/ɪ/ is produced with the front part of the tongue raised slightly less than /i/, and /ʊ/ is produced with the back part of the tongue raised not quite as high as /u/.

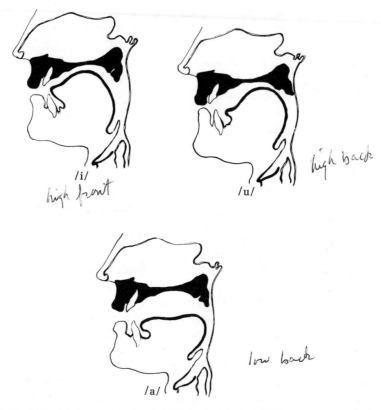

Figure 3.3 Position of the tongue for /i/ (high, front), /u/ (high, back), and /a/ (low, back).

Using these "dimensions," we can plot the American English vowels (Table 3.4). This simple classification permits us to group vowels in the following way:

high vowels: /i/, /ɪ/, /u/, /ʊ/	*front vowels:* /i/, /ɪ/, /e/, /ɛ/, /æ/
mid vowels: /e/, /ɛ/, /ə/, /o/, /ɔ/	*central vowels:* /ə/, /ʌ/
low vowels: /æ/, /ʌ/, /a/	*back vowels:* /u/, /ʊ/, /o/, /ɔ/, /a/

Just as the classes of consonants show up again and again in language rules, so do these vowel classes.

Remember that these are "broad" descriptions which do not give all the phonetic details. In English, for example, the vowels /i/, /e/, /u/, and /o/ are not "simple" vowels. Simple vowels are called **monophthongs** as opposed to **diphthongs**, which include both a vowel and a glide. These four English vowels could be phonetically symbolized more narrowly as /i/ = [ɪy], /e/ = [ɛy], /u/ = [ʊw], /o/ = [ɔw]. The more detailed pho-

Table 3.4   Dimensional classification of vowels

	Part of the Tongue Involved		
	Front	*Central*	*Back*
High	i		u
	ɪ		ʊ
Mid	e		o
	ɛ	ə	ɔ
Low	æ	ʌ	a

netic symbolization is enclosed between square brackets, as opposed to the broad or more general symbols, enclosed between slashes.

Some linguists use the terms **tense** and **lax** to distinguish between /i/ and /ɪ/, /u/ and /ʊ/, /e/ and /ɛ/, and /o/ and /ɔ/. The first vowel of each pair is tense, and the second lax. These terms are **cover terms** representing a number of phonetic properties which distinguish, for example, the tense /i/ from the lax /ɪ/. The tense vowels in English are diphthongized, are longer in duration, and are produced by a slightly higher tongue position. One reason for classifying vowels as tense and lax in English is because we can state certain generalities about the classes instead of making statements about each particular vowel pair.

Vowels are differentiated not only by tongue height, tongue part, and tenseness (or diphthongization), but also by lip position. In the production of English vowels, we round our lips when we say /u/, /ʊ/, /o/, and /ɔ/. It is true that some speakers use more lip rounding than others, but, generally speaking, the non-low back vowels in English are produced with some lip rounding.

On the other hand, front vowels are never rounded in English. This is not true in all languages. French, for example, has rounded front vowels:

/ü/   as in *tu* /tü/ "you" (singular)   The tongue position is as for /i/, but the lips are rounded

/ø/   as in *bleu* /blø/ "blue"   The tongue position is as in /e/, but the lips are rounded

/œ/   as in *heure* /œr/ "hour"   The tongue position is as in /ɛ/, but the lips are rounded

Another fact about the English vowel system is that there are no non-low back vowels which are "unrounded." In Mandarin Chinese and in many other languages there are also high back unrounded vowels:

/ɰ/ as in /sɰ/ "four"   The tongue position is as for /u/, but the lips are spread

This word in Mandarin contrasts with /su/ "speed," where the high back vowel is rounded as in English.

This shows that certain combinations of phonetic features may or may not occur in all languages. That is, in English (but not in all languages) the lip rounding of vowels is *predictable*. If you know that a vowel is non-low and back you know (can predict) that it is rounded. Rounding is not a predictable feature in either French or Mandarin.

Nasalized Vowels   Vowels, like consonants, can also be produced with a lowered velum, which permits air to escape through the nose. Such vowels are called **nasal** or **nasalized vowels.**

In English, nasal vowels occur only before or after nasal consonants. Nasality is therefore predictable. We do not need to designate by a special phonetic mark that the vowel is or is not nasal. To represent vowels in English in a more detailed way, the symbol ∼ can be placed over the vowels which are nasalized, as shown below:

> *ban* [bæ̃n], *sin* [sĩn], *keen* [kĩn]

Once more we have used the square brackets, since the phonetic transcription is a detailed or narrow symbolization. However, because in English it is *always* the case that vowels are nasalized when followed by a nasal consonant, this is a predictable feature and the vowels need not be marked this way. The reason that vowels are nasalized when they immediately precede a nasal consonant is that the velum starts to lower during the vowel production in anticipation of the following nasal consonant.

In French (and some other languages) the nasality of vowels is not always predictable phonetically. That is, nasalized vowels may occur when no nasal consonant is in the immediate phonetic neighborhood, though an unpronounced letter that would be a nasal consonant if pronounced may occur in the written word to indicate the nasal vowel. Note that the *n* in each French word below is not pronounced; thus there is no /n/ in the phonetic symbolization. The symbol ∼ indicates the nasal vowel.

> /ɛ̃/ as in *vin* [vɛ̃] "wine"
> /ɑ̃/ as in *an* [ɑ̃] "year"
> /õ/ as in *son* [sõ] "sound"
> /œ̃/ as in *brun* [brœ̃] "brown"

NATURAL CLASSES

We have now listed a number of phonetic properties which group all the speech sounds of all languages into overlapping classes. This enables us to show how one sound is both similar to and different from all other speech sounds in a language.

For example, /č/ is like the voiceless sounds /p/, /s/, /k/, and /θ/ and functions together with this class in the formation of the past tense in English. One adds a /t/ to form the past on a verb ending in /č/ in the same way as one adds a /t/ to form the past on verbs ending with those other voiceless sounds. Now /č/ is distinguished from /ǰ/ on the basis of voice. This distinction shows up in the rule of past-tense formation, where words ending in /ǰ/ take the /d/ past tense (for example, *fudged* /fʌǰd/).

But with respect to the plural rule in English, /č/ and /ǰ/ are in the same class. Both are sibilant affricates and are classed with the other sibilants /š/, /ž/, /s/, /z/. Words ending in sounds that belong to the class of sibilants add /əz/ to form plurals:

matches	/mæčəz/
ridges	/rɪǰəz/
kisses	/kɪsəz/
mazes	/mezəz/
lashes	/læšəz/
garages	/gəražəz/

It is clear that the phonetic symbols themselves do not reveal these facts. To understand how sounds "pattern" in languages, one needs to specify all the phonetic features which define the phonetic classes. We can do this by using pluses and minuses, as we have done above. This is further illustrated by Table 3.5. We see that /s/ is in the class of [−voiced] sounds together with /t/, /p/, /k/, and /š/, and is in the class of [+sibilant] sounds together with /z/, /š/, and /ž/, and is in the class of [+alveolar] sounds with /z/, /t/, and /d/, and is in the class of [−stop] sounds (or continuants) with /z/, /š/, /ž/.

If we listed all the sounds of English and all the phonetic features that specify these sounds, we would have many more intersecting or overlapping classes of sounds. It is these classes that are utilized in the "phonological rules" which constitute one's knowledge of the sound patterns of one's language.

Table 3.5   Sound groupings by phonetic classes

	/s/	/z/	/t/	/d/	/p/	/b/	/k/	/g/	/š/	/ž/
Voiced	−	+	−	+	−	+	−	+	−	+
Sibilant	+	+	−	−	−	−	−	−	+	+
Alveolar	+	+	+	+	−	−	−	−	−	−
Stop	−	−	+	+	+	+	+	+	−	−

PITCH

Speakers of all languages change the pitch of their voices when they talk. The pitch produced depends upon how fast the vocal cords vibrate; the faster they vibrate the higher the pitch.

The way pitch is used linguistically differs from language to language. In English, it doesn't much matter whether you say *cat* with a high pitch or a low pitch. It will still mean "cat." But if you say *ba* with a high pitch in Nupe (a language spoken in Nigeria), it will mean "to be sour," whereas if you say *ba* with a low pitch, it will mean "to count." The pitch "contour" *is* important in English; *John is going* as a statement is said with a falling pitch, but as a question the pitch rises at the end. Languages that use the pitch of *individual syllables* to contrast meanings are called **tone** languages. Languages that use pitch syntactically (for example, to change a sentence from a statement to a question) or in which the changing pitch of a *whole sentence* is otherwise important to the meaning are called **intonation** languages.

Tone

It is probably safe to say that most of the languages in the world are tone languages. There are more than a thousand tone languages in Africa alone; most of the Sino-Tibetan languages, such as Chinese, Thai, and Burmese, are tone languages; and many American Indian languages are tone languages.

Thai is a language that has contrasting pitches, or tones. The same string of "segmental" sounds represented by /naa/ will mean different things if one says the sounds with a mid pitch, a high pitch, a falling pitch from high to low, or a rising pitch from low to high. Thai therefore has four linguistic tones.

naa	[—]	mid tone	"rice paddy"
náa	[⎺]	high tone	"younger maternal uncle or aunt"
nâa	[\ ]	falling tone	"face"
năa	[/]	rising tone	"thick"

In Nupe, there are three tones:

bá	[⎺]	high tone	"to be sour"
bā	[—]	mid tone	"to cut"
bà	[_]	low tone	"to count"

In Twi we find contrasts between high and low pitch (tone):

dùà	[_ _]	low + low	"tail"
dùá	[_ ⁻]	low + high	"tree"
kɔ̀tɔ́	[_ ⁻]	low + high	"go buy"
kɔ́tɔ̀	[⁻ _]	high + low	"crab"

In some tone languages the pitch of each tone is "level"; in others, the direction of the pitch (whether it glides from high to low, or low to high) is important. Tones that "glide" are called **contour** tones; tones that don't are called **level** or **register** tones. In a tone language it is not the absolute pitch of the syllables which is important but the relations between the pitch of different syllables. This would have to be so, since some individual speakers have high-pitched voices, others low-pitched, and others medium-pitched. In fact, in many tone languages one finds a falling-off of the pitch, or a "down-drifting."

In the following sentence in Twi, we can see how it is the *relative* rather than the *absolute* pitch which is important:

Kòfí hwèhwé ádùàné kàkrá mà n'àdámfò bá.
"Kofi searches for a little food for his friend's child."

The tones can be specified as follows:

low high low high high low low high low high low high low high

The actual pitches of these syllables would be rather different from each other, shown as follows (the higher the number, the higher the pitch):

8.		fí				
7.			hwé á			
6.	kò			né		
5.		hwè		krá		
4.			dùà		dám	
3.				kà		bá
2.					mà nà	
1.						fò

This example shows that in analyzing tones, just as in analyzing segments, all the physical properties need not be considered; only essential features are important in language—in this case, whether the tone is "high" or "low" but not the specific pitch of that tone.

Intonation

In languages which are not tone languages, like English, pitch still plays an important role. The way we use pitch can be illustrated by a sign occasionally seen in men's lavatories:

We aim to please. You aim too, please.

Two sentences can be exactly the same phonetically except for the overall pitch contour of the utterance. The pitch contour, which is called the **intonation** of the sentence, can be used to distinguish between two different meanings. Note sentences a and b:

a. What did you put in my drink, Jane?

b. What did you put in my drink, Jane?

In sentence a the questioner is asking what Jane put in the drink. In sentence b the questioner is asking if someone put Jane in the drink. In sentence a the pitch rises sharply on the word *drink* and then falls off. In sentence b the sharp rise is on *Jane* and it continues to rise without any decrease.

Sentence c illustrates that a written sentence may be ambiguous (may have two meanings):

c. Tristram left directions for Isolde to follow.

When spoken it can be disambiguated by changing the intonation. If it means that Tristram wanted Isolde to follow him, it is pronounced with the rise in pitch on the first syllable of *follow,* followed by a fall in pitch, as in d:

d. Tristram left directions for Isolde to follow.

The sentence can also mean that Tristram left a set of directions which he wanted Isolde to use. If this is the intention, the highest pitch comes on the second syllable of directions, as in e:

e. Tristram left directions for Isolde to follow.

The way we have indicated pitch is of course highly oversimplified. Before the big rise in pitch the voice does not remain on the same monotone low pitch. These pitch diagrams merely indicate when there is a special change in pitch.

Thus pitch plays an important role in both tone languages and intonation languages but functions in different ways.

STRESS

In English and many other languages, in each content word (words other than little words like *to, the, a, of* and so on) one of the syllables is *stressed.* Stress is marked by the symbol ' over the vowel in the following examples:

súbject	noun, as in "The súbject of the story"
subjéct	verb, as in "He'll subjéct us to his boring stories."
pérvert	noun, as in "My neighbor is a pérvert."
pervért	verb, as in "Don't pervért the idea."
cómbat	noun, as in "In the heat of cómbat."
combát	verb, as in "It is not enough to combát evil."

In some words, more than one vowel may be stressed, but if so, one of these vowels receives more stress than the others. The most highly stressed vowel can be indicated by marking a ′ over the vowel (this is the vowel receiving the *primary* or main stress); the other stressed vowels can be indicated by marking a ` over the vowels (these vowels receive *secondary* stress).

rèsignátion	phònémic	sỳstemátic
phónème	fùndaméntal	introdúctory

Speakers of a language know intuitively which syllable receives primary stress, which receives secondary stress, and which are not stressed at all; it is part of their knowledge of the language.

Just as there is only one primary stress in a word spoken in isolation (for example, in a list), when words are combined into phrases only one of the vowels in the phrase (or even sentence) receives primary stress; all the other stressed vowels are "reduced." That is, a syllable which may have received the main stress when the word is not in a phrase may have only secondary stress in a phrase, as is illustrated by these examples:

hót + dóg	→ hótdòg	("frankfurter")
hót + dóg	→ hòt dóg	("an overheated dog")
réd + cóat	→ Rédcòat	("a British soldier")
réd + cóat	→ rèd cóat	("a coat that is red")
white + hóuse	→ Whíte Hòuse	("the president's house")
white + hóuse	→ whìte hóuse	("a house painted white")

In the next chapter, we shall see that there are some regular rules in English which determine where the primary stress is placed and where the secondary stress is placed.

In the English sentences used above to illustrate intonation contours, one may also describe the differences by referring to the word on which the main stress is placed. We can say, for example, that in *We àim to pléase* the primary stress is placed on the word *please,* and in *Yòu àim tóo, pléase* the primary stress is placed on the word *too.*

Stress is really a linguistic feature rather than a strictly phonetic one. To stress a syllable one may change the *pitch* (usually by raising it), make the syllable *louder,* or make it *longer.* We often use all three of these phonetic features to stress a syllable. We can, however, treat stress as a phonetic feature if we keep in mind that there are different ways of physically producing stress.

Perhaps it would be fitting to conclude this chapter by writing in phonetic transcription the two sentences we have said could greatly complicate the researches of a Martian linguist. If he found the ones given here, he would have a much easier time with the English sound system:

/dɪd hì bəlìv ðæt sìzər kʌd sì ðə pìpəl sìz ðə síz/

/ðə sìli əmìbə stòl ðə kì tu ðə məšìn/

SUMMARY

The science of speech sounds is called **phonetics.** It aims to provide the set of **features** or properties which can describe all the sounds used in human language.

When we speak, the physical sounds we produce are continuous stretches of sound, which are the physical representations of strings of **discrete linguistic segments.** To describe these speech sounds we cannot depend on the way words are spelled. The conventional spellings represent the pronunciation of words only partially. Some spellings are archaic and represent earlier pronunciations. For this reason, a **phonetic alphabet** is used, in which each phonetic symbol stands for one and only one sound. The phonetic symbols which can be used to represent the sounds of English are presented in this chapter.

All human speech sounds fall into "natural" classes according to their phonetic properties or features; that is according to how they are produced. It was shown that sounds may be either **voiced** or **voiceless; oral** or **nasal; labial, alveolar, palatal, velar, uvular,** or **glottal.** They may also be **fricatives** or **stops** and either **consonants, vowels, glides,** or **liquids.** In addition, vowels are distinguished according to the position of the tongue and lips: **high, mid,** or **low** tongue; **front, central,** or **back** tongue; **rounded** or **unrounded** lips. There are general and regular processes (rules) in languages which utilize these natural classes of sounds.

Pitch is also used phonetically. In some languages the pitch of individual syllables is as important as the phonetic properties of segments; these languages are called **tone** languages. Other **intonation** languages use pitch variations over a whole phrase or sentence. Chinese is a tone language, while English is an intonation language.

Stress is also used linguistically. Examples were provided from English to show how one may distinguish words and phrases by different stress placement. A stressed syllable is usually higher in pitch, longer in duration, and louder.

By means of these phonetic features one can describe all speech sounds, and in addition, see how the sounds are used in languages in regular patterns.

EXERCISES

1. a. Write the phonetic symbol for the *first* sound in each of the following words, according to the way you pronounce it.   Example: *ooze* [u], *psycho* [s].

1. though	6. judge
2. easy	7. Thomas
3. contact	8. physics
4. pneumonia	9. civic
5. thought	10. usury

b. Write the phonetic symbol for the *last* sound in each of the following:

1. fleece	6. cow
2. neigh	7. rough
3. long	8. cheese
4. health	9. bleached
5. watch	10. rags

c. Write the phonetic symbol for the vowel sound in each of the following:

1. coat	6. hot
2. steel	7. cut
3. play	8. put
4. fight	9. pat
5. cool	10. tease

2. Correct the phonetic description below.   The speaker may not have exactly the same pronunciation as you; there are many alternate versions.   But there is *one* major error in each line which is an impossible pronunciation for any American speaker.   Write the word in which the error occurs; circle the wrong symbol and give the correct one.   (Note: the writer of this limerick pronounced the word *didn't* as [dɪnt]; the lack of a [d] before the [n] in the transcription does not represent an error.)

1. θer wʌz wʌns
2. e lɪngwɪstɪks studɪnt
3. hu wʌz stupid
4. ænd not vɛri prudɪnt
5. ðə pronæwns hi yuzd
6. wər vɛri cʌnfyuzd
7. he wʊd se hum dɪnt
8. ɪnstɛd ʌf hu dɪnt

3. Write the symbol which corresponds to each of the following phonetic

descriptions; then give an English word which contains this sound. Example: voiced alveolar stop — [d], *dog*.

1. voiced bilabial stop
2. low front vowel
3. lateral liquid
4. lax high back rounded vowel
5. velar nasal consonant
6. voiceless alveolar fricative
7. mid central vowel
8. voiced affricate
9. palatal glide
10. tense front mid vowel
11. voiced interdental fricative
12. voiceless labiodental fricative

4. A phonetic symbol is actually a "cover term" for a composite of distinct phonetic properties or features. Define each of the symbols below by marking a + or a − for each given feature; a + if the property is present, a − if it is not. *(binary)*

1.	n	o	z	g	t	f
stop	−	−	−	+	+	−
nasal	+	−	−	−	−	−
voiced	+	+	+	+	−	−
labial	−	−	−	−	−	+
alveolar	+	−	+	−	+	−
velar	−	−	−	+	−	−

don't apply to vowel

2.	a	o	I	u	i	æ	e (ə)
high	−	+	+	+	+	−	+
low	+	−	?	−	−	+	−
back	−	+	−	+	−	−	−
tense	(+)	+	−	+	+	−	+
round	−	+	−	+	−	−	−

5. Each of the following groups of sounds consists of the members of a natural class of sounds plus one sound that is not a member of that class. A natural class of sounds is a set the members of which all

share a common property, i.e., voiced sounds, fricatives, bilabials, nasals, etc. Identify the sound that does not belong to the class; name the feature or features that define the class.

1. [g], [p], [b], [d]
2. [f], [p], [m], [θ], [v], [b]
3. [æ], [u], [i], [e], [ɛ]
4. [z], [v], [s], [ž], [g]
5. [t], [z], [d], [n], [s]
6. [m], [n], [b], [ŋ]
7. [g], [k], [b], [d], [p], [v], [t]
8. [a], [u], [e], [w], [i], [o]

6. In each of the following pairs of words the italicized sounds differ by one or more phonetic properties (features). State the differences and, in addition, state what properties they have in common. Example: ph*o*ne – ph*o*nic. The *o* in *phone* is mid, tense, round. The *o* in *phonic* is low, unround. Both are back vowels.

1. ba*th* – ba*the*
2. red*u*ce – red*u*ction
3. c*oo*l – c*o*ld
4. wi*f*e – wi*v*es
5. fa*c*e – fa*c*ial
6. h*ea*l – h*ea*lth
7. cat*s* – dog*s*
8. *im*polite – *in*decent
9. democra*t* – democra*c*y
10. m*ou*se – m*i*ce

7. Write the following in regular English spelling:

1. nom čamski ɪz ə lɪŋgwɪst hu tičəz æt ɛm ay ti.
2. fonetɪks ɪz ðə stʌdi əv spič sæwndz.
3. ɔl læŋgwɪjəz yuz sæwndz produst bay ðə ʌpər rɛspərətɔri sɪstəm.
4. ɪn wʌn dayəlɛkt kat ænd kɔt ar pronæwnct ðə sem.
5. sʌm pipəl θɪŋk fonetɪks ɪz ə bɪg bɔr.

8. a. Mark the primary stress on each of the following words by placing an acute accent (´) over the stressed syllable. Example: lánguage.

1. togéther
2. hórrible
3. mýstery
4. mystérious
5. phonétic
6. dígest (noun) – digést (verb)
7. cónvert (noun) – convért (verb)
8. spécial
9. specífic
10. spécify

b. Mark the primary stress (as above) and the secondary stress (by a grave accent (`)) on the following. Example: fùndaméntal.

1. labóratòry
2. médicìne
3. spécialìze
4. professórial
5. cònversátion
6. géneral
7. generálity
8. mýstify
9. productívity
10. expérience

c. Mark the *one vowel* which receives the primary stress in the following sentences (the meaning is given in parentheses). Example: It's a hótdog (it's a frankfurter); he's a hot dóg (the dog is overheated).

1. He's a lighthouse keeper.   (He works in a lighthouse directing ships.)
2. She's a light housekeeper.   (She is a housekeeper who is light.)
3. It's a blackboard eraser.   (an eraser for a blackboard, e.g., a black-board can be green)
4. It's a black board eraser.   (a black eraser for a board)
5. She's a French literature teacher.   (a teacher of French literature)
6. She's a French literature teacher.   (a teacher of literature who is French)

7. He's a grandfather figure.   (a "figure of a grandfather")
8. He's a grand father figure.   (a "father figure" who is grand)

References

ABERCROMBIE, DAVID. *Elements of General Phonetics.* Chicago: Aldine, 1967. A good general introductory textbook.

ABERCROMBIE, DAVID. "Forgotten Phoneticians." *Transactions of the Philological Society,* 1–34 (1948).

CHOMSKY, N., and HALLE, M. *The Sound Pattern of English,* ch. 8. New York: Harper and Row, 1968. An advanced treatment of universal phonetic theory, with a suggested set of universal distinctive features and phonetic correlates.

FIRTH, J. R. "The English School of Phonetics." *Transactions of the Philological Society,* 92–132 (1946).

INTERNATIONAL PHONETIC ASSOCIATION. *Principles of the International Phonetic Association,* rev. ed. London: IPA, 1949. The phonetic alphabet used by the IPA is given with proposed diacritics for finer phonetic distinctions.

JAKOBSON, R., and HALLE, M. *Fundamentals of Language.* Janua Linguarum 1. The Hague: Mouton, 1956. One of the first treatments of distinctive feature theory, as defined in acoustic terms.

JONES, DANIEL. *An Outline of English Phonetics,* 8th ed. Cambridge: Heffer, 1956. A comprehensive summary of traditional phonetics from the British point of view.

LADEFOGED, PETER. *Elements of Acoustic Phonetics.* Chicago: Univ. of Chicago Press, 1962. The best introduction to acoustic phonetics for those who wish to understand the physical properties of speech sounds.

LADEFOGED, PETER. *Preliminaries to Linguistic Phonetics.* Chicago: University of Chicago Press, 1971. An advanced treatment of a theory of phonetics, including data from hundreds of languages.

SWEET, HENRY. *A Primer of Phonetics.* Oxford: The Clarendon Press, 1890. Those interested in one of the most famous of the founders of "modern phonetics" would find this book by the prototype of Henry Higgins of great interest.

4
The Sound
Patterns of Language:
Phonology

*I believe that phonology is superior to music. It is more
variable and its pecuniary possibilities are far greater.*

—ERIC SATIE (from the cover of a record)

We would not encourage anyone to become a phonologist for the
reasons given by Satie. We are not sure what "pecuniary possibilities"
he had in mind, and the sound systems of the world's languages are less
varied than they are similar. It is true that speech sounds as physical
entities may be infinitely varied, but when they function as elements in a
language they are highly constrained. This is, in fact, one of the reasons
why the study of the sound systems of language is a fascinating one, for it
reveals how man's linguistic ability enables him to extract regularities
from the constantly varying physical sounds.

Linguists are interested not only in how the sound systems may vary,
but also in the phonetic universals found in all languages. We find, for
example, that the same, relatively small set of phonetic properties characterize all human speech sounds, that the same classes of these sounds
are utilized in languages spoken from the Arctic Circle to the Cape of
Good Hope, and that the same kinds of regular patterns of speech sounds
occur all over the world. Despite the infinite variations which occur
when we speak, all speakers of a language agree that certain utterances
are the "same" and others are "different." Their knowledge of the language permits such judgments.

Phonology is concerned with this kind of linguistic knowledge. Phonetics, as discussed in the previous chapter, provides the means for the
description of speech sounds, but phonology studies the ways in which
speech sounds form *systems* and *patterns* in human language.

Phonological knowledge permits a speaker to produce sounds which form meaningful utterances, to recognize a foreign "accent," to make up new words, to add the appropriate phonetic segments to form plurals and past tenses, to produce "aspirated" and "unaspirated" voiceless stops in the appropriate context, to know what is or is not a sound in one's language, and to know that different phonetic strings may represent the same "meaningful unit."   Since the grammar of the language represents the totality of one's linguistic knowledge, knowledge of the sound patterns — the phonology — must be part of this grammar.   In this chapter we shall discuss the kinds of things a speaker knows about the sound system of his language — his phonological knowledge.

PHONEMES: THE PHONOLOGICAL UNITS OF LANGUAGE

In the physical world the naive speaker and hearer actualize and are sensitive to sounds, but what they feel themselves to be pronouncing and hearing are "phonemes."

—EDWARD SAPIR, 1933

For a native speaker, phonological knowledge goes beyond the ability to produce all the phonetically different sounds of his language.   It includes this, of course.   A speaker of English can produce the sound [θ] and knows that this sound occurs in English, in words like *thin* [θɪn] or *ether* [iθər] or *bath* [bæθ].[1]   An English speaker may or may not be able to produce a "click" or a velar fricative, but even if he can, he knows that such sounds are not part of the phonetic inventory of English.   Many speakers are unable to produce such "foreign" sounds.   A Frenchman similarly knows that the [θ] is not part of the phonetic inventory of French and often finds it difficult to pronounce a word like *thin* [θɪn], pronouncing it as [sɪn].

An English speaker also knows that [ð], the voiced counterpart of [θ], is a sound of English, occurring in words like *either* [iðər], *then* [ðɛn], and *bathe* [beð].

Knowing the sounds (the phonetic units) of a language is only a small part of one's phonological knowledge.   The same set of phonetic segments can occur in two languages with different phonological systems.   For example, in the previous chapter we pointed out that in English both aspirated and unaspirated voiceless stops occur.   The aspirated stops [pʰ], [tʰ], and [kʰ] occur in the words *pill, till,* and *kill,* and the unaspirated stops [p], [t], and [k] occur in *spill, still,* and *skill.*   If one pronounced *spill* with an aspirated stop, [spʰɪl], it would still be understood as *spill,*

---

[1] The use of brackets, [ ], as opposed to slashes, / /, is further explained on page 71.

although someone hearing that pronunciation might wonder why the speaker was "spitting out" the word. [p] and [pʰ] (and the other pairs of voiceless stops) are different *phonetic* segments in English, but in spite of this, speakers consider them to be "the same." This is because the difference between the pairs of sounds is not **distinctive;** the substitution of one for the other does not change meaning. Even more than that, speakers of English "know" (unconsciously) when to produce an aspirated stop and when to produce an unaspirated stop; they know that aspirated voiceless stops occur at the beginning of a word, and unaspirated voiceless stops always occur after [s]. This is a fact about English phonology. There are two p-*sounds* which occur in English, but speakers consider the *two phonetic units* to be *one phonological unit,* which linguists call a **phoneme.**

Since the presence or absence of aspiration in English is *predictable,* aspiration is *nonphonemic;* it is a *redundant* feature of a voiceless stop which is always added in certain contexts.

When two sounds in a language are linguistically or phonologically distinctive – when the difference between them contrasts meanings – these two sounds are *separate phonemes* in the language. A phoneme is an abstract unit. We do not utter phonemes; we produce **phones,** – that is, phonetic segments.

We shall distinguish between these different kinds of segments by enclosing phonemes between two slashes, /p/, and phonetic segments (or phones) between square brackets, [pʰ] and [p]. In the last chapter we enclosed "broad transcriptions" in slashes. A phonemic transcription is like a broad transcription in the sense that all linguistically irrelevant (or predictable) features are ignored. A phoneme is, however, a unit of the phonological system of a language, and in this sense the "slash" notation represents more than a lack of phonetic detail. /p/, then, is a phoneme in English which is realized phonetically as either [p] or [pʰ]. When more than one phone is the phonetic realization of a single phoneme, these sounds have traditionally been called the **allophones** of the phoneme; [p] and [pʰ] are the allophones of the phoneme /p/.

These same phonetic segments occur in Thai, but they function differently in Thai and in English. In the chapter on phonetics we pointed out that whether a voiceless stop is aspirated or unaspirated in Thai is not predictable by a general rule. Both aspirated and unaspirated voiceless stops occur in the same position in different words:

> [paa]   "forest"   [pʰaa]   "to split"

The presence of aspiration in Thai changes the meaning of the word, and it is therefore nonredundant; aspiration is a *distinctive* or *phonemic* feature in this language.

In English a general rule can be stated: "Voiceless stops are aspirated when they occur at the beginning of a word." This cannot be a rule in the phonology of Thai, as the examples above illustrate, since if we applied it to the word [paa] "forest" we would derive a different word, [pʰaa] "to split."

Thus, the same *sounds* may exist in two languages but they may function differently. Both English and Thai include the phones [p] and [pʰ]; but in English they represent one phoneme /p/, and in Thai they represent two phonemes /p/ and /pʰ/. Aspiration as a *phonetic* feature of sounds occurs in both languages. Since aspiration is predictable in English, it is nonphonemic; since it is not predictable in Thai, it is a distinctive phonemic feature of phonological units.

Knowledge of a language includes knowing which sounds are phonemic and which are not. That may sound very complicated and abstract. Yet every speaker "intuitively" knows that different sounds may represent a single abstract phoneme. When linguists describe the phonology of a language they attempt to make such intuitive knowledge explicit.

An examination of the phonological system of English reveals other such predictable nonphonemic properties of sounds.

Every speaker of English knows that an l-sound occurs in English. There must be a phoneme /l/, since *lake* means something different from *rake, make, bake, take, cake,* and so on. Most speakers of English also believe that the same /l/ occurs in *leaf* and *feel,* and *phonemically* this is true. *Phonetically,* however, the /l/ in *leaf* and the /l/ in *feel* differ. When you pronounce *leaf,* the back of the tongue is not raised; in the pronunciation of *feel* the back of the tongue is raised toward the hard palate or velum. If you say these words aloud and concentrate on the tongue position you may feel the difference. If you can't feel the difference, and if you find it difficult to hear the difference, it is not surprising. This reflects the truth of the statement that there is only one /l/ phoneme in English. Despite the phonetic differences, the two phones seem the same. An /l/ produced with the back of the tongue raised is called a "velarized *l*" (or "hard *l*"). In Russian there is a phonemic difference between these two sounds, but in English, just as with aspiration, velarization is *predictable* or *redundant* or *nonphonemic* or *nondistinctive* (all these terms are equivalent). In English, /l/ is velarized ([ł]) *only* when it occurs before a back vowel, as in *look, Luke, lock, load,* or when it occurs at the end of a word, as in *feel, fool, pal, pull, pill.* Thus, velarization is predictable by rule, and the two phonetic l-sounds [l] and [ł] represent allophones of the single phoneme /l/.

The examples discussed so far illustrate that two segments which differ phonetically may represent the same phoneme or different phonemes. The example from Thai shows that segments which differ by *only one feature* specification may represent two phonemes. This is also true in English.

We noted above that the phonetic segments [θ] and [ð] both occur in English. In this pair, the fact that one sound is voiced and the other voiceless is a phonemic difference. Changing the value of the voicing feature changes the meaning of words, as is shown by *ether* [iθər] and *either* [iðər]. Voicing is thus a *phonemic* or *distinctive* feature in English, and /θ/ and /ð/ are distinct phonemes.

That voicing is a distinctive feature of English is also shown by the following pairs of words:

	VOICELESS		VOICED
[f]	*f*ine	[v]	*v*ine
[s]	*s*ink	[z]	*z*ink
[š]	me*sh*er	[ž]	mea*s*ure
[č]	*ch*in	[ǰ]	*g*in

Note also that in English, in addition to the two voiceless bilabial sounds, [p] and [pʰ], a voiced bilabial [b] occurs:

VOICELESS	VOICED
*p*in	*b*in
ra*p*id	ra*b*id
ri*p*	ri*b*

While the distinction between [p] and [pʰ] is nonphonemic, the distinction between these two phones and [b] is phonemic. /p/ and /b/ are distinct phonemes in English; the substitution of one for the other changes the meaning of a word. The cover symbols /p/ and /b/ do not reveal the phonemic distinction, but if we specify the features of each of these phonemes in feature matrices, the contrast becomes evident:

	/p/	/b/
Consonantal	+	+
Vocalic	−	−
Continuant	−	−
Labial	+	+
Voiced	−	+ ← distinctive difference

We did not include the nondistinctive feature "aspiration" in these phonemic matrices because aspiration is predictable. The phonemic and phonetic differences between the bilabial stops in *pit, spit,* and *bit* illustrate this:

	pit	/pɪt/	[pʰɪt]	*spit*	/spɪt/	[spɪt]	*bit*	/bɪt/	[bɪt]
Consonant		+	+		+	+		+	+
Vowel		−	−		−	−		−	−
Labial		+	+		+	+		+	+
Continuant		−	−		−	−		−	−
Voiced		−	−		−	−		+	+
Aspirated		Ø	+		Ø	−		Ø	Ø

In the phonemic representation of the word *pit* there is a blank or zero specification, Ø, for the feature "aspiration." This is because phonemically a /p/ is neither "aspirated" nor "unaspirated." The specification of this feature depends on the context of the /p/—where it occurs in a word. The general rule in English pertaining to *all* voiceless stops adds the [+aspirated] designation to the /p/ in *pit*. The feature "aspiration" is not specified for the voiced /b/ or [b] because all voiced stops are unaspirated.

In Thai, voicing is also phonemic, as is shown by the *three-way* contrast:

/paa/ "forest"; /pʰaa/ "to split"; /baa/ "shoulder."

The phonetic feature matrices for the labial stops in the three Thai words would be identical to the phonetic specifications of the labials in *spit, pit,* and *bit* in English. But the Thai phonemic specifications would differ in that the /p/ in *paa* would have to be marked [−aspirated] and the /pʰ/ in *pʰaa* would have to be marked [+aspirated], since aspiration distinguishes the two phonemes.

We see that the same phonetic segments can form different phonemic patterns in languages.

THAI PHONEMES		PHONETIC SEGMENTS		ENGLISH PHONEMES
/p/	⟵	[p]	⟶	/p/
/pʰ/	⟵	[pʰ]	↗	
/b/	⟵	[b]	⟶	/b/

The phonetic facts alone do not tell us what is distinctive or phonemic. The phonetic representation of utterances shows what speakers know about the *pronunciation* of utterances; the phonemic representation of utterances shows what the speakers know about the abstract underlying phonology. That *pot* /pat/ and *spot* /spat/ both include a /p/ reveals the fact that English speakers consider the [pʰ] in *pot* [pʰat] and the [p] in *spot* [spat] to be phonetic manifestations of the same phoneme /p/.

The phonology of a language includes rules which relate the phonemic representations of words to their phonetic representations. The phonemic representation need only include the *nonpredictable distinctive* features of the string of phonemes which represent the words. The phonetic representation includes all the *linguistically relevant phonetic* aspects of the sounds.

The phonetic representation does not include *all* the physical properties of the sounds of an utterance, since the physical signal may vary in many ways which have little to do with the phonological system. The absolute pitch of the sounds, or whether the utterance is spoken slowly or fast, or whether the speaker shouts or whispers is not linguistically significant. The phonetic transcription is thus also an abstraction from the physical signal; it includes the nonvariant phonetic aspects of the utterances, those features which remain relatively the same from speaker to speaker and from one time to another.

Given the phonemic representation of an utterance and the phonological rules of the language, one can unambiguously determine the phonetic representation:

	PHONEMIC REPRESENTATION	PHONOLOGICAL RULES	PHONETIC REPRESENTATION
"pot"	/pat/	/p/ → [pʰ] at the beginning of a word	[pʰat]

No rules can tell us that the word *pot* begins with a /p/. That is a unique characteristic of this sound-meaning unit in English. The fact that it begins with a /p/ differentiates it from *cot, not, rot, dot, sot, hot,* and so on. The grammar must then specify that English speakers know that the sound sequence that means "pot" begins with a voiceless bilabial stop, which is followed by a low back vowel and which ends with an alveolar voiceless stop. All three phonemes must be included, since *pot* also is distinguished from *pit, pat, put, pate,* and from *pod, pock, par, poll,* etc. But the phonemic representation of *pot* need not include anything about the aspiration of the /p/, since it is not distinguished from any word solely by this feature; that is, [pat] is not a word which means something different from [pʰat].

In attempting to analyze the phonemic system of a language, linguists may first look for the phonetic properties or features which account for meaning distinctions in words. Sometimes this is simple; when two words with different meanings are exactly alike phonetically except for one feature, the phonetic difference must be phonemic, since this difference alone accounts for the contrasts. Such words, called *minimal pairs,* are illustrated as follows:

see	[si]	*zee*	[zi]	The difference in meaning is due only to the voicelessness of the [s] and the voicing of the [z]. Everything else is phonetically identical.
map	[mæp]	*nap*	[næp]	The labiality of [m] and the alveolar articulation of [n] is the only phonetic difference.
rack	[ræk]	*rock*	[rak]	The two words are distinguished only because [æ] is a front vowel and [a] is a back vowel.

These minimal pairs illustrate that /s/ and /z/, /m/ and /n/, and /æ/ and /a/ are separate phonemes in English. Note that *seat* [sit] and *tease* [tiz] are *not* minimal pairs, since the order of the similar phones differ. One cannot tell from such pairs whether [s] and [z] contrast phonemically. One might wrongly conclude from such pairs that [s] and [z] are allophones of one phoneme with the voicing distinction predictable—that is, that at the beginning of a word [s] occurs, and at the end [z] occurs. Minimal pairs such as *sink/zink,* and *fuss/fuzz,* show that this is not the case in English.

If one found both [l] and [ł] at the beginning of two words with different meanings in a language, the two phones would contrast phonemically and represent two different phonemes. In English, however, one never finds [ł] at the beginning of a word followed by a non-low front vowel. Note that *leaf* [lif] and *feel* [fił] are not minimal pairs, and that *[łif] cannot occur as an English word. When two phonetically similar but distinct sounds never occur in the same phonetic environment they are said to be in **complementary distribution.** That is, if one finds one of these phones in one position in words, and the other in different positions, and if they never occur in the same position, they then complement each other, and the phonetic difference between them is predictable, making them allophones of the same phoneme.

[p] and [pʰ] are in complementary distribution, since [pʰ] never occurs after an [s], and [p] always occurs in this position.

In English, the difference between nasalized vowels and oral vowels is also nondistinctive or nonphonemic; nasalized vowels and oral vowels are in complementary distribution. Nasalized vowels occur only before nasal consonants; oral vowels occur before non-nasal consonants:

BEFORE NASALS			BEFORE NON-NASALS		
tan	/tæn/	[tʰæ̃n]	*tat*	/tæt/	[tʰæt]
tam	/tæm/	[tʰæ̃m]	*tab*	/tæb/	[tʰæb]
but not		*[tʰæn]	and not		*[tʰæ̃p]

There are phonetic nasal vowels in English, but no phonemic nasal vowels. Nasalization of vowels is predictable by a general rule: "A vowel segment is nasalized before a nasal segment."

Complementary distribution of phones is also exemplified by the fact that in English all nasal consonants are *phonemically* voiced. One might pronounce the /n/ in *snow* as an unvoiced nasal (symbolized by a small circle under the segment, [sṇo]), but such "devoiced" nasals are in complementary distribution with voiced nasals. They only occur after a voiceless segment (if at all). Once more we see that the occurrence of phonetic segments does not determine the phonemic inventory.

Suppose a linguist were attempting to analyze a language which he knew nothing about, and wrote down in a narrow phonetic transcription the sounds of a number of different words in the language, including the following:

[nat]	"girl"	[sṇat]	"boy"
[nak]	"cat"	[sṇak]	"dog"
[ṃat]	"woman"	[sṃat]	"man"
[tan]	"cow"	[taṇs]	"goat"
[tam]	"book"	[taṃs]	"tree"

Since both [n] and [m] and [t] occur at the beginning of words before [a], they occur in the same context and are not in complementary distribution; they must be separate phonemes. The minimal pair [nat] "girl" and [mat] "woman" clearly shows the phonemic contrast between /m/ and /n/. But the linguist would conclude (and perhaps by now you would also) that the [n] and [n̥] were in complementary distribution representing the single phoneme /n/, and the [m] and [m̥] similarly represent the phoneme /m/. The fact that [n̥] and [m̥] occur only when next to a voiceless segment shows that in this language the "voicelessness" is nondistinctive or nonphonemic. The devoicing of the nasals is predictable. One can reveal this in the grammar of the language by including the rules:

1 /n/ becomes [n̥] when it occurs next to a voiceless sound
2 /m/ becomes [m̥] when it occurs next to a voiceless sound.

This repetition seems needlessly cumbersome, and in fact would fail to reveal the generality which can be stated in just one rule:

3 Nasals become voiceless when next to voiceless segments.

If on further investigation the linguist found that [n̥at] did occur and meant "flower" and that [m̥at] meant "rain," he would have to change his analysis, since the occurrence of these words would show that voiced and voiceless nasals did contrast, so /n/ and /n̥/, and /m/ and /m̥/ would necessarily be phonemes in the language, and voicing would be a phonemic distinction for nasals.

This phonemic contrast does not occur in English but is found in other languages. In Burmese we find the following minimal pairs:

/ma/	[ma]	"health"	/m̥a/	[m̥a]	"order"
/na/	[na]	"pain"	/n̥a/	[n̥a]	"nostril"

Minimal pairs and complementary distribution of phonetic units are helpful clues in the attempt to discover the inventory of phonemes in a language. By themselves, however, they do not determine the phonemic representation of utterances, as will be shown below in the discussion on phonological rules.

The grammar of a language includes the kind of information we have been discussing: what the distinctive phonemic units of the language are; which phonetic features are phonemic or distinctive; and which are nonphonemic or predictable. Thus, a grammar of French would not include a /θ/ as part of the phonemic representation of any word, just as a grammar of English would not include a /x/. English would have one voiceless labial stop phoneme, /p/, but Thai would have two, /p/ and /pʰ/. Both would include /b/. The grammar of English has no voiceless nasal phonemes, but the grammar of Burmese does. These examples illustrate that two languages may have the same phonetic segments but a different set of phonemes. The grammar must account for both the phonemes in the language and the way they are pronounced.

SEQUENCES OF PHONEMES

> *If you were to receive the following telegram, you would*
> *have no difficulty in correcting the "obvious" mistakes:*
>   BEST WISHES FOR VERY HAPPP BIRTFDAY
> *because sequences such as* BIRTFDAY *do not occur in the*
> *language.*
> — COLIN CHERRY, *On Human Communication*

We demonstrated above that one's knowledge of the phonological system includes more than knowing the phonetic inventory of sounds in the language. It even goes beyond knowing the phonemes of the language.

A speaker also knows that the phonemes of his language cannot be strung together in any random order to form words. The phonological system determines which phonemes can begin a word, end a word, and follow each other.

That speakers have knowledge of such sequential rules is not too difficult to demonstrate. Suppose you were given four cards, each of which had a different phoneme of English printed on it:

| /k/ | | /b/ | | /l/ | | /ɪ/ |

If you were asked to arrange these cards to form all the "possible" words which these four phonemes could form, you might order them as:

/b/	/l/	/ɪ/	/k/
/k/	/l/	/ɪ/	/b/
/b/	/ɪ/	/l/	/k/

These are the only arrangements of these phonemes permissible in English. */lbkɪ/, */ɪlbk/, */bkɪl/, */ɪlkb/, etc., are not possible words in the language. Although /blɪk/ and /klɪb/ are not *existing* words (you will not find them in a dictionary), if you heard someone say:

"I just bought a beautiful new *blick*."

you might ask: "What's a 'blick'?" But if you heard someone say:

"I just bought a beautiful new *bkli*."

you would probably just say "What?"

Your knowledge of English "tells" you that certain strings of phonemes are permissible and others are not. After a consonant like /b/, /g/, /k/, or /p/ another similar consonant is not permitted by the rules of the grammar. If a word begins with an /l/ or an /r/, every speaker "knows" that the next segment must be a vowel. That is why */lbɪk/ does not sound like an English word. It violates the restrictions on the sequencing of phonemes.

Other such constraints also exist in English. If the initial sound of *church* begins a word, the next sound must be a vowel. [čat] or [čon] or [čækəri] are possible words in English, but *[člit] and *[čpæt] are not.

All languages have similar constraints on the sequences of phonemes which are permitted. Children learn these rules when they learn the language, just as they learn what the phonemes are and how they are related to phonetic segments. In Asante Twi, a word may end only in a vowel or a nasal consonant. /pik/ is not a possible Twi word, because it breaks the sequential rules of the language, and /ŋŋa/ is not a possible word in English for similar reasons, although it is an actual word in Twi.

Speakers of all languages have the same kinds of knowledge. They know what sounds are part of the language, what the phonemes are, and what phonemic and phonetic sequences may occur. The specific sounds or sound sequences may differ, but the phonological systems include similar *kinds* of rules.

THE RULES OF PHONOLOGY

No rule is so general, which admits not some exception.

—ROBERT BURTON

But that to come
Shall all be done by the rule.

—SHAKESPEARE, *Antony and Cleopatra*

Everyone who knows a language knows the basic vocabulary of that language. This means he knows that an object like "pot" is represented by a given sequence of phonemes, /pat/.. In other words, he knows both the sounds and the meanings of these linguistic units. This knowledge must be part of the way he "stores" these words in his mental dictionary, since when he wants to refer to the concept "pot" he doesn't produce the sounds [tʰap]. But he needn't represent the sounds of this word by including all the phonetic features of these sounds as we saw in the discussion on phonemes, as long as the relationship between the phonemic representation he has stored and the phonetic pronunciation is "rule-governed." The rules which relate the minimally specified phonemic representation to the phonetic representation form part of a speaker's knowledge of his language. They are part of his grammar. One such rule in the grammar of English was given above:

1 Voiceless stops are aspirated at the beginning of a word.

This rule makes certain predictions about English pronunciation. It specifies the class of sounds affected by the rule ("voiceless stops") and it specifies the context or phonemic environment of the relevant sounds ("at the beginning of a word"). Obviously both kinds of information must be given by a phonological rule, or we could apply it to the wrong class of sounds (for example, voiced stops) or in some environment where it is inapplicable (for example, after an /s/). Given this rule we can represent the words *pick, tick,* and *kick* phonemically as /pɪk/, /tɪk/, and /kɪk/ and *derive* the correct phonetic representation as follows:

$$/pɪk/ \longrightarrow \text{apply rule} \longrightarrow [pʰɪk]$$
$$/tɪk/ \longrightarrow \text{apply rule} \longrightarrow [tʰɪk]$$
$$/kɪk/ \longrightarrow \text{apply rule} \longrightarrow [kʰɪk]$$

We can also represent *stick,* for example, as /stɪk/. The rule will not apply, since the voiceless stop /t/ does not occur at the beginning of a word and the phonetic form is thus identical with the phonemic, [stɪk].

A separate rule was not necessary for each word or for each voiceless stop. In fact, had we given individual rules for /p/, /t/, and /k/ we would have obscured a generalization about English—that the rule applies to a *class* of phonemes. This further illustrates why individual phonemes are better regarded as combinations of features than as indissoluble whole segments.

Notice that the "aspiration rule" adds a *nondistinctive* (that is, nonphonemic) feature to the specification of phonemes in certain phonemic environments. Such rules exist in every language. A similar rule in English adds the feature "nasalization" or [+nasal] to vowels when they occur before nasal consonants. While nasalization is a phonemic feature for consonants (since *bat* contrasts with *mat,* and *nip* with *dip*), it is nonphonemic or nondistinctive for vowels, as was discussed above. This rule adds a feature which is nondistinctive for a particular class of sounds to that class in particular contexts. It was stated above as:

2 A vowel is nasalized when it occurs before a nasal consonant.

The nasalization rule is a very common one in languages of the world; it is probably a universal rule. Such a rule **assimilates** one segment to another; that is, it "copies" a feature of a sequential phoneme, making the two phonemes more similar. **Assimilation** rules are, for the most part, caused by articulatory or physiological processes.

The rule concerning the velarization of /l/ also adds a nonphonemic feature to the phoneme in certain contexts. It may be stated as:

3 Velarize an /l/ when it occurs before a back vowel or when it occurs at the end of a word.

Such rules illustrate that their function in a grammar is to provide the phonetic information necessary for the pronunciation of utterances. One may illustrate the function of phonological rules in the following way:

input   PHONEMIC (DICTIONARY) REPRESENTATION OF WORDS
IN A SENTENCE
↓
Phonological Rules (P-Rules)
↓
output   PHONETIC REPRESENTATION OF WORDS IN A SENTENCE

That is, the input to the P-Rules is the **phonemic representation;** the P-rules apply or operate on the phonemic strings and produce as output the **phonetic representation.**

This should not be interpreted as meaning that when we speak we actually apply one rule after another. What we do when we actually produce sounds is part of linguistic performance. What these rules show is what a speaker knows about the abstract and surface phonetic relationships. The rules are part of one's linguistic competence.

We have illustrated the nature of phonological rules (P-rules) by three English examples: (1) Aspiration rule; (2) Nasalization rule; (3) Velarization rule. By applying these rules to the *phonemic representation* of words in English, we can derive the *phonetic representation* of these same words. (NA means "not applicable," or "does not fit the specifications of the rule.")

PHONEMIC REPRESENTATION	/pɪl/	/spɪl/	/pɪn/	/spɪn/
Rule 1 — aspiration	pʰɪl	NA	pʰɪn	NA
Rule 2 — nasalization	NA	NA	pʰɪ̃n	spĩn
Rule 3 — velarization	pʰɪɫ	spɪɫ	NA	NA
PHONETIC REPRESENTATION	[pʰɪɫ]	[spɪɫ]	[pʰɪ̃n]	[spĩn]

The examples illustrate that phonological rules may *add features* to phonemes, but they do more than this.

In the previous chapter on phonetics, the formation of noun plurals was discussed. To form a regular plural in English one adds either a [z], [s], or [əz]. The particular sound added depends on the final phoneme of the noun. It was further pointed out that it is not necessary to learn or memorize all the sounds in each class as a list. There are regularities — "rules" — which determine the proper plural ending. That is, the addition of [s] to *cat*, and [z] to *dog*, and [əz] to *bus* is determined by the same rule as that which adds [s] to *cap, book, myth, cuff,* and which adds [z] to *cab, cad, dive, cow,* and which adds [əz] to *pause, bush, beach, judge.*

A grammar which included lists of these sounds would not reveal the regularities in the language and would fail to model what a speaker knows about the plural formation.

The regular plural rule does not work for a word like *child,* which in the plural is *children,* or for *ox,* which becomes *oxen,* or for *sheep,* which is unchanged phonologically in the plural. *Child, ox,* and *sheep* are *exceptions* to the regular rule. One learns these exceptional plurals when learning the language. If the grammar represented each unexceptional or regular word in both its singular and plural forms—for example, *cat* /kaet/, *cats* /kæts/; *cap* /kæp/, *caps* /kæps/; and so on, it would imply that the plurals of *cat* and *cap* were as irregular as the plurals of *child* and *ox.* But this is not the case. If a new toy appeared on the market called a *glick* /glɪk/, a young child who wanted two of them would ask for two *glicks* [glɪks] and not two *glicken* even if the child had never heard anyone use the plural form. This is because he would know the regular rule to form plurals. A grammar that describes his knowledge (his internalized mental grammar) must then include the general rule.

If the plural ending is phonemically represented as /z/, the regular plural rules can be stated in a simple way:

4 a. Insert an [ə] before the plural ending when a regular noun ends in a sibilant (/s/, /z/, /š/, /ž/, /č/, or /ǰ/).

　 b. Change the voiced /z/ to voiceless [s] if the regular noun ends in a voiceless sound.

Notice that it is not necessary to do anything to the /z/ if the noun ends in a nonsibilant voiced sound; its phonetic form is identical with its phonemic representation: /z/ is pronounced [z].

This phonological rule will derive the phonetic forms of plurals for all regular nouns:

PHONEMIC REPRESENTATION	*bus* + plural /bʌs +　z/	*bat* + plural /bæt + z/	*bag* + plural /bæg + z/
Rule 4a	↓ ə	NA ↓	NA
Rule 4b	NA	s	NA
PHONETIC REPRESENTATION	[bʌsəz]	[bæts]	[bægz]

As we formulated these rules, Rule 4a must be applied before Rule 4b. If we applied the two parts of the rule in reverse order we would derive incorrect phonetic forms:

PHONEMIC REPRESENTATION	/bʌs +　z/
Rule 4b	↓ s
Rule 4a	ə
PHONETIC REPRESENTATION	*[bʌsəs]

The "plural-formation" rule shows that, in addition to adding features to phonemes, *entire segments can be inserted* into a phonemic string; an [ə] is added by the first rule.

Phonological rules can also *change feature specifications.* In the previous chapter we pointed out that the phonetic form of the prefix meaning "not" is phonetically variant; it is [ɪn] before a vowel or an alveolar consonant, [ɪm] before a labial consonant, and [ɪŋ] before a velar, as illustrated in the following words:

*in*operable	[ɪnapərəbəl]
*in*discrete	[ɪndəskrit]
*im*plausible	[ɪmplɔzəbəl]
*in*conceivable	[ɪŋkənsivəbəl]

Since in all these cases the same prefix is added, one would expect it to have the same phonemic representation. If it is represented phonemically as / ɪn-/, the phonetic forms are predictable by one rule:

5 Within a word, a nasal consonant assumes the same place of articulation as a following consonant.

The rule states the class of phonemes to which it applies (all nasal consonants) and where it is to be applied (before another consonant). Like the vowel nasalization rule, this is an *assimilation* rule; the nasal assimilates its place of articulation to agree with the articulation of the following consonant. When two consonants have the same place of articulation they are called **homorganic** consonants. We can call Rule 5 the "homorganic nasal" rule.

In the examples above, *inoperable* is composed of the prefix / ɪn-/ plus *operable,* which begins with a vowel. The rule cannot apply because it specifically mentions that it is only relevant if the nasal is followed by a consonant. Thus / ɪn-/ is phonetically [ɪn]. When / ɪn-/ is prefixed to *discrete,* since the /n/ and /d/ are already homorganic (that is, they are both [+alveolar]), the rule applies vacuously; it does not change the /n/, and the phonetic form of the prefix is [ɪn-]. The / ɪn-/ is changed to [ɪm-] before *plausible,* since /n/ is alveolar and /p/ is labial, and the /n/ becomes a velar [ŋ] before the initial velar /k/ in *conceivable.* The phonetic representation of these words should also include the nasalization of the vowels that occurs before nasal consonants; this nasalization would be added by the nasalization rule given above as Rule 2.

In the previous chapter it was pointed out that the same "homorganic-nasal" rule occurs in Twi, and, in fact, this rule is found in many languages of the world. A rule such as this does not add a phonetic feature to a phoneme but *changes the feature specification* of that phoneme.

The spelling of *implausible* (or *impossible*) reflects the phonetic representation of these words, while the spelling of *incommunicable* (or *incompetent*) represents the phonemic representation. If *impossible* were spelled *inpossible,* it would still be pronounced with an [m].

There are many cases in which the English spelling represents the more abstract phonemic representation of words. This does not present problems for anyone who knows the grammar of English, since part of that grammar includes those phonological rules which relate phonemic representations to phonetic pronunciation. The spelling in these cases is actually more efficient, and represents more directly the fact that a speaker stores words phonemically in his mental dictionary.

The phonological rules of the language "tell" us how to pronounce the "same item" (like /ɪn-/) differently in different contexts. These rules apply to whole sets of words, not to just one single item, as is further illustrated by the following examples:

A		B	
sign	[sayn]	signature	[sɪgnəčər]
design	[dəzayn]	designate	[dɛzɪgnet]
malign	[məlayn]	malignant	[məlɪgnənt]

In none of the words in column A is there a phonetic [g], but in each corresponding word in column B a [g] occurs. Our knowledge of English phonology accounts for these phonetic differences. The "[g] — no [g]" alternation is regular and applies to words which one might never have heard before. Suppose someone said:

He was a *salignant* [səlɪgnənt] man.

Even if you didn't know what the word meant, you might ask (perhaps to hide your ignorance):

Why, did he *salign* [səlayn] somebody?

It is highly doubtful that you would pronounce the verb form with the *-ant* dropped as [səlɪgn]. Your knowledge of the phonological rules of English would "delete" the /g/ when it occurred in this context. The rule can be stated as:

6 Delete a /g/ when it occurs before a final nasal consonant.

Given this rule, the phonemic representation of the stems in *sign/signature, design/designation, malign/malignant* (as well as *resign/resignation, repugn/repugnant, phlegm/phlegmatic, paradigm/paradigmatic, diaphragm/diaphragmatic*) will include a *phonemic* /g/ which will be deleted by the regular rule if a suffix is not added. Notice that by stating the *class* of sounds which follow the /g/ (nasal consonants) rather than specifying any specific nasal consonant, the rule deletes the /g/ before both /m/ and /n/.

Phonological rules can therefore *delete whole segments* as well as add segments and features and change features.

There are other rules which delete segments in English. Consider the following words:

	A		B
bomb	[bam]	bombardier	[bambədir]
iamb	[ayæm]	iambic	[ayæmbɪk]
crumb	[krʌm]	crumble	[krʌmbəl]

A speaker of English knows when to pronounce a final /b/ and when not to. The relationship between the pronunciation of the A words and their B counterparts is regular and can be accounted for by Rule 7:

7 Delete a word-final /b/ when it occurs after an /m/.

The underlying phonemic representation of the A and B stems is the same.

PHONEMIC REPRESENTATION	/bamb/	/bamb + adir/	/bʌlb/
/b/ deletion rule	ø	NA	NA
vowel schwa rule²	NA	ə	NA
PHONETIC REPRESENTATION	[bam]	[bambədir]	[bʌlb]

Phonological rules which delete whole segments are found in languages throughout the world. In French, for example, as demonstrated by Sanford Schane³ word-final consonants are deleted when the following word begins with a consonant or a liquid, but are retained when the following word begins with a vowel or a glide:

Before a consonant:	petit table	[pəti tabl]	"small table"
	nos tables	[no tabl]	"our tables"
Before a liquid:	petit robe	[pəti rob]	"small dress"
	nos robes	[no rob]	"our dresses"
Before a vowel:	petit ami	[pətit ami]	"small friend"
	nos amis	[noz ami]	"our friends"
Before a glide:	petit oiseau	[pətit wazo]	"small bird"
	nos oiseaux	[noz wazo]	"our birds"

This is a general rule in French applying to all word-final consonants.⁴ In the chapter on phonetics we distinguished these four classes of sounds by the following features:

	CONSONANTS	LIQUIDS	VOWELS	GLIDES
Consonantal	+	+	−	−
Vocalic	−	+	+	−

Using these classes, we can state the French rule very simply:

8 Delete a word-final consonant when it occurs before the class of [+consonantal] segments (that is, consonants and liquids).

---

² This rule is discussed below.

³ Sanford Schane, *French Phonology and Morphology* (Cambridge: M.I.T. Press, 1968).

⁴ In Schane's complete analysis, many words that are pronounced with a final consonant actually have a vowel as their word-final segment in phonemic representation. The vowel prevents the rule of word-final consonant deletion (Rule 8) from applying. The vowel itself is deleted by another, later, rule. Thus *robe* is /robe/ phonemically and becomes [rob] phonetically.

In the grammar of French, *petit* would be phonemically /pətit/. It need not be represented additionally as /pəti/ since the rule determines the phonetic shape of the word.

We see then that it is not only in English that rules may delete segments. All the kinds of rules discussed so far are found in languages throughout the world.

Phonological rules may also move phonemes from one place in the string to another. Such rules are called **metathesis rules.** They are less common, but they do exist. In some dialects of English, for example, the word *ask* is pronounced [æks] but the word *asking* is pronounced [æskɪŋ]. In these dialects a metathesis rule "switches" the /s/ and /k/ in certain contexts.

The more we look at languages, the more we see that many aspects of the phonetic forms of utterances which appear at first to be irregular and unpredictable are actually rule-governed. We learn, or construct, these rules when we are learning the language as a child.

In the *sign/signature* examples we showed that the presence or absence of a [g] was determined by rule. Similarly the vowel differences in the pairs are predictable. Notice that in all the words in the first column below, the underlined vowel is pronounced [ay] and in the second column [ɪ].

[ay]	[ɪ]
sign	signature
malign	malignant
line	linear
sublime	sublimation
dine	dinner
rite	ritual
sacrifice	sacrificial
suffice	sufficient
divide	division
antagonize	antagonistic

These words are just a few of such pairs which show the regular alternation between phonetic [ay] and [ɪ].

Other regular vowel alternations also occur in English, as is shown by the following triplets:

[ə]		[a]		[o]	
harmony	[hárməni]	harmonic	[harmánək]	harmonious	[harmóniəs]
melody	[mélədi]	melodic	[məládək]	melodious	[məlódiəs]
symphony	[símfəni]	symphonic	[sɪmfánək]	symphonious	[sɪmfóniəs]

In all cases, the underlined [ə] in the first column corresponds to the underlined [a] in the second and to the underlined [o] in the third. There are rules in English which determine which vowels in a word should be stressed, under what conditions unstressed vowels are changed to [ə], and which also determine the particular phonetic vowel in each context. These rules account for the [ay]/[ɪ] alternation as well as the [ə]/[a]/[o] alternating vowels. They apply generally, not just to the words listed. They also, for example, account for the [i]/[ɛ] phonetic vowels in such words as these:

serene/serenity   obscene/obscenity   perceive/perception

The explicit statement of this vowel schwa rule is quite complex and goes beyond the introductory level of this discussion. But the regularities are clearly seen and illustrate the fact that a single stem may be pronounced differently when different suffixes are added to it. They further illustrate the fact that English spelling is not as irregular as some spelling reformers would lead one to think. The spelling of the three words *melody, melodic,* and *melodious* with an *o* is not accidental. The *o* symbolizes the phonemic /o/ which is changed by regular rules into phonetic [ə] and [a].

Similarly the spelling of *sign* with a *g* or *bomb* with a final *b* represents what speakers know about the phonemic representation of these words. Such "silent letters" show the relationship between these words and *signature* and *bombardier.* The pronunciation of the words is accounted for by regular rules.

You know these rules because you know the grammar of English, even if you cannot state them consciously. The phonemic representation of such words plus the phonological rules of the language determine the phonetic representations. Given the phonemic representation of the words *pornographic* and *pornography* (which is part of your linguistic knowledge), you would know that a pornographic picture could be called a *pornograph* [pɔ́rnəgræf] even though the word cannot be found in a dictionary. You would not have to hear the word pronounced to know its phonetic form.

It is not the purpose of this chapter (or this book) to describe the complex phonology of English. Examples from English are used only to illustrate the kinds of phonological rules found in languages of the world.

In the discussion on how phonemic representations of utterances are realized phonetically, it might have been concluded that each phoneme is represented by a set of allophones which "belong" only to that phoneme. That is, phoneme A is represented by the phonetic segments [a] and [a'], phoneme B by [b] and [b'], phoneme C by [c] and [c'], and so on, and phoneme A can never be realized as [b] or [c]. This would be a neat and tidy mapping of phonemic representation onto phonetic representations. But the mind is capable of greater complexities, which show up in the phonological rules of grammars. Consider the underlined vowels in the following pairs of words:

A	B
tele<u>g</u>raph	tele<u>g</u>raphy
[ə]	[ɛ]
harm<u>o</u>ny	harm<u>o</u>nic
[ə]	[a]
New<u>t</u>on	New<u>t</u>onian
[ə]	[o]
syll<u>a</u>ble	syll<u>a</u>bic
[ə]	[æ]

In column A all the underlined vowels are pronounced [ə]; yet these "reduced" vowels must be derived from different underlying phonemes, since when they are stressed they show up as different vowels in the words in column B.   If the underlined *e* in telegraph was not phonemically /ɛ/ there would be no way to account for the particular quality of the stressed vowel.   Different phonemic vowels in English, when unstressed, may all become phonetically [ə].   Thus, one might say that [ə] is an allophone of many different vowel phonemes.

We can't always tell from the phonetic transcription what the phonemic representation is.   But given the phonemic representation and the phonological rules we can always derive the correct phonetic transcription.   Another example may help to illustrate this interesting aspect of phonology.

In English, /t/ and /d/ are both phonemes, as is illustrated by the minimal pairs *tie/die* and *bat/bad*.   When a /t/ or a /d/ occurs between two vowels they both become a flap [D].   For many speakers of English, *writer* and *rider* are pronounced identically as [rayDər].   Yet speakers know that *writer* has a *phonemic* /t/ because of *write* /rayt/, and that *rider* has a *phonemic* /d/ because of *ride* /rayd/.   The "flap rule" may be stated as:

9 An alveolar stop becomes a voiced flap intervocalically (between vowels).

The application of this rule is illustrated as follows:

PHONEMIC	write	writer	ride	rider
REPRESENTATION	/rayt/	/rayt + ər/	/rayd/	/rayd + ər/
		↓		↓
"flap rule"	NA	D	NA	D
PHONETIC				
REPRESENTATION	[rayt]	[rayDər]	[rayd]	[rayDər]

We are omitting other phonetic details which are also determined by phonological rules, such as the fact that in *ride* the vowel is slightly longer than in *write* because it is followed by a voiced [d].   We are using the example only to illustrate the fact that two distinct phonemes may be realized phonetically as the same sound.

Such cases show that one cannot arrive at a phonological analysis by simply inspecting the phonetic representation of utterances. If we just looked for minimal pairs as the only evidence for phonology, we would have to conclude that [D] was a phoneme in English because it contrasts phonetically with other phonetic units: *riper* [raypər], *rhymer* [raymər], *riser* [rayzər] etc. Grammars are much more complex than this. The fact that *write* and *ride* change their phonetic forms when suffixes are added shows that there is an intricate mapping between phonemic representations of words and phonetic pronunciation.

In many cases one even requires nonphonological information in phonological rules; that is, the phonology is not totally independent of the rest of the grammar. In English we place primary stress on an adjective followed by a noun when the two words are combined in a compound noun, but we place the stress on the noun when the words are combined in a noun phrase in which the noun is modified by the adjective:

NOUN COMPOUNDS	ADJECTIVE + NOUN PHRASE
Whíte House	white hóuse
Rédcoat	red cóat
hótdog	hot dóg
bláckboard	black bóard
blúebird	blue bírd

In the previous chapter we also illustrated the stress difference in noun-verb pairs in English, as shown by:

NOUN	VERB
pérvert	pervért
pérmit	permít
cónvert	convért
réject	rejéct

The stress placement is predictable (that is, nonphonemic), given knowledge of the "word class." Actually, the stress rules are more complicated than this. These examples, as well as the others discussed above, are provided only to illustrate the *kind* of knowledge accounted for by the phonological rules of a grammar.

An examination of the phonologies of different languages shows rules which add features, change features, add segments, delete segments, and transpose or switch segments. This must mean that man's linguistic ability permits him to form such rules. Just as all possible sounds are not found in languages, so all conceivable rules are not. No language has ever been found which includes a rule specifying that all the phonemes in a word should be reversed or that every third phoneme should be deleted or that one should add an /l/ before a word just in case the word has thirteen phonemes. These are logically possible but not phonologically possible. We see then that the forms of grammars, and their phonological parts, are not as variable as Satie seemed to think. There are universal constraints on the phonological systems which man can learn.

THE FORMALIZATION OF PHONOLOGICAL RULES

Form follows function.
— Slogan of the Bauhaus school of architecture

In this chapter all the examples of phonological rules we have considered have been stated in words. That is, we have not used any special "formal devices" or "formal notations." We could, however, have stated the rules using special symbols which would make the rules look more like "mathematical" formulas.

A number of such notational devices are used as part of the theory of phonology. They do more than merely save paper or abbreviate long statements. They can express the generalizations of the language in a way which may be obscured otherwise.

For example, if we used our + and − feature value notation in the rule which nasalizes vowels before nasal consonants, it could be stated as:

$$\textbf{2}' \begin{bmatrix} +\text{vocalic} \\ -\text{consonantal} \end{bmatrix} \text{ becomes } [+\text{nasal}] \text{ before a } [+\text{nasal}].$$

This clearly shows that just one feature is changed and that it is an assimilatory rule.

Suppose we wished to write a rule which nasalized a vowel before and only before a /p/. By stating this without features, we could say: Nasalize a vowel before a /p/. This seems to be as simple and general a rule as the nasalization rule. Yet it is a strange and highly unlikely rule. To state this rule with features, we would have to write:

$$\textbf{10} \begin{bmatrix} +\text{vocalic} \\ -\text{consonantal} \end{bmatrix} \text{ becomes } [+\text{nasal}] \text{ before a } \begin{bmatrix} +\text{consonantal} \\ -\text{vocalic} \\ +\text{labial} \\ -\text{voice} \\ -\text{continuant} \end{bmatrix}$$

We can see at a glance that Rule 10 is more complex (you have to mention more features) and that the features mentioned have nothing in common. Rule 2′ seems like a "natural" rule and Rule 10 does not. But that is exactly what we want to reveal. Without the use of features the difference between the two rules is hidden. The use of such feature notation to represent phonemes is then part of the theory of phonology. The formal notation is not used merely because it is somehow more "elegant" but because it better represents what we know about phonological rules.

Instead of writing "becomes" or "occurs" we can use an arrow, $\rightarrow$, to show that the segment on the left of the arrow is or becomes whatever is on the right of the arrow:

2′′ $\begin{bmatrix} +\text{vocalic} \\ -\text{consonantal} \end{bmatrix} \rightarrow$ [+nasal] before a [+nasal].

The phonological environment or context is also important to specify in a rule. In many languages vowels are nasalized before but not after a nasal. We can formalize the notions of "environment" or "in the environment" and the notions of "before" and "after" by the following notations:

> a slash, /, to mean "in the environment of"
> a dash, $-$, placed before or after the segment(s) which determine the change.

Using these notations we can write the above rule:

2′′′ $\begin{bmatrix} +\text{vocalic} \\ -\text{consonantal} \end{bmatrix} \rightarrow$ [+nasal] / $-$ [+nasal].

This rule reads: "A vowel (that is, a segment which is specified as vocalic and nonconsonantal) becomes ($\rightarrow$) nasalized in the environment (/) before ($-$) a nasal segment.

If we write the rule as 2a,

2a $\begin{bmatrix} +\text{vocalic} \\ -\text{consonantal} \end{bmatrix} \rightarrow$ [+nasal] / [+nasal] $-$,

it reads: "A vowel becomes nasalized in the environment *after* a nasal." The fact that the dash follows the [+nasal] shows that a vowel which comes *after* it is changed.

Some of the rules discussed above state that the segment to be changed by the rule occurs at the beginning or end of a word. We can use a double cross, #, to signify a word boundary.

See if you can read the following rule:

1′ $\begin{bmatrix} +\text{stop} \\ -\text{voiced} \end{bmatrix} \rightarrow$ [+aspirated] / # $-$.

If the formal devices and notational system we have been discussing haven't completely confused you, you should be able to see that this is the same "aspiration rule" given above as Rule 1, and should be read: "A voiceless stop becomes ($\rightarrow$) aspirated in the evironment (/) after a word boundary (# $-$)" (that is, at the beginning of a word).

Rule 3 above, which velarizes a /l/, states *two* environments where the rule applies: before a non-low front vowel, and at the end of a word. We can state this formally as:

3a [+lateral] → [+velarized] / —
$$\begin{bmatrix} +\text{vocalic} \\ -\text{consonantal} \\ -\text{front} \end{bmatrix}$$

3b [+lateral] → [+velarized] / — #.

Writing two rules seems to miss some generalization, since both rules apply to /l/. To **collapse** (or combine) two rules which have *identical parts* (for example, both say that they apply to a segment that is [+lateral] and both add the feature [+velarized]), we can use another device, braces, { }, and can collapse Rules 3a and 3b into Rule 3′:

3′ [+lateral] → [+velarized] /—
$$\left\{ \begin{matrix} \begin{bmatrix} +\text{vocalic} \\ -\text{consonantal} \\ -\text{front} \end{bmatrix} \\ \# \end{matrix} \right\}$$

The braces signify that the rule applies *either* before the first segment *or* before the word boundary. Thus the brace notation permits us to express a general rule in a general fashion.

Can you "read" the following rule?

11
$$\begin{bmatrix} -\text{consonantal} \\ +\text{vocalic} \end{bmatrix} \rightarrow [+\text{long}] /-
\left\{ \begin{matrix} \begin{bmatrix} +\text{consonantal} \\ -\text{vocalic} \\ +\text{voiced} \end{bmatrix} \\ \# \end{matrix} \right\}$$

You should have read it as: "A vowel becomes long in the environment before either a voiced consonant or at the end of a word (before a word boundary)."

We mention just one other "notational device" that helps reveal generalizations in phonology. Suppose there was a rule in some language to shorten a vowel when the vowel occurs before three consonants or two consonants. We could write this rule using the brace notation:

12
$$\begin{bmatrix} +\text{vocalic} \\ -\text{consonantal} \end{bmatrix} \rightarrow$$

$$[-\text{long}] / - \left\{ \begin{matrix} \begin{bmatrix} -\text{vocalic} \\ +\text{consonantal} \end{bmatrix} \begin{bmatrix} -\text{vocalic} \\ +\text{consonantal} \end{bmatrix} \begin{bmatrix} -\text{vocalic} \\ +\text{consonantal} \end{bmatrix} \\ \begin{bmatrix} -\text{vocalic} \\ +\text{consonantal} \end{bmatrix} \begin{bmatrix} -\text{vocalic} \\ +\text{consonantal} \end{bmatrix} \end{matrix} \right\}$$

If we use V for vowels and C for consonants, this can be written as:

12′ V → [−long] / − $\left\{ \begin{matrix} \text{CCC} \\ \text{CC} \end{matrix} \right\}$.

This rule gives us the result we want; by using the braces we have collapsed two rules, both of which apply to vowels and both of which shorten the vowels. But there are identical parts in the two rules which are repeated. This seems to miss a generalization that we would want to capture. That is, we should have some notational device which clearly and simply shows that the rule applies before three or two consonants. To collapse rules like this, we use parentheses, ( ), around an "optional" segment or segments. That is, the rule really states that a vowel is always shortened before two consonants and there may or may not be a third consonant. The presence of the third consonant does not affect the rule. Using parentheses, we can state the rule as:

12a $V \rightarrow [-\text{long}] / - CC (C)$.

This rule then reads: "A vowel is shortened in the environment before three consonants (with the C in parentheses included) or before two consonants."

The importance of formal devices like feature notations, arrows, slashes, dashes, braces, and parentheses is that they enable us to express linguistic generalizations. Since the grammar that linguists write for any particular language aims to express in the most general fashion a speaker's linguistic competence, the notations which permit them to do this are part of the theory of phonology.

We have not discussed all the formalisms used in phonology to capture linguistic generalizations. Actually, our main purpose here is to help you understand the *kinds* of phonological processes (rules) found in the languages of the world. Thus this discussion of formal notations as such is brief, since it is intended mainly for those who wish to read further in phonology and may come across rules written in this way.

SUMMARY

Part of one's knowledge of a language is knowledge of the sound system—the **phonology** of that language. The phonology of the language includes the inventory of basic **phonemes** (those segments which are used to differentiate between the meanings of words) and the permissible sequences of these units. A phoneme may have different phonetic representations. The relationship between the phonemic representation of words or utterances and the phonetic representation (the pronunciation of these utterances) is determined by general **phonological rules.**

Phonological rules in a grammar apply to phonemic strings and may alter them in various ways:

1. They may add nondistinctive features which are predictable from the context. The rule which aspirates voiceless stops at the beginning of words in English is such a rule, since aspiration is a nonphonemic feature.

2. They may change the feature specification of phonemes. The "homorganic nasal" rule which changes an /n/ to an [m] or an [ŋ] before labials and velars, respectively, is such a rule.

3. They may add segments which are not present in the phonemic string. The "ə-insertion" rule which inserts an [ə] before the plural ending after sibilants illustrates this.

4. They may delete phonemic segments in certain contexts. The "g-deletion" rule which accounts for the pronunciation of *sign* without a [g] but of *signature* with a [g] is a deletion rule.

5. They may "transpose" or move segments around in a string, as illustrated by the /sk/ to [ks] rule in certain American dialects.

Such rules show that the phonemic shape of words or phrases is not identical with their phonetic form. While the rules may be very complex they are never too complex to be learned, since these rules represent what speakers of a language know. We all learn the basic phonological units of our language — the phonemic segments — and the phonemic representation of words. The phonemes are not the actual phonetic sounds, but are abstract mental constructs which are realized as sounds by the operation of rules such as those described above. No one teaches us these rules. And yet, all speakers of a language know the phonology of their language better than any linguist who tries to describe it. The linguist's job is to make explicit what we know unconsciously about the sound pattern of our language.

In the writing of rules linguists use certain formal devices to permit better generalizations of the phonological processes which occur. Features are used rather than whole segments, and other devices such as braces and parentheses collapse rules when the rules contain similar parts. Such devices are used only if they are able truly to represent what a speaker knows about the sound patterns of his language.

EXERCISES

1. The following sets of minimal pairs show that English [p] and [b] contrast in initial, medial, and final positions. A minimal pair is a pair of words which contrast in only one sound segment; all other sounds are identical and the segments are in the same order. That is, *pan* and *tan* are minimal pairs; *pan* and *tin* are not, and *tam* and *mat* are not.

INITIAL	MEDIAL	FINAL
pit-bit	rapid-rabid	cap-cab

Find similar sets of minimal pairs involving each of the following pairs of consonants in word-initial, word-medial, and word-final position:

1. [k] – [g]
2. [b] – [v]
3. [s] – [š]
4. [m] – [n]
5. [b] – [m]
6. [θ] – [ð]
7. [l] – [r]
8. [č] – [j]
9. [p] – [f]
10. [s] – [z]

2. The indefinite singular article in English is either *a* or *an*, as shown in the following phrases:

a hotel, a boy, a use, a wagon, a big man, a yellow rug, a white house, an apple, an honor, an orange curtain, an old lady.

State the rule which determines when *a* is used and when *an* is used. If possible do not list individual sound segments but make the rule as general as possible, referring to *features* or *classes* of segments.

3. The difference between the underlined sounds in column A and those in column B may be stated by one simple statement. What is the change which occurs?

A   B

wife   wives
goose   gosling
prescription   prescribe
house (noun)   house (verb)
bath   bathe

4. a. Review the rules for the "plural formation" in English. Now state the rules for the "possessive formation" in English. (For example, *boy's, cat's, cow's, judge's*.)

b. What does this tell you about the "generality" of such rules?

c. State the rules which determine the proper phonetic form of the past-tense ending on verbs. Use classes of segments, rather than listing the individual phonemes. In what ways are these rules similar to those you gave under a?

5. Below are given some data (in *phonetic* transcription) from a hypothetical language called Hip.

[tip]   "girl"   [tiben] "girls"
[pit]   "boy"   [piden] "boys"
[kip]   "child"   [kiben] "children"
[pik]   "policeman" [pigen] "policemen"
[tap]   "teacher"   [kiven] "dogs"

1. What is the *phonemic* form for "children"?

2. What is the *phonetic* form for "teachers"?

3. What is the *phonetic* form for "dog"?

4. State the rule which can account for the phonetic differences between singular and plural forms.

6. Here are some phonetic forms from another language. The words in the first column are singular nouns; those in the second column are the corresponding plurals.

SINGULAR	PLURAL
[orat]	[ēmorat]
[laz]	[ēmlaz]
[bole]	[ēmbole]
[dus]	[ēndus]
[sar]	[ēnsar]
[kipo]	[ēŋkipo]
[gola]	[ēŋgola]
[gūn]	[ēŋgūn]

1. Which of the following is the most likely phonemic representation for the plural prefix?

a. /ēm/   b. /em/   c. /ēn/   d. /en/   e. /ēŋ/   f. /eŋ/

State the reasons for your choice.

2. If the phonetic form for "girl" is [tabo], what would the *phonetic* form for "girls" be?

3. What is the *phonemic* representation for [ēŋgūn]?

4. State the phonological rules which can account for the phonetic forms.

7. In some dialects of English the following words have different vowels, as in shown by the phonetic transcriptions.

A		B		C	
bite	[bʌyt]	bide	[bayd]	tie	[tay]
rice	[rʌys]	rise	[rayz]	by	[bay]
type	[tʌyp]	bribe	[brayb]	sigh	[say]
wife	[wʌyf]	wives	[wayvz]	die	[day]
tyke	[tʌyk]	time	[taym]		
		nine	[nayn]		
		tile	[tayl]		
		tire	[tayr]		
		writhe	[rayð]		

1. How may the classes of sounds which end the words in columns

A and B be characterized? That is, what feature specifies all the final segments in A and all the final segments in B?

2. How do the words in column C differ from those in columns A and B?

3. Are [ʌy] and [ay] in complementary distribution? Give your reasons.

4. If [ʌy] and [ay] are allophones of one phoneme, should they be derived from /ʌy/ or /ay/? Why?

5. What is the *phonetic* representation of *life* and *lives*?

6. What would the *phonetic* representations of the following words be?

   a. trial   b. bike   c. lice   d. fly   e. mine

7. State the rule which will relate the phonemic representations to the phonetic representations of the words given above.

8. Below are some data from Twi, a language spoken in Ghana. The phonemic representation of the verbs is given, followed by the phonetic transcription of these verbs in affirmative and negative constructions.

"pour"	/gu/	"he pours"	[o gu]	"he doesn't pour"	[o ŋŋu]
"kill"	/kum/	"he kills"	[o kum]	"he doesn't kill"	[o ŋku]
"break"	/bu/	"he breaks"	[o bu]	"he doesn't break"	[o mmu]
"appear"	/pue/	"he appears"	[o pue]	"he doesn't appear"	[o mpue]
"eat"	/di/	"he eats"	[o di]	"he doesn't eat"	[o nni]
"scratch"	/tĩ/	"he scratches"	[o tĩ]	"he doesn't scratch"	[o ntĩ]

What are the rules that change the phonemic forms of the verbs to the phonetic forms, where the phonetic forms differ from the phonemic?

9. a. The English verbs in column A have stress on the next to last syllable (called the *penultimate*), while the verbs in column B have their last syllable stressed. State a rule which can predict where stress occurs in these verbs.

A	B
astónish	collápse
éxit	exíst
imágine	tormént
cáncel	revólt
elícit	adópt
práctice	insíst
solícit	contórt

b. In the verbs in column C, stress also occurs on the final syllable. What do you have to add to your rule which will account for this? In the forms in columns A and B the final consonants had to be considered; in the forms in column C consider the vowels.

C

expláin
eráse
surpríse
combíne
caréen
atóne
equáte

10. Below are listed 15 "words." Some of them may be English "words" and others are definitely "foreign." For each "word" state whether it could or could not be an English word. For those which you mark as "foreign" give all the reasons you can think of for making this decision.

1. [klænp]	6. [fɔlərayt]	11. [žoli]
2. [tligɪt]	7. [splad]	12. [šɛktər]
3. [prɪsk]	8. [vuzapm]	13. [θeməret]
4. [trigãn]	9. [ŋar]	14. [ǰrʊdki]
5. [æləposg]	10. [skwɨɫ]	15. [mlop]

11. State the following rules using the "formal devices" discussed at the end of the chapter.

Example: A consonant becomes zero (is deleted) after one or two consonants.

$$C \rightarrow \emptyset \: / \: C \: (C) \: -.$$

Example: Aspirate a voiceless stop consonant at the end of a word.

$$\begin{bmatrix} C \\ +stop \\ -voice \end{bmatrix} \rightarrow [+aspirated] \: / \: - \: \#.$$

1. A vowel is stressed in the environment after a word boundary (at the beginning of a word).

2. A voiced consonant becomes nasal before a nasal.

3. A voiceless segment becomes voiced between two vowels.

4. A voiced consonant becomes voiceless either before a voiceless consonant or at the end of a word.

5. A vowel is lengthened before one or two voiced consonants.

References

CHOMSKY, N., and HALLE, M. *The Sound Pattern of English.* New York: Harper & Row, 1968.

HALLE, M. "On the Bases of Phonology," in J. A. Fodor and J. J. Katz, eds., *The Structure of Language.* Englewood Cliffs, N.J.: Prentice Hall, 1964.

HALLE, M. "Phonology in Generative Grammar," in Fodor and Katz.

HARMS, R. *Introduction to Phonological Theory.* Englewood Cliffs, N.J.: Prentice Hall, 1968.

JAKOBSON, R., and HALLE, M. *Fundamentals of Language.* Janua Linguarum. The Hague: Mouton, 1956.

SCHANE, SANFORD A. *Generative Phonology.* Englewood Cliffs, N.J.: Prentice Hall, 1973.

STANLEY, R. "Redundancy rules in phonology!" *Language* 43.1 (1967).

5
What Does It Mean?

Language without meaning is meaningless.

— ROMAN JAKOBSON

For thousands of years philosophers have been pondering the meaning of "meaning." Yet, everyone who knows a language can understand what is said to him and can produce strings of words which convey meaning.

Learning a language includes learning the "agreed-upon" meanings of certain strings of sounds and learning how to combine these meaningful units into larger units which also convey meaning. We are not free to change the meanings of these words at will, for if we did we would be unable to communicate with anyone.

Humpty Dumpty, however, refused to be so restricted when he said:

> "There's glory for you!"
>
> "I don't know what you mean by 'glory,' " Alice said.
>
> Humpty Dumpty smiled contemptuously. "Of course you don't — till I tell you. I meant 'there's a nice knock-down argument for you!' "
>
> "But 'glory' doesn't mean 'a nice knock-down argument,' " Alice objected.
>
> "When *I* use a word," Humpty Dumpty said, in rather a scornful tone, "it means just what I choose it to mean — neither more nor less."
>
> "The question is," said Alice, "whether you *can* make words mean so many different things."

Alice is quite right. You cannot make words mean what they do not mean. Of course if you wish to redefine the meaning of each word as you use it you are free to do so, but this would be an artificial, clumsy use of language, and most people would not wait around very long to talk to you.   A new word may be created, but it enters the language with its sound-meaning relationship already determined.

Fortunately there are few Humpty Dumptys.   Since all the speakers of a language share the basic vocabulary—the sounds and meanings of words—we have no difficulties in using language to talk to each other.

MORPHEMES: THE MINIMAL UNITS OF MEANING

> *"They gave it to me," Humpty Dumpty continued . . .,*
> *"for an un-birthday present."*
> *"I beg your pardon?"   Alice said with a puzzled air.*
> *"I'm not offended," said Humpty Dumpty.*
> *"I mean, what* is *an un-birthday present?"*
> *"A present given when it isn't your birthday, of course."*
>
> — LEWIS CARROLL, *Through the Looking-Glass*

Copyright Los Angeles Times; reprinted with permission

DENNIS THE MENACE   **BY HANK KETCHAM**

"WHAT DOES *RETIRED* MEAN, DENNIS?"   " TIRED YESTERDAY, TIRED AGAIN TODAY...I GUESS."

Courtesy Publishers-Hall Syndicate

If language is a system which relates sounds and meanings, there must be a set of elements which represent the basic meaningful units in the language. One usually thinks of these as the words of the language, as did the pioneer movie maker, Samuel Goldwyn, when he announced: "In two words: *im-possible*." An examination of the composition of words, however, shows that many words can be broken down into smaller elements, each of which has a meaning of its own.

Notice that in the following pairs of words the meanings of all the (B) words consist of the meanings of the (A) words plus the meaning "not":

A	B
desirable	undesirable
likely	unlikely

inspired	uninspired
developed	undeveloped
sophisticated	unsophisticated

If the most elemental units of meaning are assumed to be the words of a language, it would be a coincidence that *un* has the same meaning in all the (B) words. But this is obviously no coincidence. *Undesirable, unlikely,* and the other B words consist of at least two units of meaning: *un+desirable, likely,* and so on.

The traditional term for such a unit of grammatical form is **morpheme.** The word is derived from the Greek word *morphē,* meaning "form."[1] Linguistically speaking, then, Goldwyn should have said: "In two morphemes: *im-possible.*"

A single word may be composed of more than two morphemes. A favorite word of young children is *antidisestablishmentarianism. Anti-* also occurs in words such as *antiaircraft* and *antitoxin.* It means "against." *Dis-,* meaning "reverse the process of" or "not," occurs in *disinherit, disclaim; e-* occurs in many legal terms meaning "to do," as in *escribe, estop; stable* occurs by itself as an adjective meaning "firm"; *-ish* occurs after other verbs like *burnish* and *brandish; -ment* added to verbs forms nouns, as in *achievement, shipment; -ary* (or *-ari*) is added to nouns to form adjectives like *momentary, honorary; -an* refers to a particular individual, as in *American, African;* and *-ism* at the end of words signifies "belief in something" or "system of something," as in *idealism, imperialism, Platonism.* Thus we can break the whole word down into nine parts, each with a particular meaning:

anti+dis+e+stabl+ish+ment+ari+an+ism

Sentences can also be broken down into strings of morphemes. *The boys tossed Mary's hat over the fence* can be analyzed as:

The + boy+s + toss+ed + Mary+s + hat + over + the + fence.

The is the morpheme signifying that it was some particular boys. The *-s* after boy is the "plural" morpheme; the *-ed* after toss is the "past-tense" morpheme; the *-s* after Mary signifies possession. (Notice that the same sound may represent two different morphemes, for example the plural *-s* and the possessive *-s*).

The study of the morphemic structure of words has traditionally been called **morphology,** whereas the study of the combination of words (or morphemes) into sentences has been called **syntax.** We shall see that a sharp line cannot easily be drawn between the two in all cases. But knowing a language certainly means knowing the most basic forms or morphemes of the language and what they mean.

---

[1] Another term, *formative,* is now used by some linguists. This has a slightly different meaning than *morpheme,* but the two terms are often used interchangeably.

Languages include many different kinds of morphemes, and linguists have used various ways of classifying them. They talk about **bound morphemes** and **free morphemes.** Bound morphemes are defined as those which must be attached to other morphemes, such as the "past-tense" morpheme in words like *type+d, trott+ed, giggle+d*; or the "plural" morpheme in words like *boy+s, cat+s, loss+es,* or prefixes like *pre-* in *pre+scribe, pre+conceive, pre+view.* A free morpheme can occur without a bound morpheme, but a bound morpheme must be attached to a free morpheme. *Type, walk, boy, cat* are free morphemes. Of course, we seldom use even free morphemes alone. We combine all morphemes into larger units — sentences — when we use language.

Some morphemes have been called **derivational morphemes** because when they are added to another morpheme they "derive" a new word, which is often (but not always) in a different grammatical class. One such morpheme is *-able.* When added to the verb *desire*, for example, an adjective is derived. A few other examples of derivational morphemes are: (noun to adjective) *boy+ish, virtu+ous, Elizabeth+an, pictur+esque, affection+ate, health+ful, alcohol+ic, life+like;* (verb to noun) *acquitt+al, clear+ance, accus+ation, confer+ence, sing+er, conform+ist;* (adjective to adverb) *exact+ly, quiet+ly;* (noun to verb) *moral+ize, vaccin+ate, brand+ish.*

Other derivational morphemes do not cause a change in grammatical class. Many prefixes fall into this category: *a+moral, auto+biography, ex+wife, mono+theism, re+print, semi+annual, sub+minimal.* There are also suffixes of this type: *vicar+age, fad+ism, Trotsky+ite, Commun+ist, Americ+an, music+ian.* These morphemes merely add meaning.

The classification of morphemes as derivational morphemes is usually made to distinguish them from those known as **inflectional morphemes.** Inflectional morphemes never change the grammatical category of the words to which they are affixed. Their addition to words is dictated by the syntactic rules of the language. The plural morpheme is inflectional. It does not change grammatical class, nor does the past-tense morpheme. Thus *boys* may be segmented into two morphemes *boy + plural,* and *jumped* into *jump + past.* Other inflectional morphemes are the *-er* of comparison (*big/bigger*) and the *-est* of superlative (*big/biggest*). Clearly in talking of such morphemes, we are using the notion of morphemes in a broad sense to include what may be called "grammatical meaning."

One weakness of this classification system is reflected in the paralysis that results when trying to classify the possessive suffix *-'s.* In the pair *John/John's, John's* is more like an adjective than a noun, so this morpheme has both inflectional and derivational properties.

Despite the difficulties of any classificatory scheme, it is clear that words are not the simplest, most basic elements of either meaning or grammatical form.   Morphemes are.   When you know a language you know the morphemes, and in addition you know how to form new words from these elements.   You can invent new words by using morphemes in the language, and chances are you will be understood.   New words are often coined in this way, particularly in colloquial use or slang.   When the Russian word *sputnik* came into English, the morpheme *-nik* became available to speakers of English.   Other words like *beatnik* were soon formed, and bad jokes were thought up such as: "What's a phudnik?" "A nudnik with a Ph.D."

When the Mock Turtle listed the different branches of Arithmetic for Alice — "Ambition,   Distraction,   Uglification,   and   Derision" — Alice was confused:

> "I never heard of 'Uglification,' " Alice ventured to say.   "What is it?"
>
> The Gryphon lifted up both its paws in surprise.   "Never heard of uglifying!" it exclaimed.   "You know what to beautify is, I suppose?"
>
> "Yes," said Alice doubtfully: "it means — to — make — anything — prettier."
>
> "Well, then," the Gryphon went on, "if you don't know what to uglify is, you *are* a simpleton.

We tend to feel more sympathy for the Gryphon than for Alice.

Although we have confined our discussion to English, in all languages morphemes are the most elemental units of meaning.   In Turkish, if you add *-ak* to a verb, you derive a noun, as in:

> *dur,* "to stop"   *dur+ak,* "stopping place"
> *bat,* "to sink"   *bat+ak,* "sinking place" or "marsh/swamp"

In English, in order to express reciprocal action we use the phrase *each other* as in *understand each other, love each other.*   In Turkish one simply adds a morpheme to the verb: *anla* "understand," *anla + š* "understand each other," *sev* "love," *sev + iš* "love each other."

In Piro, an Arawakan language spoken in Peru, a single morpheme *kaka* can be added to a verb to express the meaning "cause to": *cokoruha* "to harpoon," *cokoruh+kaka* "to cause to harpoon"; *salwa* "to visit," *salwa+kaka* "to cause to visit."

In Karok, an American Indian language spoken in the Pacific northwest, if you add *-ak* to a noun, it forms a locative adverbial meaning "in, on, or at": *ikrivra:m* "house," *ikrivra:m+ak* "in a house"; *?a:s* "water," *?a:s+ak* "in water."   Also in Karok, the suffix *-ara* has the same meaning as our suffix *-y,* that is, "characterized by," as in *?a:x* "blood," *?ax+ara* "bloody"; *apti:k* "branch," *aptik+ara* "branchy."

The more we examine the languages of the world, the more we see how similar they are.   Knowing English includes knowing the morphemes and how to put them together; knowing Karok means knowing the morphemes of Karok and how to put them together.

MORPHOLOGY AND SYNTAX

> "... *and even* ... *the patriotic archbishop of Canterbury*
> *found it advisable —*"
> "*Found* what?" *said the Duck.*
> "*Found* it," *the Mouse replied rather crossly:* "*of course*
> *you know what 'it' means.*"
> "*I know what 'it' means well enough, when* I *find a thing,*"
> *said the Duck:* "*it's generally a frog or a worm.   The ques-*
> *tion is, what did the archbishop find?*"
>
> — LEWIS CARROLL, *Alice's Adventures in Wonderland*

Linguists traditionally have made a distinction between *morphology,* the combination of morphemes into words, and *syntax,* the combination of words into sentences.   They tried to define a morpheme either semantically, as the "minimal unit of meaning," or phonologically, as a "recurrent sound sequence in a language."

The more deeply one examines language, the more difficult it is to classify morphemes in the ways described, or to distinguish sharply between the structure of words and the structure of sentences.

For example, if a morpheme is the minimal unit of meaning, what is the meaning of *it* in the sentence *It's hot in July* or in *the Archbishop found it advisable.*   What is the meaning of *to* in *He wanted her to go?*   One may say that *to* has a grammatical meaning, as an infinitive marker.   Yet it doesn't occur in the sentence *He heard her go* although both sentences have the same structure.

Any attempt to provide a phonological definition of a morpheme is just as hopeless.   Mario Pei has defined the morpheme as "a meaningful series of phonemes which is not further divisible save with destruction or alteration of meaning."[2]   He goes on to illustrate this: "If I take a sequence like *posts,* I can subdivide it into two morphemes, *post* and -*s.* ... It is obvious that I cannot further subdivide -*s.*   As for *post* there is no possible logical subdivision.   If I try *po-st,* I can give the first the meaning of 'the name of an Italian river,' which changes the meaning; I can do nothing with -*st.*"   He concludes that *post* "must therefore be kept intact.   It has a definite meaning and answers the definition of a morpheme."

But this definition will not work, as Dr. Pei himself must know. Thousands of years ago the Hindu grammarians recognized that some morphemes may have a **zero-form,** that is, may not have any phonological representation.   One form of the plural morpheme in English is phonologically "zero" (∅), as can be seen from the following sentences:

[2] Mario Pei, *Invitation to Linguistics* (Chicago: Henry Regnery, 1971).

The boy is going.	The boy<u>s</u> are going.
The ox is going.	The ox<u>en</u> are going.
The sheep is going.	The sheep(<u>∅</u>) are going.

The plural form of *sheep* is *sheep*.   Obviously, a morpheme cannot be defined as "a meaningful series of phonemes," since in the case of *sheep* (plural) the plural morpheme has no phonemic form.   Nor does the past-tense morpheme of the verb *hit* have a phonemic form: *He hit it yesterday.*

There are certain things we can say about morphemes:

1. A morpheme may be represented by a single sound, like the plural morpheme -*s* in *cat+s.*
2. A morpheme may be represented by a syllable, like *child* and -*ish* in *child+ish.*
3. A morpheme may be represented by more than one syllable: by two syllables, as in *aardvark, lady, water;* or by three syllables, as in *Hackensack* or *crocodile,* or by four syllables, as in *salamander.*
4. A morpheme may have no sound to represent it, as the plural of *sheep* and the past tense of *hit* demonstrate.

We have also seen that what are usually considered single words in a language may be composed of one or more morphemes:

> one morpheme — *boy, girl*
> two morphemes — *blue+bird, Red+coat*
> three morphemes — *mail+box+es, un+happi+ness*
> four morphemes — *un+desir+abil+ity*
> more than four morphemes — *un+gentle+man+li+ness*

In addition, the same sounds may represent different morphemes. We said above that the morpheme representing the plural of *boys* is the same sound as that representing the possessive in *boy's.*   Furthermore, the string of sounds which represent a morpheme in one place may not represent a morpheme when they occur elsewhere.   The morpheme -*er* means "one who does" in words like *singer, painter, lover, worker.* But in *butcher* the sounds are part of a single morpheme, since a *butcher* is not one who *butches.   (In an earlier form of English the word *butcher* was *bucker,* "one who dresses bucks."   The -*er* in this word was then a separate morpheme.)

Similarly, in *water* the -*er* is not a distinct morpheme ending.   The -*er* in *nicer* is a separate morpheme, but a different one than the -*er* in *singer,* since it represents the "comparative" in the adjective.   The *un-* in *unlikely* means "not," but *un-* in *undo* means "to reverse the process" and the *un* in *fun* does not represent a distinct morpheme.

Just as the same string of sounds may represent different morphemes, the same morpheme may have different phonetic realizations.   The morpheme *sign* occurs also in *signature.*   The morpheme meaning "not" may be pronounced *in* [ɪn] in *intolerant* and *im* [ɪm] in *impolite* and [ɪŋ] in *incomplete,* as was shown in Chapter 4.   The language system—

that is, the grammar—determines the particular pronunciation of a morpheme in different contexts. As was also discussed, you know that the *g* is not pronounced in *sign, design,* and *malign* but that it is pronounced in *signature, designate,* and *malignant,* even though the words in the second group include the same morphemes as the corresponding words in the first group.

The grammar determines the pronunciation. And the grammar determines when a particular grammatical relation will be expressed "morphologically" or "syntactically." Very often the same idea can be expressed in either way, which shows that the traditional division between morphology and syntax needs to be revised. We can see this in the following sentences:

The boy's book.	The book *of* the boy.
He love*s* books.	He is a lov*er* of books.
The planes *which* fly are red.	The fl*ying* planes are red.
He is hungri*er* than she.	He is *more* hungry than she.

Perhaps some of you form the comparative of *hungry* only by adding *-er.* There are speakers who say either. *Beastlier* or *more beastly* are often used interchangeably. We know the rule that determines when either form of the comparative can be used or when just one can be used. So does Alice: "'Curiouser and curiouser!' cried Alice (she was so much surprised, that for the moment she quite forgot how to speak good English)."

The sentences of a language are made up of sequences of morphemes. Some morphemes are pronounced; others are "silent." Some express semantic concepts; some express grammatical relations. The rules of the grammar, which are part of your knowledge of the language, permit you to use and understand the morphemes in forming sentences and understanding sentences.

THE MEANING OF MORPHEMES AND WORDS

"*My* name *is Alice . . .*"

"*It's a stupid name enough!*" Humpty Dumpty *interrupted impatiently. "What does it mean?"*

"*Must a name mean something?*" Alice *asked doubtfully.*

"*Of course it must,*" Humpty Dumpty *said with a short laugh: "my name means the shape I am—and a good handsome shape it is, too. With a name like yours, you might be any shape, almost.*"

— LEWIS CARROLL, *Through the Looking-Glass*

Not only do we know what the morphemes of our language are, we also know what they *mean*. Dictionaries are filled with words and their meanings. So is the head of every human being who speaks a language. You are a walking dictionary. You know the meaning of words like *boy, girl, ox, child, house, assassin, frighten, love, idea, democracy, problem*. Your knowledge of their meanings permits you to use them appropriately in sentences and to understand them when heard, even though you probably seldom stop and ask yourself: "What does *boy* mean?"

Each. word (and morpheme) in the language has its own meaning. We shall talk about the meaning of words, even though we already know that words may be composed of several morphemes. What we will say about the meaning of words will apply to the meaning of morphemes.

Suppose someone said:

The assassin was stopped before he got to Mr. Thwacklehurst.

If the word *assassin* is in your mental dictionary, you know that it was some *person* who was prevented from *murdering* some *important person* named Thwacklehurst. Your knowledge of the meaning of *assassin* tells you that it was not an animal that tried to kill the man and that Thwacklehurst was not likely to be a little old man who owned a tobacco shop. In other words, your knowledge of the meaning of *assassin* includes knowing that the individual to whom that word refers is *human*, is a *murderer*, and is a killer of *very important people*. These then are **semantic** properties of the word that speakers of the language will agree to. The meaning of all nouns, verbs, adjectives — the "content words" — can be similarly defined. Such knowledge about the meanings of words represents part of your semantic knowledge of the language. The study of linguistic meaning is called **semantics.**

In general, a word will have at least one special semantic "defining" property. "Horseness" is included in the meaning of *horse* as well as the meanings "animal," "four-legged," and so on. The word *mare* has all the semantic properties of *horse* plus the meaning "female." Some semantic features are common to many words; "human," for example, is part of the meaning of words such as *man, Mary, brother, infant, spinster, professor, student, deep-sea diver*, and *rock 'n' roll singer*. All these words and also words such as *dog, cat, rodent*, and *flea* are "animate," but the meanings of *stone, tree*, and *sincerity* include the fact that they refer to objects which are "nonanimate."

The semantic components of the meanings of words are not entirely independent of one another. Certain pairs of semantic properties are mutually exclusive; logically they cannot both be part of the meaning of one word. "Animate" and "nonanimate" are such properties. For most words "male" and "female" are also "contradictory" features, but *hermaphrodite* is one word which includes the semantic components "male" and "female."

Some semantic properties are predictable given the presence of others; "human" automatically means "animate" since all things which are human are also animate, but the reverse is not true, since a fly is animate but not human.

The meaning of a word, then, is specified in part by a set of semantic properties. Consider, for example, the word *kitten*. Knowing the meaning of this word means knowing that it refers to an animal, a young animal, a young feline animal, and so on. The word does not specify a particular kitten. That is, the meaning of *kitten* does not include the size or color or age of any specific kitten or what its name is or where it lives or who owns it. The meaning signifies what all kittens have in common. It defines "kittenness."

Scientists know that water is composed of hydrogen and oxygen. We know that water is an essential ingredient of lemonade or a bath. But one need not know any of these things to know what the word *water* means, and to be able to use and understand this word in a sentence.

We may know what a word means without knowing anything about the situation in which it is used in an utterance. Some philosophers deny this. Hayakawa believes that "the contexts of an utterance determine its meaning" and that "since no two contexts are ever exactly the same, no two meanings can be exactly the same. . . . To insist dogmatically that we know what a word means in *advance of its utterance* is nonsense."[3]

Nonetheless, we must insist on this "nonsense." It is not important that a word mean *exactly* the same thing each time it is used. What is important is that unless the word has essentially the same meaning from one utterance to another, two people speaking the same language could not understand each other. If we are to understand the nature of language, we must explain the fact that a speaker can and does communicate meaningfully with other speakers of his language.

Hayakawa attempts to support his view by the following example. He writes:

> . . . if John says "my typewriter" today, and again "my typewriter" to-morrow, the . . . meaning is different in the two cases, because the type-writer is not exactly the same from one day to the next (nor from one minute to the next): slow processes of wear, change and decay are going on constantly.[4]

But, we would answer, such minute changes can hardly be said to affect the *linguistic* meaning of the *word*.

We have no trouble comprehending the meaning of *typewriter*. We know that what is being talked about is an object readily recognized

---

[3] S. I. Hayakawa, *Language in Thought and Action,* rev. ed. (New York: Harcourt Brace Jovanovich, 1964).
[4] Hayakawa, op. cit.

as a "typewriter," and that the meaning of the *word* does not include the materials of which it is made, how old it is, whether it works well or not, its color, its location, or whether the owner knows how to type. Such information does not constitute the semantic properties of the word.

Linguistic knowledge means knowing the semantic meaning of a particular string of sounds. Because you know this you can use these words and combine them with other words and understand them when you hear them. This knowledge is part of the grammar of the language.

HOMONYMS (HOMOPHONES): SAME SOUNDS, DIFFERENT MEANINGS

> *"Mine is a long and a sad tale!" said the Mouse, turning to Alice, and sighing.*
> *"It is a long tail, certainly," said Alice, looking down with wonder at the Mouse's tail, "but why do you call it sad?"*
> — LEWIS CARROLL, *Alice's Adventures in Wonderland*

> *"There's a train at 4:04," said McHennie,*
> *"Four tickets I'll take, have you any?"*
> *Said the man at the door,*
> *"Not four for 4:04*
> *For four for 4:04 are too many."*

We have already said that knowing a word means knowing its sounds and meanings. Both aspects are necessary, for the same sounds can sometimes mean different things. Such words are called **homonyms** or **homophones**. The fact that two words have the same sounds can be accidental. They may not share any semantic properties. Such homonyms may create **ambiguity**. A word or a sentence is ambiguous if more than one meaning can be assigned to it.

The sentence *She cannot bear children* may be understood to mean "She is unable to give birth to children" or "She cannot tolerate children." The ambiguity is caused because *bear* represents two different meanings. Sometimes additional context can disambiguate the sentence. Thus, *She cannot bear children when they cry* is unambiguous, or practically so. The "give birth" interpretation is much less likely. On the other hand, *She cannot bear children because she is sterile* appears to be somewhat less ambiguous; yet the interpretation "She can't tolerate children because they remind her of the fact that she is sterile" is still a possible one.

In both of its meanings as used in the above sentence, *bear* is a verb.

There is another homonym, *bear,* the animal, which is a noun with very different semantic properties. The adjective *bare,* despite its different spelling, is pronounced like the above words and also has a different meaning.

When homonyms belong to different grammatical classes they normally cause less confusion. But sometimes ambiguity is caused by the fact that the same sound sequence can represent different grammatical classes in a sentence. In *I like her drawing,* there is ambiguity because *drawing* as a *verb* conveys the meaning "I like the fact that she draws" or "I like her while she draws" or "I like the way she draws," whereas *drawing* as a *noun* conveys the meaning analogous to "I like her drawing (which hangs in the hall)."

The fact that two words with different meanings may sound the same makes such words good candidates for humor, as well as for confusion.

> "How is bread made?"
> "I know *that!*" Alice cried eagerly. "You take some flour—"
> "Where do you pick the flower?" the White Queen asked. "In a garden, or in the hedges?"
> "Well, it isn't *picked* at all," Alice explained: "it's *ground*—"
> "How many acres of ground?" said the White Queen.

The humor of this passage is based on two sets of homonyms: *flower* and *flour* and the two meanings of *ground.* Alice means *ground* as the past tense of *grind,* while the White Queen is interpreting *ground* to mean "earth."

There are many other examples of sentences which are ambiguous because of the particular semantic properties which belong to some of the words of the sentence. For example,

> 1. The girl found a book on Main Street.

is ambiguous, whereas

> 2. The girl found a glove on Main Street.
>   *or*
> 3. The girl found a book on language.
>   *or*
> 4. The girl found a book in New York.

are not ambiguous. Sentence 1 can mean either:

> a. "The girl found a book which was lying on Main Street."
>   *or*
> b. "The girl found a book while she was on Main Street."
>   *or*
> c. "The girl found a book whose subject matter concerned Main Street."

The ambiguity is caused by the particular semantic properties of the words *book, on,* and *street.* The meaning of *book* includes something like "contains written information about." *On* is a homonym meaning "on the surface of" or "about" (that is, "on the subject of"). *Street* has "surface on which things may be located" among its semantic properties.

In sentence 2, *glove* does not include the meaning "contains written information about" and therefore *on* can be assigned only the meaning "on the surface of." In sentence 3, *language* does not possess any semantic property that would allow it to be used in a phrase of location, and consequently *on* can be interpreted only as meaning "about." In sentence 4, *in* is not ambiguous in the way *on* is (it lacks the semantic property "about"), so the entire phrase is unambiguous and has to do with where the book was found.

The semantic properties of these various words determine the ambiguity or lack of ambiguity of these sentences. They also reveal why in the sentence *He lectured on semantics, on* must be interpreted to mean "about" or "concerning," since *semantics* cannot be interpreted as a place; but in the sentence *He lectured on Main Street, Main Street* can be interpreted as the topic of his lecture (with *on* meaning "about") or as the place where he lectured.

The semantic properties also explain why *The girl found a glove on Main Street* is a good sentence, but **The girl found a glove on semantics* is not.

Thus we see that *on* can have two meanings in certain phrases, but only one meaning in other phrases. The semantic properties of the noun which follows it, as well as the semantic properties of the other words in the sentence, are the determining factors.

Such examples of homonyms and ambiguous sentences show that there is no one-to-one relation between sounds and meanings, and that one cannot always determine the precise meaning from the sounds alone. This is further evidence that the sound-meaning relationship in language is arbitrary, and that one must learn how to relate sounds and meanings when learning the language.

Knowing a language, however, allows one to assign possible meanings out of context. It is the fact that you know all the different meanings of the same sequence of sounds which creates ambiguities. The existence of homonyms does not mean that words have no meaning as separate entities. Quite the contrary, such words reveal our semantic knowledge.

A delightful form of humor is punning, despite the humorless view that "puns are the lowest form of humor." In a pun, one uses a homonym or near-homonym for humorous purposes. Again, Lewis Carroll's *Alice's Adventures in Wonderland* illustrates this. In reading the passage it is important to know that in British English (the English dialect spoken by Lewis Carroll) an *r* which follows a vowel is not pronounced when a consonant follows the *r*. Thus *tortoise,* pronounced [tɔrtəs] in American English, is pronounced [tɔtəs] (just like *taught us*) in British English.

> "When we were little, . . . we went to school in the sea. The master was an old Turtle — we used to call him Tortoise — "
> "Why did you call him Tortoise, if he wasn't one?" Alice asked.
> "We called him Tortoise because he taught us," said the Mock Turtle angrily.

Describing his education, the Mock Turtle explained:

> "I only took the regular course."
> "What was that?" enquired Alice.
> "Reeling and Writhing, of course, to begin with," the Mock Turtle replied; "and then the different branches of Arithmetic — Ambition, Distraction, Uglification, and Derision."

The passage illustrates how a good humorist not only substitutes similar-sounding words with different meanings, but selects words with specific semantic properties to create the humorous situation. *Reeling* for *reading* and *writhing* for *writing* — these are choices that are inspired! If Carroll had been interested merely in substituting words with similar but nonidentical sounds, he could have selected *reaping* or *reeking* for *reading* and *riding* or *rising* for *writing*. Instead, he chose words that are semantically related to creatures or activities associated with the sea. *Reeling* includes semantic properties associated with fishing, and of course fish and eels *writhe*.

The same use of like semantic properties and sound-associations is seen in the following:

> "No wise fish would go anywhere without a porpoise" [the Mock Turtle said].
> "Wouldn't it, really?" said Alice, in a tone of great surprise.
> "Of course not," said the Mock Turtle. "Why, if a fish came to *me*, and told me he was going on a journey, I should say 'With what porpoise?' "

The substitution of *porpoise* for *purpose* is particularly humorous again because of the "fishy" context.

Lewis Carroll, of course, had a great talent for *using* language. Thus he was able to take advantage of specific properties of language to create his humor. In the above examples he used the relationship between the sounds and meanings of words. Since we are not all as talented as Carroll, many of us cannot use language in this way. But our knowledge of language does permit us to enjoy the humor. Again we see the difference between language knowledge and language use, between linguistic competence and linguistic performance. We have the competence to interpret the passages as humorous because we know the meanings of the words and the sentences. Our knowledge of the meaning of words includes knowing their specific semantic properties. Our competence enables us to see the humor in the substitution of *reeling* and *writhing* for *reading* and *writing*. Carroll's competence was the same as that of other speakers of his dialect, but his performance was a reflection of his genius.

We also noted that perfect homonyms in one dialect can lead to a humorous situation that may be lost on speakers of another dialect, because for them the homonym doesn't exist. Homonyms, then, further attest to our knowledge of the semantics of our language.

SYNONYMS: DIFFERENT SOUNDS, SIMILAR MEANINGS

Does he wear a turban, a fez or a hat?
Does he sleep on a mattress, a bed or a mat, or a Cot,
The Akond of Swat?
Can he write a letter concisely clear,
Without a speck or a smudge or smear or Blot,
The Akond of Swat?

                              —EDWARD LEAR, "The Akond of Swat"

O precious codex, volume, tome,
  Book, writing, compilation, work
Attend the while I pen a pome,
  A jest, a jape, a quip, a quirk.

For I would pen, engross, indite,
  Transcribe, set forth, compose, address,
Record, submit—yea, even write
  An ode, an elegy to bless—

To bless, set store by, celebrate,
  Approve, esteem, endow with soul,
Commend, acclaim, appreciate,
  Immortalize, laud, praise, extol

Thy merit, goodness, value, worth,
  Expedience, utility—
O manna, honey, salt of earth,
  I sing, I chant, I worship thee!

How could I manage, live, exist,
  Obtain, produce, be real, prevail,
Be present in the flesh, subsist,
  Have place, become, breathe or inhale,

Without thy help, recruit, support,
  Opitulation, furtherance,
Assistance, rescue, aid, resort,
  Favor, sustention and advance?

Alas! alack! and well-a day!
  My case would then be dour and sad,
Likewise distressing, dismal, gray,
  Pathetic, mournful, dreary, bad.

Though I could keep this up all day,
  This lyric, elegiac, song.
Meseems hath come the time to say
  Farewell! adieu! good-by! so long!

— FRANKLIN P. ADAMS, "To a Thesaurus"[5]

Not only do languages contain different words which sound the same, they also contain words which sound different but have the same meanings. Such words are called **synonyms**. There are dictionaries of synonyms that contain many hundreds of such words. You find, for example: *apathetic/phlegmatic/passive/sluggish/indifferent; pedigree/ancestry/genealogy/descent/lineage.*

On the other hand it has been said that there are no perfect synonyms — that is, that no two words ever have *exactly* the same meaning. Still there seems to be very little if any difference between the sentences: *I'll be happy to come* and *I'll be glad to come*, or *He's sitting on the sofa* and *He's sitting on the couch.* One individual may always use *sofa* instead of *couch*, but if he knows the two words he will understand the sentences with either word and interpret them to mean the same thing. The degree of semantic similarity between words depends to a great extent on the number of semantic properties they share. *Sofa* and *couch* refer to the same type of object and share most if not all their semantic properties.

There are words which have many semantic features in common but which are not synonyms or near synonyms. *Man* and *boy* both refer to male humans; the meaning of *boy* includes the additional semantic property of "youth" whereby it differs from the meaning of *man*. Thus the semantic system of English permits you to say *A sofa is a couch* or *A couch is a sofa* but not *A man is a boy* or *A boy is a man* except when you wish to describe the "boylike" qualities of the man or the "manlike" qualities of the boy.

Synonyms also serve as a vehicle for humor. One story concerns the "educated" son who returns home after four years at college. His mother asks him the meaning of the word *narrative*. "It means a tale," replies the son. She also asks him the meaning of *extinguish*. "To put out," answers the son. That night, at the son's homecoming party, during a lull in the conversation the mother is heard asking her son to "grab that pesky dog by the narrative and extinguish him." The humor of this story depends on the use of the homonyms *tale/tail* and the synonyms *extinguish/put out* and also on the fact that *put out* is homonymous in that it can mean "place outside" as well as "extinguish."

If we did not know the meanings of words such stories (or any stories) would be impossible. The ability to interpret the same sounds as different in meaning or different sounds as the same in meaning shows that language is a system which relates sounds and meanings.

ANTONYMS: DIFFERENT SOUNDS, OPPOSITE MEANINGS

As a rule, man is a fool;
When it's hot, he wants it cool;
When it's cool, he wants it hot;
Always wanting what is not.

— Anonymous

It's co-existence
Or no existence.

— BERTRAND RUSSELL

The meaning of a word may be defined by saying what it is *not*. *Male* means *not female*. *Big* means *not small*. Words which are opposite in meaning are often called **antonyms**. Ironically, the basic property of two words which are antonyms is that they share all but one semantic property. The property they do not share is present in one word and absent in the other. Thus in order to be opposites, two words must be semantically very similar.

You know that *tall* is the opposite of *short* because you know that included in the semantic specification of both adjectives is the property "measures size or height on a vertical plane, indicating distance from the earth." *Short,* in addition, possesses the property "less height than average for the thing being described." Notice that the meaning of these adjectives, and other similar ones, is relational. The words themselves provide no information about absolute size. Because of our knowledge of the language, and of things in the world, this normally causes no confusion. But it does, like every aspect of language, provide a vehicle for humor. Here we are quoting a passage from *The Phantom Tollbooth* by Norman Juster (New York: Random House, 1961):

Milo and Tock walked up to the door, whose brass name plate read simply "THE GIANT," and knocked.

"Good afternoon," said the perfectly ordinary-sized man who answered the door.

"Are you the giant?" asked Tock doubtfully.

"To be sure," he replied proudly. "I'm the smallest giant in the world. . . ."

They walked to the rear of the house, which looked exactly like the front, and knocked at the door, whose name plate read "THE MIDGET."

"How are you?" inquired the man, who looked exactly like the giant.

"Are you the midget?" asked Tock again, with a hint of uncertainty in his voice.

"Unquestionably," he answered. "I'm the tallest midget in the world. . . ."

The side of the house looked very like the front and back, and the door flew open the very instant they knocked.

"How nice of you to come by," exclaimed the man, who could have been the midget's twin brother.

"You must be the fat man," said Tock, learning not to count too much on appearance.

"The thinnest one in the world," he replied brightly. . . .

Just as they suspected, the other side of the house looked the same as the front, the back, and the side, and the door was again answered by a man who looked precisely like the other three. . . .

"Are you the fattest thin man in the world?" asked Tock.

"Do you know one that's fatter?" he asked impatiently.

If meanings of words were indissoluble wholes, there would be no way to make the interpretations that we do.   We know that *big* and *red* are not opposites because they do not share all but one semantic property. They are both adjectives, but *big* possesses a semantic property involving size, whereas *red* possesses a semantic property involving color.

In English there are a number of ways to form antonyms.   You can, for example, add the prefix *un-* before a word and form its opposite, as in *likely/unlikely, able/unable.*   Or you can add *non-,* as in *entity/nonentity, conformist/nonconformist.*   Or you can add *in-,* as illustrated by *tolerant/ intolerant, discrete/indiscrete, decent/indecent.*

Because we know the semantic properties of words, which define their meanings, we know when two words are antonyms, synonyms, or homonyms or are totally unrelated as regards meaning.

COMPOUNDS AND IDIOMS

> *. . . the Houyhnhnms have no Word in their Language to express any thing that is* evil, *except what they borrow from the Deformities or ill Qualities of the Yahoos.   Thus they denote the Folly of a Servant, an Omission of a Child, a Stone that cuts their Feet, a Continuance of foul or un- seasonable Weather, and the like, by adding to each the Epithet of Yahoo.   For instance, Hhnm Yahoo, Whnaholm Yahoo, Ynlhmnawihlma Yahoo, and an ill contrived House, Ynholmhnmrohlnw Yahoo.*
>
> —JONATHAN SWIFT, *Gulliver's Travels*

> *She played upon her music-box a fancy air by chance,*
> *And straightway all her polka-dots began a lively dance.*

> *"A milkweed and a buttercup, and cowslip," said sweet*
>   *Mary,*
> *"Are growing in my garden-plot, and this I call my dairy."*
>
> —PETER NEWELL, *Pictures and Rhymes*

One of the reasons any idea in any language can be expressed is because languages have built-in mechanisms for expansion.   We have seen how one can add "derivational morphemes" to other morphemes and create new words.   We can also string together "free" morphemes, or "simple words" in a language, and create compound words.

There is almost no limit on the kinds of combinations which occur in English, as can be seen by the following examples: *dancefloor, payday, playboy, sweatshop, pickpocket, rainbow, housekeeper, easygoing, runabout, breastbone, deathbed, bedside, apronstring, clergyman, postman, lighthouse, airplane, father figure, Irishman, greenhouse, poorhouse, madhouse, goldfish, silverfish, bluejay, blackbird, Redcoat, blacklist, cold shoulder.*

One of the interesting things about a compound is that you can't always tell by the words it contains what the compound means. The meaning of a compound is *not* always the sum of the meanings of its parts.

Everyone who wears a red coat is not a Redcoat. There is quite a difference between the sentences *She has a red coat in her closet* and *She has a Redcoat in her closet.* It is true that the two sentences sound different. The words *red coat* are stressed on *coat*, whereas *Redcoat* is stressed on *Red*. But in *bedchamber, bedclothes, bedside* and *bedtime*, *bed* is stressed in all of the compounds; yet a *bedchamber* is a room where there is a bed, *bedclothes* are linens and blankets for a bed, *bedside* does not refer to the physical side of a bed but the place next to it, and *bedtime* is the time one goes to bed.

Other similarly constructed compounds show that underlying the juxtaposition of words, different grammatical relations are expressed. A *houseboat* is a boat which is a house, but a *housecat* is not a cat which is a house. A *boathouse* is a house for boats, but a *cathouse* is not a house for cats, though by coincidence some cats live in cathouses. A *jumping bean* is a bean that jumps, a *falling star* is a "star" that falls, and a *magnifying glass* is a glass that magnifies. But a *looking glass* isn't a glass that looks, nor is an *eating apple* an apple that eats, nor does *laughing gas* laugh.

Many languages have the same kinds of compounding mechanisms. In Twi, if one combines the word meaning "son" or "child," *ɔba*, with the word meaning "chief," *ɔhene*, one derives the compound *ɔheneba*, meaning "prince." Or if you add the word for "house," *ofi*, to *ɔhene*, you have a word meaning "palace," *ahemfi*.

In Thai the word for "cat" is *mææw*, the word for "watch" in the sense of "to watch over" is *fâaw*, and the word for house is *bâan*. The word for "watch cat" (like a watch dog) is the compound *mææwfâabâan*—literally "catwatchhouse."

All the above examples from English, Twi, and Thai are compounds which at least include some of the meanings of the individual words. But there are other compounds which don't seem to relate to the meanings of the individual parts at all. A *jack-in-a-box* is a tropical tree, and a *turncoat* is a traitor. A *highbrow* doesn't necessarily have a high brow, nor does a *bigwig* have a big wig, nor does an *egghead* have an egg-shaped head.

The meaning of many compounds must therefore be learned, as if they were individual simple words. Some of the meanings may be figured out, but not all. Thus if one had never heard the word *hunchback*, it might be possible to infer the meaning. But if you had never heard the word *flatfoot* it is doubtful you would know it was a word meaning "detective" or "policeman" even though the origin of the word, once you know the meaning, can be figured out.

Knowing a language obviously means knowing the morphemes, simple words, compound words, and their meanings. But in addition, there are fixed phrases, consisting of more than one word, which have meanings which cannot be inferred by knowing the meanings of the individual words. Such phrases are called **idioms.** English has many such idiomatic phrases: *sell down the river, haul over the coals, eat one's hat, let one's hair down, put one's foot in one's mouth, throw one's weight around, snap out of it, cut it out, hit it off, take for a ride, wind around one's little finger, bite one's tongue, eat one's words, make a clean breast of, give a piece of one's mind.*

There are a number of interesting things about idioms. They appear to be similar in structure to regular phrases. Thus *She put her foot in her mouth* has the same structure as *She put her bracelet in her drawer.* One can say: *The drawer in which she put her bracelet was hers* or *Her bracelet was put in her drawer.* One would hardly say **The mouth in which she put her foot was hers* or **Her foot was put in her mouth* to mean the same thing as *She put her foot in her mouth.*

Joe hit the sack meaning "Joe went to sleep" has the same structure as *Joe hit the bed,* but whereas *The bed was hit by Joe* is a good sentence and means the same thing as *Joe hit the bed, The sack was hit by Joe* cannot mean that *"Joe went to bed."* You can say *I'll eat my cake* or *I'll eat your cake,* and you can say *I'll eat my words,* but you can't say **I'll eat your words.*

We see that idioms, grammatically as well as semantically, have very special characteristics. They must be entered into one's mental dictionary as single "items," with their meanings specified, and one must learn the special syntactic restrictions on their use in sentences.

As we examine how the semantics of language expresses our thoughts we see how very complex language is. Yet we use it every day and are seldom aware of all the complexities.

SENSE AND REFERENCE

You mentioned your name as if I should recognize it, but beyond the obvious facts that you are a bachelor, a solicitor, a Freemason, and an asthmatic, I know nothing whatever about you.

—SIR ARTHUR CONAN DOYLE, "The Norwood Builder,"
The Memoirs of Sherlock Holmes

We have said that neither the linguistic meaning of a word nor its "name" need include information about any particular object or objects. The German philosopher and mathematician Gottlob Frege contributed to our understanding of linguistic meaning when he proposed a distinction between the *sense* of a word and its *reference*, that is, the thing which the word designates. Frege had read what the ancient Greek astronomers had to say about the evening star and the morning star. The Greeks did not know, as Frege did, that the reference of *evening star* and the reference of *morning star* were one and the same, namely the planet Venus. If the reference of a word comprised its total meaning, then the meanings of *evening star* and *morning star* are identical, and equal to that of *Venus*. But Frege noted that the sentence *Venus is Venus* does not have the same meaning as *The evening star is the morning star.* The former sentence is trivial and uninteresting. The latter may teach us something. The form of both sentences being identical, Frege concluded that the meaning of words involves more than just reference. He called that "something extra" *sense.* Hayakawa in his discussion of "typewriter" was referring to its reference rather than its sense. What Frege called *sense* is what we have been calling *meaning.*

It is possible then to say that a word or a sentence has a meaning but no reference. If this were not so we would be unable to understand sentences like the following:

> The present king of France is bald.
> The unicorn is in the garden.

Speakers of English have no trouble comprehending the meaning of these sentences, even though France now has no king, and unicorns do not exist.

THE "TRUTH" OF SENTENCES

> ... *having Occasion to talk of* Lying, *and* false Representation, *it was with much Difficulty that he comprehended what I meant. ... For he argued thus: That the Use of Speech was to make us understand one another and to receive Information of Facts; now if any one said the* Thing which was not, *these Ends were defeated; because I cannot properly be said to understand him. ... And these were all the Notions he had concerning that Faculty of* Lying, *so perfectly well understood, and so universally practiced among human Creatures.*
>
> —JONATHAN SWIFT. *Gulliver's Travels*

One can assign a meaning to a sentence like

> a. The Declaration of Independence was signed in 1776.

whether it was shouted from the top of a mountain, read from a slip of paper, picked up in a muddy gutter, whispered during a movie, or spoken with a mouth full of bubblegum.   One can also understand the meaning of the sentence

> b. The Declaration of Independence was signed in 1700.

even though it is a false statement.   Your ability to recognize the "falsity" of the statement depends upon your understanding its meaning and also on your knowledge of history.

Part of the meaning of a sentence, then, is knowledge of the conditions under which it can be said to be true.   Philosophers talk about the "truth value" of a sentence.   In this sense, sentence a is true and sentence b is false.   Sentence b is false because the particular event to which it refers occurred at a time other than that stated.

Consider sentence c:

> c. Rufus believes that the Declaration of Independence was signed in 1700.

This sentence is true if some individual named Rufus does indeed believe the statement, and it is false if he does not.   Your understanding of the sentence permits you to state under what conditions it is true or false.   One can understand the sentence, or any sentence — one can assign a meaning to it — even if one is unable to decide on its "truth value." Its meaning, however, partially depends on knowing what conditions would make it a true statement or a false one.

Knowledge of the external world may help you decide if the sentence is true or false, but in addition you must be able to use your linguistic knowledge to understand its meaning.   You may never have heard of the Declaration of Independence and may therefore not know whether such a declaration was signed in 1776, 1700, or 1492.   But your knowledge of the language permits you to say that sentence a means that some document called *The Declaration of Independence* was signed by someone or other in the year 1776.   Notice that your linguistic knowledge, not your knowledge about the particular event referred to, also permits you to say that sentence a means the same thing as sentence d:

> d. It was in the year 1776 that the Declaration of Independence was signed

and means the same thing as sentence e:

> e. Some person or persons signed the Declaration of Independence in 1776.

The sentence doesn't tell you who signed the document. That fact is not included in the linguistic meaning of the sentence.

Sentences a, d, and e illustrate something else about language. Not only may different words have the same meaning, but different sentences may also mean the same thing. Thus

> f. John is easy to please

means the same thing as

> g. It is easy to please John.

Clearly if two sentences mean the same thing they will have the same truth value; under identical conditions sentences f and g will both be true or false, but one cannot be true while the other is false. Similarly,

> h. Hector is my maternal uncle
> i. Hector is my mother's brother

are synonymous. We say that sentence i is a **paraphrase** of sentence h. Paraphrase and synonymity are similar concepts relating to sentences and words. We know that sentence i is a paraphrase of sentence h because we know the meanings of both sentences.

Some sentences are paraphrases of others because the meanings of the words chosen are similar. Other sentences are paraphrases only because the syntactic organization of the sentences differs, as in the following:

> j. It is easy to play sonatas on this violin.
>   Sonatas are easy to play on this violin.
>   This violin is easy to play sonatas on.
> k. Seymour used a knife to slice the salami.
>   It was a knife that Seymour used to slice the salami.
>   It was the salami that Seymour sliced with a knife.

These sentences may not be exactly synonymous; there are shades of differences. But they are clearly related and all the sentences of group j (and all those of group k) have the same truth value.

Sentences, like words, may also be related as antonyms. The negation of sentences illustrates this:

> l. Hector is my uncle.
> m. Hector is not my uncle.

Because you know the language you know that if sentence l is true, then sentence m must be false.

Your ability to assign meanings to sentences also permits you to make other judgments. For example, if someone were to say to you *"Would you like another beer?"* the meaning of that sentence implies that you have already had at least one beer. Part of the meaning of the word *an-*

other includes this *implication*. The Hatter in *Alice's Adventures in Wonderland* would not agree with us.

> "Take some more tea," the March Hare said to Alice, very earnestly.
> "I've had nothing yet," Alice replied in an offended tone, "so I can't take more."
> "You mean you can't take *less*," said the Hatter: "it's very easy to take *more* than nothing."

The humor in this passage comes from the fact that knowing the language includes knowing the meaning of the word *more*. *More* does not mean "more than nothing" but "more than something."

Knowing a language is knowing the implications inherent in the meaning of certain words and certain sentences.

MEANING, SENSE, NO SENSE, NONSENSE

> *Don't tell me of a man's being able to talk sense; everyone can talk sense. Can he talk nonsense?*
>
> —WILLIAM PITT

If in a conversation someone said to you *"My brother is an only child,"* you might think either that he was making a joke or that he didn't know the meaning of the words he was using. You would know that the sentence was strange, or **anomalous**. Yet, it is certainly an English sentence. It conforms to all the grammatical rules of the language. It is strange because it represents a contradiction; the meaning of *brother* includes the fact that the individual referred to is a male human who has at least one sibling. The sentence *That bachelor is pregnant* is anomalous for similar reasons; the word *bachelor* includes the fact that the individual is "male" and males cannot become pregnant, at least not on our planet. Such sentences violate semantic rules. If you did not know the semantic meanings of words you could not make judgments of this kind about sentences.

The semantic properties of words determine what other words they can be combined with. One sentence which has been used by linguists for the last fifteen years to illustrate this is *Colorless green ideas sleep furiously*.[6] The sentence seems to obey all the grammatical rules of English. The subject is *colorless green ideas* and the predicate is *sleep furiously*. It has the same syntactic structure as the sentence *Dark*

---

[6] Noam Chomsky, *Syntactic Structures* (The Hague: Mouton, 1957).

green leaves rustle furiously. But there is obviously something wrong *semantically* with the sentence. The meaning of *colorless* includes the semantic property "without color," but it is combined with the adjective *green,* which has the property "green in color." How can something be both "without color" and "green in color" simultaneously? Other such semantic violations also occur in the sentence.

Your knowledge of the semantic properties of words accounts for the strangeness of this sentence and sentences such as *John frightened a tree* and *Honesty plays golf.* Part of the meaning of the word *frighten* is that it can occur only with animate nouns as objects. Since you know the meaning of *tree,* and know that it is not "animate," the sentence is anomalous. Similarly, *Honesty plays golf* is anomalous because *honesty* is neither "animate" nor "human" and therefore cannot be the subject of a predicate like *play golf.*

The linguist Samuel Levin has shown that in poetry we find just such semantic violations forming strange but interesting aesthetic images. He cites Dylan Thomas's phrase *a grief ago* as an example. *Ago* is a word ordinarily used with words specified by some temporal semantic feature: *a week ago, an hour ago, a month ago, a century ago,* but not **a table ago, *a dream ago,* or **a mother ago.* When Thomas used the word *grief* with *ago* he was adding a durational-time feature to the word for poetic effect.

In the poetry of E. E. Cummings one finds phrases like *the six subjunctive crumbs twitch, a man . . . wearing a round jeer for a hat,* and *children building this rainman out of snow.* Though all of these phrases violate or break some semantic rules, one can understand them. In any case, it is the breaking of the rules that actually creates the imagery desired. The fact that you can understand these phrases while at the same time recognizing their anomalous or deviant nature shows your knowledge of the semantic system and semantic properties of the language.

Sentences which are anomalous in this way are often known as "nonsense":

> As I was going up the stair
> I met a man who wasn't there.
> He wasn't there again today —
> I wish to God he'd go away.

Nonsense sentences of verses are not strings of random words put together. The words are combined according to regular rules of the grammar. Random strings have no meaning and are also not funny. The ability to recognize "nonsense" depends on knowledge of the semantic system of the language and the meanings of words.

There are other sentences which sound like English sentences but make no sense at all because they include words which have no meaning; they are "uninterpretable." One can only interpret them if one dreams up some meaning for each "no-sense" word. Lewis Carroll's "Jabberwocky" is probably the most famous poem in which most of the content words have no meaning—they do not exist in the lexicon of the grammar. Yet all the sentences "sound" as if they should be or could be English sentences.

> 'Twas brillig, and the slithy toves
>   Did gyre and gimble in the wabe;
> All mimsy were the borogoves,
>   And the mome raths outgrabe.
>
>   .   .   .
>
> He took his vorpal sword in hand:
>   Long time the manxome foe he sought—
> So rested he by the Tumtum tree,
>   And stood awhile in thought.
>
> And as in uffish thought he stood,
>   The Jabberwock, with eyes of flame,
> Came whiffling through the tulgey wood,
>   And burbled as it came!
>
> One, two! One, two! And through and through
>   The vorpal blade went snicker-snack!
> He left it dead, and with its head
>   He went galumphing back.

You probably do not know what *vorpal* means! Nevertheless, you know that *He took his vorpal sword in hand* means the same thing as *He took his sword, which was vorpal, in hand* and *It was in his hand that he took his vorpal sword.* Knowing the language, and assuming that *vorpal* means the same thing in the three sentences (since the same sounds are used), you can decide that the "truth value" of the three sentences is identical. In other words, you are able to decide that two things mean the same thing even though you don't know for sure what either one means. You do this by assuming that the semantic properties of *vorpal* are the same whenever it is used.

We now see why Alice commented, when she had read "Jabberwocky":

> "It seems very pretty, but it's *rather* hard to understand!" (You see she didn't like to confess, even to herself, that she couldn't make it out at all.) "Somehow it seems to fill my head with ideas—only I don't exactly know what they are! However, *somebody* killed *something:* that's clear, at any rate—"

The semantic properties of words show up in other ways in sentence construction. For example, if the meaning of a word includes the semantic property "human" in English we can replace it by one sort of pronoun but not another. We have already seen that a "nonhuman" noun cannot be the subject of a predicate like *play golf.* Similarly, this semantic feature determines that we call a boy *he,* and a table *it.*

According to Mark Twain, our maternal ancestor Eve also had such knowledge in her grammar, for she writes in her diary:

> If this reptile is a man, it ain't an *it,* is it? That wouldn't be grammatical, would it? I think it would be *he.* In that case one would parse it thus: nominative *he;* dative, *him;* possessive, *his'n.*

These kinds of restrictions based on semantic properties are found in all languages. In one dialect of the Ghanaian language Twi, different numerals are used with human nouns than with nonhuman nouns. The word *baanu* meaning "two" is used exclusively with human nouns, and the word *mmienu* meaning "two" is used exclusively with nonhuman nouns. Similarly, the words for "three" are *baasa* with humans and *nsia* with nonhuman objects. Starred phrases are deviant:

HUMAN NOUNS	NONHUMAN NOUNS
nnipa baanu, "two people"	**ŋkokɔ baanu*
*nnipa mmienu	*ŋkokɔ mmienu,* "two chickens"
asɔfoɔ baasa, "three priests"	**nsem baasa*
*asɔfoɔ nsia	*nsem nsia,* "three cases"

Examples like these from English and Twi show the importance of semantic properties in the formation of sentences. It is not that one cannot understand a sentence like **I stumbled into the table, who fell over.* A Twi speaker would know what is meant by **nnipa mmienu,* "two people" with the wrong form of "two." It is just that these sentences are deviant. They violate rules based on the semantic properties of words.

The discussion in this chapter has attempted to show how much a speaker of a language knows about the meanings of words and sentences — that is, the semantic system of his language.

THE MEANING OF "MEANING"

> *"The name of the song is called 'Haddocks' Eyes.' "*
> *"Oh, that's the name of the song, is it?" Alice said. . . .*
> *"No, you don't understand," the Knight said. . . .*
> *"That's what the name is* called. *The name really is 'The Aged Aged Man.' "*
>
> —LEWIS CARROLL, *Through the Looking-Glass*

To define the meaning of a morpheme or a word we find ourselves using other words in the definition. If the meaning of the prefix *in* is "not," what does *not* mean? If the meaning of *man* is defined by such semantic properties as "male," "human," and so on, what is the meaning of *human* and *male?* It is clear that at some point we have to stop and assume that everyone "knows" the definitions of the describing terms. Those words which are left undefined are the basic **primitive semantic elements.** Anyone who has studied geometry is acquainted with this procedure. One reads a definition: "A line is the shortest distance between two points." What is a point? One assumes the knowledge of a point. "Point" is a primitive concept in geometry, just as "male," "human," "abstract," "morpheme," "phoneme," and so on are primitive terms in linguistics.

Though we are not ordinarily aware of it, language has infected us with a kind of cerebral schizophrenia. We constantly (and effortlessly) deal with the world on two levels: the level of actual objects, thoughts, and perceptions and the level of *names of* objects, thoughts, and perceptions. That is, we perceive reality on the one hand and talk about it on the other. Linguists have a tendency to become three-way schizophrenics. They not only have objects and language, but in addition they must treat language itself as an object. An anthropologist might describe a man by saying he is a bipedal, hairless primate. He is using language to talk about certain objects. A linguist wishes to describe the language used to talk about these objects. Thus, he might say that *man,* the word, is a "noun," has three "phonemes," or possesses the semantic features "male" and "human."

A language used for description is called a **metalanguage.** Ordinary English is the metalanguage used by anthropologists or botanists or physicists to describe the objects of interest to them. Linguists also have to use ordinary language as a metalanguage to describe language.

We offer an elementary illustration of these concepts which may clarify the problem (but may confuse you even further):

OBJECT (Real World)	LANGUAGE (Object for Linguists)	METALANGUAGE
	man is a bipedal hairless primate	*man* is a *noun* *man* is composed of three *phonemes* The meaning of *man* includes the semantic properties *male* and *human*

The terms *noun, phonemes, male,* and *human* are terms in the metalanguage, in the theory of language. This book is filled with such terms: *phone, allophone, phoneme, syntax, grammar, morpheme, word, sentence* . . . Thus, while the word *man* is part of our language, when we say "*man* is a word" we are using language to discuss language, and *word* is part of the metalanguage.

One can see why language has intrigued philosophers from the beginning of history. The complexities discussed only punctuate the miracle that all normal human beings learn a language, use the language to express their thoughts, and understand the meanings of sentences used by others.

SUMMARY

Knowing a language is knowing how to produce and understand sentences with certain meanings. The study of linguistic meaning is called **semantics.**

The most elemental units of meaning in a language are **morphemes,** which are combined to form words. Words then may consist of more than one morpheme. Traditionally, the combination of morphemes in the construction of words has been called **morphology.** Part of one's linguistic competence is knowledge of the morphemes, their pronunciations, their meanings, and how they may be combined.

The meanings of morphemes and words are defined by their semantic properties or features. When two words have the same sounds but differ semantically (have different meanings) they are **homonyms** or **homophones** (for example, *bear* can mean either "give birth to" or "tolerate"); two words with different sounds but which share all semantic properties are **synonyms** (for example, *couch* and *sofa*); two words which are "opposite" in meaning are **antonyms** (*open* and *close*).

Two "free" morphemes or "simple" words may combine to form **compounds.** The meaning of some compounds depends on the meanings of the individual parts (*blackbird*), but this is not so in all cases (*egghead* means "intellectual," not someone with an egg-shaped head). Words may also be combined to form phrases with meanings assigned to the whole unit; such phrases are idioms and their meanings are not the sum of their parts (for example, *put one's foot in one's mouth*).

A word or sentence may have a meaning but no **reference.** That is, we can understand the meaning of a word like *unicorn* even though unicorns do not exist.

When you know the meaning of a sentence you are able to tell under what conditions the sentence is true or false. You can understand the sentence even if it is a false statement; in fact, if you didn't understand it you could not make this judgment.

Sentences, like words, may be synonymous—that is, mean the same thing. Such sentences are related to each other as **paraphrases.** Sentences may also be homophonous — have two different meanings (be **ambiguous**) but sound the same. Sentences can also be **antonymous,** or have "opposite" meanings.

Some sentences are strange or **anomalous** in that they deviate from what we expect. *The red-haired girl has blond hair* and *The stone ran* are anomalous. Other sentences are "uninterpretable" because they contain "words" which are "nonexistent" (for example, *An orkish sluck blecked nokishly*).

Linguists have to use language to describe language. The language used for description is called a **metalanguage.** Using language to describe objects in the world, we may talk about a man, child, ostrich, and so on. But when we say *man* is a "word" or a "noun," these descriptive terms are part of the metalanguage of linguistics.

Everything one knows about linguistic meaning is included in the semantic system of one's grammar.

EXERCISES

1. Divide these words into their separate morphemes by placing a + between each morpheme.

1. moralizers	7. diachronic	13. strawberry
2. retroactive	8. synchronic	14. irreplaceable
3. inclination	9. totalitarianism	15. replacement
4. befriended	10. experiential	16. stature
5. televise	11. predetermination	17. respectability
6. endearment	12. psycholinguistics	18. introductory

2. Divide these sentences into their separate morphemes by placing a + between each morpheme.

1. The American tourists visited thirteen cities.
2. Our English literature teacher writes his grandmother daily.
3. Linguistics is the scientific study of human language.

3. Think of five morpheme suffixes. Give their meaning, what types of stems they may be suffixed to, and at least two examples of each. Example:

-er	meaning:	"doer of"; makes an agentive noun
	stem type:	added to verbs
	examples:	*rider,* "one who rides"
		teacher, "one who teaches"

4. Think of five morpheme prefixes. Give their meaning, what types of stems they may be prefixed to, and at least two examples of each.

Example:

a-	meaning:	"lacking the quality"
	stem type:	added to adjectives
	examples:	*amoral*, "lacking morals"
		asymmetric, "lacking symmetry"

5. Give five English idioms and their meanings. Example: *kick the bucket*, "to die."

6. For the following pairs of sentences, state why sentence a in each group is starred while sentence b is not. (Starred sentences are deviant or anomalous in some way.)

    1a. *He talked a blue pencil.
      b. He talked a blue streak.
    2a. *Bill held my breath.
      b. Bill held his breath.
    3a. *Bravery admires everyone.
      b. Everyone admires bravery.
    4a. *The giraffes arrested five demonstrators.
      b. The pigs arrested five demonstrators.

7. Below are some sentences in Swahili.

mtoto	amefika	"The child has arrived."
mtoto	anafika	"The child is arriving."
mtoto	atafika	"The child will arrive."
watoto	wamefika	"The children have arrived."
watoto	wanafika	"The children are arriving."
watoto	watafika	"The children will arrive."
mtu	amelala	"The man has slept."
mtu	analala	"The man is sleeping."
mtu	atalala	"The man will sleep."
watu	wamelala	"The men have slept."
watu	wanalala	"The men are sleeping."
watu	watalala	"The men will sleep."
kisu	kimepotea	"The knife was lost."
kisu	kinapotea	"The knife is lost."
kisu	kitapotea	"The knife will be lost."
visu	vimepotea	"The knives were lost."
visu	vinapotea	"The knives are lost."
visu	vitapotea	"The knives will be lost."
kikapu	kimepotea	"The basket was lost."
kikapu	kinapotea	"The basket is lost."
kikapu	kitapotea	"The basket will be lost."
vikapu	vimepotea	"The baskets were lost."
vikapu	vinapotea	"The baskets are lost."
vikapu	vitapotea	"The baskets will be lost."

One of the characteristic features of Swahili (and Bantu languages in general) is the existence of noun classes. There are specific singular and plural prefixes which occur with the nouns in each class. These prefixes are also used for purposes of agreement between the subject-noun and the verb. In the sentences given, two of these classes are included (there are many more in the language).

a. Identify all the morphemes you can detect (and give their meanings). For example:

-toto   "child"
m-   singular noun prefix attached to nouns of Class 1
a-   prefix attached to verbs when the subject is a singular noun of Class 1

Be sure to look for the other noun and verb markers including tense markers.

b. How is the "verb" constructed? That is, what kinds of morphemes are strung together and in what order?

c. How do you say the following in Swahili? (1) The child is lost. (2) The baskets have arrived. (3) The man will be lost.

8. The compounds in each of the following pairs are structurally equivalent. Some consist of a modifier plus a noun, others of a noun plus a noun, and so on. Why would a description of the superficial "structural" equivalence fail to reveal the differences in the meanings of the compounds? Example:

college president and *slave girl* are compounds both consisting of two nouns. A *college president* is a president of a college, but a *slave girl* is not a girl of a slave.

1. talking machine	eating apple
2. boiling point	washing machine
3. store-bought	company-built
4. rainbow	windmill
5. blackbird	blacksmith

9. a. The following sentence is semantically anomalous:

John is older than his sister's only brother.

Give two further examples of such sentences and explain the anomaly.

b. The following sentence is "uninterpretable":

The sklumping skrittery prog climped through the dectary.

Give two further examples of such uninterpretable sentences.

10. List as many semantic features or properties for each of the following words as you think are necessary to specify its meaning.

1. pediatrican	4. chick	7. telephone
2. giraffe	5. pot	8. wiggle
3. karate	6. sleep	9. swim

11. Give a synonym (perfect or "near") for the following words:

1. appeal	6. behavior	11. fact
2. applaud	7. graduation	12. probable
3. beg	8. lecture	13. lawyer
4. pal	9. teach	14. funny
5. generate	10. mate	15. scent

12. Provide a paraphrase for each of the following sentences (that is, a sentence which has the same meaning).

1. Columbus discovered America in 1492.
2. Gretchen adores Horace's brother.
3. The boy who lives next door to Mike is my aunt's son.
4. The President of the United States took a trip to China.
5. Phyllis snapped a picture of me.

13. For each group of words given below state what semantic feature or features are shared by the (a) words and the (b) words, and what semantic feature (or features) distinguish between the classes of (a) words and (b) words. Example:

a. widow, mother, sister, aunt, seamstress
b. widower, father, brother, uncle, tailor

The (a) and (b) words are "human"
The (a) words are "female" and the (b) words are "male"

1a. bachelor, man, son, paperboy, pope, chief
 b. bull, rooster, drake, ram
2a. table, stone, pencil, cup, house, ship, car
 b. milk, alcohol, rice, soup, mud
3a. book, temple, mountain, road, tractor
 b. idea, love, charity, sincerity, bravery, fear
4a. pine, elm, ash, weeping willow, sycamore
 b. rose, dandelion, aster, tulip, daisy
5a. book, letter, encyclopedia, novel, notebook, dictionary
 b. typewriter, pencil, ballpoint, crayon, quill, charcoal, chalk

14. Explain the semantic ambiguity of the following sentences by providing two sentences which paraphrase the two meanings. Example: *She can't bear children* can mean either *She can't give birth to children* or *She can't tolerate children.*

1. He waited at the bank.
2. Is he really that kind?

3. The proprietor of the fish store was the sole owner.
4. The long drill was boring.
5. When he got the clear title to the land it was a good deed.
6. It takes a good ruler to make a straight line.

References

AUSTIN, J. L. *How To Do Things with Words.* Cambridge: Harvard University Press, 1962.

CHAFE, WALLACE L. *Meaning and the Structure of Language.* Chicago: University of Chicago Press, 1970.

GLEASON, HENRY A. *Workbook in Descriptive Linguistics.* New York: Holt, Rinehart & Winston, 1955.

KATZ, JERROLD J. *The Philosophy of Language.* New York: Harper & Row, 1966.

MARCHAND, HANS. *The Categories and Types of Present-Day English Word Formation,* 2nd ed. Munich: C. H. Beck, 1969.

NIDA, EUGENE A. *Morphology: The Descriptive Analysis of Words,* 2nd ed. Ann Arbor: University of Michigan Press, 1949.

OGDEN, C. K., and RICHARDS, I. A. *The Meaning of Meaning,* 3rd ed. New York: Harcourt, Brace & World, 1930.

QUINE, W. V. O. *Word and Object.* New York: John Wiley, 1960.

SEARLE, J. R., ed. *The Philosophy of Language.* Oxford University Press, 1971.

WEINREICH, URIEL. "Explorations in Semantic Theory," in Thomas A. Sebeok, ed., *Current Trends in Linguistics,* Vol. III. Theoretical Foundations. The Hague: Mouton, 1966.

6
The Sentence
Patterns of Language:
Syntax

THE RULES OF SYNTAX

Everyone who is master of the language he speaks . . . may form new . . . phrases, provided they coincide with the genius of the language.

—MICHAELIS, *Dissertation* (1769)

In the previous chapters we have discussed how the grammar of a language represents the speaker's linguistic knowledge, including his knowledge of *phonetics* (the sounds of the language), *phonology* (the sound system of the language), and *semantics* (the meanings of words and sentences). Knowing a language also means being able to put words together to form sentences which express our thoughts.

The meaning of a sentence is a synthesis of the meanings of the morphemes of which it is composed. But the morphemes cannot occur haphazardly in the sentence. *The dentist hurt my teeth* does not have the same meaning as *My teeth hurt the dentist,* and the string of morphemes *my the hurt dentist teeth* has no meaning at all even though it is made up of meaningful elements. There are rules in one's grammar that determine what morphemes are combined into larger grammatical units to get intended meanings, and how these morphemes are to be combined. These are the *syntactic rules* of the language. They permit us to say what we mean, which, at least according to the March Hare, is what we should do.

"Then you should say what you mean," the March Hare went on.

"I do," Alice hastily replied: "at least—at least I mean what I say— that's the same thing, you know."

"Not the same thing a bit!" said the Hatter. "You might just as well say that 'I see what I eat' is the same thing as 'I eat what I see'!"

"You might just as well say," added the March Hare, "that 'I like what I get' is the same thing as 'I get what I like'!"

"You might just as well say," added the Dormouse . . . "that 'I breathe when I sleep' is the same thing as 'I sleep when I breathe'!"

"It *is* the same thing with you," said the Hatter.

If there were no rules of syntax it wouldn't have mattered whether Alice said "I say what I mean" or "I mean what I say." Part of the meaning of a sentence, then, is determined by the order of the morphemes. The syntactic rules of the grammar specify, among other things, such order.

This is true in all languages. In Thai, for example, *mæ̃æw hěn mǎa* means "The cat saw the dog," but *mǎa hěn mæ̃æw* means "The dog saw the cat" and *hěn mǎa mæ̃æw* is not a sentence in Thai and has no meaning. *Où est la télévision?* ("Where is the television?") is a sentence in French. **Est la où télévision?* ("is the where television?") is not a sentence in French. *ɛha yɛ hũ* ("This place is spooky") is a sentence in Twi. **Yɛ ɛha hũ* ("is place-here spooky") is not a sentence in Twi.

Strings of morphemes which conform to the syntactic rules of the language are called the **grammatical sentences** of the language, and strings which do not "obey" these rules are called **ungrammatical.**

You don't have to study "grammar" or linguistics to know which sentences are grammatical. Even a very young child knows intuitively that *The boy kissed the girl* is a "good" sentence in English but that something is wrong with the string **Girl the kissed boy the.*

According to *your* knowledge of English syntax, which of the following sentences would you mark with an asterisk (as ungrammatical)?

a. Sylvia wanted George to go.
b. Sylvia wanted George go.
c. Sylvia heard George to go.
d. Sylvia hoped George go.
e. Sylvia heard George go.
f. Clarence looked up the number.
g. Clarence looked the number up.
h. Morris walked up the hill.
i. Morris walked the hill up.

If the syntactic rules of your grammar are the same as those of our grammar (and we expect that they are), you "starred" as ungrammatical sentences b, c, d, and i.　If we agree on the "grammaticality" of any of these sentences we must be making these decisions according to some rules which we know.　Notice that the syntactic rules which account for our "intuitions" in these cases are not *just* "ordering" rules.　They "tell" us, for example, that with the verb *wanted* we must use a *to,* but with *heard* we do not use a *to.*　And they permit us to move the *up* in sentence f but not in sentence h.

These examples show that the syntactic rules permit us to make judgments about the "grammaticality" of sentences.　In other words, the sentences of a language are well-formed, grammatical strings, not just any strings of morphemes.　And it is the *syntax* of the grammar which accounts for this fact.

The syntactic rules also account for other linguistic judgments that speakers are able to make.　Consider the following sentence:

> j.　The Mafia wants protection from attack by the police.

You can't be sure whether the Mafia wants the police to protect them against the attack of some unnamed parties or whether the Mafia wants someone to protect them from the attack of the police.　The double meaning (or ambiguity) of the sentence is not due to the occurrence of any homonyms or words with two meanings, as it is in the following sentence:

> k.　Katerina gave Petruccio a sock.

In sentence k, Katerina may have given Petruccio an article of clothing or a punch.　*Sock* has two meanings.　But in sentence j the ambiguity can't be explained in this way; it must be due to the *syntactic structure* of the sentence.　Your knowledge of the syntactic rules permits you to reconstruct sentence j as meaning either

> l.　The Mafia wants the police to protect them from attack.
> *or*
> m.　The Mafia wants protection from being attacked by the police.

Sometimes the multiple meanings are not immediately apparent.　But you can usually figure out which sentences are ambiguous because of your knowledge of the syntactic rules.　We feel fairly certain that you can not only tell which of the following sentences are ambiguous but can even give the different meanings of the ones you choose:

> n.　George wanted the presidency more than Martha. ✗
> o.　Ahab wanted the whale more than glory.
> p.　Visiting professors can be boring. ✗
> q.　Complaining professors can be boring.
> r.　The matador fought the bull with courage. ✗
> s.　The matador fought the bull with swords.

If you decided that sentences n, p, and r were ambiguous (or if you see the ambiguity now that we have told you), something in your grammar must permit you to make these judgments. The phonological rules don't help, nor does your knowledge of the semantic meanings of the words. The syntax does provide this information.

The syntactic rules also account for an interesting fact about the following sentences:

    t. John is eager to please.
    u. John is easy to please.

The two sentences seem to be similar in their constructions. Yet speakers of English know that in sentence t John wants to please some-one else and in sentence u John will be pleased by someone. Knowing the syntactic rules permits you to interpret the sentences in this way. These rules also account for the fact that one can change sentence u into

    v. It is easy to please John

without altering the meaning of the sentence, but sentence t cannot be similarly changed into

    w. *It is eager to please John.

These examples illustrate the role of syntactic rules in a grammar:

1. They account for the grammaticality of sentences.
2. They determine the ordering of morphemes.
3. They reveal ambiguities.
4. They determine the relations between different parts of a sentence (the *grammatical relations*).
5. They can relate one sentence to another without changing the meaning.

We have been discussing the syntactic rules which you (and every speaker of a language) must "know." As we stated in the first chapter, to account for this linguistic knowledge linguists write descriptive grammars. Insofar as the linguist's grammar accounts for your knowledge, it will be a good description of the language. If you know certain rules, these rules must be stated in a clear way. In the next sections we will attempt to describe the kinds of syntactic rules which are found in all languages. For the most part we will illustrate them by using English examples, but no one should think that we are presenting the grammar of English. Our aim is rather to look at the kinds of regularities that can be explained by syntactic rules.

PHRASE-STRUCTURE RULES

Who climbs the grammar-tree distinctly knows
Where noun and verb and participle grows.

                —JOHN DRYDEN, "Juvenal's Satire," vi

We said above that everyone knows what a sentence in his language is. But what is it? Most schoolchildren learn that "every sentence has a subject and a predicate." That's a pretty good definition, and every speaker is aware of this even if he hasn't learned it consciously. All the ten strings of morphemes listed here as group 1 have subjects and predicates, and they are all sentences of English:

SUBJECT *(NP)* *Noun phrase*	PREDICATE *(VP)* *Verb phrase*
1 a. It	frightens me.
b. Sally	frightens me.
c. The man	frightens me.
d. The fat man	frightens me.
e. The fat man who is whistling	frightens me.
f. He	fell.
g. John	went fishing.
h. Several friends of mine	threw a party.
i. This book	is fascinating.
j. Flying planes	can be dangerous.

The subject may assume various forms, some more complex than others, but all of them are **referring expressions**; that is, they point out some entity. *John* points out the individual named John; *this book* points out a particular book; *it* points out something that the hearer is assumed to know (perhaps by previous discourse). Linguists call such expressions **noun phrases** (NP), since they contain at least one noun or pronoun.

The predicate is a **relating expression** in that it relates the subject to some action or some property. In sentences 1a to 1e, the various noun phrases (NPs) are related to the action "frighten." In sentence 1i, "this book" is related to the property of "being fascinating." Since the predicate always contains at least a verb (and may contain other elements, such as the direct object *me*) it is called a **verb phrase** (VP).

If every sentence of a language must include a noun phrase as subject and a verb phrase as predicate, the grammar must include a rule which can be stated as:

1 Every Sentence (S) consists of a Noun Phrase (NP) and a Verb Phrase (VP).

This rule can be abbreviated, or stated formally as:

1' S → NP VP.   *means*

This reads: A Sentence "is a" (or "rewrites as") as Noun Phrase followed by a Verb Phrase. We know Rule 1 is a rule of English because it "explains" why the strings under sentence group 2 are not sentences:[1]

2 a. *frightens me

---

[1] Certain "subjectless" sentences will be discussed later. We shall see that what may appear to be a grammatical sentence without a subject actually has an "understood" subject.

    b. *the man
    c. *the man that is whistling
    d. *jumped into the pool without his clothes on

The order of the NP and the VP must also be as given in the rule to account for the ungrammaticality of the sentences in group 3:

3 a. *frightens me it
    b. *frightens me the fat man
    c. *went fishing John
    d. *can be dangerous flying planes

Verb phrases may consist of subparts just as sentences do, as we can see from the sentences in groups 4 and 5.

4 a. The wind howled.
    b. The wind blew.

5 a. The wind frightened Mary.
    b. The wind frightened the girls.
    c. The wind frightened the little kitten.
    d. The wind frightened several old ladies who were drinking tea in the living room of the haunted house.

Notice that in the sentences of group 4 the verb phrase consists of a verb alone, but in those of group 5 the verb is followed by a noun phrase. Since these are all grammatical sentences in the language, the rule stating what a verb phrase is must account for this. This rule can be stated:

2 A Verb Phrase may consist of a Verb (V) alone, or of a Verb followed by a Noun Phrase.
2′ VP → V (NP).

The parentheses in Rule 2′ denote that the NP is optional, that is, may or may not occur in a verb phrase. Rule 2′ really abbreviates two rules:

2′ a. VP → V.
    b. VP → V NP.

As we add rules we are clearly defining what it is a speaker knows about sentences. If we just defined a sentence as consisting of an NP VP, that would not tell us what these two categories are. Furthermore we see by Rule 2′ that all the expressions that can be subjects also have the potential of being objects of verbs (and vice-versa).[2] This is an important general property of language, for it allows speakers to reuse in a different context what they know already. When a child is learning his language he need only learn what a noun phrase is, and learn that an NP

---

[2] There are, of course, restrictions which depend on the semantic and syntactic properties of the words used. This is why we said "have the potential." *Several old ladies frightened the wind* is an anomalous sentence, but *several old ladies* can occur as the subject NP in *Several old ladies frightened the little kitten.*

can occur either as a subject or an object. Furthermore, by using the same symbol, NP, in two rules we show that the same kinds of phrases occur in different parts of the structure.

Knowing the syntactic rules of English, you know that verbs may be in the *present tense* or the *past tense*.[3] We can express this knowledge by Rule 3:

> **3** A verb consists of a verb *stem* and an abstract morpheme designating tense: present (Pres) or past (Past).
>
> $$3'\ V \rightarrow V_{stem} \begin{Bmatrix} \text{Pres} \\ \text{Past} \end{Bmatrix}.$$

The braces, { }, indicate that either Pres or Past must follow the verb stem. Notice that once again we have used an abbreviating device which collapses two rules which could have been stated:

> **3**′a. $V \rightarrow V_{stem}$ Pres.
> b. $V \rightarrow V_{stem}$ Past.

By writing one rule with braces we are able to state this more generally.

The rules "defining" a verb phrase or a sentence do not yet give enough information; we haven't said what a noun phrase is. Speakers of all languages know what constitutes a noun phrase even if they never heard the term *noun phrase*. They know the different linguistic forms that can be referring expressions, and they know that only that type of linguistic form can be a subject and occur in an environment like "_____ was lost" or be an object and occur in an environment like "Who found _____?"

> **6** a. The kitten was lost.   Who found the kitten?
> b. The blond haired girl was lost.   Who found the blond-haired girl?
> c. It was lost.   Who found it?
> d. Sally was lost.   Who found Sally?

As the (c) sentences show, an NP may be a pronoun, since a pronoun (Pro) is a referring expression that can be a subject or an object. And the (d) sentences show that an NP can be a proper noun (the name of a *particular* person or place or object), for all proper nouns refer to someone or something and can serve as subjects or objects, as Alice pointed out:

> "What's the use of their having names," the Gnat said, "if they won't answer to them?"
>
> "No use to *them*," said Alice, "but it's useful to the people that name them, I suppose. If not, why do things have names at all?"

A noun phrase can also be a noun (N) preceded by such morphemes as *a, the, some, several, every, each, many, my,* and so on. Of these, we

---

[3] The *future tense* in English is expressed by the use of the "auxiliary verbs" *shall, will,* and *going to,* not by changing the tense of the verb. Remember that we are not including all the rules of English syntax but merely illustrating what kinds of syntactic rules exist and what they do in the grammar.

will only consider the articles (Art) *a* and *the*. An NP can of course be much more complex than what has been described so far, since it includes phrases such as *several old ladies who were drinking tea in the living room of the haunted house.*

NPs occur in all languages, although some of the details may differ. Thai, for example, has no articles (*phŏm hĕn dèg* is literally "I see boy"), and in Danish the article follows the noun as a suffix (*bog,* "book"; *bogen,* "the book"). The particular rule which "rewrites" NP, that is, which states what it is, will differ somewhat from language to language, but all grammars will include an "NP rule."

An oversimplified version of the English NP rule may be stated:

4 A Noun Phrase may be a pronoun (Pro) or a proper noun (N_{prop}) or a noun (N) preceded by an article (Art) or a noun preceded by one or more adjectives (Adj) all of which are preceded by an article.

The more complicated these rules get, the more difficult it is to understand them when they are written out in this way. Formally we can abbreviate this rule as:

$$\textbf{4}' \ NP \rightarrow \begin{Bmatrix} Pro \\ N_{prop} \\ Art \ (Adj)^* \ N \end{Bmatrix}.$$

Once more the braces designate the optional choice between a pronoun, a proper noun, and an expression containing a noun. When braces are used, one of the items enclosed must be chosen. That is, an NP must be something. Thus the braces differ from parentheses, which designate that the item enclosed may be selected or may be omitted. We added another device, the asterisk after the adjective, $(Adj)^*$. This notation means "zero or more adjectives." It clearly states that a noun phrase of this type can include no adjectives (*the man*); one adjective (*the old man*); two adjectives (*the dirty old man*); three adjectives (*the bearded dirty old man*); ? adjectives (*the skinny, red-haired, lecherous, bearded, . . . dirty old man*).

Further evidence that Rule 4 is a syntactic rule of English comes from the fact that English speakers know all the expressions in group 7a are noun phrases, and that none of the expressions in group 7b are:

7 a. he   the dwarf
      you   a good boy
      Sally   an elegant old table
      Chicago   the cross-eyed bear
      Waterloo   a noun phrase
   b. man the   run
      the man old   a blue whale is abaft the binnacle
      an it   of a mouse
      the Sally   an oaken

You know much more about noun phrases than is shown by this rule. You know, for example, that most nouns can be singular or plural (*boy/boys, man/men*),[4] and that a prepositional phrase can follow the noun (*the cousin of my aunt, the hole in the bottom of the sea*). Clearly a complete grammar of English would have to include all this syntactic information about noun phrases, verb phrases, prepositional phrases, and so on.

All the rules given so far have counterparts in other languages, although there may be certain differences. In Korean, *The wind the girl frightened* is a sentence and the VP rule would look like:

2K   A Verb Phrase consists of a Verb alone, or a verb *preceded* by a Noun Phrase.

2′K VP → (NP)   V.

The NP in French differs in detail from its English counterpart in that French adjectives normally follow the noun. Thus Rule 4′F would be part of the NP rule of French to account for the order in the following phrases:

8 a. le gateau délicieux   "the delicious cake"
   b. une femme intelligente   "an intelligent woman"

4′F NP → Art N (Adj).

Though languages may differ in such details, they all have referring phrases (NP) and relating phrases (VP), and their sentences must contain at least one of each. They all have nouns, pronouns, and verbs, and they all require the morphemes of a sentence to occur in certain orders specified by the rules of syntax.

Rules 1 through 4 are valid for English (though not complete), and every speaker "knows" these rules whether he is aware that he knows them or not. He wasn't ever taught them by his mother, his teachers, or anyone else. Nor did he learn them from a book (illiterate speakers of English know them also). The rules are a part of the syntactic system of the language, and they are "learned" by children when language is acquired.

These rules are called **phrase-structure rules.** They show us what a sentence is, what a noun phrase is, what a verb phrase is, and so on. They also show that sentences are more than strings of morphemes which follow one after the other. The morphemes are grouped into substructures called **constituents.** The constituents are in a hierarchical arrangement showing what each constituent is composed of. For example, the constituent *sentence* is composed of a noun phrase and a verb phrase; the constituent *verb phrase* may be made up of a single verb, or a verb followed by a noun phrase; a *verb* consists of a verb stem followed by a

---

[4] Some nouns do not ordinarily specify "number," such as *rice* and *molasses.*

morpheme of tense.   The phrase-structure rules also reveal *grammatical relations*.   They tell us that the first noun phrase is the *subject* of the sentence, but a noun phrase that occurs after the verb is the *direct object* of the sentence.   Knowledge of the grammatical relations of a sentence is extremely crucial to comprehension of meaning: *cats eat bats* is quite different from *bats eat cats!*

A sentence can be represented in a diagram called a **phrase-structure tree** or a **phrase marker** that reveals the constituent structure and the grammatical relations.   Such diagrams of sentences 9a, 9b, and 9c are shown in Figures 6.1, 6.2, and 6.3, respectively.

9 a. The wind howled.
  b. The wind frightened me.
  c. A cold wind brings cold rainy weather.

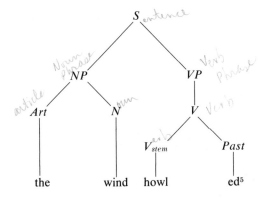

Figure 6.1 Phrase marker of sentence 9a.

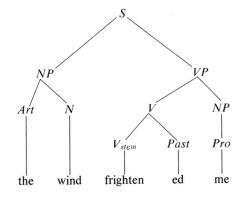

Figure 6.2 Phrase marker of sentence 9b.

Notice that such a phrase-structure tree (or phrase marker: PM)

---

[5] The phonetic representation of the grammatical morphemes like Past would be determined by the phonological rules of the language.

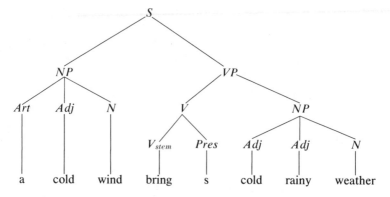

Figure 6.3 Phrase marker of sentence 9c.

visually represents what you know about these sentences. Starting from the topmost structure of Figure 6.1, the tree shows that an S is composed of two parts, an NP and a VP, that the NP consists of an Art and an N, that the VP consists of a V_{stem} and the tense Past. If you trace the "branches" of the tree from the bottom up, the diagram shows that *the* is an Art, that *wind* is an N, that *howl* is a V_{stem}, that *-ed* is the Past morpheme, that *the wind* is an NP, and *howled* is a V, and that *the wind howled* is an S. In addition, if you look at all three trees (Figures 6.1–6.3), you can see that *the wind, a cold wind, me,* and *cold rainy weather* are all NPs (since the label NP is at the points or *nodes* in the trees from which they all come). Of course you know this is true, but the diagrams reveal this knowledge.

These rules and the phrase-structure trees which can be constructed from them show what speakers know about the structures of the sentences of their language.

FITTING THE MORPHEMES IN

We next went to the School of Languages, where three Professors sat in Consultation upon improving that of their own Country.

The first Project was to shorten Discourse by cutting Polysyllables into one, and leaving out Verbs and Participles; because in Reality all things imaginable are but Nouns.

The other was a Scheme for entirely abolishing all Words whatsoever; and this was urged as a great Advantage in Point of Health as well as Brevity. For it is plain, that

every Word we speak is in some degree a Diminution of our
Lungs by Corrosion. . . .

   — JONATHAN SWIFT, "A Voyage to Laputa," *Gulliver's Travels*

The learned Professors of Languages in Laputa proposed a scheme for abolishing all words, thinking it would be more convenient if "Men [were] to carry about them, such Things as were necessary to express the particular Business they are to discourse on."   We would venture to say that this scheme never came to fruition, even in Laputa.

   Our thoughts expressed in sentences are conveyed by the particular morphemes or words we combine into the grammatical strings permitted by the syntactic rules.   But none of the rules we have given show how the actual words and morphemes get into the phrase-structure trees.   The rules given so far would produce trees like the one in Figure 6.4.

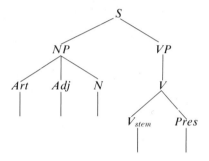

Figure 6.4

To complete this tree we need to use our knowledge of the syntactic category (the "part of speech") of individual words and morphemes. And we do have this knowledge, as the following exercise will show:

> Classify the following words into four classes according to their "part of speech":
>
> man,   hot,   run,   you,   droop,   boy,   he,   walk,   water,   funny

A speaker of English who understood the "directions" would probably come up with these four classes:

N	ADJ	V	PRO
man	hot	run	he
boy	funny	walk	you
water		droop	

   One needn't know how to label these classes to know that the words under N are words of the same type, those under Adj are words of the same type, and so on.   If a speaker didn't know this he might form a sentence such as *water you droop hot.   This kind of knowledge must also be part of one's grammar.

Obviously when you know a language you know its <u>vocabulary of morphemes and words (which</u> is called the **lexicon**).   Each lexical item is specified in the lexicon as to its phonological features and its semantic properties.   In addition, each item must also be specified as to its syntactic category: *man* — N, *hot* — Adj, *run* — V$_{stem}$, *he* — Pro and so on.   The syntactic rules of the grammar include **lexical-insertion rules.**   Among other things, these rules match the syntactic categories at the bottom of a phrase-structure tree with lexical items of the same category, and then place those words or morphemes under the corresponding node of the tree.   Of course the choice of a particular noun, verb, or other part of speech depends on the intended meaning of the sentence.

Phrase-structure trees with lexical items in place correspond to the "sentence diagrams" that some students learn to construct in English classes.   More importantly, they represent what speakers *know* about sentences of their language.

THE INFINITUDE OF LANGUAGE: RECURSIVE RULES

> *Normal human minds are such that . . . without the help of anybody, they will produce 1000 [sentences] they never heard spoke of . . . inventing and saying such things as they never heard from their masters, nor any mouth.*
>
> — HUARTE DE SAN JUAN (c. 1530–1592)

We observed in Chapter 1 that speakers of any language can produce and understand sentences they have never said or heard before and that the grammar must therefore account for this creative aspect of language.   The phrase-structure rules do just this.   You may never have heard sentence 10 before reading it now:

10 The young orangutan strummed the old red banjo.

We feel sure you can understand it, for you know its structure, you know what the noun phrases refer to, what the adjectives modify, and that the verb relates *the young orangutan* to *the old red banjo* through the action of "strumming" (see Figure 6.5).

When you consider all the possible NP subjects, adjectives, verbs, and NP objects that can be constructed from Rules 1, 2, 3, and 4 and the huge lexicon every speaker knows, you can begin to appreciate how a few simple rules of grammar permit us to understand a huge number of sentences.   And we have only looked at a tiny, oversimplified fraction of the grammar of English.

The rules of the grammar also account for the fact that speakers can

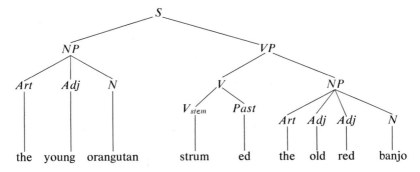

Figure 6.5 Phrase marker of sentence 10.

produce single sentences of unlimited length. Notice we said *can,* not *do.* This was also discussed in Chapter 1, when we pointed out that a person's ability (his linguistic competence) is not identical with how he uses that ability (his linguistic performance). Even a five-year-old child has the linguistic competence to understand quite long sentences, as is evident from the children's rhyme about the house that Jack built:

> This is the farmer sowing the corn,
> That kept the cock that crowed in the morn,
> That waked the priest all shaven and shorn,
> That married the man all tattered and torn,
> That kissed the maiden all forlorn,
> That milked the cow with the crumpled horn,
> That tossed the dog
> That worried the cat
> That killed the rat
> That ate the malt
> That lay in the house that Jack built.

In fact, you have the linguistic ability to make this sentence, or any sentence, longer. This shows that there is no longest sentence in a language. For every sentence of a given length, you can produce a sentence of greater length. You can, for example, add any of the following to the beginning of the rhyme and still end up with a grammatical sentence:

11 I saw that . . .
> What is the name of the unicorn that noticed that . . .
> Ask someone if . . .
> Do you know whether . . .

So far, the rules of syntax that we have discussed account for such indefinitely long sentences in only a trival way. We showed that one cannot limit the number of adjectives in principle:

12 The seedy battered rundown old red wooden shack fell down.

This was accounted for by the (Adj)* in our NP rule. But such a rule could not account for the example above, and many other examples. One could provide another perfectly grammatical (though rather stilted) version of the poem:

13 This is the farmer sowing his corn,
and the farmer kept the cock that crowed in the morn,
and the cock waked the priest all shaven and shorn,
and the priest married the man all tattered and torn,
and the man kissed the maiden all forlorn,
and the maiden milked the cow with the crumpled horn,
and the cow tossed the dog,
and the dog worried the cat,
and the cat killed the rat,
and the rat ate the malt,
and the malt lay in the house and Jack built the house.

The ability of any speaker of English to identify this poem as a single sentence must somehow be reflected in the grammar. We can do this by positing another phrase-structure rule:

5 A Sentence may consist of any number of Sentences, each joined by the conjunction *and*.
5′ S → S (and S)*.

We are again using the abbreviation of parentheses followed by an asterisk to mean that zero or more of whatever is enclosed in the parentheses may occur. In this case Rule 5′ states that S may rewrite simply as S or as S *and* S or as S *and* S *and* S, and so on.

An abbreviated phrase-structure tree for the new version of the poem is given as Figure 6.6. Other rules of syntax reflect the other ways of getting indefinitely long sentences, such as a rule which would account for the original version of the poem.

Rules such as Rule 5 are called **recursive** rules because their basic element (S in this case) recurs. It is because of such rules that we have the ability to produce an infinite set of sentences with our finite brains and

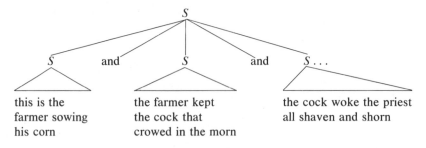

Figure 6.6 Phrase marker of sentence 13.

finite set of linguistic rules. Recursive rules occur in all the grammars of all languages because the facts already given are not unique to English. In fact, Rule 5 or some variant of it is a "universal" rule occurring in all grammars. Here is an example of such a **conjoined** sentence from Thai

14 măă	kin	hŭahɔɔm	láe	mæææw	kin	plaa	láe . . .
the dog	ate	onions	and	the cat	ate	fish	and . . .

Another recursive rule in English is Rule 6:

> **6** A Noun Phrase may consist of two Noun Phrases joined by either the conjunction *and* or the conjunction *or*.

6' $NP \rightarrow NP \left(\left\{ \begin{matrix} and \\ or \end{matrix} \right\} NP \right).$

This rule accounts for the fact that the phrases in group 15a are noun phrases but those in group 15b are not.

15 a. Antony and Cleopatra
N P   The cowboys and the Indians
The Democrats or the Republicans
The red flag or the old blue stocking
b. *John Mary and
*run and play
*the or house barn
*the girl or dreamed

Further proof that Rules 1 through 6 are realistic symbolizations of a speaker's knowledge is illustrated by sentences with nonsense words. In Chapter 5 we discussed such nonsense sentences and noted that though they were "uninterpretable" they sound as if they *should* be English sentences. This is because they "obey" the syntactic rules of the language.

For instance, if a speaker of English were told that a *tove* is a noun and *slithy* an adjective, he would know that *the slithy tove* was a noun phrase because he knows Rule 4. If he were told that *The slithy tove gyred* was a sentence of English he would know that *The slithy tove* was the subject of the sentence in which *gyre* + Past was the predicate, for he knows Rule 1. He would also know that *The slithy tove* is a noun phrase, and from Rule 4 he could deduce that *slithy* was an adjective modifying the noun *tove*. If you added to his knowledge the hypothetical fact that *The mimsy borogove gimbled* was also a sentence of English, then he would know that *The slithy tove gyred and the mimsy borogove gimbled* was a sentence simply because he knows Rule 6; he would also know from Rule 6, that *the tove and the borogove* would be a noun phrase, for he could deduce that *tove* and *borogove* were nouns. This is possible only because of our knowledge of syntactic rules.

AMBIGUITY REVISITED

A smile is the chosen vehicle for all ambiguities.

—HERMAN MELVILLE, *Pierre*, iv

At the beginning of this chapter we mentioned that the syntactic part of the grammar accounts for our ability to recognize the multiple meanings of ambiguous sentences. Why is it, for example, that speakers know that a sentence such as sentence 16 is ambiguous?

16 Mary and Joe or Bill frightened the dog.

Sentence 16 has the two meanings shown in sentences 17a and 17b.

17 a. Mary and Joe frightened the dog or Bill frightened the dog.
   b. Mary and Joe frightened the dog or Mary and Bill frightened the dog.

Since sentence 16 is syntactically ambiguous (that is, the double meaning is not due to any ambiguous words), we should be able to construct two phrase-structure trees, one for each meaning, and we can (Figures 6.7 and 6.8). Figure 6.7 can be read aloud: *MaryandJoe* [pause] *or Bill frightened the dog.* Figure 6.8 can be read: *Mary* [pause] *andJoeorBill frightened the dog.* Notice that in both sentences the pause comes between the two main subject NPs. That is, you don't pause until you say everything under NP₁; in Figure 6.7 that includes *Mary and Joe,* but in Figure 6.8 it includes only *Mary.* The phrase-structure rules and the corresponding phrase-structure trees thus capture the knowledge that speakers have about how elements of such sentences are grouped. In this case the groupings (the constituents) correspond to different structures and thus have different meanings.

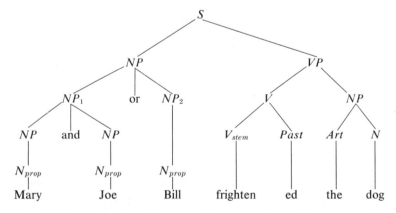

Figure 6.7 Phrase marker of sentence 16 as paraphrased by sentence 17a.

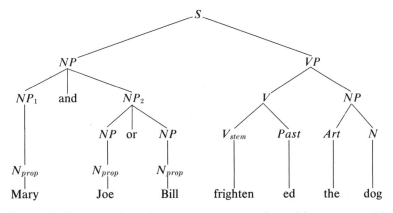

Figure 6.8 Phrase marker of sentence 16 as paraphrased by sentence 17b.

Sentence 18 also is ambiguous:

18 They are moving sidewalks.

It could mean either 19a or 19b:

19 a. They (those things over there) are sidewalks that move.
   b. They (the workmen) are relocating sidewalks.

The meaning of sentence 19a can be revealed by the tree diagram in Figure 6.9.[6] To diagram sentence 18 correctly as 19b, we have to include another branch of the V — the *ing* of the progressive aspect (see Figure 6.10). Don't worry if you don't know what an aspect is or what *progressive* means. All we want you to see is that the two trees are structurally

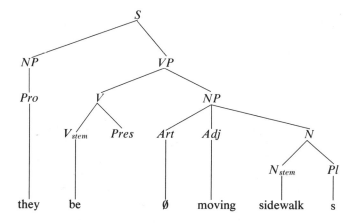

Figure 6.9 Phrase marker of sentence 18 as paraphrased by sentence 19a.

---

[6] The Art in the NP of the verb phrase is "null," a case we have not explicitly discussed. Nor have we included in our rules the plural (Pl) morpheme attached to the noun. Also note that *be + Pres* is converted to *are* when the subject is plural.

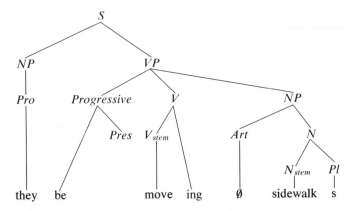

Figure 6.10 Phrase marker of sentence 18 as paraphrased by sentence 19b.

different. The differences between Figures 6.9 and 6.10 again show that sentences have structure and are not merely morphemes strung together like beads on a string. Speakers must know (in some sense) the structures because they can interpret sentence 16 as 17a or 17b and sentence 18 as 19a or 19b.

Speakers' awareness of ambiguity must be reflected in their grammars and in the grammars we write to describe their competence. We see that we can do this (in certain cases) by means of phrase-structure rules.

GENERATIVE GRAMMARS

> . . . the only thing that is important is whether a result can
> be achieved in a finite number of elementary steps or not.
>
> —JOHN VON NEUMANN

Phrase-structure rules are a very important part of a grammar, as we have seen. They account for much of our knowledge of the syntactic structures of the language, and they do this in a clear and explicit fashion. One doesn't have to "guess" what it is they are describing. In fact, one can view rules such as this as a machine which "cranks out" or generates sentences. A grammar including such rules is called a generative grammar. Each rule applies that can apply in the following fashion: Start with S and substitute for S (or *rewrite* S) with the symbols that appear on the right side of the arrow. Rewrite each successive category according to the appropriate phrase-structure rule, stopping only when no more rules apply.

We can see how such a "machine" works with a little grammar consisting of just a simplified version of Rules 1–4 given above (but in a different order) and a small lexicon.

PHRASE STRUCTURE RULES	LEXICON	
1 S → NP VP	Pro:	you
2 NP → $\begin{Bmatrix} \text{Pro} \\ \text{N}_{prop} \\ \text{Art (Adj) N} \end{Bmatrix}$	N:	boy, girl, unicorn
	Art:	the, a
	Adj:	big, little
3 VP → V NP	V$_{stem}$:	kiss, hit
4 V → V$_{stem}$ $\begin{Bmatrix} \text{Pres} \\ \text{Past} \end{Bmatrix}$	N$_{prop}$:	John, Mary

To generate a sentence by this grammar we write down the initial symbol *S* and then "rewrite" it using any rule that applies and keep doing this until there are no symbols appearing in our string which also appear on the left side of an arrow.

	S				
NP	VP				by applying Rule 1
N$_{prop}$	VP				by applying Rule 2
N$_{prop}$	V	NP			by applying Rule 3
N$_{prop}$	V	Art	Adj	N	by applying Rule 2
N$_{prop}$	V$_{stem}$	Past	Art Adj N		by applying Rule 4

No further phrase-structure rules apply, so lexical-insertion rules match each category in the string with a lexical item designated as belonging to that category. In this way we can generate:

> John hit the little unicorn.
> Mary hit the big boy.   *and so on*

We can also generate the phrase-structure tree in the same way, starting with S, as in Figure 6.11.

Figure 6.11 S expanded by Rule 1.

We can now expand NP by Rule 2, as in Figure 6.12.

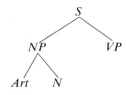

Figure 6.12 S expanded by Rules 1 and 2.

Proceeding in the same fashion, we can generate the phrase-structure tree shown in Figure 6.13.

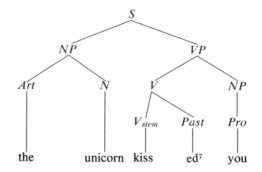

Figure 6.13 S expanded by Rules 1, 2, 3, and 4.

With just these four simple rules and a lexicon of ten items we can generate 1,764 sentences. Of course, if we had included any recursive rules, we could generate an infinite set of sentences.

Phrase-structure generative grammars are therefore powerful devices for generating the sentences of a language and associating a structure for each sentence. They can generate an infinite set of sentences by means of recursive rules and thereby account for a speaker's ability to do this. They can show the hierarchical structures of sentences, as the tree diagrams illustrate. By providing labels (the category symbols) for syntactic categories, they show similar strings as being similar (for example, NPs such as *you, the unicorn, Mary, the little boy*). They even are able to show why certain sentences are ambiguous by providing two different phrase-structure trees for a single ambiguous sentence. It is clear that every grammar needs such rules, since they account for much of what we know about our language.

TRANSFORMATIONAL RULES

Our life passes in transformation.

— RAINER MARIA RILKE, *Duineser Elegien,* vii

Phrase-structure rules are necessary but not sufficient to adequately account for *all* our knowledge of syntax. To show this let us consider sentences like those in group 20.

---

[7] The -ed is added by the phonological rules.

THE WIZARD OF ID   by Brant parker and Johnny hart

By permission of John Hart and Field Enterprises, Inc.

20 a.   The detective tracked *down* the murderer.

    b.   Friday Foster threw *over* Mwenye Nguvu.

    c.   A teacher called *up* the university.

The italicized elements are called **verbal particles** (Prt). They differ from prepositions (even though they sound like them) in that they can occur on either side of the direct object NP, as shown in group 21.

21 a.   The detective tracked the murderer *down*.

    b.   Friday Foster threw Mwenye Nguvu *over*.

    c.   A teacher called the university *up*.

Now compare these with the following:

22 a.   The crook sped *down* an alley.

    b.   *The crook sped an alley *down*.

If you agree that the sentences in groups 20 and 21 are grammatical, and that sentence 22a is grammatical and 22b is not, then clearly the grammar must reflect the difference between particles and prepositions.

One way we might be able to generate sentences with particles is to change Rule 2 in the following way:

2a A Verb Phrase may consist of a Verb alone, a Verb followed by a Verbal Particle, a Verb followed by a Noun Phrase, or a Verb followed by a Verbal Particle followed by a Noun Phrase.

2′a VP → V (Prt) (NP).

The parentheses, as usual, designate optionality. Each choice corresponds to an actual sentence-type in the language:[8]

V	John left.
V Prt	John came over.
V NP	John loved Mary.
V Prt NP	John looked up the address.

While Rule 2a will account for sentence group 20, it doesn't account for sentence group 21, and so the grammar is incomplete in this respect. We need another rule:

2b VP → V (NP) (Prt).

If we collapse Rules 2a and 2b, we get:

$$\textbf{2c} \quad \text{VP} \rightarrow \text{V} \begin{cases} (\text{Prt}) & (\text{NP}) \\ (\text{NP}) & (\text{Prt}) \end{cases}.$$

This rule will produce the right strings. But every speaker knows that sentences 20a, b, and c and 21a, b, and c are related; they mean the same thing and each seems to be a stylistic variant of the other. Using Rule 2c, we are unable to show the relatedness of these sentences, since each sentence in group 20 would be generated independently of its counterpart in group 21 and vice versa.

In addition, we see from the phrase-structure trees (phrase markers) that groups 20 and 21 have different structures (Figures 6.14 and 6.15).

When we discussed ambiguous sentences we observed that different phrase-structure trees correspond to the speaker's knowledge that the meanings of the sentences represented by those trees are different. Knowing that two sentences are different in meaning is a basic part of our linguistic competence. We represented this knowledge in the gram-

---

[8] Not all verbs, particles, and noun phrases can co-occur freely. *I ate over the number* is ungrammatical. Only certain verbs can go with certain particles, and not all verbs take an NP object. We have been oversimplifying throughout. The rules that select lexical items and insert them into the phrase-structure trees (lexical-insertion rules) are actually quite discriminating, and only allow those combinations that speakers find grammatical. We are using these examples and these rules to exemplify the *nature* of syntactic rules, not the rules as they actually exist in the grammar of English.

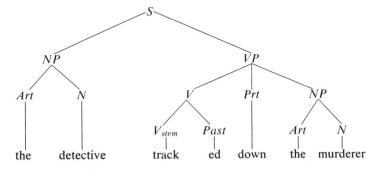

Figure 6.14 Phrase marker of sentence 20a.

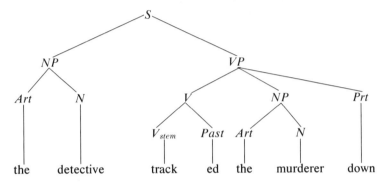

Figure 6.15 Phrase marker of sentence 21a.

mar by providing different phrase-structure trees for sentences with different meanings.

But if we retain Rule 2c in the grammar, this generalization will be lost, for sentences 20a and 21a have different phrase-structure trees but they do not have different meanings, even though the words are the same.[9]

Then we have to reject Rule 2c because it does not tell us that sentences 20a and 21a are related, and it suggests falsely that pairs such as these have different meanings. Yet there is no other way to derive these sentences with phrase-structure rules. This situation repeats itself many times in English and in all languages. Clearly, other means are needed if the grammar is truly to reflect what speakers know when they know a language.

What we need is a rule which can change a phrase-structure tree such as that for sentence 20a into one like that for sentence 21a. The new tree would not be generated by phrase-structure rules, and we can account

---

[9] There are, of course, sentences which are synonymous even though their phrase markers are different. The synonymy is due to different words or phrases which are synonymous — for example, *John is my sister's husband* and *John is my brother-in-law*. The sentences we are discussing here, however, are composed of the same morphemes.

for the similarity in meaning by the fact that sentence 21a derived from sentence 20a. The meaning of such sentences would then be generally specified by the original trees generated by the phrase-structure rules. A rule which can change or **transform** one phrase-structure tree into another is called a **transformational rule.** The original phrase-structure tree, which was generated by the phrase-structure rules, is called the **deep structure.** Deep structures are acted upon by transformations to give **surface structures,** which are then acted upon by phonological rules to produce the sentences speakers actually utter.

The deep structures of sentences are abstract representations which most clearly reflect the meaning of the sentence. No one speaks deep structures, just as no one speaks phonemes; we produce or utter surface structures just as we utter phones.

Before we discuss in any detail the form of transformational rules, it is important to see that they are truly needed in a grammar. The facts about "particle movement" illustrated this necessity to a small degree.

We showed above that some ambiguous sentences could be accounted for by phrase-structure rules (PS rules). There are, however, many ambiguous sentences which cannot be so explained. Some of the sentences mentioned at the beginning of this chapter cannot be handled by PS rules, such as:

23 John loves Richard more than Martha.

This sentence has two meanings, as indicated in 24:

24 a. John loves Richard more than Martha loves Richard.

b. John loves Richard more than John loves Martha.

There is a transformational rule (T rule) in the grammar that in certain cases deletes identical elements in a "more than" clause. Thus, assuming that the sentences in 24 are the *deep structures* underlying sentence 23, by applying this transformation we can account for the two meanings of sentence 23.

24a John *loves Richard* more than Martha *loves Richard.*
$$\Downarrow$$
T rule: Delete identical elements in the second clause.
$$\Downarrow$$
23 John loves Richard more than Martha.

24b *John loves* Richard more than *John loves* Martha.
$$\Downarrow$$
T rule: Delete identical elements in the second clause.
$$\Downarrow$$
23 John loves Richard more than   Martha.

Without transformations we would be unable to explain the ambiguity of sentence 23. A transformational rule such as this one changes two different deep structures (and therefore two different meanings) into two identical surface structures, or one sentence with two meanings.

We can now also explain why although sentence 25 has the same *surface structure* as sentence 23, it is not an ambiguous sentence:[10]

25 John likes doughnuts more than bagels.

Sentence 25 is not ambiguous because it is not derived from two different deep structures. This is shown by the fact that sentence 26a is grammatical but sentence 26b is not:

26 a.   John likes doughnuts more than John likes bagels.
   b.   *John likes doughnuts more than bagels like doughnuts.

Since only sentence 26a is possible as the deep structure for sentence 26, only one meaning can be assigned to sentence 26.

There are other pairs of sentences with similar surface phrase-structure trees which *must* be derived from different deep structures. Consider, for example, the sentences under 27:

27 a. Tarzan promised Jane to kill the lion.
   b. Tarzan persuaded Jane to kill the lion.

There is no question as to who will be the killer in each sentence; in sentence 27a it will be Tarzan, but in sentence 27b it will be Jane. There is no way that the surface phrase-structure trees can show this important difference. Both trees will look something like Figure 6.16.

Certainly the meaning of sentence 27a includes knowing that *Tarzan*

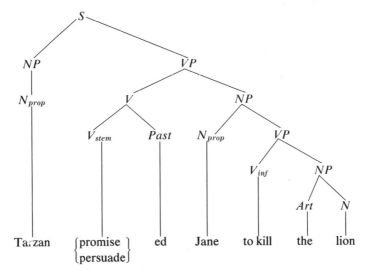

Figure 6.16 Surface structure of sentences 27a and 27b.

[10] Note that the *structures* are the same even if the particular lexical items are different.

is the logical subject of *to kill,* and the meaning of sentence 27b includes knowing that *Jane* is the logical subject of *to kill.* The deep structures of sentences 27a and 27b must make explicit the differences in meaning between the two sentences. An oversimplified diagram of the deep struc-

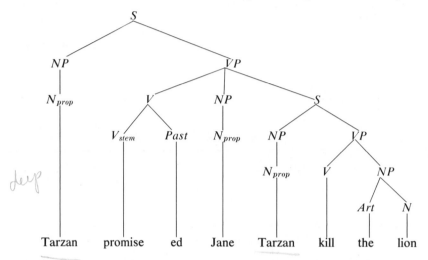

Figure 6.17 Deep structure of sentence 27a.

ture of sentence 27a is given in Figure 6.17.[11] This deep structure tree shows that *Tarzan* is the subject of *kill.* Transformations would apply to the tree to give the surface structure of sentence 27a.

The deep structure of sentence 27b is shown in Figure 6.18. In this

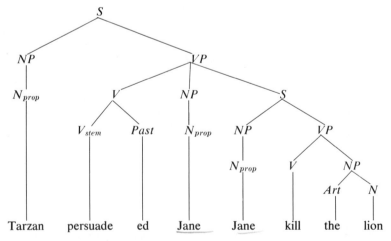

Figure 6.18 Deep structure of sentence 27b.

[11] Don't be concerned about the presence of the "embedded" S node, which hasn't been discussed.

deep structure, *Jane* (not *Tarzan*) is the subject of *kill*. Again transformations will apply to the deep structure tree to derive the surface structure of sentence 27b. Without positing these deep structures, we cannot explain the important logical differences between sentence 27a and sentence 27b. Once more we see that two different deep structures can be changed into similar surface structures by transformational rules.

Transformational rules can also change a single deep structure into many different surface structures, as the sentences in group 28 illustrate:

28 a. Mattie has been fasting and Hattie has been fasting too.
   b. Mattie has been fasting and Hattie has been too.
   c. Mattie has been fasting and Hattie has too.
   d. Mattie has been fasting and Hattie, too.

If all these sentences had to be generated by different rules to produce these distinct surface sentences, there would clearly be something wrong with the grammar. All the sentences in group 28 can be derived from the same deep structure by means of another *deletion* transformation. This transformation then explains how, in spite of the "missing elements," speakers understand sentences 28b, c, and d as synonymous with sentence 28a.

MORE NONSENSE

> *When sporgles spanned the floreate mead*
> *And cogwogs gleet upon the lea,*
> *Uffia gopped to meet her love*
> *Who smeeged upon the equat sea.*
>
> — HARRIET R. WHITE, "Uffia"

The use of nonsense morphemes shows that the transformational rules really do correspond to what speakers know about the syntactic structures of their language. If a speaker of English is told that *The flangmotter gribbled up a snark* and that *The flangmotter gribbled a snark up*, he knows that these are sentences which have the same meaning because the particle-movement transformation is part of his linguistic competence. That he has no idea what *gribble up* means doesn't matter.

Transformations relate all kinds of sentences syntactically. *Mary saw a hobo* means essentially the same thing as *A hobo was seen by Mary*, suggesting that active sentences and their corresponding passives are transformationally related. To see how complex our knowledge of syntactic structures is and how complex the system of transformations in a grammar is, observe that the simple sentence 29a is closely related to all the other sentences in group 29:

29 a. Mary glipped a snoozle.
   b. It's a snoozle that Mary glipped.
   c. What Mary glipped was a snoozle.
   d. It was Mary who glipped a snoozle.
   e. The one who glipped a snoozle was Mary.
   f. A snoozle was glipped by Mary.
   g. It's a snoozle that was glipped by Mary.
   h. What was glipped by Mary was a snoozle.
   i. It was Mary who a snoozle was glipped by.
   j. The one who a snoozle was glipped by was Mary.

In each of these sentences it is understood that the grammatical relationships among *Mary, glip,* and *a snoozle* are unvarying. That is, Mary is the one doing the "glipping" in all cases, just as it is "a snoozle" that gets "glipped" in all cases. To account for all these various syntactic forms, and at the same time reveal that the grammatical relationships are the same in each case — hence that the sentences are all nearly synonymous — is obviously too much of a job for the phrase-structure rules alone.

If we let the phrase-structure rules account for the basic structure of sentence 29a and let transformations derive the other nine surface sentences, we can explain the fact that in spite of the variance of syntactic forms all the sentences mean basically the same thing.

Such sentences explain why Alice often felt "dreadfully puzzled" in Wonderland. "The Hatter's remark seemed to have no meaning in it, and yet it was certainly English." By choosing "words" that have sound sequences which obey the phonological rules of English and by constructing sentences that have structures which obey the syntactic rules of English, one can, in effect, simulate the language.

WHAT A TRANSFORMATIONAL RULE LOOKS LIKE

We hope that by now you are convinced that a grammar consisting solely of phrase-structure rules would not be adequate to account for what all speakers of a language know. But a grammar cannot consist entirely of transformational rules either, since these require structures on which to operate. Besides, we saw above that the PS rules do account for a good part of what we know about sentences, and they provide, in addition, the deep structures which more or less represent the meanings of sentences.

One has to know just which deep structures can be changed by specific T Rules. That is, we want the "particle transformation" to change sentence 30a into 30b, but we don't want it to change sentence 31a into 31b.

30 a.   Merlin called off the Genie.
   b.   Merlin called the Genie off.

31 a.   Merlin jumped off the roof.
   b.   *Merlin jumped the roof off.

A transformational rule must then state specifically which structures it can apply to (the **structural description** or SD of the rule), and the change or transformation which is to be made (the **structural change** or SC of the rule).

We can state the particle-movement transformation to illustrate such rules:

> T$_{Prt}$: If the Verb Phrase in a phrase-structure tree consists of a Verb followed by a Verbal Particle followed by a Noun Phrase (the SD), then one can move the Verbal Particle to the position after the Noun Phrase (the SC).

Just as we abbreviated phrase-structure rules, we can state T$_{Prt}$ in a more formal fashion:

> T$'_{Prt}$:   SD: $V - Prt - NP$.
>
>   SC: $V - NP - Prt$.

Notice that the SD does not state any particular string of morphemes. Because of its generality it can apply to any phrase-structure tree which includes V followed by Prt followed by NP and will produce a corresponding tree in which the V is followed by NP which is followed by Prt.

All the sentences under A in group 32 can be operated on by this T rule to produce the sentences under B:

32   A   B

Aladdin cleaned up his lamps $\rightarrow$ Aladdin cleaned his lamps up
   V   Prt   NP   *V   NP   Prt*
A cow kicked over the bucket $\rightarrow$ A cow kicked the bucket over
   V   Prt   NP   *V   NP   Prt*
The Huns hauled off the loot $\rightarrow$ The Huns hauled the loot off
         V   Prt   NP   *V   NP   Prt*

We don't have to learn a separate transformational rule for each particular sentence. We learn *general* rules which apply to classes of phrase-structure trees.

This can be further illustrated by a transformational rule which derives the most common form of imperative sentences. The presence of this T rule will also support our statement given earlier in the chapter that all sentences have an NP followed by a VP. What we should have said was that the deep structures of all sentences have an NP followed by a VP.

In English one can give an order by saying either the sentences under A or those under B in group 33:

33	A	B
	You put out the cat!	Put out the cat!
	You stop crying!	Stop crying!
	You shut up!	Shut up!
	You never darken my doorstep again!	Never darken my doorstep again!
	You leave!	Leave!
	John, you get out!	John, get out!

Notice that you never give an order like *John and Mary, they get out!* In the sentences under B, "you" is understood. A command is always addressed to a "second person" (or to "second persons"), who is then the subject of the verb phrase of that command. The pronoun in English which corresponds to the "second person singular or plural" is *you*. Since the sentences under A in group 33 are synonymous with those under B, both sets must be derived from the same deep structures. The sentences under B, without the subject *you*, result from a transformational rule applied to the sentences under A.

We can state this rule as T_{Imp}:

$$T_{Imp}: \qquad SD: \qquad you - V_{imperative}$$

$$SC: \qquad \overset{(delete)}{\phi} - V_{imperative}$$

The $\emptyset$ means "zero" or "delete." That is, if there is a deep structure with *you* as the NP subject of an imperative verb, the subject *you* may be deleted.

The transformational rules T_{Prt} and T_{Imp} provide simple illustrations of what transformational rules do. These particular rules derive two different synonymous surface structures from a single deep structure. Other transformational rules change two different deep structures into a single surface structure that will then be ambiguous, with each meaning corresponding to one of the deep structure sources. We have not given a specific illustration of such a transformation, but we noted that the ambiguity of sentence 23 must be accounted for in this way. In all cases these transformational rules constitute part of what we know when we know a language.

A TRANSFORMATIONAL-GENERATIVE GRAMMAR

We are now able to describe in general terms the grammar of any language. Such a grammar exists in the head of any speaker of any language. It represents what a speaker knows about his language—his linguistic competence. From what has been discussed so far we can therefore list some of the properties of grammars:

1. All grammars have semantic rules which characterize the meanings of sentences in the language.
2. All grammars have phonological rules which specify the sound patterns of the language and how sentences are pronounced.
3. All grammars have a system of syntax which mediates between meaning and sound, and which contains phrase-structure rules, lexical-insertion rules, and transformational rules.
4. All grammars have a lexicon which contains the "vocabulary" (words and morphemes) of the language. Each lexical item is specified by its phonological, syntactic and semantic properties.

A generative grammar is not a "production" model. It does not indicate that speakers produce utterances by first "thinking" S, then "thinking" NP VP, . . . then "inserting" the lexical items, then "transforming" the deep structure into a surface structure, then applying phonological rules, and so on. Indeed, we are quite certain that speakers do not produce sentences in this way. The generative grammar is meant to represent the knowledge that speakers bring to bear in the production and comprehension of sentences, rather than the way they actually do this. This knowledge is intricate and complex and to a great extent can be described by a generative grammar.

SUMMARY

Speakers of a language recognize the grammatical sentences of their language, know how the morphemes in a grammatical sentence must be arranged, and can detect ambiguities. All this knowledge, and much more, is accounted for in the grammar by **syntactic rules.**

Phrase-structure rules are one kind of syntactic rule. They reflect the knowledge that all sentences are made up of various parts (**constituents**) such as noun phrases, verb phrases, nouns, adjectives, verbs, and so on. The rules also show the hierarchical relations between the constituents of a sentence. These relationships are expressed explicitly in the **phrase-structure tree (phrase marker).**

Lexical-insertion rules are responsible for placing lexical items in phrase structure trees. These rules select from the **lexicon** a word or morpheme of the appropriate syntactic category and appropriate meaning and "insert" it under a terminal node of the tree.

We showed that just a few simple phrase-structure rules, in conjunction with the lexicon, can account for the production of huge numbers of sentences. We also showed that by using a special kind of phrase-structure rule called a **recursive rule**, the grammar would account for the fact that our linguistic competence permits us to produce sentences of indefinitely great length. That is, there is no longest sentence in any language. Thus the very important fact that speakers can understand and produce totally new sentences, possibly of great length, is explained.

Phrase-structure rules are not sufficient to account for *all* the syntactic knowledge speakers have. Transformational rules are needed to account for sentences that are stylistic variants of each other, such as sentences a and b:

  a. We called up Pizza Granny.
  b. We called Pizza Granny up.

They are also needed to account for the ambiguity of sentences such as sentence c (as well as the lack of ambiguity in similar sentences such as sentence d):

  c. Richard loves power more than Pat.
  d. Richard loves power more than wealth.

And they are needed to account for how speakers understand sentences with missing elements, such as sentence e:

  e. Dad's going to the football game and Gramps is too.

For these reasons, among many others, we hypothesize that abstract **deep structures** of sentences are **generated** by the phrase-structure rules. These are **acted on by transformational rules** to give **surface structures,** which are what speakers actually utter.

With such a **transformational-generative grammar,** we account for the knowledge that speakers have about the syntactic structures of their language.

EXERCISES

1. Consider the following sentences:

  1. I hate war.
  2. You know that I hate war.
  3. He knows that you know that I hate war.

  a. Write another sentence which includes sentence 3.
  b. What does this ability you have demonstrated reveal about the nature of language?
  c. How is this characteristic of human language related to the difference between linguistic competence and performance?

2. In all languages, sentences can occur within sentences. For example, in Exercise 1, sentence 2 contains sentence 1 and sentence 3 contains sentence 2; or sentence 1 is *embedded* in sentence 2 and

sentence 2 is embedded in sentence 3. Sometimes embedded sentences appear slightly changed from their "normal" form, but you should be able to recognize and write down the embedded sentences in the sentences below:

1. Becky said that Jake would play the piano.
2. Yesterday I noticed my accountant repairing the toilet and my plumber computing my taxes.
3. I deplore the fact that bats have wings.
4. That Guinevere smells bad is known to all my friends.
5. Who promised the teacher that Max wouldn't be absent?
6. It's ridiculous that he washes his own face.
7. The girls pleaded for Charlie to leave them alone.
8. The person who spilled this soft drink on my new mink coat is banished to Los Angeles.
9. The idea of Romeo beating his wife is disconcerting.
10. I gave my hat to the nurse who was helping me with the bedpan.
11. For your wife to spend all your royalty payments is a shame.
12. Give this water pipe to the girl whom Ralph Mintz is growling at.
13. khăw chŷa   wâa khruu   maa.
    he   believe   teacher come
    He believes the teacher is coming.
14. Je me demande quand il   partira.
    I me ask   when he will leave
    I wonder when he'll leave.

3. Using the "mini-grammar" on page 155, construct phrase-structure trees for the following sentences:

1. A boy kissed a girl.
2. The little unicorn kisses the girl.
3. John hit a little boy.

4. a. Show that the "mini-grammar" used in Exercise 3 cannot produce the surface structure of the sentence *Kiss the unicorn!*
   b. Add to this grammar the imperative transformation (T Imp). Construct the *deep* structure tree for *Kiss the unicorn!*

5. a. Modify the mini-grammar used in Exercises 3 and 4 to generate the sentences below. You may change or add phrase-structure rules, add to the lexicon, and introduce transformational rules.

1. The wolf ate up Little Red Riding Hood.
2. The unicorn ate up the little girl.
3. The wolf ate Little Red Riding Hood up.
4. The unicorn ate the little girl up.

   b. Give deep-structure phrase markers for sentences 1 and 3.
   c. Give surface-structure phrase markers for sentences 2 and 4.

6. Paraphrase each of the following sentences in two different ways to show that you understand the ambiguity involved.

    1. Smoking grass can be nauseating.
    2. Dick finally decided on the boat.
    3. The professor's appointment was shocking.
    4. Old men and women are hard to live with.
    5. I saw the boy studying in the library.

7. Consider the following two sentences:

    1. John is eager to please.
    2. John is easy to please.

  a. In terms of the notion "grammatical relationship," explain the difference in meaning between sentences 1 and 2.
  b. Now consider sentence 3:

    3. The chickens are ready to eat.

This sentence is ambiguous. Show that one of its paraphrases is analogous to sentence 1 and the other to sentence 2.

8. Consider the "active" sentences in group 1 and the corresponding "passive" sentences in group 2:

    1. John kissed Mary.
       John found Mary.
       John loves Mary.
    2. Mary was kissed by John.
       Mary was found by John.
       Mary is loved by John.

  a. Who is the "doer" of the action in group 1? Who is the "recipient" of that action?
  b. Who is the "doer" of the action in group 2? Who is the "recipient"?
  c. Are the grammatical relations the same in groups 1 and 2?
  d. What do the answers to Questions a, b, and c of this exercise suggest to you about an active sentence and its corresponding passive in terms of a transformational grammar?

9. Here is a sentence in Malagasy that typifies a basic sentence pattern in the language.

    manasa ny zaza ny vehivavy.
    washes the child the woman
    The woman washes the child.

Give the equivalent of phrase-structure rules 1 and 2 for Malagasy.

10. Consider the following sentences from Thai (the diacritics are tone marks):

    1. dèg   maa.   The boy comes.
       boy   come

2. dèg   hĕn   mŭu.   The boy sees the pig.
   boy   see   pig
3. mǎa   maa.   The dog comes.
   dog   come
4. mǎa   hĕn   mŭu.   The dog sees the pig.
   dog   see   pig
5. mŭu   maa.   The pig comes.
6. dèg   chɔ̂ɔb mǎa.   The boy likes the dog.
   boy   like   dog
7. mǎa   chɔ̂ɔb dèg.   The dog likes the boy.
8. *maa   dèg.
9. *dèg   mŭu   hĕn.
10. *chɔ̂ɔb mǎa   dèg.

a. Write a grammar to generate these sentences using phrase-structure rules and a lexicon.
b. List three other sentences that your grammar generates. Be sure
   that your grammar doesn't generate any ungrammatical strings.
Add the following sentences to those listed above:

11. dèg   khon   níi   maa.
    boy   classifier this come
    This boy comes.
12. dèg   khon   níi   hĕn   mŭu tua   nán.
    boy   classifier this see   pig classifier that
    This boy sees that pig.
13. mǎa   tua   nán maa.
    dog   classifier that come
    That dog comes.
14. mǎa   tua   níi   hĕn   mǎa tua   nán.
    dog   classifier this see   dog classifier that
    This dog sees that dog.
15. dèg   khon   nán chɔ̂ɔb mŭu tua   níi.
    boy   classifier that like   pig classifier this
    That boy likes this pig.
16. *khon níi dèg maa.
17. *mǎa níi tua hĕn mŭu tua nán.
18. *dèg níi maa.

c. Extend your grammar to generate sentences 11–15. (*Classifier* is
   a syntactic category in Thai. Don't worry about what it means —
   just make sure your grammar generates it in the right place. You
   will notice that certain classifiers go with certain nouns. The
   lexical-insertion rules — which needn't concern you — will take care
   of this.)
d. List three other sentences that your new grammar generates,
   being sure that the classifier *tua* goes with the animals, and
   khon with the humans.
Add the following sentences to sentences 1–18:

19. dèg maa khon   níi.
    boy come classifier this
    This boy comes.
20. mǎa maa tua   nán.
    dog come classifier that
    That dog comes.

e. As you can see, sentences 11 and 19 and 13 and 20 are syntactic variants of each other. Extend your phrase-structure grammar into a transformational grammar by adding a transformation to account for sentences 19 and 20. Write out in words what the transformation does, specifying the structural description (SD) and the structural change (SC). Then give your transformation in formal notation.

References

BACH, E. *An Introduction to Transformational Grammar.* New York: Holt, Rinehart & Winston, 1964.

BOLINGER, D. *Aspects of Language.* New York: Harcourt, Brace & World, 1968.

CHAFE, W. *Meaning and the Structure of Language.* Chicago: University of Chicago Press, 1970.

CHOMSKY, NOAM. *Language and Mind.* New York: Harcourt, Brace & World, 1968.

CHOMSKY, NOAM. *Syntactic Structures.* The Hague: Mouton, 1957.

FODOR, J., and KATZ, JERROLD. eds. *The Structure of Language: Readings in the Philosophy of Language.* Englewood Cliffs, N.J.: Prentice-Hall, 1964.

GRINDER, J., and ELGIN, SUZETTE. *Guide to Transformational Grammar.* New York: Holt, Rinehart & Winston, 1973.

HERNDON, JEANNE. *A Survey of Modern Grammars.* New York: Holt, Rinehart & Winston, 1970.

JACOBS, R., and ROSENBAUM, PETER. *English Transformational Grammar.* Lexington, Mass.: Xerox College Publishing, 1968.

LANGACKER, R. *Language and Its Structure.* New York: Harcourt, Brace & World, 1968.

LEES, R. "Review of Syntactic Structures." *Language* 33:375–407 (1957). Also available in Bobbs-Merrill reprint series.

LESTER, M. *Introductory Transformational Grammar of English.* New York: Holt, Rinehart & Winston, 1971.

LYONS, J. *Introduction to Theoretical Linguistics.* Cambridge, England: Cambridge University Press, 1969.

POSTAL, P. *Constituent Structure: A Study of Contemporary Models of Syntactic Description.* The Hague: Mouton, 1964.

REIBEL, D., and SCHANE, SANFORD. eds. *Modern Studies in English.* Englewood Cliffs, N.J.: Prentice-Hall, 1969.

WARDHAUGH, R. *Introduction to Linguistics.* New York: McGraw-Hill, 1972.

7
Animal "Languages"

No matter how eloquently a dog may bark, he cannot tell you that his parents were poor but honest.

— BERTRAND RUSSELL

The articulated signs of human language are not like the expression of emotions of children or animals. Animal noises cannot be combined to form syllables.

— ARISTOTLE

If animals could talk, what wonderful stories they would tell. The eagle already knew the earth was round when men were still afraid of falling off its edge. The whale could have warned Columbus about a barrier between Europe and India and saved that explorer a lot of anxiety. Justice would be more properly served if animals could give testimony. There would be a reduction in crime, no doubt, and quite possibly an increase in the divorce rate. All of us would have to alter our behavior in some way or another, for our environment would be considerably changed.

The idea of talking animals is as old and as widespread among human societies as language itself. No culture lacks a legend in which some animal plays a speaking role. All over West Africa, children listen to folk tales in which a "spider-man" is the hero. "Coyote" is a favorite figure in many American Indian tales. And there is hardly an animal who does not figure in Aesop's famous fables. Many authors have exploited the idea successfully, among them Hugh Lofting, the creator of the famous Doctor Dolittle. The good doctor's forte was animal communication, and he is no doubt fiction's most prodigious language learner. Still, Doctor Dolittle and his adventures are fantasies for children, and the idea of communicating with our fellow animal tenants of this globe as we communicate with our fellow human tenants is absurd. Or is it?

Whether language is the exclusive property of the human species is an interesting question. The answer depends on what properties of hu-

173

man language are considered. If language is viewed only as a system of communication, then obviously many species communicate. Humans also use systems other than their language to relate to each other and to send "messages." To understand human language one needs to see what, if anything, is special and unique to language. If we find that there are no such special properties, then we will have to conclude that language, as we have been discussing it, is not, as claimed, uniquely human.

We have already mentioned a number of linguistic universals. All normal humans who acquire language utilize speech *sounds* to express meanings. Are such sounds a necessary aspect of language? Obviously not. Children that are born deaf cannot learn to speak vocally without very special training. These unfortunate children are nonetheless able to learn language. Many learn the sign language **Deaf Sign** (or **Sign**). Sign utilizes the hands and fingers as the "organs of articulation." For some words, for example proper names, a finger spelling system is used; there is a different gesture representing each letter of the alphabet. But many other words, in fact most words, have a special symbol which stands for their meaning. Users of Sign are in no way linguistically deprived. Poetry of high quality has been "written" in Sign, and plays are acted out in Sign. Certain individuals, cured of their deafness as adults and able to use language vocally, nevertheless prefer Sign, since this is their "native language."

Just as speech sounds have "distinctive features," which we discussed in the chapters on phonetics and phonology, so Sign also utilizes a set of distinctive properties. Speech sounds may be distinguished by their "place of articulation" — that is, a *p*, articulated at the lips, is distinguished from a *t*, which is produced by the tongue tip, and from a *k*, which is produced by the back of the tongue raised to the palate. Analogously, signs are also differentiated by "place of articulation" — the particular part of the body where the gesture is placed. Sign also distinguishes meanings by the particular configuration of the fingers, and by the direction of the movement of the "articulators." The sentences produced in sign are also "rule-governed" by the particular syntactic system of the language. And of course Sign has a semantic system as part of its grammar. Sign is undoubtedly a system comparable to human spoken language. It is human language. But Sign is not vocal. Therefore, the use of speech sounds is not a key property of human language.

If this is so, then the squeaking of dolphins, the dancing of bees, and the manipulation of plastic chips by chimpanzees may represent systems similar to human language. That is, if we decide that animal communication systems are *not* languages similar to human languages, it will not be because they fail to have speech sounds.

Conversely, if animals vocally imitate human utterances, this does not mean they possess language. We have already seen that language is a system by which sounds and meanings (or gestures and meanings) are related. "Talking" birds such as parrots and mynah birds are capable of flawlessly enunciating words and phrases of human language. The birds imitate what they have heard. But when a parrot says "Polly wants a cracker" she may really want a ham sandwich or a drink of water or nothing at all. A bird that has learned to say "hello" or "goodbye" is as likely to use one as the other, regardless of whether people are arriving or departing. The bird's "utterances" carry no meaning. They are neither speaking English nor their own language when they sound like us.

A mynah bird trained by the animal ethologist W. Thorpe "spoke" excellent English. Then a new laboratory assistant was hired who spoke English with a Hungarian accent. When the bird began to repeat his phrases, she sounded as though she were practicing for a part in a Hollywood Dracula movie. This illustrates the imitative nature of the bird's utterances. The parrot or mynah bird is not "dissecting" the sounds into discrete units. *Polly* and *Molly* do not "rhyme" for a parrot. They are as different as *hello* and *goodbye* (or as similar). One property of all human languages is the "discreteness" of the units which are ordered and reordered, combined and split apart. A parrot says what it is taught, or what it hears, and no more. If Polly learns "Polly wants a cracker" and "Polly wants a doughnut" and also learns to imitate the single words *whiskey* and *bagel,* she will not produce "spontaneously," as children do, "Polly wants whiskey" or "Polly wants a bagel." If she learns *cat* and *cats* and *dog* and *dogs* and then learns *bird* and *parrot,* she will be unable to "form the plural" by adding a [z] to *bird* to form *birds* (as in *dogs*) and an [s] to *parrot* to form *parrots* (as in *cats*).

A parrot does not "take speech to pieces," nor can she form an unlimited set of utterances from a finite set of units. All humans can. We have already discussed this "creative" aspect of language use.

Thus, the ability to produce sounds similar to those used in human language cannot be equated with the ability to learn a human language.

In the seventeenth century, the philosopher and mathematician René Descartes pointed out what we have been discussing here: that the ability to use language is not based on the physiological abilities to produce speech or speech-like sounds. He concluded:

> It is not the want of organs that [prevents animals from making] . . . known their thoughts . . . for it is evident that magpies and parrots are able to utter words just like ourselves, and yet they cannot speak as we do, that is, so as to give evidence that they think of what they say. On the other hand, men who, being born deaf and dumb, are in the same degree, or even more than the brutes, destitute of the organs which serve the others for talking, are in the habit of themselves inventing certain signs by which they make themselves understood.[1]

---

[1] René Descartes, "Discourse on Method," part v, *The Philosophical Works of Descartes,* trans. by E. S. Haldane and G. R. T. Ross, Vol. I, 116.

We shall examine various animal communication systems to see whether other creatures share with man the ability to learn and use languages creatively.

THE BIRDS AND THE BEES

The birds and animals are all friendly to each other, and there are no disputes about anything. They all talk, and they all talk to me, but it must be a foreign language, for I cannot make out a word they say.

— MARK TWAIN, *Eve's Diary*

Most animals possess some kind of "signaling" communication system. Among the spiders there is a complex system for courtship. The male spider, before he approaches his lady love, goes through elaborate gestures to inform her that he is indeed a spider and not a crumb or a fly to be eaten. These gestures are invariant. One never finds a "creative" spider changing or adding to the particular courtship ritual of his species.

A similar kind of "gesture" language is found among the fiddler crabs. There are forty different varieties, and each species uses its own particular "claw-waving" movement to signal to another member of its "clan." The timing, movement, and posture of the body never change from one time to another or from one crab to another within the particular species. Whatever the signal means, it is fixed. Only one meaning can be conveyed. There is not an "infinite set" of fiddler crab sentences. Nor can the signal be "broken down" into smaller elements, as is possible in any utterance of human language.

The "language" of the honeybees is far more complex than that of the spiders or fiddler crabs. When a forager bee returns to the hive, if it has located a source of food it does a dance which communicates certain information about that source to other members of the colony.

The dancing behavior may assume one of three possible patterns: *round, sickle,* and *tail-wagging*.[2] The determining factor in the choice of dance pattern is the distance of the food source from the hive. The round dance indicates locations near the hive, within twenty feet or so. The sickle dance indicates locations at an intermediate distance from the hive, approximately twenty to sixty feet. The tail-wagging dance is for distances that exceed sixty feet or so.

In all the dances the bee alights on a wall of the hive and literally dances on its feet through the appropriate pattern. For the round dance, the bee

---

[2] A species of Italian honeybee is described here. Details differ from species to species. We might say that different species have different "dialects" of honeybee "language."

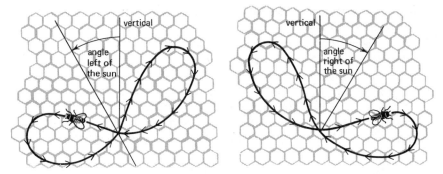

Figure 7.1 The sickle dance.   In this case the food source is 20–60 feet from the hive.

describes a circle.   The only other semantic information imparted by the round dance, besides approximate distance, is the quality of the food source.   This is indicated by the number of repetitions of the basic pattern that the bee executes, and the vivacity with which it performs the dance.   This feature is true of all three patterns.

To perform the sickle dance the bee traces out a sickle-shaped figure-eight on the wall.   The angle made by the direction of the open end of the sickle with the vertical is the same angle as the food source is from the sun.   Thus the sickle dance imparts the information: approximate distance, direction, and quality (see Figure 7.1).

The tail-wagging dance imparts all the information of the sickle dance with one important addition.   The number of repetitions per minute of the basic pattern of the dance indicates the precise distance: the slower the repetition rate, the longer the distance (see Figure 7.2).

The bees' dance is an effective system of communication, capable, in

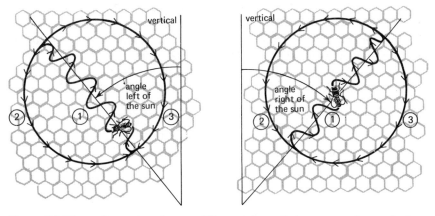

Figure 7.2 The tail-wagging dance.   The number of times per minute the bee dances a complete pattern (1–2–1–3) indicates the distance of the food source.

principle, of infinitely many different messages, and in this sense the bees' dance is infinitely variable, like human language. But unlike human language, the communication system of the bees is confined to a single subject, or thought. It is frozen and inflexible. For example, an experimenter forced a bee to walk to the food source. When the bee returned to the hive, it indicated a distance twenty-five times farther away than it actually was. The bee had no way of communicating the special circumstances or taking them into account in its message. This absence of *creativity* makes the bees' dance qualitatively different from human language.

The bees' dance does give us a chance to illustrate another very interesting property that every natural language of the world possesses, as already discussed in Chapter 1. We called this property the **arbitrariness of the linguistic sign**. In every system of communication that has a semantic system, each basic unit has two aspects, the **form** and the **meaning**. In the case of human language, the morpheme is usually this basic unit. Its form is the actual string of sounds that make up its pronunciation. Its meaning, or linguistic meaning, is of course determined by whatever language it belongs to. The sound and the meaning are like the head and tail of the same coin — distinct but inseparable. An example taken from the English language is the word *tree*. The linguistic sign is the string of sounds [t], [r], [i]; the linguistic meaning is the concept "tree." The same concept or meaning is expressed by different sounds in other languages. To take an example that does not involve language, consider a red traffic signal. The sign is the physical object, a red light. The meaning is "stop — danger."

When we say that the linguistic sign is arbitrary, we mean that there is no connection between the linguistic form and its corresponding linguistic meaning. There is no connection between the sounds of the word *tree* and the concept "tree." Likewise there is no connection between a red light and the notion "stop — danger." The relationship in this case is a cultural matter that developed by pure chance. In all human languages the relationship between the sounds and meanings of the overwhelming majority of words or morphemes is an arbitrary one.

What about the bees' dance? What are the forms of the sign, and to what meanings do they correspond? Are the relationships arbitrary or nonarbitrary? Consider the tail-wagging dance. One linguistic sign is the vivacity of the dance, with a corresponding meaning "quality of food source." The relationship is clearly arbitrary, for there is nothing inherent about vivaciousness that indicates good or bad quality. In fact, we have been careful not to say whether more vivacity indicates a greater or lesser quality source of food. Because the relationship is arbitrary, there is no a-priori way of telling.

What about distance? The question here is more complicated. Remember that the slower the repetition rate, the greater the distance.

On the surface this relationship may seem arbitrary, but let's use a little physics to reword the relationship: The longer it takes to complete the basic pattern, the longer it will take a bee to fly to the source. Thus we see that this sign is in some sense nonarbitrary. Similarly, the direction-determining aspect of the dance is perfectly nonarbitrary.

It should be remembered, however, that there are many communication systems, other than language, which contain signs that are arbitrarily related to the meanings they stand for. "Arbitrariness" is not enough to make a system a language in the sense of human language.

We have talked about the "language" systems of the spiders, the crabs, and the bees. What about the birds? It is known that the songs of certain species of birds have definite meanings. One song may mean "let's build a nest together," another song may mean "go get some worms for the babies," and so on. But the bird cannot make up a new song to cope with a new situation, nor can it vary an old song to reflect some nuance of meaning.

Two French scientists have studied the songs of the European robin.[3] They found that the songs are very complicated indeed. But, interestingly, the complications have little effect on the "message" which is being conveyed. The song which was studied was that which signaled the robin's possession of a certain territory. The scientists found that the rival robins paid attention only to the alternation between high-pitched and low-pitched notes, and which came first didn't matter at all. The message varies only to the extent of expressing how strongly the robin feels about his possession and how much he is prepared to defend it and start a family in that territory. The different alternations therefore express "intensity" and nothing more. The robin is creative in his ability to sing the same thing in many different ways, but not creative in his ability to use the same "units" of the system to express many different "utterances" all of which have different meanings.

Bird songs, then, seem to be no more similar to human language than are the movements of the spider, the claw waving of the crab, or the dancing of the bees. All these systems are "fixed" in terms of the messages which can be conveyed. They lack the creative element of human language.

A study of higher animals also reveals no "language" systems that are creative in the way human language is. Wolves use many facial expressions, movements of their tails, and growls to express different degrees of threats, anxiety, depression, and submission. But that's all they can do. And the sounds and gestures produced by nonhuman primates, the monkeys and apes, show that their signals are highly stereotyped and

[3] R. G. Busnel and J. C. Bremond, "Recherche du support de l'information dans le signal acoustique de défense territoriale du Rougegorge," *C. R. Acad. Sci. Paris* 254, 2236–2238 (1962).

limited in terms of the messages which they convey. Most importantly, studies of such animal communication systems reveal that the basic "vocabularies" produced by either sounds or facial expressions occur primarily as emotional responses to particular situations. They have no way of expressing the anger they felt "yesterday."

Descartes pointed out more than three hundred years ago that the communication systems of animals are qualitatively different from the language used by men!

> it is a very remarkable fact that there are none so depraved and stupid, without even excepting idiots, that they cannot arrange different words together, forming of them a statement by which they make known their thoughts; while, on the other hand, there is no other animal, however perfect and fortunately circumstanced it may be, which can do the same.[4]

Descartes goes on to state that one of the major differences between man and animal is that man's use of language is not just a response to external, or even internal, emotional stimuli, as are the grunts and gestures of animals. He warns against confusing human use of language with "natural movements which betray passions and may be . . . manifested by animals."

All the studies of animal communication systems provide evidence for Descartes' distinction between the fixed stimulus-bound messages of animals and the linguistic creative ability possessed by the human animal.

DOLPHINS

I kind of like the playful porpoise
A healthy mind in a healthy corpus
He and his cousin, the playful dolphin,
Why they like swimmin like I like golphin.

— OGDEN NASH, "The Porpoise"[5]

Researchers are still trying to prove Descartes wrong. For a while the dolphin, the "monkey of the sea," appeared to be a good candidate for refuting the claim that language is unique to man. The dolphin has a brain comparable in size to the human brain. Its surface, the cerebral cortex, is

---

[4] René Descartes, op. cit.
[5] "The Porpoise," copyright 1942 by Ogden Nash. From *Verses from 1929 On* by Ogden Nash, by permission of Little, Brown and Co. Also by permission of The Estate of Ogden Nash and J. M. Dent and Sons.

very wrinkled, like the surface of the human brain. However, the wrinkling is due to the thinness of the cerebral cortex; the dolphin's brain is even less complex than that of a rabbit, having fewer nerve cells.

But the dolphin does indeed use sounds to communicate. Dolphins produce clicking sounds. However, these are not produced to communicate with other dolphins. They are radar detection sounds; that is, dolphins produce them to help locate position and objects which may get in their way, just as bats do. Dolphins also produce squawky sounds and whistles. The analysis of these "sound units" shows that like other animals' signals, they are closely related to emotional situations. Thus a falling-pitch whistle represents the dolphin's call of distress, and also at times the mating call of the male.

A number of experiments have been conducted with dolphins. Jarvis Bastian developed an elaborate experiment to see if dolphins would communicate messages to each other.[6] A male and a female dolphin were kept in a special tank. The female was shown either a continuous light or a flashing light. The male could see neither the lights nor the female. The task was as follows: If the continuous light was shown, the female had to press a right-hand paddle and "inform" the male by her calls to press his right-hand paddle too. If a flashing light appeared, the female had to press the left-hand paddle and again call out to the male to press his left-hand paddle. Only if both responded correctly would they be rewarded with fish. Remember that the male could not see either the light or the female. His response had to result solely from the signals he received from the female. It first appeared that the dolphins were indeed signaling each other. But later it became clear that they had learned their tasks as "conditioned responses," and had behaved more like Pavlov's dogs than communicating humans.

The great Russian physiologist Pavlov trained dogs to salivate when they heard a bell by giving them food whenever a bell rang, repeating this action over a long period of time. They became "conditioned" to salivate whenever they heard bells ringing, whether or not food followed the bells. Similarly, the female dolphin kept on pushing her paddles and producing her calls even when the male could see the lights for himself, and in fact even when the male was taken out of the tank. Her calls therefore had little to do with her desire to communicate with the male. She performed because she had been conditioned into believing the paddle-pressing and signal-giving would reward *her* with fish. She didn't really seem to care whether the male was fed or not. The male was no smarter. He had become conditioned to associate a certain paddle with a certain call, having learned that that would fill his stomach.

---

[6] See Claire Russell and W. M. S. Russell, "Language and Animal Signals" in *Linguistics at Large,* Noel Muhnis, ed. (New York: Viking Press, 1971), 159–194.

Such studies of animal communication systems provide evidence for Descartes' distinction between the fixed stimulus-bound messages of animals, and the creative linguistic ability possessed by the human animal.

CLEVER HANS

The two Creatures stood silent while I spoke, seeming to listen with great attention; and when I had ended, they neighed frequently towards each other, as if they were engaged in serious Conversation.

—JONATHAN SWIFT, *Gulliver's Travels*

At the beginning of this century a famous horse named Hans appeared to disprove the ideas of the uniqueness of human language. Hans's fame spread from Berlin, where he lived, throughout the world. According to his owner and trainer, Herr von Osten, Hans was able to understand what was said to him and to respond appropriately by tapping his foot. He tapped out answers to arithmetic problems—four hoofbeats when asked to add 2 and 2, and so on. He would answer 4/16 as the sum of 1/8 and 2/16 by first tapping the 4, and then the 16. When he was "taught" a code, relating a certain number of hoofbeats for each letter of the alphabet, he spelled out answers to nonarithmetical questions. It is no wonder that "Clever Hans" became a famous "personality." Committees of learned scholars were appointed to investigate his miraculous behavior. The first committee concluded, after testing Hans with von Osten out of the room, that Hans indeed "understood" language. A second commission, however, found to the disappointment of von Osten, and Hans's many believers, that Hans was responding to visual cues, which were used by the questioners unconsciously. One member of the investigating committee, O. Pfungst, discovered that Hans could only provide answers to questions when the answers were known by the interrogator. That is, the questioner would unconsciously make some kind of movement when the correct number of hoofbeats had been tapped out, and this movement was a signal to Hans to stop. When this was realized and the movement was deliberately made at the wrong time, Hans would give wrong answers. He understood neither the questions nor the answers. He, like the dolphins, was trained to give conditioned responses. Hans was indeed clever, but not clever enough to learn human language.[7]

---

[7] O. Pfungst, *Clever Hans, The Horse of Mr. Von Osten* (New York: Holt, 1911).

GUA, VIKI, WASHOE, SARAH

Children, behold the Chimpanzee:
He sits on the ancestral tree
From which we sprang in ages gone.
I'm glad we sprang: had we held on,
We might, for aught that I can say,
Be horrid Chimpanzees to-day.

—OLIVER HERFORD, "A Child's Primer of Natural History"

The more animal communication systems we examine, the more sure we become that language is a human characteristic. Animal systems seem to be either a nonproductive limited set of fixed messages, or emotionally conditioned cries.

The attempt to teach animals to communicate failed in the case of the Dolphins and in the case of Hans. There are other cases which have proved to be somewhat more successful. In the 1930s Winthrop and Luella Kellogg raised their infant son together with an infant chimpanzee named Gua.[8] Gua understood about a hundred words at sixteen months, more words than their son at that age. But she never went beyond that. And as we have already seen, comprehension of language involves much more than understanding the meanings of isolated words. When their son could understand the difference between *I say what I mean* and *I mean what I say*, Gua could not understand what either sentence meant.

A chimpanzee named Viki was raised by Keith and Cathy Hayes, and she too learned a number of individual words.[9] She even learned to "articulate" with great difficulty the words *mama, papa,* and *cup.* But that was the extent of her perception and production of language.

Allen and Beatrice Gardner recognized that one disadvantage suffered by the primates is the absence of a sufficiently complex system of articulatory organs necessary for producing aural contrasts. They therefore decided to teach sign language to a very clever chimp named Washoe.[10] By the age of three, Washoe understood and produced about thirty-four signs, which represented such meanings as "more," "eat," "listen," "gimme," "please," "key," "you," and "me." This is very good for a chimp; but a child of three is already putting words together according to the syntactic rules of the language to produce an unlimited set of sen-

---

[8] W. N. Kellogg and Luella A. Kellogg, *The Ape and the Child* (New York: McGraw-Hill, 1933).

[9] Catherine Hayes, *The Ape in Our House* (New York: Harper, 1951).

[10] R. A. Gardner and B. T. Gardner, "Teaching Sign Language to a Chimpanzee," *Science* 165 (Aug. 1969).

tences. This Washoe cannot do. Her use of language is limited to the fixed number of words in her vocabulary, and few new words are being added, if any. She is, however, capable of combining two signs together. In these "complex sentences" such as "gimme key" and "key gimme" there is no fixed word order. Neither sentence is "ungrammatical" to her. She has no way of distinguishing between *John hit Mary* and *Mary hit John*. Washoe has learned a great deal, but what she has learned is not equivalent to the complex grammars learned by children.

A more remarkable chimp, named Sarah, is now being taught a language very similar to English by David Premack, a psychologist at the University of California, Santa Barbara.[11] The units of Sarah's "language" consist of differently shaped and colored plastic symbols which are metal-backed. Sarah and her trainers "talk" to each other by arranging these symbols on a magnetic board. Sarah has been taught to associate particular symbols with particular meanings. These symbols are the "words" or "morphemes" of Sarah's language. Thus a small red square means "banana" and a small blue rectangle means "apricot." Some of these symbols are shown in Figure 7.3. These and others reveal that Sarah has words for nouns, adjectives, and verbs. She even has symbols for abstract concepts like "same as" and "different from," "negation," and even a symbol to represent "question."

The forms of these symbols are *arbitrarily* related to their meanings. For example, the color red is represented by a gray chip, and the color yellow by a black chip. Sarah has learned the concepts "name of" and "color of." Premack is able to ask Sarah for "the color of name of blue" (that is, the color of the plastic chip that means "blue"). Sarah selects the gray plastic chip which means "red," since red is the color of the chip that means "blue." We can see that Sarah is even capable of using language as a metalanguage to describe her language. If you're confused, remember that a "dumb" chimpanzee named Sarah has no difficulty with this task.

Indeed, such "conversations" occasionally bore Sarah. During a particularly tedious drill one time, Sarah reached out and stole all the plastic tokens. Then, as if to suggest "let's get the whole thing over with," she wrote out all the questions she was being asked as well as the corresponding answers. This was very clever, showing that Sarah knew the questions and the answers. But she did not (and probably could not) write out "no questions" even though she had a "word" for "no" and one for "question." She is able to form new sentences, but only in the exact form of those she has been carefully taught.

Yet, Sarah seems to have mastered some rules of syntax. And like children, no one specifically teaches her these rules. She must generalize from the data. For example, given the sentence *If Sarah put red on green,*

[11] Ann James Premack and David Premack, "Teaching Language to an Ape," *Scientific American* (Oct. 1972).

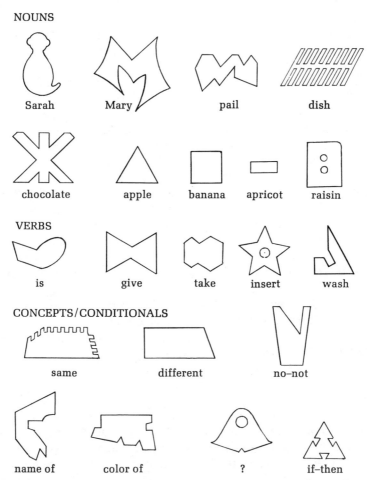

Figure 7.3 Plastic symbols that varied in color, shape, and size were chosen as the language units to be taught to Sarah. The plastic pieces were backed with metal so they would adhere to a magnetic board. Each plastic symbol stood for a specific word or concept. A "Chinese" convention of writing sentences vertically from top to bottom was adopted because at the beginning of her training Sarah seemed to prefer it. Sarah had to put the words in proper sequence, but the orientation of the word symbols was not important. Actually, most of these symbols were colored. (Adapted from "Teaching Language to an Ape" by Ann James Premack and David Premack, *Scientific American,* Oct. 1972. Copyright © 1972 by Scientific American, Inc. All rights reserved)

Mary give Sarah chocolate, Sarah will dutifully place a red card on top of a green card and collect her reward. The sentence *If Sarah put green on red, Mary give Sarah chocolate* also evokes the correct response. Sarah is quite obviously sensitive to word order—that is, the "syntax" of the sentences.

Sarah is also able to understand some complex sentence structures. She was taught to respond correctly to sentences such as *Sarah insert apple pail* (that is, "Sarah, insert the apple in the pail"), *Sarah insert banana pail, Sarah insert apple dish,* and *Sarah insert banana dish.* These sentences were then combined into *Sarah insert apple pail Sarah insert banana dish.* Sarah performed both tasks. Then a "transformational rule" was performed on this sentence by the trainer, which deleted the second occurrence of *Sarah insert* (see Chapter 6 on syntax for similar rules in our language). This transformed sentence given Sarah was *Sarah insert apple pail banana dish.* Sarah still performed the complicated instruction, showing that she "understood" the "underlying" compound sentence. She correctly grouped together *apple* with *pail* and *banana* with *dish* rather than incorrectly grouping *pail* with *banana,* and she did not put the apple, pail, and banana in the dish, as the word order would suggest. Thus we see that when Sarah processes a sentence she does more than link words in simple linear order. She imposes a hierarchical structure, just as we do. Sarah's grammar apparently possesses a transformational rule, which associates Figure 7.4 with Figure 7.5.

Does Sarah disprove the notion that only humans can learn language? Sarah's language certainly seems to include many of the properties of human language: arbitrariness of the linguistic sign, "open-endedness" or "creativity," hierarchical structure, transformational rules.

One major difference between the way Sarah has learned her language and the way children learn theirs is that each new rule has been introduced in a deliberate, highly constrained way. When parents speak to children they do not confine themselves to a few words in a particular order for months, rewarding the child with a chocolate bar or a banana each time the child correctly responds to a command. Nor do they wait until the child has "mastered" one rule of grammar before going on to a different structure.

Young children require no special training. Children brought up with little adult "reinforcement" or encouragement will acquire all the complexities of their language. This is demonstrated by children brought up in orphan homes or institutions. Of course, exposure to language is required. Feral children such as those raised by animals do not learn language, as pointed out in Chapter 2. Normal children, while they require exposure to language, are not taught language the way Sarah is being taught.

Furthermore, Sarah does not "initiate" any conversations. Her use of the language being taught her is in response to her trainers' questions. Sarah responds because she is rewarded. The reward may be food, or it may be approval from her trainers. She does not use language the way humans do.

It would be interesting to see what would happen if another chimp were taught Sarah's language. Would they communicate with each other

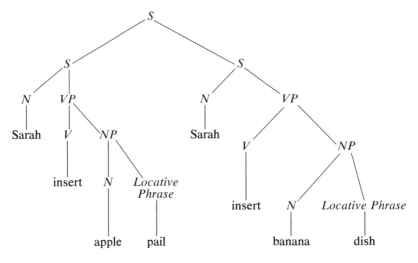

Figure 7.4

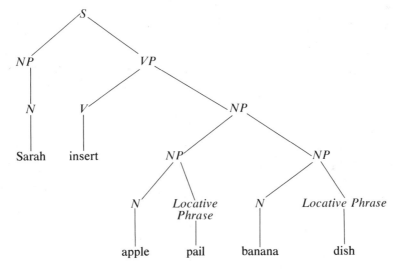

Figure 7.5

using this language? And if they were mated and bore baby chimps, could they teach their babies the new chimp language? If such could happen we would then know the origin of "Chimpanese."

The differences between Sarah's language acquisition and that of normal human children in no way negate the great achievement on Sarah's part and also on the part of Dr. Premack. At this time we do not know how much more Sarah will learn. We do know that a child by the age of four has already learned complex rules and a grammar qualitatively beyond what Sarah has mastered.

When we try to compare Sarah's language with human language we immediately perceive the impossibility of separating linguistic ability from general intelligence. The human animal appears to possess a brain capable of far greater analytic and synthetic abilities than does the chimpanzee, or any other animal. "Stupid" humans are far "smarter" than "smart" chimpanzees. If language is the result of superior brain mechanisms, then the kind of language learned and used by humans remains unique to the species.

SUMMARY

If language is defined merely as a system of communication, then language is not unique to man. There are, however, certain characteristics of human language which are not found in the communication systems of any other species. A basic property of human language is its creative aspect—a speaker's ability to string together **discrete units** to form an **infinite** set of "well-formed" sentences. Furthermore, children need not be taught language in any controlled way; they require only linguistic input to enable them to form their own grammar.

The fact that deaf children learn language shows that the ability to hear or produce sounds is not a necessary prerequisite for language learning. And the ability to "imitate" the sounds of human language is not a sufficient basis for the learning of language, since "talking" birds imitate sounds but can neither segment these sounds into smaller units nor understand what they are imitating.

Birds, bees, crabs, wolves, dolphins, chimpanzees, and most other animals communicate in some way. Limited information is imparted, and emotions such as fear, and warnings, are emitted. But the communication systems are fixed and limited. They are **stimulus-bound.** This is not so of human language. Experiments to teach animals more complicated language systems have historically failed. Recently, however, some chimps have demonstrated an ability to master some subset of a human language. It is possible that the higher primates have the limited ability to be taught *some* complex rules. To date, however, language still seems to be unique to man.

EXERCISES

1. What do the barking of dogs, the meowing of cats, and the singing of birds have in common with human language? What are some of the basic differences?

2. What is meant by the "arbitrary nature of the linguistic sign"? Describe at least one animal system of communication which includes arbitrary signs. Describe any communication system in which all the signs are nonarbitrary. State the reasons for your choices in all cases.

3. Suppose you heard someone say: "My parrot speaks excellent English. He even says such complicated sentences as *I want jam with my cracker*." Give reasons for or against this assertion.

4. A wolf is able to express very subtle gradations of expression by different positions of the ears, the lips, and the tail. There are eleven postures of the tail which express such emotions as self-confidence, confident threat, lack of tension, uncertain threat, depression, defensiveness, active submission, complete submission. This seems to be a complex system. Suppose there were a thousand different emotions which could be expressed in this way. Would you then say a wolf had language similar to a human? If not, why not?

5. Suppose you taught a dog to *heel, sit up, beg, roll over, play dead, stay, jump,* and *bark* on command, using the italicized words as cues. Would you be teaching it language? Why or why not?

6. What are the properties of Sarah's language which make it more like human language than like other animal languages?

References

BRONOWSKI, J., and BELLUGI, URSULA. "Language, Name, and Concept." *Science* 168 (May 1970).

BUSNEL, R. H. G., ed. *Animal Sonar Systems: Biology and Bionics,* Vol. 2. Jouy-en-Josas, France: 1966.

BUSNEL, R. G., and BREMOND, J. C. "Recherche du support de l'information dans le signal acoustique de défense territoriale du Rougegorge." *C. R. Acad. Sci. Paris* 254 (1962).

GARDNER, R. A., and GARDNER, B. T. "Teaching Sign Language to a Chimpanzee." *Science* 165 (Aug. 1969).

HAYES, CATHERINE. *The Ape in Our House.* New York: Harper, 1951.

KROUGH, AUGUST. "The Language of the Bees," in *Scientific American Reader.* New York: Simon and Schuster, 1953.

LILLY, JOHN C. *Man and Dolphin.* New York: Pyramid Publications, 1969.

LILLY, JOHN C. *The Mind of the Dolphin: A Nonhuman Intelligence.* New York: Avon Books, 1969.

PFUNGST, O. *Clever Hans, The Horse of Mr. von Osten.* New York: Holt, 1911.

PREMACK, ANN J., and D. "Teaching Language to an Ape." *Scientific American.* (Oct. 1972), 92–99.

PREMACK, DAVID. "The Education of Sarah: A Chimp Learns the Language." *Psychology Today*, 4 (Sept. 1970).

PREMACK, DAVID. "Language in Chimpanzee?" *Science* 172. 3985 (May 1971).

SEBEOK, T. A., and RAMSAY, ALEXANDRA, eds. *Approaches to Animal Communication.* The Hague: Mouton, 1969.

THORPE, W. H. "Animal Vocalization and Communication," in *Brain Mechanisms Underlying Speech and Language,* C. H. Millikan and F. L. Darley, eds. New York: Grune and Stratton, 1967.

VETTER, HAROLD J. "Sign Language of the Deaf." *Language Behavior and Communication: An Introduction.* Itasca, Ill.: F. E. Peacock, 1969.

VON FRISCH, K. *The Dance Language and Orientation of Bees,* trans. by C. E. Chadwick (London: 1967)

8
The Syllables of Time: Language Change

The language of this country being always upon the flux, the Struldbruggs of one age do not understand those of another, neither are they able after two hundred years to hold any conversation (farther than by a few general words) with their neighbors the mortals, and thus they lie under the disadvantage of living like foreigners in their own country.

—JONATHAN SWIFT, *Gulliver's Travels*

All languages change with time. It is fortunate for us that though languages change, they do so rather slowly compared to the human life span. It would be inconvenient to have to relearn our native language every twenty years. In the field of astronomy we find a similar situation. Because of the movement of individual stars, the stellar configurations we call constellations are continuously changing their shape. Fifty thousand years from now we would find it difficult to recognize Orion or the Big Dipper. But from year to year the changes are not noticeable. Linguistic change is also slow, in human if not astronomical terms. If a person were to turn on a radio and miraculously receive a broadcast in his "native language" from the year 3000, he would probably think he had tuned in some foreign language station. Yet from year to year, even from birth to grave, we hardly notice any change in our language at all.

Where languages have written records it is possible to see the actual changes that have taken place. We know quite a bit about the history of the English language, because about a thousand years of English is preserved in writing. Old English, spoken in England around the end of the first millennium, is scarcely recognizable as English. (Of course our linguistic ancestors didn't call their language Old English!) A speaker of modern English would find the language unintelligible. There are college courses in which Old English is studied in much the same way as any foreign language like French or Swahili.

The following example from *Caedmon's Hymn* of Old English spoken and written in the period between 658 and 680 A.D. will reveal why it must be studied as a "foreign" language:

Nū sculon herian	heofon-rīces Weard,
Now we must praise	heaven-kingdom's Guardian
Meotodes meahte	and his mōd-ġeþanc
the Creator's might	and his mind-plans,
weorc Wuldor-Fæder,	swā hē wundra ġehwæs,
the work of the Glory-Father,	when he of wonders of every one
ēċe Dryhten	ōr astealde
eternal Lord,	the beginning established.

The tenth-century epic *Beowulf,* written in Old English, further exemplifies the need for a translation, as students of English literature well know (the letter þ is pronounced like the *th* in *think*):

Wolde guman findan þone þe him on sweofote sare geteode.
He wanted to find the man who harmed him while he slept.

Almost four hundred years later, Chaucer wrote *The Canterbury Tales.* The language used by Chaucer, now called Middle English, was spoken from around 1100 to 1500; as one might expect, it is more easily understood by present-day readers, as is seen by looking at the opening of the *Tales:*

Whan that Aprille with his shoures soote
The droghte of March hath perced to the roote . . .

When April with its sweet showers
The drought of March has pierced to the root . . .

Two hundred years after Chaucer, in a language that can be considered an earlier dialect of Modern English, Shakespeare's Hamlet says:

A man may fish with the worm that hath eat of a king, and eat of the fish that hath fed of this worm.

Shakespeare wrote in the sixteenth century. A passage from *Everyman,* written about 1485, further illustrates why it is claimed that Modern English was already spoken by 1500:

The Summoning of Everyman called it is,
That of our lives and ending shows
How transitory we be all day.
The matter is wonder precious,
But the intent of it is more gracious
And sweet to bear away.

The division of English into Old English (449–1100 A.D.), Middle English (1100–1500), and Modern English (1500–present) is somewhat arbitrary, being marked by the dates of events in English history which profoundly influenced the English language. Thus the history of English and the changes that occurred in the language reflect, to some extent, nonlinguistic history.

The English language had a beginning. When the Romans invaded and occupied Britain in the first century, the inhabitants of that island did not speak English. They were people of Celtic stock who were themselves earlier invaders. Despite the Celts' resistance, the Roman legions prevailed. Under Roman rule the Celtic civilization flourished, with a Roman flavor. During this period the Scots and the Picts, fierce tribes of northern Britain, raided and plundered Celtic villages to the south. As long as Rome was powerful the Celts were relatively secure. As the strength of the Roman Empire waned, the Roman troops were withdrawn, and by the fifth century A.D. the last Roman legion had dissolved. The Celtic King Vortigern of Britain hired mercenaries to repel the Scots and Picts. These hired soldiers were the Jutes, powerful warriors of Teutonic origin. After beating back the invaders, the Jutes proceeded to disfranchise their Celtic "employers" and settled down on the rich and fertile island. The year was 449 A.D.

The new conquerors spoke German. Other German-speaking peoples arrived to occupy and settle the lands left vacant by the Celts, who fled to Wales, Ireland, Scotland, and the west coast of France. (Welsh, Irish, Scottish Gaelic, and Breton are all Celtic languages.) Among the Germanic tribes that joined the Jutes in Britain were the Saxons and the Angles, from whose name the word *England* is derived.

Britain's new inhabitants were isolated from their old home in northern Germany. As time passed, the German spoken in England and the German spoken on the continent changed, but independently of each other. The languages used became, first, different dialects of German — different but mutually intelligible. By 1066, they were no longer so; there were two languages where once there had been only one. Thus in the year 449 A.D., one could say that English was born.

In 1066 another important event — the Norman conquest of England by William the Conqueror — caused major changes in the English language. French was used as the state language, since the French-speaking Normans were the ruling class. English continued to be spoken by the masses, but was influenced in many ways by French. Vast changes in all aspects of the language took place during this period. One major change is referred to as the Great Vowel Shift (discussed below). Other changes also occurred, and by 1500, English had become very similar to the language spoken today. Since the English spoken after 1500 is more intelligible to modern speakers than that spoken before that time, Modern English is dated from that year.

An examination of the changes that have occurred during the 1500 years since the "birth" of English shows that the sound system has changed, the syntactic rules have changed, and the semantic system has changed. Since a speaker's knowledge of his language is represented by his grammar, the changes that occur in a language are changes in the grammar; all parts of the grammar may change. Although we have discussed linguistic change only in relation to English, the histories of other languages show that similar changes occur in all languages.

KINDS OF LANGUAGE CHANGE

Phonological Change

> *Etymologists . . . for whom vowels did not matter and who cared not a jot for consonants.*
>
> —VOLTAIRE

In Chapters 1 and 4 we discussed the kinds of knowledge one has about the phonological system. This includes knowledge of the phonological units in the language, the phonetic pronunciation of morphemes, and the phonological rules. Any of these aspects of the phonology is subject to change.

Inventory of Sounds If you know modern English you know that /x/, the velar fricative, is not part of the English sound system. One of the changes that occurred in the history of our language was the loss of this particular sound. *Night* was once pronounced [nixt], *drought* was pronounced [druxt], and *saw* was pronounced [saux]. A phonological change—the loss of /x/—took place sometime between the times of Chaucer and Shakespeare. All the words which were once pronounced with a /x/ no longer include this sound. In some cases the /x/ became /f/, as in *rough* and *tough*. In other cases it disappeared leaving no trace, as in *night* and *light*. In other cases the /x/ became a /k/, as in *elk* (written as *eolh* [εlx] in Old English). In some cases it was "vocalized"—that is, it became a vowel, as in *hollow* (Old English *holh* [holx]) or *sorrow* (Old English [sorx]). There are British dialects, such as Scottish, that have kept the /x/ sound in some of these words.

This example shows that the **inventory** of sounds can be changed. English *lost* a phoneme. The inventory can also change by the *addition* of new phonemes to the language. Old English and Middle English did not have the phoneme /ž/. When words like *azure, measure,* and *rouge* were borrowed from French, this sound was added to the inventory of phonological units.

A phonetically predictable sound may also become distinctive or contrastive and be elevated in status to an independent phonological unit, that is, a phoneme. In Old English, for example, the phoneme /f/ was pronounced as [f] in initial and final position of words, but as

[v] between two vowels. Just as [p] and [pʰ] are variants of the same /p/ phoneme in modern English, [f] and [v] were variants of the phoneme /f/ in Old English. Later, when English borrowed words from French with an initial [v], such as *veal*, the [v] was pronounced, since English already had a phonetic [v]. *Veal* now contrasted with *feel;* the voicing of the labiodental consonant in initial position became distinctive, and [v] became a separate phoneme /v/.

These examples show that phonemes may be lost (for example, /x/), or added (for example, /ž/), or may "split" to become two phonemes (for example, /f/ > /f/ and /v/).

Such changes occur in all languages. Two examples may illustrate this. At one time the language Xhosa had no click sounds. It is suggested that all the different clicks were borrowed from the languages spoken by the Bushmen and the Hottentots. The language spoken by the ancestors of all Indo-European language speakers is said to have had "laryngeal" sounds which are no longer present in any Indo-European language.

Phonological Rules   We know that the phonological system includes more than the set of sounds in the language; it also includes the rules which show the different pronunciations of the same morpheme when these morphemes occur in different contexts. These rules "tell" us to pronounce the /t/ which occurs at the end of *democrat* as a [t] but to pronounce it as an [s] in *democracy.*

In the course of linguistic change, such rules can be made more general. At one time, for example, the nouns *house* and *bath* were differentiated from the verbs *house* and *bathe* by the fact that the verbs ended with a short vowel sound (still reflected in the spelling of *bathe*). Furthermore, there was a rule in English (mentioned above in relation to [f] and [v]) which said: "When a voiceless consonant occurs between two vowels, make that consonant voiced." Thus the /s/ in the verb *house* was pronounced [z] and the /θ/ in the verb *bathe* was pronounced [ð]. Then a rule was added to the grammar of English which first "weakened" and then "deleted" unstressed short vowels in certain contexts. The final vowel sound was thus deleted from the verb *house* (that is, we do not pronounce it [hæwzə] but [hæwz]) and also from *bathe.* The deletion of the vowels also resulted in the new phonemes /z/ and /ð/, which prior to this change were simply the phonetic realizations of the phonemes /s/ and /θ/ between vowels.

Eventually, the "intervocalic-voicing" rule was "dropped" from the grammar of English, showing that the set of phonological rules can change by loss of a rule.

One hundred years ago, Fante, a language of Ghana, did not have the sounds [ts] or [dz]. The addition of a phonological rule to the language "created" these sounds; this rule said: "Change a /d/ to [dz] and a /t/ to [ts] when these sounds occur before /i/." The addition of this rule to the grammar of Fante did not create new phonemes; [dz] and [ts] are predictable phonetic realizations of the underlying phonemes /d/ and /t/. The grammar, however, was changed—a new rule was added.

At the time of the English colonization of America, the colonial settlers, like their countrymen who remained in England, pronounced the *r* wherever it was spelled: *farm, mother,* and *margin* were pronounced [farm], [mʌðər], and [marjən]. Between 1607 and 1900 a phonological rule was added to the grammar of British English. The same rule was added to the grammars of the English spoken by the American settlers in Boston, perhaps largely because of the close commercial contact which was maintained between the British and Boston merchants, but it was not added to the grammars of many other Americans. This rule said: "Pronounce an *r* only when the *r* occurs before a vowel."

Thus by 1900, British and Bostonian speakers pronounced *farm* [fam], *mother* [mʌðə], and *margin* [majən]: this pronunciation is part of what we call a "Boston accent," or Boston dialect. All English speakers continued to pronounce the *r* in words like *Mary* and *breakfast.* This added rule did not change the phonological representation of these words. When *four* [fɔ], for example, is followed by a word which begins with a vowel, the /r/ shows up, as in *four acts* [fɔrækts]. Thus the word must be phonemically /fɔr/. The new phonological rule in the grammars of speakers of this "*r*-less" dialect "deletes" the *r* only when it does not precede a vowel.

The addition of phonological rules can affect the pronunciation of words, resulting in dialect differences, and may cause changes in the phonological inventory as well.

The Great Vowel Shift   The most dramatic change that English underwent involved the vowels. The Great Vowel Shift started right around the death of Chaucer in 1400 and was still taking place when Shakespeare died in 1616. The seven long or tense vowels of Middle English underwent the following change:

MIDDLE ENG.		MODERN ENG.		MIDDLE ENG.		MODERN ENG.	
[i:]	→	[aɪ]		[mi:s]	→	[mays]	*mice*
[u:]	→	[æw]		[mu:s]	→	[mæws]	*mouse*
[e:]	→	[i:]		[ge:s]	→	[gi:s]	*geese*
[o:]	→	[u:]		[go:s]	→	[gu:s]	*goose*
[ɛ:]	→	[e:]		[brɛ:ken]	→	[bre:k]	*break*
[ɔ:]	→	[o:]		[brɔ:ken]	→	[bro:k]	*broke*
[a:]	→	[e:]		[na:mə]	→	[ne:m]	*name*

Some reflection of this vowel shift is seen in the alternating forms of morphemes in English: *please, pleasant; serene, serenity; sane, sanity; crime, criminal; sign, signal;* and so on.

Only the long tense vowels were affected. The low vowels became mid vowels ([a:] → [e:], [na:mə] → [ne:m] *name*), the mid vowels became high ([e:] → [i:], [te:θ] → [ti:θ] *teeth;* [o:] → [u:], [to:θ] → [tu:θ] *tooth*). The high vowels became low and diphthongal, and also later shifted from front to back and vice versa ([i:] → [ay], [wi:f] → [wayf] *wife;* [u:] → [æw], [hu:s] → [hæws] *house*).

Syntactic Change

> *Of all the words of witch's doom*
> *There's none so bad as which and whom.*
> *The man who kills both which and whom*
> *Will be enshrined in our Who's Whom.*
>
> — FLETCHER KNEBEL

Just as changes occur in the phonological component of the grammar, they also occur in the syntactic component. Some rules are dropped from the grammar; others may be added or changed. We can observe some of these changes by looking at different dialects.

For example, an advertising slogan has caused a great deal of furor among language "purists" in America. They insist that "Winston tastes good like a cigarette should" is "bad" English, because they say that there is a "rule" in our grammar stating that *like* can only be followed by a "noun phrase" and cannot be used as a conjunction to introduce an embedded sentence. According to them, the slogan should read "Winston tastes good *as* a cigarette should." But the grammar of many speakers of English has changed, so that *like* is now a conjunction, and for them the Winston jingle is a perfectly grammatical sentence.

For a number of centuries, English speakers had no more trouble deciding when to use *who* and *whom* than they had deciding when to use *he* or *him*. The rule which once governed the occurrence of *who* and *whom* is slowly fading out of the language. Some speakers say *I don't know who to give it to;* others still use *whom*. Some speakers are not quite sure which pronoun to use. We are able to witness this change in progress.

Many syntactic changes have occurred in the history of English (and the histories of all languages). An examination of Chaucer's English (end of the fourteenth century) and even Shakespeare's English (beginning of the seventeenth century) makes us aware of some of these changes.

We look again at the opening line of *The Canterbury Tales:*

Whan that Aprille with *his* shoures *soote* . . .

Literally:

When that April with his showers sweet . . .

In modern English, the pronoun *it* is used to replace *April*. *His* would only be used with an "animate masculine" noun: the "agreement" rule has been changed.

The syntactic rules relating to the English negative construction underwent a number of changes from Old English to the present. In Modern English, negation is expressed by adding *not* or *do not*. One may also express negation by adding words like *never*[1] or *no:*

> I am going → I am not going.
> I went → I did not go.
> I go to school → I never go to school.
> I want meat → I don't want any meat; I want no meat.

In Old English the main negation element was *ne*. It usually occurred before the auxiliary of the verb (or before the main verb if there was no auxiliary), as illustrated by these examples from Old English manuscripts:

1. þæt he *na*   sippan geboren *ne* wurde
   that he never after   born   not would-be
   that he should never be born after that

2. ac hie *ne* dorston þær on cuman
   but they not dared   there on come
   but they dared not land there[2]

Notice in example 1 that not only is the word order different from that in Modern English, but that there are two negatives: *na* (a contraction of *ne* + *a* "ever" = "never") and *ne*. This use of a "double negative" which occurred in Old English is considered by some grammarians to be "substandard" and "ungrammatical" today. Whether it is grammatical depends upon the rules of one's own grammar; it was grammatical in Old English, as it is in certain English dialects of modern times.

In addition to the contraction of *ne* + *a* → *na*, other negative contractions occurred in Old English; *ne* could be attached to *habb-* "have," *wes-* "be," *wit-* "know," *will-* "will" to form *nabb-, nes-, nyt-, nyll-,* respectively.

We also have "contraction" rules which change *do* + *not* or *did* + *not* into *don't* and *didn't;* other contraction rules are similar to those found in Old English: *not* + *ever* → *never, will* + *not* → *won't, can* + *not* → *can't,* and so on. Notice that in our contractions the phonetic form of the negation element in *won't, can't, haven't, isn't,* and *wasn't* always comes at the end of the word. This is because in modern English the gram-

---

[1] From a contraction of *not ever*.

[2] From E. C. Traugott, *The History of English Syntax* (New York: Holt, Rinehart and Winston, 1972).

matical word order puts the *not* after the auxiliary. In Old English the negative element shows up at the beginning, since it typically preceded the auxiliary. The rules of word order have changed.

As late as the fifteenth and sixteenth centuries, one could merely add *not* at the end of an affirmative sentence to negate it. One finds such sentences in the writings of Malory at the end of the fifteenth century:

> He saw you not.

Similarly, such sentences are found in Shakespeare:

> I love thee not, therefore pursue me not.

In modern English, *not* must precede the main verb of the clause, and a *do*, marked for the proper tense, must be inserted.

> He saw you → he did not see you.
> I love you, therefore pursue me → I do not love you, therefore don't pursue me.

Another change which has occurred in English since Malory's time affected the rules of "comparative" and "superlative" constructions. Today we form the comparative by adding *-er* to the adjective or inserting *more* before it; the superlative is formed by adding *-est* or inserting *most*. In Malory one finds many examples of double comparatives and superlatives which are now ungrammatical: *more gladder, more lower, moost royallest, moost shamefullest*. These would be "starred" forms today.

When we study a language whose only source is written records, such as Elizabethan English, we see only sentences that are grammatical unless the author is *deliberately* using ungrammatical sentences. There being no native speakers of Elizabethan English around for us to query, we can only infer what sentences were ungrammatical. Such inference leads us to believe that expressions like *the Queen of England's crown* were ungrammatical in former versions of English. Shakespeare would have said *the Queen's crown of England* or *the crown of the Queen of England*. Modern English, on the other hand, allows some rather complex constructions that involve the possessive marker. It is not uncommon to hear an English speaker use possessive constructions such as *The girl whose sister I'm dating's roommate is really pretty,* or *The man from Boston's hat fell off.* Older versions of English would have to resort to an *of* construction to express the same thought (*The hat of the man from Boston fell off*). It is clear that a syntactic change took place that accounts for the extended use of the possessive morpheme *s*.

To appreciate fully the extent to which the syntactic component of a grammar may change we can look beyond English, or even the family of Germanic languages, and consider other Indo-European languages. In Classical Latin, as well as in Russian, Lithuanian, and other languages, one finds an extensive system of *case endings* on nouns. Whenever a speaker of Latin used a noun, he had to add the correct case suffix to the noun stem, according to the function of the noun in the sentence (all of which a native speaker would do without thinking, of course). Latin had six cases. Below are the different forms (the declension) for the noun *lupus,* "wolf":

CASE	NOUN STEM		CASE ENDING		
nominative	lup	+	us	lupus	The *wolf* runs.
genitive	lup	+	ī	lupī	A sheep in *wolf's* clothing.
dative	lup	+	ō	lupō	Give food *to the wolf.*
accusative	lup	+	um	lupum	I love the *wolf.*
ablative	lup	+	ō	lupō	Run *from a wolf.*
vocative	lup	+	e	lupe	*Wolf,* come here!

In *Alice's Adventures in Wonderland,* Lewis Carroll has Alice give us a brief lesson in grammatical case. Alice, greatly shrunken, is swimming around in a pool of her own tears with a mouse, whom she wishes to befriend:

> "Would it be of any use, now," thought Alice, "to speak to this mouse? Everything is so out-of-the-way down here, that I should think very likely it can talk: at any rate, there's no harm in trying." So she began: "O Mouse, do you know the way out of this pool? I am very tired of swimming about here, O Mouse!" (Alice thought this must be the right way of speaking to a mouse: she had never done such a thing before, but she remembered having seen in her brother's Latin Grammar, "A mouse — of a mouse — to a mouse — a mouse — O mouse!")

Alice gives us an English "translation" of the nominative, genitive, dative, accusative, and vocative cases (she omits the ablative).

Such an extensive case system (of which we have seen only part) was present in Latin, Ancient Greek, and Sanskrit. We are certain that it was present in Proto-Indo-European, the ancestor of all these languages. Modern languages such as Lithuanian and Russian retain much of the Indo-European case system, but these languages are in the minority. In most modern Indo-European languages, changes have all but obliterated the case system. English still retains the genitive case, calling it possessive (in *a sheep in wolf's clothing,* the noun *wolf* is in the genitive case). Pronouns retain a few more traces: *he* is nominative, *him* is accusative and dative (note the *m* in the Latin accusative), and *his* is genitive. (English has replaced its depleted case system with an equally expressive system of prepositions, and stricter constraints on word order.)

Old English also had a rich case-ending system, as illustrated by the following:

1. CASE	MODERN ENGLISH	OE SIN- GULAR	OE PLURAL
nominative	stone/stones	stān	stānas
genitive	stone's/stones'	stānes	stāna
dative	stone/stones	stāne	stānum
accusative	stone/stones	stān	stānas

2. CASE	MODERN ENGLISH	OE SIN- GULAR	OE DUAL	OE PLURAL
nominative	I/we two/we	ic [ič]	wit [wɪt]	wē [we:]
genitive	my-mine/our-ours	min [mɪn]	uncer [unker]	ūre/ūser
dative	me/us	mē [me:]	unc [unk]	ūs [u:s]
accusative	me/us	mec [meč]	uncit [unkit]	ūsic [u:sɪč]

In these examples, *stone* represents the principal "strong" masculine noun declension. There were "weak" declensions also. The interesting thing is that the plural of this "strong" declension in the nominative and accusative cases became generalized to all the English regular nouns, another example of historical change.

We have mentioned a phonological rule which weakened certain short unstressed vowels. When the vowel was dropped in the plural form of "stones" [sta:nas], it became [sta:ns], and when the "weak" syllables representing case endings in the singular forms were dropped, English lost much of its case system.

With the loss of these case endings, new syntactic rules regulating word order entered the language, possibly so that ambiguities would not result. In Old English, word order was not as crucial, because the language was so highly inflected. The doer of the action (that is, the subject) and the object of the action were revealed unambiguously by various case endings. This does not mean that there was no preferred word order, but even if the normal order was violated, the sentence meaning was perfectly clear. Thus, the following sentences all meant "The man slew the king":

Se man sloh thone kyning.
Thone kyning sloh se man.
Se man thone kyning sloh.
Thone kyning se man sloh.
Sloh se man thone kyning.
Sloh thone kyning se man.

Se was a definite article used only with the subject noun, and *thone* was the definite article used only with the object noun.

Notice how only the first literal (word-for-word) translation of these Old English sentences would mean what the original meant:

> The man slew the king.
> The king slew the man.
> *The man the king slew.
> *The king the man slew.
> *Slew the man the king.
> *Slew the king the man.

Furthermore, the last four sentences would not be grammatical in Modern English—the syntactic rules which determine proper word order are violated.

Thus we see that the syntactic parts of grammars undergo change just as do the phonological components.

Lexical Change

Curl'd minion, dancer, coiner of sweet words.

— MATTHEW ARNOLD, *Sohrab and Rustum*

Hold fast the form of sound words.

— The Bible

Knowing a language means knowing what words and morphemes are in the language, and that means knowing what they "mean." As discussed in Chapter 5, these basic units of meaning constitute the vocabulary or *lexicon*, which is part of the grammar. Changes in the lexicon can include the loss of words, the addition of words, or changes in the meanings of words.

When speakers start to use a new word—that is, when a word is *added*—the change is quite obvious and relatively abrupt. When speakers fail to use a word—that is, when a word is *lost* from the lexicon—the process takes place gradually over the course of several generations.

Word Coinage A new word can come into a language in many ways. It can be coined—created outright to fit some purpose. Madison Avenue has added many new words to English in this way, showing the truth of the old proverb "Necessity is the mother of invention." *Kodak, nylon, Orlon,* and *Dacron* were names made up for certain consumer items. Specific brand names such as *Xerox, Kleenex, Jell-o, Frigidaire, Brillo,* and *Vaseline* are now often used as the general name for many brands of the actual product. Notice that some of these words were created from existing words: *Kleenex* from the word *clean, Jell-o* from *gel, Frigidaire* from *frigid* plus *air.*

Acronyms are words derived from the initials of several words. Such words are pronounced as the spelling indicates: NASA as [næsə], UNESCO as [yunɛsko], and CARE as *care. Radar* from "*radio detecting and ranging*"; and *laser* from "*light amplification by stimu-*

lated *e*mission of *r*adiation" show the creative efforts of word coiners, as does *snafu,* which is rendered in polite circles as "*s*ituation *n*ormal, *a*ll *f*ouled *u*p."

Compounding Recombining old words to form new ones, with new meanings, is a productive source of lexical additions. Thousands of common English words entered the language via this process. To name a few: *afternoon, bigmouth, chickenhearted, drumstick, egghead, five-and-ten, grapevine, highball, icecap, jetset, longshoreman, moreover, nursemaid, offshore, pothole, quarterhorse, railroad, sailboat, tentpeg, underworld, verbform, waterpipe, x-axis, yachtsman, zoo-ecology.*

Blends Blends are compounds that are "less than" compounds. *Smog,* from *smoke + fog; motel,* from *motor + hotel; broasted,* from *broiled + roasted;* and *urinalysis* from *urine + analysis* are examples of blends that have attained full lexical status in English. Lewis Carroll's *chortle,* from *chuckle + snort,* has limited acceptance in the language. Carroll was famous for both the coining and the blending of words. In *Through the Looking-Glass* he described the "meanings" of the made-up words he used in "Jabberwocky" as follows:

> . . . "Brillig" means four o'clock in the afternoon—the time when you begin *broiling* things for dinner. . . . "Slithy" means "lithe and slimy." . . . You see it's like a portmanteau—there are two meanings packed up into one word. . . . "Toves" are something like badgers—they're something like lizards—and they're something like corkscrews. . . . also they make their nests under sun-dials—also they live on cheese. . . . To "gyre" is to go round and round like a gyroscope. To "gimble" is to make holes like a gimlet. And "the wabe" is the grass-plot round a sun-dial. . . . It's called "wabe" . .,. because it goes a long way before it and a long way behind it. . . . "Mimsy" is "flimsy and miserable" (there's another portmanteau for you).

Carroll's "portmanteaus" are what we have called blends, and such words can become part of the regular lexicon.

Abbreviations Abbreviations of longer words or phrases also may become "lexicalized": *nark* for *narcotics agent, tec* (or *dick*) for *detective, telly,* the British word for *television, prof* for *professor, teach* for *teacher,* and *doc* for *doctor* are just a few examples of such "short forms" which are now used as whole words.

Borrowings Loans from other languages are an important source of new words. Most languages are borrowers, and the lexicon of any language can be divided into native and non-native words (often called **loan words**). A **native word** is one whose history (or etymology) can be traced back to the earliest-known stages of the language.

A language may borrow a word *directly* or *indirectly.* A *direct* borrowing means that the borrowed item is a native word in the language it is borrowed from. The native Middle French word *festa* (Modern French *fête;* the Old French was *feste* from Latin *festa*) was directly borrowed by Middle English, and has become Modern English *feast*. On the other hand, the word *algebra* was borrowed from Spanish, which in turn had borrowed it from Arabic. English borrowed *algebra* indirectly from Arabic, with Spanish as an intermediary.

Some languages are heavy borrowers; Albanian has borrowed so heavily that few native words are retained. On the other hand, many American Indian languages have borrowed but lightly from their neighbors.

English has borrowed extensively. Of the 20,000 or so words in common use, about three-fifths are borrowed. However, the figure is misleading. Of the 500 most frequently used words, only two-sevenths are borrowed, and since these "common" words are used over and over again in sentences, the actual frequency of appearance of native words is much higher than the statistics on borrowing would lead one to believe. "Little" words such as *and, be, have, it, of, the, to, will, you, on, that,* and *is* are all native to English, and constitute about one-fourth of the words regularly used. Thus it is not unreasonable to suppose that more than four-fifths of the words commonly used in speaking English are native to the language.

One can almost trace the history of the English-speaking peoples by studying the kinds of loan words in the language and when they entered the language. Up until the Norman Conquest in 1066, the Anglo-Saxons borrowed few words. The German spoken by the Anglo-Saxons and Jutes was almost completely undiluted by foreign elements. It stayed that way for some time. The conquerors adopted some Celtic place names, but the Celts were so thoroughly vanquished that their language had little effect on the language of the invaders.

For three centuries after the Norman Conquest, French was the language used for all affairs of state and for most commercial, social, and cultural matters. The West Saxon literary language was abandoned, but regional varieties of English did continue to be used in the homes of the people, and in their churches when they worshipped, and even in the market places of their small villages. During these three centuries, vast numbers of French words entered English, of which these are but a few: *government, crown, prince, state, parliament, nation, jury, judge, crime, sue, attorney, property, miracle, charity, court, lechery, virgin, saint, pray, mercy, religion, value, royal, money, society.*

Until the Norman invasion, when an Englishman slaughtered an ox for food, he ate *ox*. If it was a pig, he ate *pig*. If it was a sheep he ate *sheep*. But "ox" served at the Norman tables was *beef* (*boeuf*), "pig" was *pork* (*porc*) and "sheep" was *mutton* (*mouton*). The French language also gave English the food-preparing words *boil, broil, fry, stew,* and *roast.*

Many languages supplied words for English to borrow and assimilate. Between 1500 and 1700, the time of the Renaissance in England, there was much study of the Greek and Roman classics, and "learned" words from these sources entered our lexicon. In 1476 the printing press was introduced to England by William Caxton, and by 1640, 55,000 books had been printed in English. The authors of these books made free use of many Greek and Latin words, and some people grasped hungrily at this source of erudition. As a result, many words of Ancient Greek and Latin came into the language.

From Greek came *drama, comedy, tragedy, scene, botany, physics, zoology, atomic,* and many other words. Greek roots have also provided English with a means for coining new words. *Thermos* "hot" plus *metron* "measure" give us *thermometer.* From *akros* "topmost" and *phobia* "fear" we get *acrophobia,* "abnormal dread of heights." An ingenious American cartoonist, Robert Osborn, has "invented" some phobias, each of which he gives an appropriate name:

logizomechanophobia	"fear of reckoning machines" from Greek *logizomai* "to reckon or compute" + *mekhane* "device" + *phobia*
ellipsosyllabophobia	"fear of words with a missing syllable" from Greek *elleipsis* "a falling short" + *syllable* "syllable" + *phobia*
pornophobia	"fear of prostitutes" from Greek *porne* "harlot" + *phobia*[3]

Here is a sampling of words borrowed by English from Latin: *convention, animal, bonus, maximum, alumnus, quorum, exit, scientific, interrogatory, orthography, debt, describe, advantage, rape, violent.*

Latin, like Greek, has also provided prefixes and suffixes that are used productively with both native and non-native roots. The prefix *ex-* comes from Latin: *ex-husband, ex-boss, ex-wife, ex-sister-in-law, exhibit, extend, export, exhale, exterminate, exclude, exalt.* The suffix *-able/-ible* is also Latin and can be attached to almost any English verb: *writable, readable, answerable, movable, kissable, intelligible, trainable, laughable, typewritable, operable, questionable.*

During the ninth and tenth centuries, the Scandinavian raiders who first raided and then settled on the British Isles left their traces in the English language. In fact, the pronouns *they, their,* and *them* were borrowed from the Scandinavians. This is the only time that English ever borrowed pronouns. Many English words beginning with [sk] are of Scandinavian origin: *scatter, scare, scrape, skirt, skin, sky.*

Ass, bin, flannel, clan, slogan, and *whisky* are all words of Celtic origin, borrowed at various times from Welsh, Scots-Gaelic, and Irish.

From Dutch we borrowed such words as *buoy, freight, leak, pump, yacht.*

[3] From *An Osborn Festival of Phobias.* Copyright © 1971 by Robert Osborn. Text copyright © 1971 by Eve Wengler. Reprinted by permission of Liveright, Publishers, New York.

From German: *cobalt, quartz, sauerkraut, lager, beer.*

From Italian: *opera, sonata, piano, allegro, virtuoso, balcony, corridor, mezzanine.*

From Arabic: *alcohol, algebra, cipher, sugar, zero.*

With the settlement of the "New World," the English-speaking Americans borrowed from Indian languages as well as from Spanish.

From American Indian languages: *pony, hominy, squash, chipmunk, moose, opossum, raccoon, skunk, moccasin, tomahawk, wigwam, papoose, squaw, totem, powwow, hickory.*

From Spanish: *alligator, barbecue, cigar, cockroach, guitar, key* ("reef"), *mosquito, Negro, adobe, canyon, cinch, lariat, mesa, patio, ranch, taco.*

Hundreds of "place names" in America are of non-English origin. One certainly can't call Indian names "foreign," except in the sense that they were foreign to English.

American Indian place names: *Connecticut, Potomac, Ohio, Mississippi, Erie, Huron, Michigan, Alleghenies, Appalachians, Ozarks, Massachusetts, Kentucky, Wisconsin, Oregon, Texas, Chattanooga, Chicago, Milwaukee, Omaha, Passaic, Hackensack.*

Spanish place names: *Rio Grande, Colorado, Sierra Nevada, Santa Fe, Los Angeles, San Francisco, Santa Barbara, San Jose, Santa Cruz.*

Dutch place names: *Brooklyn, Fishkill, Catskills, Amsterdam.*

The influence of Yiddish on English is interesting when one realizes that Yiddish words are used by many non-Jews, as well as non-Yiddish-speaking Jews in America. There was even a bumper sticker quite popular (at least in Los Angeles) reading "Marcel Proust is a yenta." *Yenta* is a Yiddish word meaning "gossipy woman" or "shrew." *Lox* "smoked salmon," *bagel* "a hard roll resembling a doughnut," and *matzo* "unleavened cracker" belong to American English, as well as a number of Yiddish expressions introduced via comedians: *schmaltz, shlemiel, shmoe, kibbitz.*

Other languages also borrow words. Twi speakers drank palm wine before the white man arrived in Africa. Now they also drink [bia] "beer," [hwiski] "whiskey," and [gɔrdɔn jin] "Gordon's gin."

French, a language from which English has borrowed heavily, now borrows from English. *Weekend, picnique, bar, club, hit parade, flashback,* and *tanker* are but a few of these Anglicisms. The French government, as of the beginning of 1973, has been strongly urging the people to purge these items from the "pure" French language. If the history of hundreds of languages is any indication, the attempt to "purify" French will fail dismally.

Loss of Words   So far in this section we have discussed how words are *added* to a language. It is also true that words can be *lost* from a language, though a word's departure is never as dramatic as a new word's arrival. When a new word comes into vogue, its very presence draws attention.   But a word is lost by the act of inattention—nobody thinks of it; nobody uses it; and it fades out of the language.

English has lost many words, which a reading of any of Shakespeare's works will quickly make obvious.   Here are a few taken from *Romeo and Juliet: beseem* "to be suitable," *mammet* "a doll or puppet," *wot* "to know," *gyve* "a fetter," *fain* "gladly" or "rather," *wherefore* "why."

Semantic Change

His talk was like a stream which runs
With rapid change from rocks to roses.
It slipped from politics to puns;
It passed from Mahomet to Moses.

—WINTHROP MACKWORTH PRAED, *The Vicar*

We have seen that a language may gain or lose lexical items.   It is also common for lexical items to shift in meaning, providing yet another way in which languages change.   There are three ways in which a lexical item may change semantically.   Its meaning may become broader; its meaning may become narrower; its meaning may shift.

Broadening   When the meaning of a word becomes broader, that word means everything it used to mean, and then some.   The Middle English word *dogge* meant a specific breed of dog, much like the word *dachshund* in Modern English.   The meaning of *dogge* was broadened to encompass all members of the species "Canis familiaris."   The word *holiday* originally meant "holy day," a day of religious significance. Today, of course, the word signifies any day on which we don't have to work.   *Butcher* once meant "slaughterer of goats" (and earlier "of bucks"), but its modern usage is more general.   Similarly, *picture* used to mean "painted representation," but today you can take a picture with a camera.   A *companion* used to mean a person with whom you shared bread, but today it's a person who accompanies you.   *Quarantine* once had the restricted meaning "forty days' isolation," and *bird* once meant "young bird."   The invention of steam-powered boats gave the verb *sail* an opportunity to extend its dominion to boats without sails, just as the verb *drive* widened in meaning to encompass self-propelled vehicles.

Narrowing   In the King James version of the Bible (1611), God says of the herbs and trees, "to you they shall be for meat" (Genesis 1, 29). To a speaker of seventeenth-century English, *meat* meant "food," and *flesh* meant "meat."   Since that time, semantic change has **narrowed** the meanings of these words to what they are in Modern English.   The word *deer* once meant "beast" or "animal," as its German cognate *Tier* still does.   The meaning of *deer* has been narrowed to a particular kind of animal.   Similarly, the word *hound* used to be the general term for "dog," like the German *Hund*. Today *hound* means a special kind of dog. Before the Norman Conquest, as we have pointed out before, the words *ox, pig, calf,* and *sheep* meant both the animal and the meat of that animal. The Normans brought with them the words *beef, pork, veal,* and *mutton,* which were borrowed into English, thus narrowing the meaning of *ox, pig, calf,* and *sheep*. The Old English word that occurs as modern *starve* once meant "to die." Its meaning has narrowed to become "to die of hunger." *Token* used to have the broad meaning "sign," but long ago was specialized to mean a physical object that is a sign, such as a *love token*. *Liquor* was once synonymous with *liquid, reek* used to mean "smoke," and *girl* once meant "young person of either sex."

Meaning Shifts   The third kind of semantic change that a lexical item may undergo is a shift in meaning. The word *bead* originally meant "prayer." During the Middle Ages the custom arose of repeating one's prayers (that is, *beads*) over and over and counting them by means of little wooden balls on a rosary. The meaning of *bead* shifted from "prayer" to the visible manifestation of a prayer. The word *knight* once meant "youth" but was elevated in meaning in time for the age of chivalry. *Lust* used to mean simply "pleasure," with no negative or sexual overtones. *Lewd* was merely "ignorant," and *immoral* meant "not customary." *Silly* used to mean "happy" in Old English. By the Middle English period it had come to mean "naïve," and only in Modern English does it mean "foolish." The overworked Modern English word *nice* meant "ignorant" a thousand years ago. When Juliet tells Romeo, "I am too *fond*," she is not claiming she likes Romeo too much. She means "I am too *foolish*."

Slang   The use of slang, or colloquial language, introduces many new words into the language, by recombining old words into new meanings. *Spaced out, right on, hangup,* and *rip-off* have all gained a degree of acceptance. More rarely, slang will come up with an entirely new word for the language, such as *barf, flub,* and *pooped*. Slang often consists of using old words with totally new meanings ascribed to them. *Grass* and *pot* have widened their meaning to "marijuana"; *pig* and *fuzz* are derogatory terms for "policeman"; *rap, cool, dig, stoned, bread,* and *split* have all extended their semantic domain. The words we have cited sound "slangy" because they have not gained total acceptability. Words such as *dwindle, freshman, glib,* and *mob* are former slang words that in time lost their "unsavory" origin. It is not always easy to know where to draw the line between "slang" words and "regular" words. This seems always to have been true. In 1890, John S. Farmer, co-editor with W. E. Henley of *Slang and Its Analogues*, remarked: "The borderland between slang and the 'Queen's English' is an ill-defined territory, the limits of which have never been clearly mapped out."

Euphemisms   Undoubtedly, the pinnacle of human linguistic ingenuity is achieved with the **euphemism**. A euphemism is a word or phrase which replaces a taboo word or a taboo idea, as is illustrated by Virginia

Woolf's reference to the "comfortably padded lunatic asylums which are known, euphemistically, as the stately homes of England."   Ogden Nash's poem "Ode to the Four-Letter Words" exhorts against such pruderies:

> When in calling, plain speaking is out;
> When the ladies (God bless 'em) are milling about,
> You may wet, make water, or empty the glass;
> You can powder your nose, or the "johnny" will pass.
> It's a drain for the lily, or man about dog
> When everyone's drunk, it's condensing the fog;
> But sure as the devil, that word with a hiss
> It's only in Shakespeare that characters – – – –.

The linguist Jay Powell has made an interesting study of euphemisms used by Australian speakers of English.[4]   The expressions which revolve around the idea "toilet" or the functions connected with it show that there is more than "prudery" involved, as is illustrated by the Australian euphemisms which replace the verb *urinate:*

> drain the dragon
> syphon the python
> water the horse
> squeeze the lemon
> drain the spuds
> see if the horse has kicked off his blanket
> wring the rattlesnake
> shake hands with wife's best friend
> point Percy at the porcelain
> train Terence on the terracotta

Similar "metaphors" exist for *have intercourse:*

> shag
> root
> crack a fat
> dip the wick
> play hospital
> hide the ferret
> play cars and garages
> hide the egg roll (sausage, salami)
> boil bangers
> slip a length
> go off like a beltfed motor
> go like a rat up a rhododendron
> go like a rat up a drainpipe
> have gin on the rocks
> have a northwest cocktail

[4] Paper delivered at Western Conference of Linguistics meeting, University of Oregon, 1972.

When such colorful idioms are added to the language, we can be happy that language does change.

WHY DO LANGUAGES CHANGE?

Stability in language is synonymous with rigor mortis.

— ERNEST WEEKLEY

No one knows exactly how or why languages change. Certainly linguistic changes do not happen suddenly. It is not the case that all speakers of English awoke one morning and decided to use the word *beef* for "ox meat." Nor is it true that all the children of one particular generation grew up to adopt this new word usage. Changes are more gradual, particularly changes in the phonological and syntactic system.

Of course certain changes may occur instantaneously for any one speaker. For example, when a speaker acquires a new word, he doesn't "gradually" acquire it. Even when a new rule is incorporated into his grammar, the rule is either in or not in his grammar. It may at first be an optional rule; he may use it only some of the time, its use perhaps being determined by social context. What is gradual is the spread of certain changes over the entire speech community.

A basic cause of change can be attributed to the way children acquire the language. No one teaches the child the rules of the grammar; each child constructs his grammar on his own, generalizing rules from the linguistic input he receives. As will be discussed in Chapter 12, observations of the language used by children show stages in the development of their grammars. The early simple grammars become more and more complex until they approximate the grammars used by adults. The child's grammar is never exactly like the adults'. He receives input from many dialects used around him, many individual styles, and so on. The features of these grammars may then merge. Certain rules may be simplified or overgeneralized.

The older generation may be using "variable" rules. For example, at certain times they may say "It's I" and at other times "It's me." The less formal style is usually used with children. The next generation may use only the "me" form of the pronoun in this construction. In such cases, the grammar will have changed.

The reasons for some changes are relatively easy to understand. Before the advent of television there was no such word as *television* in the language. It soon became a common lexical item. We have already seen how words may be coined and borrowed, and their entry into the language is not mysterious. Other changes are more difficult to explain. For example, no one knows why vowels shifted in English.

We have also discussed how external borrowing—loans from other languages—can affect the phonological system of a language as well as the lexicon. Thus, when English borrowed French words containing /ž/ and /v/, they were eventually added to the inventory of English phonemes. Metaphorically, we can say that English borrowed /z/ and /v/ from French.

We have some plausible explanations for some of the phonological changes in languages. Some of these changes are due to physiological mechanisms. Some sounds and combinations of sounds are "easier to pronounce" than others. For example, it is universally the case that vowels are nasalized before nasal consonants. This is because it is difficult to time the lowering of the velum to produce the nasal sound so that it coincides exactly with the production of the consonant. In anticipation of the nasal consonant, then, the velum is lowered during the vowel and the result is a nasalized vowel. As stated in Chapter 3, the effect of one sound on another is called *assimilation;* the vowel *assimilates* to the nasality of the nasal consonant. Once the vowel is nasalized, the contrast that the nasal consonant provided can be equally well provided by the nasalized vowel alone, and the redundant consonant may be deleted. The contrast between oral and nasal vowels which exists in many languages of the world today results from just such a historical sound change.

In French, at one time, *bol* "basin," *botte* "high boot," *bog* "a card game," *bock* "Bock beer," and *bon* "good" were pronounced [bɔl], [bɔt], [bɔg], [bɔk] and [bɔn], respectively. Notice that in *bon* there was a final nasal consonant which *conditioned* the nasalization of the preceding vowel. Today, *bon* is pronounced [bɔ̃]; the nasal vowel effectively maintains the contrast with the other words.

Another example from English illustrates how such assimilative processes can change a language. In English when we say *key,* the /k/ is articulated forward in the mouth in anticipation of the high front "palatal" vowel /i/. But when we say the /k/ in *cot,* the [k] is backed in anticipation of the low back vowel [a]. The /k/ in *key* is thus "palatalized." In Old English there were a number of words which began with a palatalized /kʸ/. When these were followed by /i/ they developed into our modern palatal affricate /č/ as is illustrated by the following:

OLD ENGLISH [kʸ]		MODERN ENGLISH [č]
ciese	→	cheese
cinn	→	chin
cild	→	child

The same process that produced the /č/ in English—the palatalization of the /k/—is also found in many other languages. In Twi, for example, the word meaning "to hate" was once pronounced [ki]. The [k] became [kʸ] and then finally a [č], so that today it is pronounced [či].

Such assimilative processes at work in languages gave rise to a "theory of least effort" to explain linguistic change. According to this theory, sound changes are primarily due to linguistic "laziness"; we exert as little effort as possible in speaking. We might call this the "mumbling tendency." We tend to assimilate one sound to another, to drop out unstressed syllables, and so on.

Linguistic history reveals that many exceptional morphemes lost their special status because of a different kind of "laziness." This kind of change has been called **internal borrowing** — that is, we "borrow" from one part of the grammar and apply the rule generally. It has also been called **analogic change.** One could say that it is by analogy to *foe/foes* and *dog/dogs* that speakers started saying *cows* as the plural of *cow* instead of the earlier plural *kine*. By analogy to *reap/reaped, seem/seemed,* and *ignite/ignited,* children and adults are presently saying *I sweeped the floor, I dreamed that I went to the Presidential Ball in my Maidenform Bra, She lighted the bonfire,* instead of using *swept, dreamt,* and *lit.*

The same kind of analogic change is exemplified by our "regularization" of exceptional plural forms. We borrowed words like *datum/data, agendum/agenda, curriculum/curricula, memorandum/memoranda, medium/media, criterion/criteria, bandit/banditti, virtuoso/virtuosi,* to name just a few. The irregular plurals of these nouns have been replaced by regular plurals among many speakers: *agendas, curriculums, memorandums, criterias, bandits, virtuosos.* Notice that in some cases the borrowed original plural forms were considered to be the singular (as in *agenda* and *criteria*) and that the new plural is therefore a "pluralplural." Also, many speakers now regard *data* and *media* as mass nouns like *rice* or *milk.*

The "theory of least effort" does seem to account for some linguistic changes, but it cannot account for others. Simplification of grammars occurs, but so does elaboration or complication.

Simplification often reduces redundancies, but some redundancy is required to make language efficient. When case endings are lost, confusion can result unless the grammar compensates for the loss; stricter word-order constraints are thus placed on the grammar. Thus while one sees a tendency toward greater simplification, one also finds a counter tendency, the desire to be intelligible.

Thus we find many factors which contribute to linguistic change — simplification of grammars, elaboration (to maintain intelligibility), borrowing, lexical additions. Basically, however, it must be remembered that it is the children learning the language who finally incorporate the ongoing changes or create new changes in the grammar of the language. The exact reasons for linguistic change are still elusive. Perhaps language changes for the same reason all things change: that it is the nature of things to change. As Heraclitus pointed out, thousands of years ago, "All is flux, nothing stays still. Nothing endures but change."

THE STUDY OF LANGUAGE CHANGE

. . . Philologists who chase
A panting syllable through time and space,
Start it at home, and hunt it in the dark,
To Gaul, to Greece, and into Noah's Ark.

—COWPER, *Retirement*

But, for mine own part, it was Greek to me.

—SHAKESPEARE, *Julius Caesar*

That branch of linguistics which deals with how languages change, what kinds of changes occur, and why they occurred is called **historical and comparative linguistics.** It is *historical* because it deals with the history of particular languages; it is *comparative* because it deals with relations between languages.

The main linguistic work in the nineteenth century was historical-comparative research. In that century, Darwin's theory of evolution had a profound influence on all areas of science, linguistics included, which led to theories of language and language development that were analogous to biological theories. Language was considered to have a "life cycle" and to develop according to evolutionary laws. In addition, it was believed that language, like man, has a "genealogical tree"—that is, that each language can be traced back to a common ancestor. This theory of biological naturalism is known by the name of the *Stammbaum* ("family tree") theory. In the next chapter, we will discuss the Indo-European family tree.

The nineteenth-century historical and comparative linguists based their theories on three major premises: that there is a resemblance between languages; that this resemblance is not due to chance but is rather due to a relationship between languages; and that the relationship which exists is a genealogical or genetic one.

The chief goal of the nineteenth-century historical-comparativists was to develop and elucidate the genetic relationships which exist among the world's languages. They aimed to establish the major language families of the world and to define principles for the classification of languages. Their work grew out of earlier research.

In the eighteenth century, scholars had already begun to look closely at a number of languages. Sir William Jones (a British scholar who found it best to reside in India because of his sympathy for the rebellious American colonists) delivered a paper in 1786 in which he observed that Sanskrit bore to Greek and Latin "a stronger affinity . . . than could possibly have been produced by accident." Jones suggested that these three languages had "sprung from a common source" and that probably

Germanic and Celtic had the same origin. The classical philologists of the time attempted to disprove the idea that there was any genetic relationship between Sanskrit, Latin, and Greek, since if such a relationship existed it would make their views on language and language development obsolete. A Scottish philosopher, Dugall Stewart, for example, put forth the hypothesis that Sanskrit and Sanskrit literature were inventions of Brahmans, who used Greek and Latin as models to deceive Europeans. This "scholar" wrote on this complex question without knowing a single Sanskrit character, whereas Jones was an eminent Sanskritist.

The work of Jones was supported by many scholars. Friedrich Schlegel was the first to use the term **comparative grammar**. He stressed that if one looked at the "inner structures" of languages, genetic relationships would be revealed.

About thirty years after Jones delivered his important paper, the German linguist Franz Bopp pointed up the relationship between Sanskrit, Latin, Greek, Persian, and Germanic. At the same time, a young Danish scholar named Rasmus Rask corroborated these results, and brought Lithuanian and Armenian into the relationship as well. Rask was the first scholar to describe formally the regularity of certain phonological differences between related languages.

Rask's investigation of these regularities was followed up by the German linguist Jakob Grimm (of fairy-tale fame), who published a four-volume treatise (1819–1822) which specified the regular sound correspondences between Sanskrit, Greek, Latin, and the Germanic languages. It was not only the similarities that intrigued Grimm and the other linguists, but the systematic nature of the differences. Where Latin has a [p], English often has a [f]; where Latin has a [t], English often has a [θ]; where Latin has a [k], English often has a [h].

Grimm pointed out how these "sound shifts" must have occurred in what came to be known as "Grimm's law," which can be diagramed as shown in Figure 8.1.

The correspondences between the Romance (Latin) sounds and the Germanic (English) sounds are easily revealed:

SANSKRIT	LATIN	ENGLISH
[p]	[p] *p*ater	[f] *f*ather
[t]	[t] *t*res	[θ] *th*ree
[k]	[k] *c*or	[h] *h*eart
[b]	[b] la*b*ium	[p] li*p*
[d]	[d] *d*uo	[t] *t*wo
[g]	[g] a*g*er	[k] a*c*re
[bh]	[f] *f*rater	[b] *b*rother
[dh]	[f] *f*acio	[d] *d*o
[gh]	[h] *h*ortus	[g] *g*arden

We can see from the above that the voiced sounds became voiceless (*duo* → *two*], that the voiceless stops became fricatives (*pater* → *father*), and that the fricatives became voiced stops (*frater* → *brother*).

Exceptions can be found to these regular correspondences, and Grimm was aware of this. In fact, he did not call it a "law" but stated: "The sound shift is a general tendency; it is not followed in every case." Karl Verner in 1875 was able to explain some of the exceptions to Grimm's law; "Verner's law" accounted for the fact that Indo-European [p], [t], and [k] became [f], [θ], and [x] when the root syllable was accented, but [b], [d], and [g] in other cases.

A group of young linguists who became known as the New Grammarians went beyond the idea that such sound shifts represented only a tendency, and claimed that sound laws have no exception. They viewed linguistics as a natural science, and therefore believed that laws of sound change were universal natural laws. The laws which they put forth were often stated with respect to specific languages and times and places, and consequently they are not as universal as claimed. But the work of these linguists provided important data and insights into the changes which occurred and, in some cases, why such changes do occur.

Sherlock Holmes would have made an excellent linguist. This famous detective's attention to detail and his ability to make *all* his observations fit a consistent pattern have given him much fame in the realm of fictional criminology. Bopp, Rask, and Grimm were to historical linguistics what Holmes was to criminology. These men collected linguistic clues and by clever deduction and ingenuity pieced together a theory of historical linguistics. The linguists saw a number of similarities among a dozen or so modern spoken languages, plus Classical Latin, Ancient Greek, and Sanskrit, for which they had written records. They also perceived regularities in the differences among these languages. Their first conclusion was that all these languages evolved from a single language, which they called **Indo-Germanic** or **Indo-Aryan**. Later, less nationally minded scholars used the term we employ presently, **Indo-European**. In any case, the point was clear: A single language, through the mechanism of linguistic change, spawned languages that covered the geographical area of northern India and Europe, and everything in between.

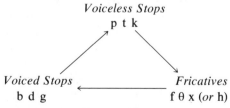

Figure 8.1 Diagram of Grimm's law.

HISTORICAL EVIDENCE

You know my method. It is founded upon the observance
of trifles.

—SIR ARTHUR CONAN DOYLE, "The Boscombe Valley Mystery"

One might wonder how we know about all these phonological changes.
How do we know how Shakespeare or Chaucer or the writer of Beowulf
pronounced their versions of English? Obviously, we have no phono-
graph records or tape recordings that would give us direct knowledge
of the pronunciation used.

We mentioned that for many languages there are historical records
which go back more than a thousand years. These records are studied
to find out how languages were pronounced long ago. The spelling in
early manuscripts tells us a great deal about the sound systems of older
forms of modern languages. If certain words are always spelled one way,
and other words another way, it is logical to conclude that the two groups
of words were pronounced differently, even if the precise pronunciation
is not known. For example, if you didn't know English, but you con-
sistently found that the word which meant "deep hole" was written as *pit,*
and the word for a domesticated animal was written as *pet,* it would be
safe to assume that these two words were pronounced differently. Once
a number of orthographic contrasts are identified, good guesses can be
made as to actual pronunciation. These guesses are greatly assisted by
certain common words which show up in all stages of the language, al-
lowing their pronunciation to be traced from the present, step by step,
into the past.

Another clue to earlier pronunciation is provided by non-English words
used in the manuscripts of English. Suppose a French word which
scholars know contains the vowel [o:] is borrowed into English. The
way the borrowed word is spelled reveals a particular spelling-sound
correspondence. A number of spelling symbols were related to certain
sounds in this way.

Other documents can be examined for evidence. Private letters are a
great source of data. Linguists care little for the gossip they contain
but cherish the linguistic information provided. Linguists prefer letters
written by "naïve" spellers, since they will misspell words according
to the way they pronounce them. For instance, at one point in English
history all words spelled with *er* were pronounced as if they were spelled
with *ar.* Naïve spellings show this to be the case. Some poor letter
writer kept writing *clark* for *clerk,* which did his reputation as a scholar
little good, though it helped linguists to uiscover the older pronunciation.

Clues are also provided by the writings of scholars interested in the
correct spelling and correct pronunciation of the language of their period.

Between 1550 and 1750, there existed a group of people in England known as orthoepists, who desired to preserve the purity of English. They busied themselves telling people what they should say, and in so doing they told us how the people of their time actually pronounced words. Suppose an orthoepist lived today who wished all speakers in America to pronounce words "correctly." He might write in his manual: "All those who pronounce *Cuba* with a final *r* are wrong! *Cuba* should not be pronounced as if it were spelled *Cuber*." In the future, scholars would know that there were speakers of English who did pronounce the word in this way.

Probably some of the best clues to earlier pronunciation are provided by puns and rhymes in literature. Two words rhyme if the vowels and final consonants of these words are the same. When a poet rhymes the verb *found* with the noun *wound*, it strongly suggests that the vowels of these two words were identical:

> BENVOLIO: . . . 'tis in vain to seek him here that means to not be found.
> ROMEO: He jests at scars that never felt a wound.
>
> *— Romeo and Juliet*

Shakespeare's rhymes are very helpful in reconstructing the sound system of Elizabethan English:

> When shall we three meet again
> In thunder, lightning, or in rain?
>   . . .
> Where's the place? Upon the heath
> There to meet with Macbeth
>
> *— Macbeth*

> But since he died, and poets better prove
> Theirs for their style I'll read, his for his love.
>
> *— Sonnet 32*

In the speech of Shakespeare's Elizabethan audience, *again* [əgen] rhymed with *rain* [ren], *heath* [hɛ:θ] with *Macbeth* [məkbɛθ], and *prove* [prov] with *love* [lov]. In modern English these words do not rhyme. The pronunciation of *again, heath, prove,* and *love* has changed as a result of changes in the sound system of English.

Dialect differences may provide clues as to what earlier stages of a language were like. There are many dialects of English spoken around the world, including a fair number in the United States. By comparing the pronunciations of various words in several dialects, we can "reconstruct" earlier forms and see what changes took place in the inventory of sounds and in the phonological rules. When we study different dialects it becomes apparent that all language change is not "hidden." We can actually observe some changes in progress.

For example, since some speakers of English pronounce *Mary, merry,* and *marry* with three different vowels (that is, [meri], [mɛri], and [mæri] respectively), we suspect that at one time all speakers of English did so. (The different spellings are also a clue.) For some dialects, however, only one of these sounds can occur before /r/, namely the sound [ɛ], so we can "see" a change taking place. When language historians hundreds of years from now are trying to reconstruct the various dialects of English they will be helped by the "drinking song" sung by the students of the University of California:

> They had to carry Harry to the ferry
> And the ferry carried Harry to the shore
> And the reason that they had to carry Harry to the ferry
> Was cause Harry couldn't carry any more.

This song was written by someone who rhymed *Harry, carry,* and *ferry*. It doesn't sound quite as good to those who do not rhyme *Harry* and *ferry*.

One can see such changes taking place. The linguist William Labov has studied "language change in progress" in New York City, and is now studying contemporary linguistic change in the Philadelphia community.

The historical-comparativists working on Indo-European languages, and other languages with written records, had a difficult job, but not nearly so difficult as those scholars who are attempting to discover genetic relationships among languages with no written history. Linguists have, however, been able to establish language families and reconstruct the histories of such individual languages. They first study the grammars of the languages and dialects spoken today and compare the sound systems, the vocabularies, and the syntax, seeing what correspondences exist. By this method, Major John W. Powell, Franz Boas, Edward Sapir, Mary Haas, and others have worked out the complex relationships of American Indian languages. Other linguists have worked with African languages, and have established seven major and five minor language families in Africa, each containing many subgroups. About a thousand different languages are involved in these twelve families.

LINGUISTIC PALEONTOLOGY

History is too serious to be left to historians.
— IAIN MACLEOD, in the *Observer* (July 16, 1961)

A fascinating application of historical linguistics is deducing information about the culture and location of an ancient civilization for which we have no written history, using as data its partially reconstructed language. Such studies are known as **linguistic paleontology**, and have been carried out extensively on Indo-European.

We have no direct written knowledge of the Indo-European peoples.

They are prehistoric. Yet with Holmesian ingenuity and tenacity, linguists have deduced quite a few things about the ancestors of many of us. For instance, in reconstructing Proto-Indo-European, we find a word for "daughter-in-law," but no word for "son-in-law." This leads us to believe that when a couple "married," they lived closer to the man's family than to the woman's family. This in turn indicates that these people did not form matriarchal families.

We find that the Indo-Europeans had terms for "cow," "sheep," "goat," "pig," "dog," "wolf," "duck," "bee," "oak," "beech," "willow," and "grain." But the lack of terms for vegetables or for special kinds of grain indicates a nonagricultural people that relied heavily on animal sources for food.

The words for "beech," "oak," "salmon," and "wolf," which are known to have existed in Proto-Indo-European, have been used in an attempt to pinpoint the geographical location of the Indo-European speech community. The lack of terms for trees of the Mediterranean or Asiatic areas such as the olive, cypress, and palm, coupled with the presence of terms for beech and oak trees, which are indigenous to eastern and central Europe, suggests an Indo-European homeland near those places, though this homeland might well have extended as far east as the Volga River. This hypothesis is supported by the presence of terms for "wolf" and "salmon," creatures of that geographic area, and the lack of terms for animals indigenous to Asia. Archeological discoveries in Rumania and the Ukraine support this hypothesis.

Knowing that Proto-Indo-European had no terms for silver, gold, and iron, we can deduce that they were a pre-iron-age peoples, placing them in time before 4000 B.C.

For language families without any written history, the attempt to reconstruct an earlier language from several modern languages shown to be related may be the only way of gaining any information about the history of the speakers of those languages. This method has proved modestly effective in the case of American Indian languages, though we may never achieve any detailed knowledge. But we get a rough picture of where peoples were at what point in time. Knowing that two languages are closely related, but widely separated geographically, tells us that one or the other group of speakers migrated (or they both migrated in opposite directions). By linguistic means we can determine approximately when the languages separated, hence when the peoples themselves separated. In addition to increasing linguistic knowledge, the study of linguistic change brings with it auxiliary rewards of knowledge in other fields.

A study of linguistic change could have been the inspiration for Shelley, who pointed out in his poem "Mutability" that

> Man's yesterday may ne'er be like his morrow;
> Nought may endure but Mutability.

SUMMARY

In this chapter we discussed the fact that all languages change through time. Linguistic change is a change in the grammar of a language. Examples were provided to illustrate that all parts of a grammar may change; that is, **phonological, syntactic, lexical,** and **semantic** changes occur. The particular types of changes were discussed: phonemes, phonological and syntactic rules, and words may be added, lost, or altered. The meanings of words also change.

No one knows all the causes for linguistic change. Basically, change comes about through children's restructuring of the grammar. Grammars are both simplified and elaborated; the elaborations may arise to counter the simplifications which could lead to unclarity and ambiguity.

It was shown that some sound changes result from physiological, **assimilative** processes. Others, like the Great Vowel Shift, are more difficult to explain. Grammatical changes may be explained, in part, as **analogic** changes. External borrowing from other languages also affects the grammar of a language.

The study of linguistic change is called **historical and comparative linguistics.** Linguists of the eighteenth and nineteenth centuries studied the internal changes which occurred in a language. They also compared languages, reconstructed earlier forms of particular language families, and classified languages according to their "family trees."

Historical-comparative linguists use many methods and a wide variety of data. Old written records are studied. Differences between related dialects and languages provide important clues to earlier stages. By studying various dialects of a language it is sometimes possible to partially reconstruct the linguistic prehistory of a people.

Finally, we saw that knowledge of the linguistic prehistory of peoples may provide clues to knowledge in other areas of prehistory.

EXERCISES

1. Many changes in the phonological system have occurred in English since 449 A.D. Below are some Old English words (given in their spelling and phonetic forms), and the same words as we pronounce them today. What sound changes have occurred in each case? Example:

   OE: hlūd [xlu:d] → Mod E: loud

   Change: (1) the [x] was lost; (2) the long vowel [u:] became [æw].

	OE			MOD E
1.	crabbe	[krabba]	→	crab
2.	fisc	[fɪsk]	→	fish
3.	fūl	[fu:l]	→	foul
4.	gāt	[ga:t]	→	goat
5.	lǣfan	[læ:van]	→	leave
6.	tēþ	[te:θ]	→	teeth

2. The Great Vowel Shift in English left its traces in modern English in such pairs as:
   1. ser*e*ne/ser*e*nity ([i]/[ɛ])
   2. div*i*ne/div*i*nity ([ay]/[ɪ])
   3. s*a*ne/s*a*nity ([e]/[æ])

   List as many pairs as you can which relate [i] and [ɛ] as in example 1, [ay] and [ɪ] as in example 2, and [e] and [æ] as in example 3.

3. At one time in English, the initial *k* and the final *g* of the following words were pronounced: *knight, know, knit; sing, long, bring.* Did a change take place in the phonemic inventory? the phonetic inventory? the phonological rules? Why?

4. Below are given some sentences taken from Old English, Middle English, and early Modern English texts, illustrating some changes which have occurred in the syntactic rules of English grammar. (Note: In the sentences, the earlier spelling forms and words have been changed to conform to modern English. That is, the OE sentence *His suna twegen mon brohte to bǣm cyninge* would be written as *His sons two one brought to that king,* which in Modern English would be *His two sons were brought to the king.*) Underline the parts of each sentence which differ from Modern English. Rewrite the sentence in Modern English. State, if you can, what changes must have occurred. Example:

   It *not* belongs to you.
   — SHAKESPEARE, *Henry IV*

   Mod. Eng: *It does not belong to you.*
   Change: It was once possible to negate a sentence by merely adding the negative morpheme *not* before the verb. Today, one must insert a *do* (in its proper morphological form) in addition to the *not.*

   1. It nothing pleased his master.
   2. He hath said that he would lift them whom that him please.
   3. I have a brother is condemned to die.
   4. I bade them take away you.
   5. I wish you was still more a Tartar.
   6. Christ slept and his apostles.
   7. Me was told.
   8. That is never without battle not was.

5. The vocabulary of English consists of "native" words and also thousands of borrowed words. Look up the following words in a dictionary which provides the etymologies (history) of words. State the source of each of them.

1. size	8. robot	15. skunk	22. pagoda
2. royal	9. check	16. catfish	23. khaki
3. aquatic	10. banana	17. hoodlum	24. shampoo
4. heavenly	11. keel	18. filibuster	25. kangaroo
5. skill	12. fact	19. astronaut	26. bulldoze
6. ranch	13. potato	20. emerald	
7. blouse	14. muskrat	21. sugar	

6. Make up ten new "compounds" which are not found in the dictionary but which could easily become new English words. Examples: *coldcat* "baloney" (see: *hotdog*); *dribbledoer* "basketball player who dribbles" (see: *goaltender*); *glassass* "someone who is accident prone."

7. Make up ten blends. Example: *nunday* "never on Sunday."

8. Words may shift in their meanings by becoming "narrower" or "wider." Look up the following words in a dictionary and state how the meanings have changed.

1. fowl	3. corn	5. record	7. paper
2. wife	4. virtue	6. queen	

9. The following are some different pronunciations of the same utterances. How do these illustrate some possible causes for language change? What happens in each case?

1. lots of money	lota money
2. I've got to	I gotta
3. John and Mary	John an Mary
4. why don't you?	whyncha?
5. do you want to eat?	wanna eat?
6. how would you?	howdja [hæwǰə]
7. how do you do	[hadu]
8. did you eat?	[ǰit]

References

BAUGH, A. C. *A History of the English Language*, 2nd ed. New York: Appleton-Century-Crofts, 1957.

BLOOMFIELD, L. *Language*. New York: Holt, Rinehart & Winston, 1933.

BLOOMFIELD, L., and HOIJER, H. *Language History* (from *Language*). New York: Holt, Rinehart & Winston, 1965.

BLOOMFIELD, M. W., and NEWMARK, LEONARD. *A Linguistic Introduction to the History of English.* New York: Knopf, 1963.

HOENIGSWALF, HENRY M. *Language Change and Linguistic Reconstruction.* Chicago: University of Chicago Press, 1960.

JESPERSEN, OTTO. *Growth and Structure of the English Language,* 9th ed. New York: Doubleday, 1955.

JESPERSEN, OTTO. *Language, Its Nature, Development, and Origin.* London: 1922; New York: Norton, 1964.

KING, ROBERT D. *Historical Linguistics and Generative Grammar.* Englewood Cliffs, N.J.: Prentice-Hall, 1969.

LASS, ROGER, ed. *Approaches to English Historical Linguistics: An Anthology.* New York: Holt, Rinehart & Winston, 1969.

LEHMANN, W. P. *Historical Linguistics: An Introduction.* New York: Holt, Rinehart & Winston, 1962.

MCKNIGHT, GEORGE H. *The Evolution of the English Language.* New York: Dover, 1968.

PEDERSEN, H. *The Discovery of Language.* Bloomington, Ind.: University of Indiana Press, 1962.

PYLES, THOMAS. *The Origins and Development of the English Language.* New York: Harcourt, Brace & World, 1964.

ROBERTSON, STUART, and CASSIDY, FREDERICK G. *The Development of Modern English.* Englewood Cliffs, N.J.: Prentice-Hall, 1969.

STURTEVANT, E. H. *Linguistic Change.* Chicago: University of Chicago Press, 1917.

TRAUGOTT, ELIZABETH CLOSS. *A History of English Syntax.* New York: Holt, Rinehart & Winston, 1972.

9
The Tower of Babel: Languages of the World

Let us go down, and there confound their language, that they may not understand one another's speech.

— The Book of Genesis

How many people of the world can be brought together so that no one person understands the language spoken by any other person? Considering that there are billions of people in the world, the number of mutually unintelligible languages is rather small — "only" about 3,000, according to one suggestion, and as many as 8,000, according to another. Table 9.1 at the end of this chapter lists some of these languages. Despite the seemingly large number of languages spoken in the world today, three-fourths of the world's population (2,500,000,000 people) speak but thirteen languages. As the figures in the table show, if you spoke Chinese,[1] English, Hindi, and Russian, you could communicate with approximately 1,600,000,000 people.

Of the 400,000,000 English speakers, 280,000,000 speak English as a first language and another 120,000,000 speak it as a second language. In addition, about 60 percent of the world's radio stations broadcast in English and more than half the periodicals of the world are published in English. This dominance of course reflects political and social factors as well as linguistic ones.

But even if you knew English, Chinese, Russian, and Hindi, you would be unable to talk to monolingual speakers of Arabic, Xhosa, Persian, Tamil, Navajo, and the several thousand other languages.

[1] Actually you would have to know the seven major dialects of Chinese, each of which is for the most part unintelligible to speakers of any of the others.

If we consider the superficial differences among these individual languages, the situation appears to be chaotic indeed. This has led some people to conclude that languages can differ in infinite or innumerable ways. If this were the case, then the attempt to understand the nature of human language would be doomed to failure, since one human language could differ from another to as great an extent as one human language could differ from, say, the "language" of the bees. Fortunately, this does not seem to be the case. The more we learn about the grammars of these languages, the more we see how basically similar they are. By understanding the similarities, and the limitations on the ways languages may differ, we begin to understand the nature of human language in general.

LANGUAGE UNIVERSALS

In a grammar there are parts which pertain to all languages; these components form what is called the general grammar. . . . In addition to these general (universal) parts, there are those which belong only to one particular language; and these constitute the particular grammars of each language.
— DU MARSAIS (c. 1750)

Throughout the ages, philosophers and linguists have been divided on the question of whether there are universal properties which hold for all human languages and are unique to them. Most modern linguists are on the side of the "universalists," since common, universal properties are found in the grammars of all languages. Such properties may be said to constitute a "universal" grammar of human language.

In 1588, the German philosopher Alsted first used the term *general grammar* as distinct from *special grammar*. He believed that the function of a *general grammar* was to reveal those features "which relate to the method and etiology of grammatical concepts. They are common to all languages." Pointing out that "general grammar is the pattern 'norma' of every particular grammar whatsoever," he implored "eminent linguists to employ their insight in this matter."[2]

Three hundred years before Alsted, the scholar Robert Kilwardby put forth the view that linguists should be concerned with discovering the nature of language in general. So concerned was Kilwardby with universal grammar that he excluded considerations of the characteristics

[2] V. Salmon, review of *Cartesian Linguistics* by N. Chomsky, *Journal of Linguistics* 5, 165–187.

of particular languages, which he believed to be as "irrelevant to a science of grammar as the material of the measuring rod or the physical characteristics of objects were to geometry."[3]   In a sense, Kilwardby was too much of a universalist, for the particular properties of individual languages are relevant to the discovery of language universals, and are, in addition, of interest for their own sake.

The emphasis these scholars placed on the universal properties of language may lead someone attempting to study Latin, Greek, French, or Swahili as a second language to assert, in frustration, that those ancient scholars were so hidden in their ivory towers that they confused reality with idle speculation.   Yet, if we summarize some of what has already been discussed in previous chapters, we may better understand the universalist's position.   The following list of "linguistic universals" is far from complete; literally hundreds of entries could be added:

1. Wherever man exists, language exists.
2. There are no primitive languages—all languages are equally complex and equally capable of expressing any idea in the universe. The vocabulary of any language can be expanded to include new words for new concepts.
3. All languages change through time.
4. All human languages utilize sounds to express meaning, and the relationships between sounds and meanings are for the most part arbitrary.
5. All human languages utilize a finite set of discrete sounds which are combined to form "meaningful" elements (morphemes), which themselves are combined to form "whole thoughts" (sentences).
6. All grammars contain phonological and syntactic rules of a similar kind.
7. Similar grammatical categories (for example, noun, verb) are found in all languages.
8. There are universal semantic concepts found in every language in the world.   Every language has a system of tense, the ability to negate, the ability to form questions, and so on.
9. Speakers of all human languages are capable of producing and comprehending an infinite set of sentences.
10. Any normal child, born anywhere in the world, of any racial, geographical, social, or economic heritage, is capable of learning any language to which he is exposed.   The differences we find among languages cannot be due to biological reasons.

It seems that Alsted and Du Marsais (and we could add many other "universalists" from all ages) were not spinning idle thoughts.   We all speak "human language."

---

[3] V. Salmon, op. cit.

HOW LANGUAGES DIFFER

He that understands grammar in one language, under-
stands it in another as far as the essential properties of
Grammar are concerned. The fact that he can't speak, nor
comprehend, another language is due to the diversity of
words and their various forms, but these are the accidental
properties of grammar.

— ROGER BACON (1214–1294)

The "accidental properties" of which Bacon spoke make it impossible for a French speaker and an Arabic speaker to converse and understand each other. What are these "properties" which differentiate between languages?

The **phonological systems** of languages differ. Different languages have different inventories of sounds, though all languages will have some of the same sounds; in fact, certain sounds are found in every language. All languages have vowels and consonants, and the consonants always include stops and continuants, while the vowels always include a high front vowel.

Consider, for example, English and Twi, two widely different languages from two distinct language families. They both contain the consonants /p/, /t/, /k/, /b/, /d/, /g/, /m/, /n/, /ŋ/, /f/, /s/, /h/, /r/, /w/, /y/, /č/, and /ǰ/ and the vowels /i/, /ɪ/, /e/, /ɛ/, /u/, /ʊ/, /o/, /ɔ/, and /a/. There are sounds in English not found in Twi, such as /z/, /v/, /θ/, /ð/, and /l/, and there are sounds in Twi not found in English, such as /čʷ/ (which is like the *ch* sound in *church* but with your lips rounded) or /ǰʷ/ (like the *j* sound in *judge* with the lips rounded).

Languages may also differ as to the particular **phonological rules** in their grammars, although the rules often refer to the same classes of sounds. In English there is a rule that aspirates voiceless stops if they are word-initial. In Thai there is a rule that states: "Voiceless stops are 'unreleased' (unexploded) in word-final position." The following rule is found in English and in many other languages: "When two similar consonants come together, simplify them into one consonant." Thus when we combine *big* /bɪg/ with *girl* /gərl/ we delete one *g:*

/bɪg gərl/ → [bɪgərl].

This rule is not found in all languages, but the rule in English which states that a vowel is nasalized before a nasal consonant is probably a universal rule. In English, from /bæn/ *ban* we get the phonetic [bæ̃n]; in Twi from /kum/ "kill" we get the phonetic [kũm]. This phonological rule seems to be conditioned by general physiological constraints.

The syntactic rules of languages may also differ. The basic phrase-structure rules, which produce the "deep structures" of sentences, are more similar across languages than the transformational rules, which alter word order, add elements, delete elements, and so on. We find in all languages that sentences contain a noun-phrase subject (S), a verb or predicate (V) and possibly a noun-phrase object (O). In some languages the basic or "preferred" order of these elements is subject-verb-object (SVO). Many familiar languages, such as French, Spanish, and English, are examples. Other languages, such as Japanese and Korean, have the preferred order subject-object-verb (SOV). Still others, such as Hebrew and Welsh, are VSO languages, and rarely one finds a language like Malagasy (spoken on Madagascar), which is VOS.

No language has been discovered that is OSV or OVS. Phrase-structure rules produce only the four preferred orders, indicating a "universal" rule: "In the preferred word order of all languages, the object is never first."

The transformational rules, however, may cause the production of a nonpreferred order, as in the "cleft" sentence *It's a wombat that Willy whipped.* In general, transformations may produce any word order, so these rules vary more from language to language than the phrase-structure rules.

Languages may also differ syntactically in the way questions are formed. Many languages (including English) may form a simple "yes-no" question merely by changing the pitch contour of the sentence. A declarative sentence is spoken with a falling pitch at the end:

   You are going.

The question is spoken with a rising pitch at the end:

   You are going?

This intonational distinction seems to be universal. That is, in languages which can use pitch alone to distinguish statements from questions, one inevitably finds the rising pitch at the end of the question. If one uses a change in word order in English, however, it is the word order which marks the "interrogative," and the pitch may fall, as in the neutral or declarative sentence:

   Are you going?

Other languages use other means to form yes-no questions. Thai, for example, adds an interrogative particle to the end of a sentence that would otherwise be a declarative statement:

   khăw cà maa "he'll come" → *khăw cà maa măj* "will he come?"

Măj [măy] is virtually a phonetic question mark. Yoruba and Twi behave like Thai, and Zapotec, an Indian language of Mexico, adds a particle at the beginning of the interrogative sentence, or one at the beginning and one at the end, much like the question mark of Spanish orthography.

In English, as in most Indo-European languages, a common way of forming a yes-no question is to change word order:

> He is mad. → Is he mad?
> John is mad. → Is John mad?

In French one finds a similar "transformation." The same sentences in French are:

> Il est fou. → Est-il fou?
> Jean est fou. → Jean est-il fou?

In all these languages there must be a special transformational rule specifying just what must be done to form yes-no questions. The specifics of the individual rules differ. Notice that in French, word order is changed as in English when the subject is a pronoun; but when the subject is not a pronoun the rule does not change the position of the subject, but inserts a pronoun after the verb.

Despite the differences in specific rules, all languages have a rule for yes-no question formation. This *type* of rule, then, is "universal."

There are many other syntactic differences which are found. Language is so complex that this should not be surprising. There are languages where the auxiliary (such as the English words *will, may,* and so on) precedes the verb, and other languages where the auxiliary follows the verb (for example, Japanese). There are languages where noun modifiers (adjectives) normally precede the noun in a noun phrase:

> English: the *red* book
> Russian: *interesnaya* gazeta ("interesting newspaper")

There are languages where the modifier usually follows the noun:

> French: le livre rouge ("the book red")
> Igbo: éféré úkwú ("plate large")

There appear to be systematic relations between syntactic differences. Joseph Greenberg has proposed (as a starter) forty-five universals which relate to syntax and word formation. One of his universals is: "In languages with dominant order SOV an inflected auxiliary always follows the main verb."[4] So even certain differences between languages are "regular."

The relations between particular strings of sounds and particular meanings *(lexical differences)* are the most obvious differences between languages, as is illustrated by the following translations of *water: wasser* (German), *agua* (Spanish), *uisce* (Irish), *maji* (Swahili), *nsu* (Twi),

---

[4] Joseph Greenberg, *Universals of Language.* Cambridge: M.I.T. Press, 1963.

pani (Hindi), *voda* (Russian), *šuudek* (Pima), *čaʔak* (Nootka), *náam* (Thai), *shuǐ* (Mandarin Chinese), *oyu* (Japanese).

We have seen that languages may differ phonologically, syntactically, and lexically. The differences one finds in the grammars of languages of the world play an important role when we try to define "human language." A theory of language must be able to account for just those differences that actually exist, as well as for all the universal properties which are found.

TYPES OF LANGUAGES

> *All the Oriental nations jam tongue and words together in the throat, like the Hebrews and Syrians. All the Mediterranean peoples push their enuciation forward to the palate, like the Greeks and the Asians. All the Occidentals break their words on the teeth, like the Italians and Spaniards. . . .*
>
> — ISADORE OF SEVILLE (7th century A.D.)

In order to determine the similarities and differences which exist between languages, it is helpful to put some order into the apparent chaos. Many different classification schemes have been devised.

One system classifies languages according to various properties they possess. In such a "typological" classification, August Schleicher, an outstanding linguist of the nineteenth century, set up a tripartite division of language classification: *isolating, agglutinating,* and *inflecting.*

According to this system, in **isolating** languages, typified by Chinese, both grammatical relationships, and syntactic functions are indicated by word order rather than by derivational or inflectional affixes. In Chinese, one morpheme equals one word (and usually one syllable), and a morpheme rarely undergoes a change in its phonological shape. The morpheme *kuaile,* for example, is pronounced the same whether it is used as a noun, verb, or adjective. It can mean "to be happy" or "happiness" or "happy." In isolating languages, prefixes or suffixes are rarely found. Even in Chinese, however, this is an oversimplified picture. The tone (pitch) of a morpheme may be changed when the word class is changed.

In **agglutinating** languages, various morphemes are combined to form a single word; each element maintains a distinct and fixed meaning. In such languages, prefixes, suffixes, and even "infixes" are used over and over again to build new words. They usually keep their same phonological shape, except for phonetic changes resulting from the regular phonological rules of the language.

English, according to this definition, is somewhat agglutinating. The suffix *-ness,* for example, can be attached to virtually any adjective to form a noun: *good/goodness, red/redness, tired/tiredness.* The prefix *in-* is another example; it produces negative adjectives: *incomplete, intolerant, indecisive, inescapable, indispensable.* Of course, as we have already pointed out, the phonological rules of English change the phonetic shape of /in-/ according to the sound that follows.

Turkish and Swahili are agglutinating languages; Swahili mostly by prefixing, Turkish mostly by suffixing. In Turkish, the word for "tooth" is *diš* and the word for "house" is *ev.* The following examples illustrate the "agglutinating" character of the language.

diš "tooth"   dišim "my tooth"   dišimde "in my tooth"
ev "house"   evim "my house"   evimde "in my house"

The suffixes *-im* and *-de* can be attached to most noun stems and carry the meaning of "my" and "in the" respectively. In Turkish several suffixes may be attached to a stem, resulting in a complex polymorphemic word (which may be a whole sentence). Thus:

kɨr + ɨl + ma + dɨ + lar + mɨ (kɨrɨlmadɨlarmɨ)
Were they not broken?

In this case,

kɨr = "break"
ɨl = passive voice
ma = negative
dɨ = past tense
lar = plural
mɨ = interrogative

The stem "break" has been modified by the addition of five distinct morphemes to give the meaning shown above. To accomplish the same effect in English we must do the following:

Concept: *break*
Passive voice: *to be broken*
Negative: *to not be broken*
Past tense: (it) *was not broken*
Plural: (they) *were not broken*
Question: *were* (they) *not broken?*

It is clear that English is not an "agglutinating" language to the degree that Turkish is, although from the examples above it appears to have some agglutinating characteristics.

Swahili would also be classified as "agglutinating" by the definition given, but it is a "prefixing" rather than a "suffixing" language, as the following examples illustrate

ni + na + penda	"I" + present tense + "love" ("I love")
ni + na + sema	"I" + present tense + "speak" ("I speak")
ni + li + penda	"I" + past tense + "love" ("I loved")

An examination of the languages of the world shows that there are many languages which use only suffixes as their "additive" elements, but very few which use only prefixes. Swahili uses mostly prefixes but also uses some "infixes" (morphemes inserted into the middles of words). Thai, often considered an isolating language, does use prefixes when it uses any affixes at all, but this is truly exceptional.

The third type of language in this classificatory scheme is **inflectional.** In such languages, a word or morpheme undergoes a change in form when its grammatical function in the sentence is changed. Morphemes are added to lexical stems, but these added elements fuse with the stem and have no independence.

Modern English is somewhat inflectional. Some adjectives and their corresponding nouns reveal this "fusion": *deep/depth, long/length, wide/width.*

At one time, as was discussed in Chapter 8, Old English was highly inflectional. Many inflectional endings were lost and English became more "isolating"; the syntactic information provided by these endings was then supplied by other syntactic means (for example, more use of prepositions and stricter word order). The remnants of English inflection are exemplified by the different forms of the first-person-singular pronoun:

I: when it occurs as the subject NP of a sentence.
       I love you.
me: when it occurs as the object of a verb or preposition.
       You love *me*. Give it to *me*.
mine: when it occurs as the possessive pronoun.
       The book is *mine*.
my: when it occurs as the possessive pronominal adjective.
       My book is lost.

The different forms for the first-person-singular pronoun demonstrate how difficult it would be to separate out the individual syntactic and semantic features that are fused into one morpheme. This is also revealed in English by the inflectional ending -*s* added to the present-tense form of the verb after a third-person-singular subject (pronounced differently, of course, according to the last sound in the verb stem):

I hit	you hit	he/she/it hit +s	we hit	they hit
I love	you love	he/she/it love +s	we love	they love
I catch	you catch	he/she/it catch +es	we catch	they catch

This inflectional ending — one of the few remaining in English — combines the meaning "third person," "present tense," and "singular" in an indissoluble form.

On the other hand, the ▪-*d* attached to the verb to form the past tense means only "past tense." Neither the singular or plural distinction nor the "person" is specified in the -*d* suffix. This is, then, an "agglutinative" suffix.

Latin and Greek are highly inflected languages. In Latin the verb stem is inflected for person, number, and tense:

amo	first person, singular, present tense	"I love"
amas	second person, singular, present tense	"you love"
amat	third person, singular, present tense	"he/she loves"
amamus	first person, plural, present tense	"we love"
amatis	second person, plural, present tense	"you love"
amant	third person, plural, present tense	"they love"

Notice that the -*o* in *amo* represents "first person" + "singular" + "present." One cannot separate out these elements as independent units.

Schleicher proposed that these three types represent different stages in the evolution of languages. Like many other nineteenth-century linguists, he was strongly influenced by Darwin. He believed that each language has a "life cycle" and like plants and animals is subject to "natural" evolution—that is, a language is born, lives, gives birth to a new language (a daughter) which in turn replaces it, and the daughter in time will also be replaced by its progeny. Schleicher also assumed that the inflection stage represents the highest level of a language; when a language reaches this stage it has nowhere to go but down. This idea was compatible with the classicist notion that Greek and Latin represented the highest, most beautiful forms of language.

Schleicher also supported his view by analogies with nature. According to him, each stage corresponds with one of the basic forms of the world. Languages in the isolating stage correspond to the crystals found in nature; the agglutinating stage he related to plants; and the inflecting stage he correlated with animal life.

The last scholar to pay serious attention to this kind of development was Otto Jespersen, but he suggested that the development was just the opposite from that put forth by Schleicher. According to Jespersen, the highest stage a language could reach was the isolating stage.

Linguists have discovered that no language is purely one type or another. Also, despite their differences, languages of the three "types" have much in common. They all have similar syntactic categories, and although transformational rules "look" different in languages of one type or another, they often perform the same function. Thus, possession may be expressed on the surface by an inflectional form (for example, *the book's cover*) or by an isolating form (*the cover of the book*), but the basic relationship remains the same.

WHY LANGUAGES DIFFER AND
YET REMAIN THE SAME

Get used to thinking that there is nothing Nature loves so well as to change existing forms and to make new ones like them.

— MARCUS AURELIUS, *Meditations*

The ways in which languages change account to a great extent for the kinds of differences one finds in the world's languages. Even when languages are in one language family, different changes occur in each.

We can illustrate how many of the world's languages arose by a rather oversimplified hypothetical situation. Consider a community of people speaking one language. If they all stay in the same place, communicate with one another, send their children to the same schools, go to the same movies, and watch the same television shows, the changes that occur will be reflected in the whole community. No one will notice them.

But suppose from among this one language community, a group of people decide that the hunting or the farming or the climate is better over the mountains, and so set off to settle new regions. Suppose, further, that they settle very far from the first group and have no way of communicating.

Group A, the people that "stay put," and Group B, the travelers, start out speaking the same language, L. Once they are separated, some changes occur in L spoken by Group A, and other changes occur in language L spoken by Group B. After some time, say a hundred years, Group A will speak L_1 and Group B will speak L_2. At this point they will probably still understand each other. They will thus be speaking two dialects of L. But in five hundred years the changes may be so great that the two dialects are no longer mutually understandable. Thus two languages have arisen from one parent language.

This hypothetical case reflects what happened over the thousands of years of man's wandering around the earth. In earlier periods of history when a group took off for a new place, regular contact with the motherland (and the mother tongue) was broken, and the language was free to change independently in both groups.

German, for example, changed in different ways than did its sister, English. German retained more "inflectional" processes than English, and German syntax differs from English syntax with regard to the position of the verb and auxiliary verbs, which often come at the end of the sentence. This particular characteristic of German inspired Mark Twain to say:

> Whenever the literary German dives into a sentence, that is the last you are going to see of him till he emerges on the other side of the Atlantic with his verb in his mouth.[5]

Languages differ in their particular elements and rules because elements and rules change, are added, or are dropped from grammars. Meanings change and all aspects of the sound system also change. But the changes which occur are all within the limits which constrain human languages and their grammars. No language will ever be without vowels, nor will the syntactic rules of a language ever change to allow it to become an object-verb-subject (OVS) language.

We have seen that the "preferred" order of the subject, verb, and object may differ from one language to another. We have also seen that transformational rules may switch the order of elements:

> Unicorns are stunning → Are unicorns stunning?
> My sheepdog loves to eat popcorn → It's popcorn my sheepdog
> loves to eat.
> Spiro sent a letter to the president → Spiro sent the president a letter.

But we never find in any language of the world a rule which says "Reverse the order of all the words in the sentence" or "Reverse the sounds of an adjective to get its opposite." Such rules are not possible rules. An adequate theory of language must not allow such rules, as it is the nature of human language not to have them.

Similarly we find in many languages a type of rule that permits the deletion of certain elements. Thus, syntactic rules of English permit the following:

> I know that he is coming late → I know θ he is coming late.
> Joanne is lazier than I am → Joanne is lazier than I. θ
> or
> Joanne is lazier than me.

But we never find in any language a rule that says "Delete every other word of a sentence" or "Delete all final words." Again we see that there are universal constraints on what can occur. If there were no holds barred where language diversity is concerned, there would not be such universal restrictions.

Knowing that universal constraints on rules exist in all languages may help when one is trying to learn a foreign language. An English speaker studying French for the first time may have to learn that the NP expansion rule in French is: NP → Art + N + Adj, whereas the English rule he already knows says NP → Art + Adj + N, but he already intuitively knows what an NP is, what an article is, and how nouns differ from adjectives.

[5] Mark Twain, *A Connecticut Yankee at King Arthur's Court.*

This is the meaning of Bacon's statement that "a person knowing grammar in one language knows the grammar of all languages, except for accidental differences."

THE GENETIC CLASSIFICATION OF LANGUAGES

The Sanskrit language, whatever be its antiquity, is of a wonderful structure, more perfect than the Greek, more copious than the Latin, and more exquisitely refined than either, yet bearing to both of them a stronger affinity, both in the roots of verbs and in the forms of grammar, than could possibly be produced by accident; so strong, indeed, that no philologer could examine all three, without believing that they have sprung from some common source, which, perhaps, no longer exists . . .

—SIR WILLIAM JONES (1786)

Languages, like ~~men~~, are created equal. But it seems that, also like ~~men~~, some languages are "more equal" than others. A French speaker can learn Spanish more easily than he can learn Russian, although that wouldn't be true of a Bulgarian speaker. This is because French and Spanish are both modern forms of Latin, just as Russian and Bulgarian are modern forms of an earlier Slavic language. It is not surprising that languages in the same family resemble each other more than languages descending from a different branch of the genealogical tree.

The languages of the world belong to families and bear offspring. Chapter 8 discussed how different languages are "born" from one language, and how historical and comparative linguists classify languages into families and reconstruct earlier forms of the ancestral language. When we examine the languages of the world, we perceive similarities and differences among them that provide further evidence for the "genetic" relatedness we know exists.

Counting to five in English, German, and Pima (a southwestern American Indian language) shows similarities between English and German not shared by Pima:

ENGLISH	GERMAN	PIMA
one	eins	hermako
two	zwei	gohk
three	drei	waik
four	fier	giik
five	fünf	hetasp

This similarity between English and German is pervasive. Sometimes it is extremely obvious (*man/Mann*), other times a little less obvious (*child/ Kind*).

Because German and English are human languages, we expect to find certain similarities between them. But there are more similarities than in other languages. It is not the case that they are related because they are highly similar, however. Rather, they are highly similar because they are related. They are related because at one time in history they were the same language, namely the language spoken by the German tribes that settled in Britain in the fifth century. Languages which are related were, at some point in the past, one language.

Fifth-century German is the parent of Modern English and Modern German, which are its daughters; English and German are sisters. Sisterhood is the fundamental genealogical relationship between languages. Similarly, Latin has mothered the Romance languages; French, Spanish, Portuguese, Italian, and Romanian are daughters of Latin and sisters to one another.

Where there are mothers and sisters, there must be *cousins*. At one time, well over two thousand years ago, an early form of the German from which English ultimately descended and an early form of Latin were sisters. The respective offspring are cousins. The five Romance languages listed above are cousins to English. The numbers from one to three in the three languages reveal this relationship:

SPANISH	FRENCH	ENGLISH
uno	un	one
dos	deux	two
tres	trois	three

Norwegian, Yiddish, Danish, Icelandic, and Dutch are all close relatives of English. They, like English, descended from an early form of German. Greek is a somewhat more distant cousin. The Celtic language gave birth to Irish, Scots Gaelic, Welsh, and Breton, all cousins of English. Breton is spoken by the people living in the northwest coastal regions of France called Brittany. It was brought there by Celts fleeing the Germans in the fifth century from Britain, and preserved as a second language for some Celtic descendants ever since. Russian is also a distant cousin, as are its sisters, Bulgarian, Serbo-Croatian, Polish, and Czecho-Slovak. The Baltic language, Lithuanian, is related to English, as is its neighboring language, Latvian. A third neighbor, Estonian, however, is not a relative. Sanskrit, as pointed out by Sir William Jones, as far removed from the European languages as it appears to be, is a distant cousin of these languages, as are its daughters, Hindi, spoken in India, and Bengali, spoken primarily in Bangladesh. Even Modern

Persian, the language of Iran in the Middle East, is a distant cousin of English.

All the languages mentioned in the last paragraph, except for Estonian, are related, more or less distantly. As such they must have evolved from a single ancient language, spoken at one time in the distant past — approximately eight thousand years ago. It is called Indo-European by linguists. No one knows what name, if any, its speakers used for it.

Figure 9.1, an abbreviated "family tree" of the Indo-European family of languages, gives a genealogical and historical classification of the languages shown. All the languages of the world may be similarly classified. This diagram of the Indo-European family is actually somewhat over-simplified. For one thing, the "dead-ends" — languages that evolved and died, leaving no offspring — are not included. A language dies when no children learn it. This may come about in two ways: either all the speakers of the language are annihilated by some tragic event, perhaps a volcanic eruption or a war, or, more commonly, the speakers of the language are absorbed by another culture that speaks a different language. The children, at first bilingual, grow up using the language of the dominant culture. Their children, or their children's children, fail to learn the old language, and so it dies. This is what has become of many American Indian languages. Cornish, a Celtic language akin to Welsh, met a similar fate in England in the last century. In fact, all the Celtic languages left in the world today, Irish, Scots Gaelic, Welsh, and Breton, are relentlessly being squeezed out of existence by English and French, which are dominant where these languages are spoken. Today, however, there are "revival" movements among these people to "resurrect" their old languages. In Brittany, for example, many of the popular singers use only Breton.

One "dead" language has been reborn. For over two millennia Hebrew had been used only as a religious language. The Jewish Book of Laws, the Talmud, is read ceremonially in Hebrew, and prayers are recited in Hebrew, just as Latin, Classical Arabic, and Sanskrit are used in other religions. Because of the persecution of the Jews in history and their spread throughout the world, there was no opportunity until recently for Hebrew to be revived. But with the establishment of Israel, Hebrew had a place to flourish as a national language, and many determined Jews learned it as a second language and adapted it for daily use in the twentieth century. These new Israelites used only Hebrew in the presence of their children, who learned it as their native language. With that, Hebrew rejoined the living languages of the world after being dead for more than two thousand years.

The diagram also fails to show a number of intermediate stages that must have existed in the evolution of modern languages. Languages do not evolve abruptly. It is difficult to determine precisely when a "new" language appears. There is evidence that Germanic had at first three

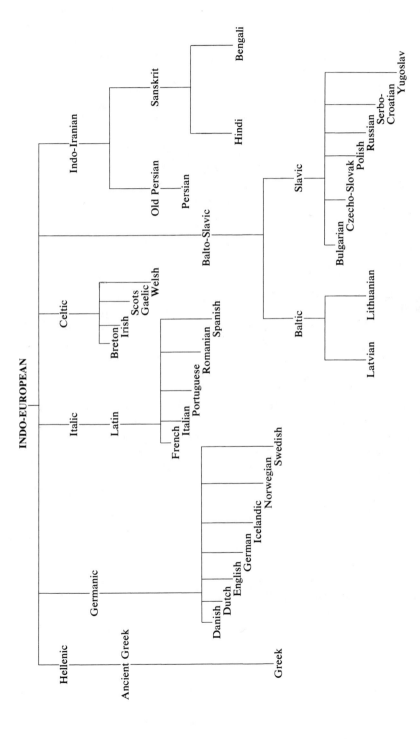

Figure 9.1 The Indo-European family of languages.

daughters. From the northernmost daughter, the Scandinavian languages evolved; English, German, and Dutch evolved from the westernmost daughter.

The diagram is also inadequate in that it fails to show a number of Indo-European languages that are spoken by only a handful of people today. Faeroese, a sister of English spoken on the Faeroe Islands north of Scotland, has a few thousand speakers. Yiddish, spoken in various forms by a fairly large number of Jews all over the world, developed from twelfth-century German. It can be considered a sister language of Modern German.

The final deficiency of the diagram arises out of our lack of knowledge concerning the status of certain languages. Albanian is not in this Indo-European family tree, although many linguists think it is an Indo-European language. There are some linguists, however, who think it is unrelated.

Many mysteries still remain in this best-studied language family, even though most of the Indo-European languages have left written records of their history.

Obviously, most of the world's languages do not belong to the Indo-European family. Linguists have also attempted to classify the non-Indo-European languages according to their genetic relationships. The task is to identify the languages which constitute a family, and the relationships which exist among those languages.

The results of this research are often surprising; faraway Bengali is an Indo-European language, whereas Hungarian, surrounded on all sides by Indo-European languages, is not.

For linguists interested in the nature of human language, the number of languages in the many different language families provides necessary data. Although these data are diverse in many ways, they are also remarkably similar in many ways. We find that the languages of the "wretched Greenlanders," the Maoris of New Zealand, the Hottentots of Africa, and the people of North America have similar sounds, similar phonological and syntactic rules, and similar semantic systems. There is evidence, then, that we need a theory of language which aims at universality as well as specificity.

In Mark Twain's *Huckleberry Finn,* the slave Jim showed himself to have a real understanding of universal grammar. (In the following passage it should be noted that Twain was attempting to capture the vernacular used by the slaves at that time. That he was in no way making fun of such a dialect is evident from the passage itself and, of course, from his strong antislavery position.)

> "Why, Huck, doan' de French people talk de same way we does?"
> "No, Jim, you couldn't understand a word they said—not a single word—"
> "Well, now, I be ding-busted! How do dat come?"

"I don't know, but it's so. I got some of their jabber out of a book. S'pose a man was to come to you and say Polly-voo-franzy. What would you think?"

"I wouldn't think nuffn, I'd take en bust him over de head — dat is, if he warn't white." . . .

"Shucks, it ain't calling you anything. It's only saying, do you know how to talk French?"

"Well, den, why couldn't he say it?"

"Why he *is* a-saying it. That's a Frenchman's *way* of saying it."

"Well, it's a blame ridicklous way, en I doan' want to hear no mo' bout it. Dey ain't no sense in it."

"Looky here, Jim, does a cat talk like we do?"

"No, a cat don't."

"Well, does a cow?"

"No, a cow don't nuther."

"Does a cat talk like a cow, or a cow talk like a cat?"

"No, dey don't."

"It's natural and right for 'em to talk different from each other, ain't it?"

"Course."

"And ain't it natural and right for a cat and a cow to talk different from us?"

"Why mos sholy it is."

"Well, then, why ain't it natural and right for a Frenchman to talk different from us? You answer me that."

"Is a cat a man, Huck?"

"No."

"Well, den, dey ain't no sense in a cat talkin' like a man. Is a cow a man? er is a cow a cat?"

"No, she ain't either of them."

"Well, den, she ain't got no business to talk like either one er the yuther of 'em. Is a Frenchman a man?"

"Yes."

"Well, den. Dad blame it, why doan he *talk* like a man? You answer me *dat*."

What Jim did not know was that he and a Frenchman did both talk like men — and to a great extent spoke the same language, human language — except for the "accidental differences."

Table 9.1   Some Languages of the World

Language family	Language	Principal geographic areas where spoken	Rank in number of speakers if in top 13	
		INDO-EUROPEAN (see Figure 9.1)		
Germanic	Danish	Denmark	_____	
	Dutch[a]	Netherlands, Indonesia	_____	
	English	North America, Great Britain, Australia, New Zealand	(2)	400,000,000
	Faeroese	Faeroe Islands	_____	
	Flemish[a]	Belgium	_____	
	German	Germany, Austria, Switzerland	(7)	120,000,000
	Icelandic	Iceland	_____	
	Norwegian	Norway	_____	
	Swedish	Sweden	_____	
	Yiddish	(diffuse)	_____	
Italic — Latin	Catalan	Spain	_____	
	Dalmatian	Adriatic coast (Yugoslavia	_____	
	French	France, Belgium, Switzerland, Quebec, Haiti, Algeria, Morocco	(12)	85,000,000
	Italian	Italy, Switzerland, Libya	(13)	65,000,000
	Portuguese	Portugal, Brazil, parts of Africa	(9)	105,000,000
	Provençal	Southern France	_____	
	Rhaeto-Romanic	Switzerland, Italy	_____	
	Romanian	Romania, parts of the Balkans	_____	
	Sardinian	Sardinia	_____	
	Spanish	Spain, Latin America	(5)	205,000,000
Celtic	Breton	Brittany (France)	_____	
	Irish	Ireland	_____	
	Scots Gaelic	Scotland	_____	
	Welsh	Wales	_____	
Hellenic	Greek	Greece	_____	

[a] Dutch and Flemish are dialects of the same language.

Table 9.1   Some Languages of the World — *continued*

Language family	Language	Principal geographic areas where spoken	Rank in number of speakers if in top 13	
Balto-Slavic	Bulgarian	Bulgaria	————	
	Czecho-Slovak	Czechoslovakia	————	
	Latvian	Latvia (USSR)	————	
	Lithuanian	Lithuania (USSR)	————	
	Polish	Poland	————	
	Russian	USSR	(4)	210,000,000
	Serbo-Croatian	Yugoslavia	————	
	Yugoslav	Yugoslavia	————	
Indo-Iranian	Bengali	Bangladesh	(10)	100,000,000
	Hindi (including Urdu)	Northern India, Pakistan	(3)	240,000,000
	Persian	Iran	————	
(?)	Albanian	Albania, Southern Italy	————	
Armenian	Armenian	Asia Minor, Caucasus	————	

OTHER THAN INDO-EUROPEAN

Language family	Language	Principal geographic areas where spoken	Rank in number of speakers if in top 13	
Basque	Basque	Pyrenees	————	
Finno-Ugric	Estonian	Estonia (USSR)	————	
	Finnish	Finland	————	
	Hungarian	Hungary	————	
	Lap	Northern parts of Norway, Finland, Sweden, Russia	————	
Altaic	Mongolian	Mongolia	————	
	Turkish (a number of languages spoken in the Caucasus)	Turkey	————	
Japanese (?)	Japanese	Japan	(8)	110,000,000
Korean (?)	Korean	Korea	————	

Table 9.1   Some Languages of the World—*continued*

Language family	Language	Principal geographic areas where spoken	Rank in number of speakers if in top 13	
Sino-Tibetan	Burmese	Burma	_____	
	Cambodian	Cambodia	_____	
	Chinese (actually 7 mutually un-intelligible "dialects")	China, Formosa	(1)	800,000,000
	Laotian	Laos	_____	
	Thai	Thailand	_____	
	Vietnamese	Vietnam	_____	
	Tibetan	Tibet	_____	
Dravidian	Malayalam	Southern India	_____	
	Kanarese	Southern India	_____	
	Tamil	Southern India	_____	
	Telugu	Southern India	_____	
Malayo-Polynesian	Formosan	Formosa	_____	
	Fiji	Fiji Islands	_____	
	Hawaiian	Hawaiian Islands		
	Indonesian (Malay)	Indonesia, Malasia	(11)	80,000,000
	Javanese	Island of Java	_____	
	Malagasy	Madagascar	_____	
	Samoan	Samoan Islands	_____	
	Tagalog	Philippines	_____	
	Tahitian	Tahitian Islands		
Niger-Congo	Akan (Twi)	Ghana, Ivory Coast	_____	
	Ibo	Nigeria (Biafra)	_____	
	Yoruba	Nigeria	_____	
	Luganda	Uganda	_____	
	Swahili	East Africa	_____	
	Zulu	Southern Africa	_____	
	Bambara	Mali		
Khoisan ("click" languages)	Bushman	Southern Africa	_____	
	Hottentot	Southern Africa	_____	
	Xhosa	Southern Africa	_____	

Table 9.1   Some Languages of the World — *continued*

Language family	Language	Principal geographic areas where spoken	Rank in number of speakers if in top 13	
Afro-Asiatic includes Semitic languages)	Amharic	Ethiopia	_____	
	Arabic	North Africa, Middle East	(6)	130,000,000
	Berber	Morocco	_____	
	Chad	Central North Africa	_____	
	Galla	Somaliland, Ethiopia	_____	
	Hausa	West Central Africa	_____	
	Hebrew	Israel	_____	
	Somali	Somaliland, Ethiopia	_____	
Quechua	Quechua (Incan)	Peru	_____	
Mayan	Mayan	Yucatan Peninsula, Central America	_____	
Eskimo-Aleut	Eskimo	Continental rim, from the Aleutians to Greenland	_____	
Athabaskan	Chipewyan	Pacific Northwest	_____	
	Sarsi		_____	
	Tlingit		_____	
	Apache	American Southwest	_____	
	Navaho		_____	
Algonkian	Arapaho	Eastern and central	_____	
	Blackfoot	Canada, Great Lakes	_____	
	Cheyenne	region	_____	
	Cree		_____	
	Delaware		_____	
	Illinois		_____	
	Menomini		_____	
	Miami		_____	
Iroquoian	Cherokee	Tennessee, North Carolina,	_____	
	Erie	in and around the three		
	Huron	easternmost Great Lakes	_____	
	Iroquois		_____	
	Mohawk		_____	

Table 9.1   Some Languages of the World—*continued*

Language family	Language	Principal geographic areas where spoken	Rank in number of speakers if in top 13
Siouan	Crow	Great Plains	———
	Iowa		———
	Omaha		———
	Missouri		———
Uto-Aztecan	Aztec	Mexico	———
	Comanche	Southwestern United	———
	Hopi	States	———
	Paiute		———
	Pima		———
	Ute		———
Hokan	Karok	California	———
	Shasta		———
Mosan	Bella Coola	Southwestern Canada	———
	Nootka	Vancouver Island	———

Note: Obviously, we have omitted thousands of languages. These are given merely to provide some examples of the languages in some of the language families.

SUMMARY

There are more than three thousand languages spoken in the world. Despite the differences among these languages, they are surprisingly similar. There are common universal properties found in the grammars of all human languages.

Languages may differ in their phonetic inventory, in their phonological rules, in their syntactic rules, and in their lexicons. The large number of sounds utilized by the world's languages can be specified by a relatively small set of universal phonetic features. Syntactically, certain restrictions constrain the rules of grammars. Since any idea or concept which can be expressed in one language can also be expressed in any other language, we know that the semantic systems of languages are similar.

Languages may be classified by type or by genetic relationships. Typological classification has traditionally been based on word formation: **isolating languages** are those defined as consisting of individual, non-combinable morphemes; **agglutinative languages** are those in which words are composed of independent, "immutable" strings of morphemes;

inflectional languages are those in which the strings of morphemes are fused with each other and with the lexical stem.

In *isolating* languages grammatical relationships are indicated by word order. Morphemes in such languages rarely undergo a change in phonological shape, and often one morpheme equals one word. In *agglutinative* languages, words are composed of strings of morphemes "glued together." Each such morpheme is generally reused over and over again to form other words. *Inflectional* languages are those in which grammatical relationships are often indicated by prefixing or suffixing operations. The strings of morphemes that are fused with each other and with the lexical stem to form words often change their "underlying" shape.

Languages are classified genealogically according to their "life history." The ancestors of the language are specified, including the source or "mother" language. Sisters and cousins, which all sprang up at different points in time from the original source language, are also noted in a "family tree" similar to Figure 9.1. Different language types may be found in a single language family.

In spite of the differences between languages, which we are acutely aware of when we try to learn a foreign language, there are a vast number of ways in which languages are alike. That is, there are language universals as well as language differences.

EXERCISES

1. Here is a list of possible language universals. Which of them do you think are truly universal? Which are not? Give your reasons in each case.

   1. All languages have kinship terms (that is, words that refer to parents, siblings, inlaws, etc.).
   2. All languages have three nasal phonemes.
   3. All languages have idioms.
   4. All languages have a "syntactic plural" (a way of changing the form of a noun to indicate that it is plural).
   5. All languages have pronouns.
   6. All languages have phonological rules that delete unstressed vowels.
   7. All languages have glides in their phonemic inventory.
   8. All languages have a phonological rule that aspirates voiceless stops in word-initial position.
   9. All languages have a "syntactic past tense" (a way of changing the form of the verb to indicate that it is in the past tense).
   10. All languages have rules that determine what sounds can occur next to each other.

2. Suppose you are a native speaker of a language in column A. List the languages in column B in the order that they would (most likely) be the easiest to learn as a second language.

A	B
1. Bulgarian	Lithuanian Russian Greek
2. Dutch	Bulgarian English Indonesian
3. English	Navaho Russian Persian
4. Persian	Serbo-Croatian Arabic Bengali
5. Russian	Yugoslav English Latvian Finnish
6. Hungarian	Russian Finnish Twi
7. Welsh	French Breton Estonian
8. Spanish	English Arabic Romanian

3. Here is how to count to five in a dozen languages. Six of these languages are Indo-European and six are not. Identify which is which.[6]

	LG. 1	LG. 2	LG. 3	LG. 4	LG. 5	LG. 6
1	en	jedyn	i	eka	ichi	echad
2	twene	dwaj	liang	dvau	ni	shnayim
3	thria	tři	san	trayas	san	shlosha
4	fiuwar	štyri	ssu	catur	shi	arba?a
5	fif	pjec	wu	pañca	go	chamishsha

[6] Data from John Algeo and Thomas Pyles, *Problems in the Origins and Development of the English Language* (New York: Harcourt Brace Jovanovich, 1966).

LG. 7	LG. 8	LG. 9	LG. 10	LG. 11	LG. 12
1 mot	un	hana	yaw	uno	nigen
2 hai	duos	tul	daw	dos	khoyar
3 ba	trais	set	dree	tres	ghorban
4 bon	quatter	net	tsaloor	cuatro	durben
5 nam	tschinch	tasŏt	pindze	cinco	tabon

4. Here are some data from five languages.   Identify which languages are isolating, which agglutinative, and which inflectional.

   1. Miwok (American Indian language of California).[7]

yilim	I am biting	ʔinim	I am coming
yilis	you are biting	ʔinis	you are coming
yili	he is biting	ʔini	he is coming
yilimas	we are biting	ʔinimas	we are coming
yilitos	you (pl.) are biting	ʔinitos	you (pl.) are coming
yilip	they are biting	ʔinip	they are coming

   2. Serbo-Croatian.[8]

	read	drink	smoke
I	ya čitam	ya piyem	ya pušim
you (sg.)	ti čitaš	ti piyeš	ti pušiš
he	on čita	on piye	on puši
we	mi čitamo	mi piyemo	mi pušimo
you (pl.)	vi čitate	vi piyeye	vi pušite
they	oni čitayu	oni piyu	oni puše

   3. Thai

	eat	am eating	will eat
I	chăn kin	chăn kamlang kin	chăn cà kin
you	khun kin	khun kamlang kin	khun cà kin
he	khăw kin	khăw kamlang kin	khăw cà kin
she	thəə kin	thəə kamlang kin	thəə cà kin
we	raw kin	raw kamlang kin	raw cà kin

   4. Efik (Nigeria).[9]

ńsìn	I am laying	mbè	I am passing
ésìn	he is laying	ébè	he is passing
ésìn	they are laying	ébè	they are passing
ńyésín	I will lay	ńyébĕ	I will pass
éyésín	he will lay	éýebĕ	he will pass
éyésín	they will lay	éýebĕ	they will pass
ŋkésín	I laid	ŋkébĕ	I passed

---

[7] Data from Henry Allen Gleason, Jr., *Workbook in Descriptive Linguistics* (New York: Holt, Rinehart & Winston, 1955), 45.

[8] Data from R. Langacker, *Fundamentals of Linguistic Analysis* (New York: Harcourt Brace Jovanovich, 1972), 68.

[9] Data from Gleason, op. cit., 37.

ékésín	he laid	ékébě	he passed
ékésín	they laid	ékébě	they passed

5. Spanish

yo cazo	I hunt	yo cacé	I hunted
tú cazas	You (fam.) hunt	tú cazaste	you (fam.) hunted
el caza	he hunts	el cazó	he hunted
nosotros cazamos	we hunt	nosotros cazamos	we hunted
ustedes cazáis	you (pl.) hunt	ustedes cazasteis	you (pl.) hunted
ellos cazan	they hunt	ellos cazaron	they hunted

5. State at least three differences between English and the following languages, using just the sentence(s) given. Ignore lexical differences — that is, the different vocabulary. Example:

Thai:	dèg khon	níi	kamlang	kin
	boy *classifier*	this	*progressive aspect*	eat

This boy is eating.

măa tua	nán	kin	khâw
dog *classifier*	that	eat	rice

That dog ate the rice.

The three differences are: (1) Thai has "classifiers." They have no English equivalent. (2) The demonstratives "this" and "that" follow the noun in Thai, but precede the noun in English. (3) The "progressive" is expressed by a separate word in Thai. The verb doesn't change form. In English, the progressive is indicated by the presence of the verb *to be* and the adding of *-ing* to the verb.

1. French:

cet	homme	intelligent	arrivera
this	man	intelligent	will arrive

This intelligent man will arrive.

ces	hommes	intelligents	arriveront
these	men	intelligent	will arrive

These intelligent men will arrive.

2. Japanese:

watasi	ga	sakana	o	tabete	iru
I	*subject marker*	fish	*object marker*	eat (*ing*)	am

I am eating fish.

3. Swahili:

mtoto	alivunja	kikombe				
m-	toto	a-	li-	vunja	ki-	kombe
the	child	he	*past*	break	the	cup

The child broke the cup.

watoto	wanavunja		vikombe				
wa-	toto	wa-	na-	vunja	vi-		kombe
the (*pl.*)	child	they	*present*	break	the (*pl.*)		cup

The children break the cups.

4. Korean:

kɨ	sonyɔn-nɨn		wɨyu-lɨl		masi-ass-ta		
kɨ	sonyɔn-	nɨn	wɨyu-	lɨl	masi-	ass-	ta
the	boy	*subject marker*	milk	*object marker*	drink	*past*	*assertion*

The boy drank milk.

kɨ-nɨn	muɔs-lɨl		mɔk-ass-nya			
kɨ-	nɨn	muɔs-	lɨl	mɔk-	ass-	nya
he	*subject marker*	what	*object marker*	eat	*past*	question

What did he eat?

6. We have stated that more than three thousand languages exist in the world today. State one reason why this number might grow larger and one reason why it might grow smaller. Do you think the number of languages will increase or decrease in the next one hundred years? Why?

References

BOAS, FRANZ. *Handbook of American Indian Languages.* Washington, D.C.: Smithsonian Institution, Bureau of American Ethnology, Bulletin 40, 1911. Introduction, with foreword by C.I.J.M. Stuart, reprinted, Washington, D.C.: Georgetown University Press, 1964.

CHOMSKY, N. *Cartesian Linguistics.* New York: Harper & Row, 1966.

GREENBERG, J. *Studies on African Linguistic Classification.* New Haven: Yale University Press, 1955.

GREENBERG, J. *Universals of Language.* Cambridge: M.I.T. Press, 1963.

GREENBERG, J., ed. *Universals of Language.* Cambridge: M.I.T. Press, 1966.

JESPERSEN, O. H. *Language: Its Nature, Development and Origin.* London: Allen and Unwin, 1922.

MEILLET, A., and COHEN, MARCEL. *Les langues du Monde,* new ed. 2 vols. Paris: Champion, 1952.

MULLER, S. H. *The World's Living Languages.* New York: Unger, 1964.

PEDERSEN, H. *Linguistic Science in the Nineteenth Century.* Translated by John Spargo. Bloomington: Indiana University Press, 1931.

SAPIR, E. *Language.* New York: Harcourt Brace Jovanovich, 1921.

10
The Diversity of Language

DIALECTS

I have noticed in traveling about the country a good many differences in the pronunciation of common words. . . . Now what I want to know is whether there is any right or wrong about this matter. . . . If one way is right, why don't we all pronounce that way and compel the other fellow to do the same? If there isn't any right or wrong, why do some persons make so much fuss about it?

— Letter quoted in "The Standard American" in

J. V. WILLIAMSON and V. M. BURKE, eds., *A Various Language*

All speakers of English can talk to each other and pretty much understand each other. Yet no two speakers speak exactly alike. Some differences are due to age, sex, state of health, size, personality, emotional state, and grammatical idiosyncrasies. That each person speaks somewhat differently from all others is shown by one's ability to recognize an acquaintance by hearing him talk. Thus every speaker of a language has his own "dialect" (called an *idiolect*); English may then be said to consist of 400,000,000 idiolects.

Even beyond these individual differences, the language of a group of people may show regular variations from that used by other groups. English spoken in different geographical regions and different social groups shows systematic differences. Such groups are said to speak different dialects of the same language. A language is composed of its dialects in much the same way that a baseball league is composed of its individual teams. No single team is the league; no single dialect is the language.

Dialectal diversity tends to increase proportionately to the degree of communicative isolation between the groups. Communicative isolation refers to such a situation as existed between America, Australia, and England in the eighteenth century. There was some contact through commerce and emigration, but an Australian was less likely to talk to an Englishman than to another Australian. Today the isolation is less pronounced because of the mass media and jet airplanes. But even within one country, regionalisms persist. Children learn the language spoken to them and reinforce the unique features characteristic of the dialect used.

The changes which occur in the language spoken in one area are not necessarily spread to another area. The variability of linguistic changes accounts, to a great extent, for the early dialect splits. Within a single group of speakers who are in regular contact with one another, the changes are spread among the group and "relearned" by their children. When some communication barrier separates groups of speakers—be it a physical barrier like an ocean or a mountain range, or social barriers of a political, racial, class, or religious kind—linguistic changes are not easily spread and dialectal differences are reinforced.

It is not always easy to decide whether the language differences reflect two dialects or two different languages. A rule-of-thumb definition can be used: "When dialects become mutually unintelligible, they are different languages." But to define "mutually intelligible" is itself a difficult task. Danes speaking Danish and Norwegians speaking Norwegian can converse with each other. Yet Danish and Norwegian are considered separate languages because they are spoken in separate countries and because there are regular differences in their grammars. Similarly, Hindi and Urdu are mutually intelligible "languages" spoken in Pakistan and India; both religious and national boundaries separate the speakers, who prefer to consider their languages distinct.

The continuum of intelligibility that exists between dialects makes an objective definition difficult. We shall, however, use the rule-of-thumb definition and refer to dialects of one language as mutually intelligible versions of the same basic grammar, with systematic differences between them.

REGIONAL DIALECTS AND ACCENTS

> *The educated Southerner has no use for an* r *except at the beginning of a word.*
>
> — MARK TWAIN, *Life on the Mississippi*

Most Americans have had some exposure to regional dialects in the United States. The phonological or phonetic distinctions are often referred to as different "accents." A person is said to have a Boston accent, a Brooklyn accent, a Southern accent, a Midwestern drawl, and so on. Diversity of pronunciation is what accounts for such "accents."

A tongue-in-cheek *Language Guide to Brooklyn* illustrates the kinds of pronunciation differences that exist:

earl: a lubricant
oil: an English nobleman

tree: the numeral that precedes four
doze: the ones yonder
fodder: male parent

A similar glossary was published to "translate" a Southern dialect:

sex: one less than seven, two less than eh-et, three less than noine, foe less than tin.

American regional dialects remain a constant source of humor. A sports writer, Jim Murray, discussing the Southern regional dialect in a column entitled "Berlitz of the South," begins: "When the North conquered the South in the late unpleasantness between the two, it tore down the rebel flag, broke up the Confederacy, sent the carpetbaggers in, but it never could do much about the language."[1] He then provides "a few common translations you may want to have" if you are ever in the South, including:

watt: primary color, as in "the flag is raid, watt, and blue."
height: where you don't like someone
pa: something good to eat
bike: what you do with a pa
mine: principal or chief
mane: Homo sapiens, your best friend is your mine mane
rod: what you do in auto

These regional dialects tell us a great deal about how languages change. Their origins can be traced to the history of the people who first settled America. American English, in all its varieties, derived principally from the English spoken in southern England in the seventeenth and eighteenth centuries.

An example of how regional dialects developed may be illustrated by examining changes in the pronunciation of words with an *r*.

In Chapter 8 we pointed out that the English colonists who first settled this country pronounced an *r* wherever it was spelled. In the seventeenth century, Londoners and Jamestowners pronounced *farm* as [farm] and *father* as [faðər]. By 1800 the citizens of London deleted *r* in places where it was formerly pronounced; an *r* was now pronounced only when it occurred before vowels. *Farm* had become [fa:m] and *father* [fa:ðə] and *far* [fa:]. In New England and along the Southern Atlantic Seaboard, close commercial (and linguistic) ties with England were maintained. In these areas, American English reflected the same "*r*-dropping" that occurred in England, but in other regions the change did not enter the language, which is why most Americans today pronounce *r* before consonants as did our English ancestors two hundred years ago.

By the time of the American Revolution, there were three major dialect

[1] *Los Angeles Times*, April 5, 1973.

areas in America: the Northern dialect spoken in New England and around the Hudson river; the midland dialect spoken in Pennsylvania; and the Southern dialect. These dialects differed from each other in systematic ways and from the English spoken in England. Some of the changes that occurred in British English spread to America; others did not. Pioneers from all three dialect areas spread westward. The intermingling of their dialects "leveled" or "submerged" many of their dialectal differences, which is why the language used in large sections of the Midwest and the West is very similar. Many of the features which characterized seventeenth-century British persisted in the States long after these were changed in England, as is shown in Table 10.1.

Table 10.1

Seventeenth-century London	*Nineteenth-century London*
1. *r* was pronounced wherever it was spelled: *farm* [farm], *father* [faðər], *farther* [farðər] (Standard American English of today retains this pronunciation)	1. *r* was only pronounced when it occurred before a vowel: *farm* [fa:m], *father* [fa:ðə], farther [fa:ðə] (in New England and the South, a similar change occurred)
2. The vowel in words like *half, last, path,* and *laugh* was [æ] (this is the vowel still used in these words in Standard American)	2. The vowel [æ] in these words changed to the back vowel [a:] (a similar change occurred in New England: *laugh:* British [la:f], New England [laf].
3. The vowel in *due, duty, true* was a diphthong: *due* [dyu]	3. The diphthong was maintained except after *r* (the [yu] was also maintained in New England and the South; in Standard American the [yu] became [u] after an alveolar: *due* [du])
4. The *h* in *which, when, what, where* signified a voiceless *w* /ʍ/; *which* contrasted with *witch* (the contrast was maintained in areas of the Midwest and West)	4. The voiceless /ʍ/ was lost; all *wh* words were pronounced with a voiced /w/; *which* and *witch* became homophones (this change spread to many regions of America)
5. Words like *laboratory, dictionary, cemetery* were given both primary and secondary stress: *laboratory* [lǽbərətɔ̀ri] (American dialects preserved this stress pattern)	5. Secondary stress was lost in such words with subsequent syllable loss, and stress shifted to the second syllable: *laboratory* [ləbɔ́rətri]

Other regional changes took place in the United States, further separating American regional "accents." In the Southern dialect, for example, when the r was dropped it was replaced by a "schwa-like" glide: *farm* is pronounced as two syllables [faəm], as are *four* [foə] and *poor* [poə]. This led Jim Murray to end his column cited above with the admonition: "Also remember, there is no such thing as a one-syllable word." This, of course, is not so, as his own examples show, but it is true that many words which are monosyllabic in Standard American are disyllabic in the Southern dialect: the word *right,* pronounced as [rayt] in the Midwest, New England, and the Middle Atlantic states and in British English is pronounced [raət] in many parts of the South.

Regional dialects also differ in the words people use for the same object. Hans Kurath, an eminent American dialectologist, opens his paper, "What Do You Call It?" by asking: "Do you call it a *pail* or a *bucket?* Do you draw water from a *faucet* or from a *spigot?* Do you pull down the *blinds,* the *shades,* or the *curtains* when it gets dark? Do you *wheel* the baby, or do you *ride* it or *roll* it? In a *baby carriage,* a *buggy,* a *coach,* or a *cab?*"[2] One takes a *lift* to the *first floor* (our *second floor*) in England, but an *elevator* in America; one gets five gallons of *petrol* (not *gas*) in London; in Britain a *public school* is "private" (you have to pay) and if a student showed up there wearing *pants* ("underpants") instead of *trousers* he would be sent home to get dressed. If you ask for a *tonic* in Boston you will get a drink called a *soda* or *soda-pop* in Los Angeles, and a *freeway* in Los Angeles is a *thruway* in New York, a *parkway* in New Jersey, a *motorway* in England, and an *expressway* or *turnpike* in other dialect areas.

Systematic syntactic differences also distinguish dialects. In most American dialects sentences may be conjoined as follows:

John will eat and Mary will eat → John and Mary will eat.

But in the Ozark dialect this transformation is also possible:

John will eat and Mary will eat → John will eat and Mary.

In some American dialects the past tense of *see* is *seen,* as in *I seen it;* for other dialects this would be a starred (ungrammatical) sentence. American speakers often use *gotten* in a sentence such as *He should have gotten to school on time.;* in British English, only the form *got* occurs. In a number of American dialects the pronoun *I* occurs when *me* would be used in British English; in other dialects this is ungrammatical.

Am. between you and I	*Br.* between you and me
Am. Won't he permit you and I to swim?	*Br.* Won't he permit you and me to swim?

---

[2] Hans Kurath, "What Do You Call It?" in Juanita V. Williamson and Virginia M. Burke, eds., *A Various Language: Perspective on American Dialects* (New York: Holt, Rinehart & Winston, 1971).

The use of articles (*the* and *a*) is different in British and American English. In London someone may be *in hospital* or *have toothache*. In America we always use an article in such phrases: *in the hospital, have a toothache*. In both dialects we can omit the article in other phrases: *in school, have appendicitis*.

In British English a syntactic transformation permits the deletion of the pronoun in the sentence. *I could have done it* to form *I could have done*, which is not permitted in the American grammar.

With all such differences we still are able to understand the speakers of another dialect. Even though dialects differ as to pronunciation, vocabulary, and syntactic rules, these are minor differences when compared with the totality of the grammar. The largest part of the vocabulary, the sound-meaning relations of words, and the syntactic rules are shared, which is why the dialects are mutually intelligible.

THE "STANDARD"

We don't talk fancy grammar and eat anchovy toast. But to live under the kitchen doesn't say we aren't educated.

— MARY NORTON, *The Borrowers*

Even though every language is a composite of dialects, many people talk and think about a language as if it were a "well-defined" fixed system with various dialects diverging from this norm. This is analogous to equating the American Baseball League of the 1950s to the New York Yankees. The Yankees enjoyed so much success in that decade that many baseball enthusiasts did just that. Similarly, a particular dialect of a language may enjoy such prestige that it becomes equated with the language itself.

The prestigious dialect is often that used by political leaders and the upper socio-economic classes; it is the dialect used for literature or printed documents; it is taught in the schools, used by the military, and propagated by the mass media. Once a dialect gets a head start, it often builds up momentum. The more "important" it gets, the more it is used; the more it is used, the more important it becomes. Such a dialect may be that spoken in the political or cultural center of a country and may spread into other regions. The dominance in France of the Parisian dialect, and in England (to a lesser extent) of the London dialect, is attributable to this cause.

Such a dominant dialect is often called the **standard dialect. Standard American English** (SAE) is a dialect of English which many Americans *almost* speak; divergences from this "norm" are labeled "Philadelphia dialect," "Chicago dialect," "Black English," etc.

When two languages are compared, it is necessary to compare one of the dialects of each language. The "standards" are usually used. When American and British English are compared, SAE and the British spoken by educated Britishers, called Received Pronunciation (RP),[3] are the dialects used for this purpose. The standard dialect is taught to non-native speakers and is usually the most widespread; speakers of all dialects usually understand it easily even if they do not use it. Speakers of different dialects use the standard as the written form, since this dialect is the accepted literary language.

In France, a notion of the "standard" as the only correct form of the language is propagated by an official academy of "scholars" who determine what usages constitute the "official French language." All deviations from the standard are frowned on by the academy, which attempts to *legislate* what words, rules, and pronunciations are to be used. The Parisian dialect was selected as the basis for this norm, at the expense of the hundreds of local village dialects (called *patois*). Many of these *patois* are actually separate languages, derived from Latin (as are French, Spanish, and Italian). A Frenchman from the provinces who wishes to succeed in French society must nearly always be bi-dialectal. The academy, acting as self-appointed guardians of the purity of French, may pull out their hair, rail against the language's corruption, and proclaim against all deviations from the "official" standard, but they have not been able to prevent the standard from changing or determine how speakers of the standard actually do speak. The younger members of the academy sometimes let some new "corrupt" usage slip in, and fifty or a hundred years after the fact, the "official" language is updated to conform with the language used by the people.

A standard dialect is in no *linguistic* way "superior." The standard dialect may have social functions—to bind people together or to provide a common written form for multi-dialectal speakers. It is, however, neither more expressive, more logical, more complex, nor more regular than any other dialect. Any judgments, therefore, as to the superiority or inferiority of a particular dialect are social judgments, not linguistic ones.

BLACK ENGLISH

> *For some blacks and some whites (notice the infamous all has been omitted) it is not a matter of you say* e-*ther and we say* i-*ther, but rather:*
> *. . . You kiss your children, and we give 'em some sugar. . . .*

[3] Received Pronunciation (commonly called RP) is the British pronunciation that is "received" (accepted as "proper") at the royal court.

You cook a pan of spinach, and we burn a mess of greens. You wear clothes, and we wear threads. . . . You call the police, and we drop a dime. You say wow! We say ain't that a blip. You care, love and hurt, and we care, love and hurt.

The differences are but a shade.

—SANDRA HAGGERTY, "On Digging the Difference"
(Los Angeles *Times*, April 2, 1973)

Those who interpret "standard" literally and consider nonstandard dialects as inferior are not confined to Paris. While the majority of American dialects are free from stigma to a great extent, especially the many regional dialects, one dialect of American English has been a victim of prejudicial ignorance. This is the dialect spoken by a large section of non-middle-class American blacks; it is usually referred to as Black English (BE) or Negro English or Non-standard Negro English. The distinguishing features of this English dialect persist for social, educational, and economic reasons. The historical discrimination against black Americans has created ghetto living and segregated schools. Where social isolation exists, dialect differences are intensified. In addition, particularly in recent years, many blacks no longer consider their dialect to be inferior and it has become a means of positive black identification.

LUTHER   **BY BRUMSIC BRANDON, JR.**

Copyright Los Angeles Times; reprinted with permission

Since the onset of the civil-rights movement, Black English has been the focus of national attention. There are those who attempt to equate the use of Black English with inferior "genetic" intelligence and "cultural deprivation," and justify these incorrect notions by stating that BE is a "deficient, illogical, and incomplete" language. Such epithets cannot be applied to any language and are as unscientific in reference to BE as to Russian, Chinese, or Standard American English. The cultural-deprivation myth is as false as the idea that some dialects or languages are inferior. A person may be "deprived" of one cultural background but very rich in another.

There are people, white and black, who think they can identify an unseen person's race by hearing him talk, believing that different races inherently speak differently. This assumption is equally false; a black child raised in an upper-class British household will speak RP English. A white child raised in an environment where Black English is spoken will speak Black English. Children construct grammars based on the language they hear.

There are, however, systematic differences between BE and SAE, just as there are systematic differences between Australian and American English. We have seen above that dialect differences show up in the phonological rules of the grammars. British grammar has a rule which can be stated as: "Delete the /r/ except before a vowel." Black English has the same rule (as does nonblack Southern dialect). Words like *guard* and *god, nor* and *gnaw, sore* and *saw, poor* and *pa, fort* and *fought,* and *court* and *caught* are pronounced identically in BE because of the presence of this phonological rule in the grammar.

Other words that do not rhyme in SAE do rhyme in BE: *yeah* and *fair, idea* and *fear.* In BE (and other Southern dialects) the "*r*-deletion" rule has been extended in some cases, so that it is also deleted between vowels. *Carol* is pronounced identically with *Cal,* and *Paris* with *pass.* For some speakers of BE, an "*l*-deletion" rule also occurs, creating homophones like *toll* and *toe, all* and *awe, help* and *hep* [hɛp].

A regular phonological rule which exists in BE and not in SAE simplifies consonant clusters, particularly at the end of words and when one of the two consonants is an alveolar (/t/, /d/, /s/, /z/). The application of this rule may delete the past-tense morpheme; *past* and *passed* (*pass + ed*) are both pronounced *pass.* When a speaker of this dialect says *I pass the test yesterday* he is not showing an ignorance of past and present, but is pronouncing the past tense according to the rule present in his grammar:

"passed" /pæs + t/ → apply rule → [pæs]

Because of this consonant rule, *meant* and *mend* are both pronounced the same as *men.* And when combined with the "*l*-deletion" rule, *told, toll,* and *toe* have identical pronunciations.

	told	*toll*	*toe*
Phonemic Representation	/told/	/tol/	/to/
Consonant cluster			
simplification rule	∅	NA	NA
l-deletion rule	∅	∅	NA
Phonetic Representation	[to]	[to]	[to]

There are other systematic differences between the phonology of BE and SAE. BE shares with many regional dialects the lack of any distinction between /ɪ/ and /ɛ/ before nasal consonants, producing identical pronunciations of *pin* and *pen*, *bin* and *Ben*, *tin* and *ten*, and so on. The vowel used in these words is roughly between the [ɪ] of *pit* and the [ɛ] of *pet*.

In BE the phonemic distinction between /ay/ and /æw/ has been lost, both having become /a/. Thus *why* and *wow* are pronounced [wa]. Another change which has occurred has replaced the /ɔy/ (particularly before /l/) to the simple vowel [ɔ] without the glide, so that *boil* and *boy* are pronounced [bɔ]. One other regular feature is the change of a final /θ/ to [f] so that *Ruth* is pronounced [ruf] and *death* [dɛf].

Notice that these are all systematic changes and "rule-governed." The kinds of changes which have occurred are very similar to sound changes which have taken place in languages all over the world, including Standard English. Some dialects of Black English drop final nasal consonants. The preceding vowel, however, retains its nasalization, so the words end in nasalized vowels. (Note the rule in Standard English that nasalizes a vowel before a nasal consonant, discussed in Chapter 4.) This is precisely how French developed nasal vowels. Linguistic change caused final nasal consonants to be dropped, leaving behind a nasal vowel to distinguish the word.

Every dialect of every language has its own lexical items and its own phonological rules. The preponderance of likenesses of Black English to Standard English — the two dialects share most lexical forms and rules — is what makes the differences so conspicuous. If Black English were as incomprehensible as Russian, many Americans would probably have more respect for it.

Syntactic differences, as noted above, also exist between dialects. Recently linguists like William Labov have begun to investigate the syntactic structures of Black English. It is the syntactic differences that have often been used to illustrate the "illogic" of BE, and yet it is just such differences that point up the fact that BE is as syntactically complex and as "logical" as SAE.

Following the lead of early "prescriptive" grammarians, some "scholars" and teachers conclude that it is illogical to say *he don't know nothing* because two negatives make a positive. Since such negative constructions occur in BE, it has been concluded by some "educators" that speakers of BE are deficient because they use language "illogically." Consider the following sentences from BE and SAE:

		SAE	BE
1.	*Affirmative:*	He knows something.	He know something.[4]
	Negative:	He doesn't know anything.	He don't know nothing.
		He knows nothing.	He know nothing.
2.	*Affirmative:*	He likes somebody.	He like somebody.
	Negative:	He doesn't like anybody.	He don't like nobody.
		He likes nobody.	He like nobody.
3.	*Affirmative:*	He has got some.	He got some.
	Negative:	He hasn't got any.	He ain't got none.
		He's got none.	He got none.

In Black English when the verb is negated the indefinites *something, somebody,* and *some* become the negative indefinites *nothing, nobody,* and *none.* The rule is simple and elegant and quite common in the world's languages. This was the rule which existed in earlier periods for all dialects of English. In Standard English, if the verb is negated the indefinites become *anything, anybody,* and *any.* If in the negative sentences in SAE the forms *nothing, nobody,* and *none* are used, then the verb is not negated. The speakers of both SAE and BE know how to negate sentences. The rules are essentially the same, but differ in details. Both dialects are strictly rule-governed, as is every syntactic process of every dialect in the world.

It has also been said that BE is "illogical" because the copula (that is, the verb *to be*) is deleted in sentences such as *He nice.* Consider the following sentences from SAE and BE:

SAE	BE
4. He is nice/He's nice.	He nice.
5. They are mine/They're mine.	They mine.
6. I am going to do it/I'm gonna do it.	I gonna do it.

Note that wherever the standard can use a contraction (he + is → he's), Black English can delete the copula. The following sentences, however, will show that where a contraction *cannot* be used in SAE, the copula *cannot* be deleted in BE:[5]

SAE	BE
7. *He is as nice as he says he's.	*He as nice as he say.

---

[4] As the examples in this list show, Black English also regularizes the present tense verb forms. In SAE the third person singular verb forms are inflected by adding to the verb the particular phonetic form that is the same as the plural ending (for example, $/z/$ as in *loves* or *knows,* $/s/$ as in *kicks,* or $/əz/$ as in *kisses*). The deletion of this ending in Black English may be the result of the application of phonological rules such as those discussed above.

[5] Sentences taken from W. Labov, "The Logic of Nonstandard English" (Georgetown University, 20th Annual Round Table, No. 22, 1969).

8. *How beautiful you're.   *How beautiful you.
9. *Here I'm.   *Here I.

These examples further illustrate that syntactic rules may operate slightly differently from one dialect to another, but that the surface forms of the sentences are derived by rule — they are not strings of words randomly put together.   It is interesting to note that many languages allow such copula deletion.   In Russian the copula is never used in such sentences.   In Swahili, *mimi ni mwanafunzi* "I am a student" is grammatical and so is *mimi mwanafunzi* "I a student" with the copula, *ni*, missing.

In BE, the possessive morpheme *-'s* is absent whenever possession is redundantly specified by word order:

SAE	BE
10. That is John's house.	That John house.
11. That is your house.	That you house.
12. That house is John's.	That house John's.
(but not	*That house John.)
13. That house is yours.	That house yours.
(but not	*That house your.)

There is nothing "illogical" about the presence of such a rule; when word order suffices to indicate possession, the possessive ending is "superfluous."   Thai works like Black English:

14. nân   John   bâan.   nân   kun   bâan.
    that   John   house   that   you   house
    That's John's house.   That's your house.

Other BE sentences that are formed by syntactic rules different from those in the grammar of SAE are:

15. He done told me.
16. I been seen it.
17. I ain't like it.
18. I been washing the car.

These are not "corruptions" of the standard but dialect sentences that appear strange to a nonspeaker, although not as strange as sentence 19 appears to a nonspeaker of French:

19. Il me l'a   donné.
    he me it has   gave
    He gave it to me.

There are many more differences between the grammars of BE and SAE than those we have discussed.   But the ones we have listed are enough to show the "regularity" of BE and to dispel the notion that there is anything "illogical" or "primitive" about this dialect.

The study of Black English is important for linguists, of course, but it is also important for nonlinguists. When a teacher in an American school teaches French or German or Russian, we expect him to know both English and the language he is teaching. Yet, in many schools in our country where the students are primarily speakers of Black English, instruction seldom if ever takes place in Black English. There is nothing inherently wrong with attempting to teach the standard dialect in all schools for nonlinguistic reasons, but the standard will be learned much more easily by speakers of other dialects if teachers are aware of the systematic differences and permit children to use their own dialect to express themselves. Certainly, there would be less of a communication breakdown between students who speak Black English (not to mention other speakers of nonstandard dialects) and their teachers if these nonstandard dialects were not considered to be inferior versions of the standard. A child who reads *your brother* as *you bruvver* is using his own pronunciation rules. He would be more likely to respond positively to the statement "In the dialect we are using, the /ð/ is not pronounced [v], as it is in yours" than he would be to an attitude of contempt toward his grammar. To give another example, when a speaker of BE does not add the -*'s* in possessive phrases like *Mary hat* (instead of *Mary's hat*), an attempt to "correct" him which assumes that he does not understand possession as a *concept* creates serious problems for both the child and the teacher. The child knows perfectly well what he means, but the teacher may not know that he knows, and the child does not know why the teacher cannot understand him and keeps telling him he is "wrong." Thus a linguistic study of the systematic differences between dialects may, hopefully, repair some of the damage which has been done in situations like these — whatever the motivations of those involved.

Another important reason for studying these dialects is that such study provides rich data for an understanding of the extent to which dialects differ and leads to a better knowledge of human language. Furthermore, the history of any dialect reveals important information about language change in general.

Take the history of Black English as an example. It is simple enough to date its beginning — the first blacks arrived in Virginia in 1619. There are, however, different theories as to the factors which led to the systematic differences between Black English and other American English dialects.

One view suggests that the origins of Black English can be traced to the fact that the Negro slaves learned English from their white masters as a second language. The difficulties of second-language learning for an adult are all too clear to anyone who has attempted to do this. The basic grammar may be learned, but many surface differences persist. These differences, it is suggested, were reflected in the grammars constructed by the children of the slaves, since they heard English primarily from the slaves. Had they been exposed to the English spoken by the whites as children, their grammars would have been less different from regular Southern speech. The dialect differences persisted and grew because the black in America was isolated by social and racial barriers as important as the geographic barriers which isolated the New Zealander from other English speakers. The proponents of this theory point to the fact that Black English and Standard American are basically identical in their deep structures; that is, they suggest that the phrase-structure rules are the same but transformational rules and phonological rules change sentences to produce surface differences.

A second view suggests that many of the particular features found in Black English are traceable to influences of the African languages spoken by the slaves. During the seventeenth and eighteenth centuries, Africans who spoke different languages were purposefully grouped together by the slave traders to discourage communication between the slaves, the idea being to prevent slave revolts. This theory suggests that in order to communicate with each other the slaves were forced to use the one common language all had access to, namely, English, and used a simplified form—called a *pidgin*—with various features from West African languages. According to this view, the differences between BE and other dialects are due more to "deep" syntactic differences than to surface distinctions.

That Black English is closer to the Southern dialect of English than to other dialects is quite apparent. This fact does not favor either of the opposing views. The theory which suggests that the Negro slaves imitated the English of their white Southern masters explains the similarities in this way. One might also explain the similarities by the fact that for many decades a large number of Southern white children were raised by black women and played with black children. It is not unlikely that many of the distinguishing features of the Southern dialect were acquired from Black English in this way. A publication of the American Dialect Society in 1908–1909 makes this point clearly:

> For my part, after a somewhat careful study of east Alabama dialect, I am convinced that the speech of the white people, the dialect I have spoken all my life and the one I tried to record here, is more largely colored by the language of the negroes than by any other single influence.[6]

The two-way interchange still goes on. Standard American English is constantly enriched by words, phrases, and usage originating in Black English, and Black English, whatever its origins, is one of the many dialects of English, influenced by the changes which go on in the other dialects.

[6] L. W. Payne, "A Word-List from East Alabama" (*Dialect Notes*, 3:279–328, 343–391).

LINGUA FRANCAS

Language is a steed that carries one into a far country.

— Arab proverb

Many areas of the world are populated by people speaking divergent languages. In such areas, where groups desire social or commercial communication, one language is often used by common agreement. Such a language is called a **lingua franca.**

In medieval times, a trade language came into use in the Mediterranean ports. It consisted of Italian mixed with French, Spanish, Greek, and Arabic, and was called Lingua Franca, "Frankish language." The term *lingua franca* was generalized to other languages similarly used. Thus, any language can be a lingua franca.

English has been called "the lingua franca of the whole world," French, at one time, was "the lingua franca of diplomacy," and Latin and Greek were the lingua francas of Christianity in the West and East, respectively, for a millennium. Among Jews, Yiddish has long served as a lingua franca.

More frequently, lingua francas serve as "trade languages." East Africa is populated by hundreds of tribes, each speaking its own dialect, but most Africans of this area learn at least some Swahili as a second language, and this lingua franca is used and understood in nearly every marketplace. A similar situation exists in West Africa, where Hausa is the lingua franca.

From early times, Malay was the commercial language of the East Indies, providing a linguistic bridge that stretched around a quarter of the globe. So pervasive was this lingua franca that it is now the native tongue of nearly 80,000,000 people, and the official language of Indonesia and Malaysia.

Hindustani is the name of the lingua franca of the Indian subcontinent, and is basically Hindi (=Urdu) with a few contributions from local dialects. So complex is the linguistic situation of this area that there are often regional lingua francas—usually a popular dialect near some commercial center. The same situation existed in Imperial China, and persists to some extent in present-day China. Mandarin Chinese is the major lingua franca, and is used by Koreans, Manchurians, Mongolians, and Tibetans, not to mention half a billion Chinese.

PIDGINS AND CREOLES

Big Name watchem sheepysheep. Watchum blackfella.
No more belly cry fella hab. Big Name makum camp
alonga grass, takum blackfella walkabout longa, no fightem

no more hurry wata.   Big Boss longa sky makum inside
glad; takem walkabout longa too much goodfella.

— *Psalms* 23, 1–3

A lingua franca is typically a language with a broad base of native speakers, likely to be used and learned by persons whose native language is in the same language family.   Often in history, however, missionaries and traders from one part of the world have visited and attempted to communicate with peoples residing in another area.   In such cases the contact is too sporadic, and the cultures too widely separated for the usual kind of lingua franca to arise.   Instead, the two groups use their native languages but simplify and coalesce them into a rudimentary language of few lexical items and "straightforward" grammatical rules. Such a "marginal language" is called a **pidgin.**

The most notable pidgin that exists today is called Melanesian Pidgin English.   It is widely used in Australian New Guinea and the nearby South Seas islands.   Like most pidgins, many of its lexical items and much of its structure are based on just one language of the two or more contact languages, in this case English.   Melanesian Pidgin English has about 1,500 lexical items, of which about 80 percent are derived from English.

When the English whalers and traders were sailing the South Seas, they encountered a maze of different languages — more than five hundred. There was need for a lingua franca.   The local islanders who were trading with the Europeans tried to learn enough English to communicate with the foreigners.   They repeated words and phrases that they heard, somewhat imperfectly, as is to be expected.   The English traders were not linguistically sophisticated, nor did they even attempt to speak a South Seas language.   They considered the English used by the islanders as "baby talk," which they concluded was the extent of the natives ability (reflecting an unfortunate attitude that non-Europeans are simple and childlike).   The English repeated this "baby talk" and it became the "trade language" regularly used.

Although pidgins are in some sense rudimentary, they are not devoid of grammar.   The phonological system is rule-governed, as in any human language.   The inventory of phonemes is generally small, and each phoneme may have many allophonic pronunciations.   In Melanesian Pidgin, for example, [č], [š], and [s] are all possible pronunciations of the phoneme /s/; [masin], [mašin] and [mačin] all mean *machine*.   When a New Guinean says [masin] and an Englishman says [mašin], the difference in Pidgin is nondistinctive and no more serious than the different *p*'s in *gap* [gæp] and [gæpʰ], that is, they are freely variant.

Although case, tense, mood, and voice are generally absent from pidgins (as from many non-pidgin languages), one cannot speak an English pidgin by merely using English without inflecting verbs or declining pronouns.   Pidgins are not "baby talk" or Hollywood "Injun talk."

Me Tarzan, you Jane may be understood, but it is not pidgin as it is used in West Africa.

Pidgins are simple, but are rule-governed. In Melanesian Pidgin, verbs that take a direct object must have the suffix -*m*, even if the direct object is absent in surface structure; this is a "rule" of the language:

> Me dream kill'*m* onefella snake.
> I dreamed I killed a snake.
> Bandarap 'em 'e cook'*m*.
> Bandarap cooked (it).

Other rules determine word order, which, as in English, is usually quite strict in pidgins because of the lack of case endings on nouns.

With their small vocabularies, pidgins are not very good at expressing fine distinctions of meaning. Many lexical items bear a heavy semantic burden, with context being relied upon to remove ambiguity. Much circumlocution is necessary. All of these factors combine to give pidgins a unique flavor. What could be a friendlier definition of friend than the Australian aborigine's *him brother belong me,* or more poetic than his description of the sun, *lamp belong Jesus?* A policeman is *gubmint catchum-fella,* whiskers are *grass belong face,* and when a man is thirsty *him belly allatime burn.* And who can top this classic announcement by a Chinese servant that his master's prize sow had given birth to a litter: *Him cow pig have kittens?*

Pidgin has come to have negative connotation, perhaps because the best-known pidgins are all associated with European colonial empires. The *Encyclopaedia Britannica* once described Pidgin English as "an unruly bastard jargon, filled with nursery imbecilities, vulgarisms and corruptions." It no longer uses such a definition, since in recent times there is greater recognition of the fact that pidgins reflect human creative linguistic ability. Melanesian Pidgin, which is sometimes referred to as Neo-Melanesian to avoid the pejorative word *pidgin,* has its own writing system, its own literature, and its own newspapers and radio programs, and it has even been used to address a United Nations meeting.

Some people would like to eradicate Melanesian Pidgin. A pidgin spoken on New Zealand by the Maoris was replaced, through massive education, by Standard English, and the use of Chinese Pidgin English was forbidden by the government of China. It, too, has died out. The linguist Robert A. Hall points out that a New Guinean can learn Melanesian Pidgin well enough in six months to begin many kinds of semi-professional training.[7] To learn English for the same purpose might require ten times as long. In an area with well over five hundred mutually unintelligible languages, Melanesian Pidgin plays a vital role in unifying similar cultures.

----

[7] Robert A. Hall, *Hands Off Pidgin English* (New South Wales: Pacific Publications, 1955).

During the seventeenth, eighteenth, and nineteenth centuries many pidgins sprang up along the coasts of China, Africa and the New World to accommodate the Europeans. Chinook Jargon is a pidginized American Indian language used by various tribes of the Pacific Northwest to carry on trade. The original Lingua Franca was an Italian-based pidgin used in Mediterranean ports, and Malay, the language of Indonesia and Malaysia, has been highly influenced by a Dutch-based pidgin. Some linguists have even suggested that Proto-Germanic was originally a pidgin, arguing that ordinary linguistic change cannot account for certain striking differences between the Germanic tongues and other Indo-European languages. They theorized that in the first millennium B.C., the primitive Germanic tribes that resided along the Baltic Ocean traded with the more sophisticated, seagoing Asian cultures. The two peoples communicated by means of a pidgin, which either grossly affected Proto-Germanic, or actually became Proto-Germanic. If this is true, English, German, Dutch, and Yiddish had humble beginnings as a pidgin.

The distinguishing characteristic of pidgin languages is that no one learns them as native speakers. When a pidgin is learned by a child as his first language, that language is called a **creole**; the pidgin has become creolized. A creole arises when a speech community comes to rely entirely on a pidgin, using it exclusively and passing it on to their children. This was the case on slave plantations in certain areas where Africans of many different tribes could communicate only via the plantation pidgin. Haitian Creole, based on French, developed in this way, as did the "English" spoken in parts of Jamaica. Gullah is an English-based creole spoken by the descendants of African slaves on the islands off the coast of Georgia and South Carolina. Louisiana Creole, a dialect of Haitian Creole, is spoken by large numbers of blacks and whites in Louisiana. Krio, the language spoken by 40,000 Sierra Leoneans, developed from an English-based pidgin.

The development of pidgins with subsequent creolization may account for much of the linguistic diversity—the multiplicity of languages—in the world today.

ARTIFICIAL LANGUAGES

La inteligenta persono lernas la interlingvon Esperanto rapide kej facile. (Esperanto for: "The intelligent person learns the international language Esperanto rapidly and easily.")

Since the scattering at Babel, many men have hoped for a return to the blissful state when everyone would speak a universal language. Lingua francas are a step in that direction, but none has gone far enough. Since the seventeenth century, scholars have been inventing artificial languages with the hope that they would achieve universal acceptance and that universal language would bring universal peace. With stubborn regularity the world has rejected every attempt. Perhaps the world has seen too many civil wars to accept this idea.

The obituary column of artificial languages indicates the constant attempts and regular failures: Bopal, Kosmos, Novial, Parla, Spokil, Universala, and Volapuk are but a few of the deceased hundreds. Most artificial languages never get beyond their inventors, because they are abstruse and difficult and uninteresting to learn.

One artificial language has enjoyed some success. **Esperanto** ("hope") was invented by the Polish scholar Zamenhof. He gave his "language" the advantages of extreme grammatical regularity, ease of pronunciation, and a vocabulary which was based mainly on Latin-Romance, Germanic, and Greek. Esperanto is spoken, it is claimed, by several million speakers throughout the world, including some who learned it as one of their native languages. There is a literature written in it, a number of institutions teach it, and it is officially recognized by some international organizations.

Esperantists claim that their language can be understood by any intelligent person. But despite the claims of its proponents, it is not maximally simple. There is an obligatory accusative case (*Ni lernas Esperanton* "We're learning Esperanto"), and adjectives and nouns must agree in number (*inteligenta persono* "intelligent person," but *inteligentaj personoj* "intelligent persons"). Speakers of Chinese or Malaysian (and even English) would find this very different from the rules of their grammars. Esperanto is regular insofar as all nouns end in *-o*, with plural *-oj;* all adjectives end in *-a*, with plural *-aj;* the present tense of all verbs ends in *-as,* the future in *-os,* and the past in *-is;* and the definite article is always *la*. But for a language like Thai that does not have a definite article at all, Esperanto is far from "simple," and speakers of the many languages that indicate tenses without verb endings (as English indicates the future tense with *shall* or *will*) will find Esperanto as difficult as learning any language.

A modification of Esperanto, called **Ido** ("offspring" in Esperanto), has further simplified the language by eliminating the accusative case and abolishing adjective and noun agreement, but the basic problem remains. Esperanto is essentially a Romance-based pidgin with Greek and Germanic influence. It remains totally foreign and difficult to speakers of most languages, none of whom, regardless of intelligence, would have the foggiest notion of what the passage quoted above in Esperanto means. To a Russian or a Hungarian, or a Nigerian or a Hindu, Esperanto is as unfamiliar as French or Spanish.

The problems besetting the world community are basically nonlinguistic, despite the linguistic problems that do exist. Language problems may intensify social and economic problems, but they do not generally cause wars, unemployment, poverty, pollution, disease.

ARGOT, CANT, JARGON, SLANG

. . . but there was no law yet against prodding some of the new veshches which they used to put into the old moloko, so you could peet it with vellocet or synthemesc or drencrom or one or two other veshches which would give you a nice quiet horrorshow fifteen minutes admiring Bog And All His Holy Angels and Saints in your left shoe with lights bursting all over your mozg. Or you could peet milk with knives in it, as we used to say, and this would sharpen you up and make you ready for a bit of dirty twenty-to-one, and that was what we were peeting this evening I'm starting off the story with.

—ANTHONY BURGESS, *A Clockwork Orange*

You were probably not surprised to learn that your language is "spoken differently" in the different parts of the world; dialects are a common phenomenon. But you may not be aware that you speak two or more "dialects" of your own language. When you are out with your friends, you talk one way; when you go on a job interview, you talk differently. These "situation dialects" are called styles.

Nearly everybody has at least an informal and a formal style. In an informal style the rules of contraction are used more often, the syntactic rules of negation and agreement may be altered, and many words are used that do not occur in the formal style. Many speakers have the ability to use a number of different styles, ranging between the two extremes of formal and informal. Speakers of minority dialects sometimes display virtuosic ability to slide back and forth along a continuum of styles that may range from the informal patterns learned in a ghetto to "formal standard." When William Labov was studying Black English used by Harlem youths he encountered difficulties because the informants (subconsciously) adopted a different style in the presence of white strangers. It took time and effort to gain the confidence of these youths to the point where they would "forget" that their conversations were being recorded and so use their normal style.

Many cultures have rules of social behavior that strictly govern style. In some Indo-European languages there is the distinction between "*you* familiar" and "*you* polite." German *du* and French *tu* are to be used only with "intimates"; *Sie* and *vous* are more formal and used with non-intimates. French even has a verb *tutoyer* which means "to use the 'tu' form."

Other languages have a much more elaborate code of style usage. In Thai one uses *kin* "eat" to his intimates, and very informally; but he uses *thaan* "eat" informally with strangers, and *rábpràthaan* on formal occasions or when conversing with dignitaries or esteemed persons (like one's parents). Thai also has a style for talking about Buddhist monks. The verb "eat" is *chăn* when said of a monk. The ordinary third-person pronoun in Thai is *khăw* "he, she, it, they," but if the person referred to is a monk a Thai must use *thăn*. Japanese and Javanese are also languages with elaborate styles that must be adhered to in certain social situations.

One mark of an informal style is the frequent occurrence of slang. We have talked about slang in several places in this book, always casually, for a good definition is elusive. One linguist has defined slang as "one of those things that everybody can recognize and nobody can define."[8] Even this doesn't help, since one man's slang is not another man's slang. *Hippie* and *pot* are no longer recognized as slang by some persons, but are by others. Also, one generation's slang is not another generation's slang. *Fan* (as in "Dodger fan") was once a slang term, short for *fanatic*. *Phone*, too, was once a slangy, clipped version of *telephone*, as *TV* was of *television*. In Shakespeare's time, *fretful* and *dwindle* were slang, and recently *goof*, *blimp*, and *hot dog* were all hard-core slang.

The use of slang varies from region to region, as one would expect, so slang in New York and slang in Los Angeles are not identically the same. Interestingly, the word *slang* is slang in British English for "swindle."

Slang words and phrases are often "invented" in keeping with new ideas and customs. They may represent "in" attitudes better than the more conservative items of the vocabulary. Their importance is shown by the fact that it was thought necessary to give the returning Vietnam prisoners of war a glossary of eighty-six new slang words and phrases, from *acid* to *zonked*. The words on this list—prepared by the Air Force—had come into use during only five years. Furthermore, by the time this book is published, many of these terms may have passed out of the language, and many new ones will have been added.

Cant is a term that means "slang used by the underworld." It was once defined as "the Sicilian dialect of Italian" before ethnic jokes fortunately became passé. *To two-finger* ("to pickpocket"), *snow* ("cocaine"), and *lugger* ("con man"—from "confidence man") are some cant terms. Other such terms have made their way from underground to overground, and are understood by nearly all, though most are considered slang: *payola*, *C-note*, *G-man*, *to hang paper* (write "bum" checks), *sawbuck*.

Cant and **argot** are nearly synonyms. One speaks of a "thieves' cant" or a "thieves' argot." But the term *argot* may also be applied to the specialized terminology of a profession or trade. Linguistic argot, some

---

[8] Paul Roberts, *Understanding English* (New York: Harper & Row, 1958), 342.

of which is used in this book, consists of terms such as *phoneme, morpheme, case, lexical item, rule, style,* and so on. The existence of argots is illustrated by the story of a seaman witness being cross-examined at a trial, who was asked if he knew the plaintiff. Indicating that he didn't know what *plaintiff* meant brought a chide from the attorney: "You mean you came into this court as a witness and don't know what *plaintiff* means?" Later the sailor was asked where he was standing when the boat lurched. "Abaft the binnacle," was the reply, and to the attorney's questioning stare he responded: "You mean you came into this court and don't know where *abaft the binnacle* is?"

Jargon, in one of its meanings, has the non-cant definition of argot. Practically every conceivable profession, trade, and occupation has its own jargon: truck drivers, doctors, linguists, soda "jerks," mechanics, schoolteachers, lumberjacks, firemen, lawyers all use special terms of their trade.

Like every aspect of language, jargon changes. A recent newspaper article on gambling casinos discussed the dying out of gambler's jargon:

> "Tom" and "George" were signals casino employees used to describe a player.
>
> "Here comes George" meant a good tipper or "live one."
>
> "Tom" meant an approaching person was a poor tipper, a "stiff," a wiseguy, or possibly an irate husband.
>
> Now, the old-timers say, when they occasionally use one of the old signals from habit, the less experienced dealers just stare blankly, or reply, "I didn't know his name was Tom."[9]

Many jargon terms pass into the standard language. Jargon spreads from a narrow group until it is used and understood by a large segment of the population, similar to slang. Eventually, it may lose its special status as either jargon or slang and gain entrance into the respectable circle of formal usage.

LANGUAGE GAMES

All-may as-way urned-tay o-tay ollity-jay and-may ames-gay.

—JOHN MILTON, *Paradise Lost* (in Pig Latin, Dialect 1)

Once you know a language you can use it to speak to others, to write, to read, to make speeches, to think, to tell secrets. Man's creative use of language is also revealed by "distorting" his language in *regular* ways to create "secret" languages. In all languages, children (and adults) play

[9] Los Angeles *Times,* Nov. 19, 1972.

language games.   To the uninitiated, the language is transformed into gibberish, but for the players the distortion hardly interferes with communication and adds special amusement.

Pig Latin is the most common language game of English.   Children teach it to one another by some such instruction as: "Take the first sound of each word and put it at the end, and then add *a* [e]."   Even Pig Latin has a number of dialects.   In one version, if two or more consonants precede the first vowel, the whole "cluster" goes to the end: *strike* [strayk] becomes *ike-stray* [aykstre].   In another only the first phoneme is moved: *strike* becomes *trikesay* [traykse].   The invention of such "rules" shows that speakers of the language clearly can segment a word into its individual segmental parts, even breaking up consonant clusters, revealing their linguistic competence.

There are at least three Pig Latin dialects, with different rules applying when a word begins with a vowel:

> Dialect 1: Insert an *m* between the end of the word and the *a* sound: *at* becomes *at-may; eat* becomes *eat-may.*
> Dialect 2: Insert an *h: at* becomes *at-hay; eat* becomes *eat-hay.*
> Dialect 3: Insert nothing; just add the *a: at* becomes *at-ay; eat* becomes *eat-ay.*

Speakers of Pig Latin have no problem in "breaking up" words with more than one syllable because they know the language.   More than phonology is concerned.   *Detective* becomes *etective-day,* but football becomes *oot-fay all-bay.*   Even though *football* is one word, its compound composition is known by English speakers.

Thousands of such language games exist.   In "G gibberish" or "L gibberish" a *g* or *l* suffix is added to each word:

> How do you do → Howg dog youg dog
> → Howl dol youl dol

In many languages, these games include the addition of a "one-sound" or whole-syllable suffix.   Sometimes a syllable is inserted after each syllable:

> Better late than never → Beteeztereez lateez thaneez neveezereez
> → Betalterfal late-fal thanal nefalverfal

In other languages, prefixes are added:

> English: You can talk skimono jive → skyou sk-can sk-talk sk-skimono sk-jive
> Russian: Ja idu v kino → Kata-ja kata-i kata-du kata-və kata-ki kata-no

There are rhyming games, as in this French example:

> Crois-tu qu'il m'aime → Croisvois tuvu qu'ilvil m'aimevaime

There are reversals of phonemes, transpositions of phonemes, insertions of syllables, and various combinations of all of these "rules."

One of the most fascinating language games is used by the Walbiri, who are natives of central Australia.   The adults use a secret language that may be described as "upside-down talk."   Unlike games such as Pig Latin which distort the phonology, upside-down talk distorts meaning. In this language, all nouns, verbs, pronouns, and adjectives are replaced by their semantic opposites.   The phonology and syntax remain otherwise unaffected.   The sentence *These things are small* means *That one is big; Another is standing on the sky* would mean *I am sitting on the ground*, and *They are just beginning* means *We have come to the end*.

The study of such "secret languages" has provided evidence for linguists wishing to understand the grammars of different languages and language in general.   We find support for the assumption that words are stored in abstract phonological representations, that distinct semantic features are specified, that rules exist.   The players of these language games reveal over and over that all language is rule-governed.

Research on regional dialects, social dialects, dialect changes, and language games is of linguistic and social interest.   The more we look at the fascinating diversity, the more we find that man everywhere communicates in basically the same way.

SUMMARY

Every person has his own **idiolect** reflecting the particular idiosyncratic features of his language.   Besides the individual linguistic differences, the language used by groups of speakers may show sytematic differences, which are called **dialects**.   Dialects develop and are reinforced because languages change and the changes which occur in one group or area may differ from those which occur in another.   Regional dialects and social dialects develop for this reason.

The regional dialects in America are the result of historical differences. All American dialects derive from the seventeenth-century English used by the early settlers.   Some of the changes that took place in British English were spread to the American areas which maintained close contact with England, whereas in other areas the earlier forms were preserved.

Dialect differences include pronunciation differences (often called "accents"), vocabulary distinctions, and syntactic rule differences. The grammar differences between dialects are not as great as the parts which are shared, thus permitting speakers of different dialects to communicate with each other.

In most countries one dialect assumes the role of being the **standard**. While this particular dialect is not linguistically superior it may be considered by some to be the only "correct" form of the language.   Such a view has unfortunately led to the idea that some nonstandard dialects are "deficient," as is erroneously suggested regarding Black English, the dialect used by large numbers of black Americans. A study of Black English shows it to be as logical, complete, rule-governed, and expressive an any other dialect.

In areas where many languages are spoken, the people often use one language as a **lingua franca** to communicate with each other. In other cases, the language spoken by one group may be simplified lexically, phonologically, and syntactically to become a **pidgin.** When a pidgin becomes the language learned natively, it is **creolized.** Such creole languages exist in many parts of the world.

The communication barriers which exist because of the thousands of languages used in the world have led to the invention of artificial languages which, the inventors hope, could be used universally. All such attempts have failed. Most of such languages, including the most widely known, Esperanto, are not "universal" in any sense but are pidgins based on a small number of languages from one language family, and are as difficult to learn as any other language.

Besides regional and social dialects, speakers may use different **styles** of their dialect depending on the particular context. **Slang** may not be used in formal papers or situations, but is widely used in colloquial talk. **Cant** is the term used to describe the language of the "underword"; **argot** and **jargon** are words used to describe the special terms used by a professional or trade group.

The development of cants, argots, jargons, and slang attests to man's creative linguistic ability. Similarly, the language games played by children and the "secret languages" which are constructed in most cultures further reveal that all languages have built-in mechanisms for expansion and are all rule-governed.

Dialect differences are fascinating to study and lead to a greater understanding of the ways in which languages can differ while remaining essentially the same.

EXERCISES

1. Each pair of words below is pronounced as shown phonetically in at least one American dialect. State whether you pronounce them in this way. If not, state how your pronunciations would differ.

   1. "horse"   [hɔrs]   "hoarse"   [hors]
   2. "morning" [mɔrnɪŋ] "mourning" [mornɪŋ]
   3. "for"   [fɔr]   "four"   [for]
   4. "ice"   [ʌyc]   "eyes"   [ayz]
   5. "knife"   [nʌyf]   "knives"   [nayvz]
   6. "mute"   [myut]   "nude"   [nyud]
   7. "pin"   [pɪn]   "pen"   [pɛn]
   8. "hog"   [hɔg]   "hot"   [hat]

9. "marry"	[mæri]	"merry"	[mɛri]
10. "cot"	[kat]	"caught"	[kɔt]
11. "father"	[faðə]	"farther"	[faðə]
12. (to) "lease"	[lis]	(to) "grease"	[griz]
13. "what"	[ʌat]	"Watt"	[wat]
14. "ant"	[ænt]	"aunt"	[ant]
15. "creek"	[krik]	"sick"	[sɪk]

2. Following is a paragraph from a sermon delivered by the Reverend M. G. M. Cole in Sierra Leone Krio. See how much of it you can understand before reading the translation. What are some of the ways in which Krio resembles English? What differences can you find in this one passage?

> Today the country happ. Make dis thing go as ee do go, en den de go. Nor cause any trouble. Nor gee the president headache . . . oona nor amborgin am . . . nor forget two party. We nor want one party."
>
> *Translation:* Today the country is happy. Let's continue things as it is, as they are. Don't cause any trouble. Don't give the president a headache . . . Don't you humbug him . . . Don't forget the two-party system. We don't want a one-party state.

3. In the period from 1890 to 1904, the book *Slang and Its Analogues* by J. S. Farmer and W. E. Henley was published in seven volumes. The following entries are included in this dictionary. For each item: (1) state whether the word or phrase still exists; (2) if not, state what the modern slang term would be; (3) if the word remains but its meaning has changed, provide the modern meaning.

> *all out* — entirely, completely, as in "All out the best." (The expression goes back to as early as 1300)
>
> *to have apartments to let* — to be an idiot; one who is empty-headed.
>
> *been there* — as in "Oh, yes, I've been there." Applied to a man who is shrewd and who has had many experiences.
>
> *belly-button* — the navel.
>
> *berkeleys* — a woman's breasts.
>
> *bitch* — the most offensive appellation that can be given to a woman, even more provoking than that of whore.
>
> *once in a blue moon* — extremely seldom.
>
> *boss* — a master; one who directs.
>
> *bread* — employment. (1785 — "out of bread" = "out of work.")
>
> *claim* — to steal.
>
> *cut dirt* — to escape.
>
> *dog cheap* — of little worth. (Used in 1616 by Dekker: "Three things there are Dog-cheap, learning, poorman's sweat, and others")
>
> *funeral* — as in "It's not my funeral." "It's no business of mine."
>
> *to get over* — to seduce, to fascinate.
>
> *grub* — food.
>
> *groovy* — settled in habit; limited in mind.
>
> *head* — toilet (nautical use only).

hook — to marry.
hump — to spoil.
hush money — money paid for silence; blackmail.
itch — to be sexually excited.
jam — a sweetheart or a mistress.
to lift a leg on — to have sexual intercourse.
leg bags — stockings.
looby — a fool.
to lie low — to keep quiet; to bide one's time.
malady of France — syphilis (used by Shakespeare in 1599).
nix — nothing.
noddle — the head.
old — money. (1900 — "Perhaps it's somebody you owe a bit of the old to, Jack.")
to pill — to talk platitudes.
pipe layer — a political intriguer; a schemer.
poky — cramped, stuffy, stupid.
pot — a quart; a large sum; a prize; a urinal; to excel.
puny — a freshman.
puss-gentleman — an effeminate.

4. Suppose someone said, "I don't got nothin' " and you heard someone say to him, "That's an illogical statement since two negatives make a positive." How would you argue with the "corrector"?

5. Suppose someone asked you to help him compile items for a new dictionary of slang. List ten "slang" words that you use regularly and provide a dictionary definition for each.

6. Find someone who speaks a dialect of English different from yours. See if you can list some of the *systematic* (regular) differences in the pronunciation of words.

7. Below are given some words used in British English for which different words are usually used in American English. See if you can find the American equivalents.

1. clothes peg	11. biscuits
2. braces	12. queue
3. lift	13. torch
4. pram	14. underground
5. waistcoat	15. high street
6. shop assistant	16. crisps
7. sweets	17. chips (fish and chips)
8. boot (of car)	18. lorry
9. bobby	19. holiday
10. spanner	20. tin

8. Compile a list of argot (or jargon) terms from some profession or trade (for example, *lawyer, musician, doctor, longshoreman,* etc.). Give a definition for each term in "non-jargon" terms.

9. Below are listed some sentences representing different English language games. Write each sentence in its undistorted form; state the language-game "rule."

    1. Io tooko myo dogo outo to-o the-o country-o.
    2. this-ly is-ly a-ly more-ly com-ly-pli-ly-cate-ly-ed-ly game-ly.
    3. Mary-shmary can-shman talk-schmalk in-shmin rhyme-shmyme.
    4. betpeterper late-pate thanpan nevpeverper.
    5. kool ta eth namow.
    6. thop-e fop-oot bop-all stop-a dop-i opum.
      [ðapə fapʊt bapɔl stape dapi ap əm]

10. Invent a secret language; state the rule(s) which must be used and give five examples.

11. "Translate" the first paragraph of any well-known document or speech, such as the Declaration of Independence, the Gettysburg Address, or the Preamble to the Constitution into informal, colloquial language.

References

ANDERSON, W. L., and STAGEBERG, N. C., eds. *Introductory Readings on Language,* 3rd ed. New York: Holt, Rinehart & Winston, 1970. Articles in Section 8: Dialectology.

BURLING, ROBBINS. *Man's Many Voices.* New York: Holt, Rinehart & Winston, 1970.

DILLARD, J. L. *Black English: Its History and Usage in the United States.* New York: Random House, 1972.

HYMES, DELL, ed. *Language in Culture and Society.* New York: Harper & Row, 1964.

HYMES, DELL, ed. *Pidginization and Creolization of Languages.* Cambridge: Cambridge University Press, 1971.

KRAPP, G. P. *The English Language in America,* 2d ed. New York: Ungar, 1960.

LABOV, W. "The Logic of Nonstandard English." Georgetown University 20th Annual Round Table, Monograph Series on Languages and Linguistics, No. 22, 1969.

LABOV, W. "The Study of Nonstandard English." National Council of Teachers of English, Champaign, Ill., 1970.

PARTRIDGE, ERIC. *A Dictionary of Slang and Unconventional English,* 7th ed. New York: Macmillan, 1970.

REED, CARROLL E. *Dialects of American English.* Cleveland: World, 1967.

SHERZER, JOE. "Talking Backwards in Cuna: The Sociological Reality of Phonological Descriptions." Southwestern Journal of Anthropology 26, 343–53 (1970).

WILLIAMSON, JUANITA V., and BURKE, VIRGINIA M. *A Various Language: Perspectives on American Dialects.* New York: Holt, Rinehart & Winston, 1971.

11
The ABCs of Language: Writing

The Moving Finger writes; and, having writ,
Moves on: nor all thy Piety nor Wit
  Shall lure it back to cancel half a Line,
Nor all thy Tears wash out a Word of it.

—OMAR KHAYYAM, *Rubáiyát*

The development of writing was one of the great inventions of man. Writing allows human knowledge to transcend time and space. It is the wheel of man's words, the time machine of his thoughts.

For many of us it is hard to imagine language without writing; the spoken word seems intricately tied to the written word. But children speak before they learn to write. And millions of people in the world speak languages with no written form. Among these people oral literature abounds, and crucial knowledge is memorized and passed between generations. But human memory is short-lived, and the brain's storage capacity is finite. Writing was developed to overcome such problems and to allow man to communicate across the miles and through the years.

"The palest ink is better than the sharpest memory," according to an ancient Chinese proverb. The reason for this was stated by the Roman poet Horace: "Once a word has been allowed to escape, it cannot be recalled." Writing permits a society to permanently record its poetry, its history, and its technology.

It might be argued that today we have electronic means of recording sound and cameras to produce films and television, and thus writing is becoming obsolete. If writing became extinct, there would be no knowledge of electronics for TV technicians to study; there would be, in fact, little technology in years to come. There would be no film or TV scripts,

no literature, no books, no mail, no newspapers, no science. There would be some advantages: no bad novels, junk mail, poison-pen letters, or "unreadable" income-tax forms, but the losses would far outweigh the gains. The historian Arnold Toynbee has summed up the importance of writing:

> Man has lived the greater part of his existence on earth, which today is estimated as having lasted between 600,000 and 1 million years, as a "savage." It was only in the comparatively recent blossoming of civilizations in the last six thousand years that the various procedures of dictating and preserving graphic annotations were invented—the art which made man for the first time aware of the "philosophical contemporaneity" of all human evolutions. Thanks to writing, he realized that there was nothing new under the sun, but that he could also descend into the depths of "unhappy, far-off things," and exploit the treasures which countless generations had amassed, guarded and preserved down the ages to grasp at last . . . "the splendors and miseries of man."[1]

THE HISTORY OF WRITING

One picture is worth a thousand words.

—Chinese proverb

There are almost as many legends and stories on the invention of writing as there are on the origin of language. Legend has it that Cadmus, Prince of Phoenicia and founder of the city of Thebes, invented the alphabet and brought it with him to Greece. (He later retired to Illyria and was changed into a snake.) In one Chinese fable the four-eyed dragon-god T'sang Kie invented writing, but in another, writing first appeared to man in the form of markings on a turtle shell. In an Icelandic saga, Odin was the inventor of the runic script. In other myths, the Babylonian god Nebo and the Egyptian god Thoth gave man writing as well as speech. The Talmudic scholar Rabbi Akiba believed that the alphabet existed before man was created, and according to Islamic teaching, the alphabet was created by Allah himself, who presented it to man but not to the angels.

While these are delightful stories, it is evident that before a single word was ever written, uncountable billions were spoken; it is highly unlikely that a particularly gifted ancestor awoke one morning and decided "today I'll invent a writing system." Momentous inventions are rarely conceived in a moment.

---

[1] Arnold J. Toynbee, *An Historian's Approach to Religion* (New York: Oxford University Press, 1956).

Pictograms and Ideograms

It is widely believed that the early drawings made by ancient man were the seeds out of which writing developed. Cave drawings such as those found in the Altamira cave in northern Spain, drawn by men living over twenty thousand years ago, can be "read" today. They are literal portrayals of aspects of life at that time. We have no way of knowing why they were produced; they may well be esthetic expressions rather than communication messages. Later drawings, however, are clearly "picture writing," or **pictograms.** Unlike modern writing systems, each picture or pictogram is a direct image of the object it represents. There is a **nonarbitrary** relationship between the form and meaning of the symbol. Comic strips, minus captions, are pictographic — literal representations of the ideas to be communicated. This early form of "writing" did not have any direct relation to the language spoken, since the pictures represented objects in the world, rather than the linguistic names given to these objects; they did not represent the sounds of spoken language. Pictographic "writing" has been found among people throughout the world, ancient and modern; among African tribes, American Indians, Alaskan Eskimos, the Incas of Peru, the Yukagirians of Siberia, the people of Oceania. Pictograms are used today, in international roadsigns, and signs on public toilets showing which is for men and which for women. The advantage of such symbols is that since they do not depend on the sounds of any language, they can be understood by anyone. The signs used by the National Park Service exemplify this. One does not need to know any English to understand them. Some of the concepts conveyed in these signs are relatively complicated, in fact; see, for example, the symbol for "environmental study area" in Figure 11.1.

In the course of time the pictogram's meaning was extended, in that the picture represented not only the original object but attributes of that object, or concepts associated with it. Thus, a picture of a sun could

Figure 11.1 Six of seventy-seven symbols developed by the National Park Service for use as signs to indicate activities and facilities in parks and recreation areas. These are: environmental study area; grocery store; men's restroom; women's restroom; fishing; amphitheater. Certain symbols are available with a "prohibiting slash" — a diagonal red bar across the symbol that means the activity is forbidden. (National Park Service, U. S. Department of the Interior)

represent "warmth," "heat," "light," "daytime," and so on. It is easy to understand how this came about. Try to imagine a drawing to represent "heat" or "daytime." Pictograms thus began to represent *ideas* rather than objects, and such pictograms are called **ideograms** ("idea pictures" or "idea writing").

Later, the pictograms or ideograms became stylized, probably because of the ambiguities which could result from "poor artists" or "abstractionists" of the time. The simplifying conventions which developed so distorted the literal representations that it was no longer easy to interpret these new symbols without learning the system.

By this period in time, the form and the meaning of a pictogram were fixed in an *arbitrary* relationship. The pictograms were now *linguistic* symbols; since their forms departed drastically from the objects they represented, they became instead symbols for the sounds of these objects—that is, for the words of the language. This stage represents a revolutionary step in the development of writing systems.

A word-writing system of this kind relates the symbol to the sounds of a word, but the symbol still stands for the concept rather than representing the sounds directly. Such identical symbols could be used to represent the words in any language, no matter how they were pronounced. The possible advantages of such a "universal" writing system stimulated a Dutch journalist, Karel Johnson, and a German professor, André Eckardt, soon after World War II, to develop a pictographic system called Picto. In Picto, the phrase *I have a house in town* (or *Ich habe ein Haus in der Stadt* or *J'ai une maison en ville*) would look like this:

$\mathcal{I}$	$\vert+$	$\Box$	$\boxdot$	$\overline{\overline{\underline{\odot}}}$
I	have	house	in	town
Ich	haben	Haus	in	Stadt
je	avoir	maison	en	ville

Unfortunately such a system is only effective when concrete ideas are communicated. Suppose one tried to translate into Picto the following sentence from Kierkegaard's *Fear and Trembling:*

> If there were no external consciousness in a man, if at the foundation of all there lay only a wildly seething power which writhing with obscure passions produced everything that is great and everything that is insignificant, if a bottomless void never satiated lay hidden beneath all—what then would life be but despair?

The difficulty is apparent.

Had pictographic writing been adequate to the task, there would have been no reason for it to have developed into the modern writing systems.

Cuneiform Writing

Much of our information on the development described above stems from the records left by the Sumerians, an ancient people of unknown origin who built a civilization in southern Mesopotamia over five thousand years ago. Their writing system is the oldest one known. It appears that they were a commercially oriented people, and as their business deals became increasingly complex the need for permanent records arose. An elaborate pictography was developed along with a system of "tallies." Some examples are shown here:

star, sky, God	hand	corn	5 oxen[2]	13 fish

Over the centuries their pictography was simplified and conventionalized. The characters or symbols were produced by using a wedge-shaped stylus which was pressed into soft clay tablets, made from the clay found on the land between the Tigris and Euphrates rivers. This form of writing is called **cuneiform** — literally "wedge-shaped" (from Latin *cuneus*). Here is an illustration of how Sumerian pictographs evolved to cuneiform:

star

hand

fish

Notice that the cuneiform "words" do little to remind one of the meaning represented. As cuneiform evolved, its users began to think of the symbols more in terms of the *name* of the thing represented, than the actual thing itself. Ultimately cuneiform script came to represent words of the language, and the Sumerians were in possession of a true writing system, called a **word-writing system.**

[2] The pictograph for "ox" evolved much later, into our letter *A*.

The Rebus Principle

When a graphic sign no longer has any visual relationship to the word it represents, it becomes a symbol for the sounds which represent the word. A single sign can then be used to represent all words with the same sounds—the homophones of the language. If, for example, the symbol

⊙   stood for *sun* in English, it could then be used in a sentence like

My ⊙ *is a doctor.* If the symbol ⌀ stood for *purse,* it could

be combined with ⊙ to form *person:* ⌀⊙. Using symbols which originally represented one-syllable words to represent individual syllables in many-syllable words is constructing words according to the **rebus principle.**

A rebus is a representation of words or syllables by pictures of objects whose names *sound like* the intended syllables. Thus ◁⊙▷ might represent *eye* or the pronoun *I.* The sounds of the two monosyllabic words are identical, even though the meanings are not. In the same way,

🐝🍃   could represent *belief* (*be* + *lief* = *bee* + *leaf* = /bi/ + /lif/),

and   🐝🍃🍃 could be the verb form, *believes.*

This is not a very efficient system, since the words of many languages do not lend themselves to subdivision into sequences of sounds which represent independent meaning. It would be difficult, for example, to represent the word *English* (/iŋ/ + /glɪš/) in English according to the rebus principle. *Eng* by itself does not "mean" anything, nor does *glish.* The rebus system, however, led to a syllabic-writing system which had many advantages over word-writing.

Syllabic Writing Systems

The cuneiform writing system was borrowed by a number of peoples, most notably by the Assyrians (or Babylonians) when they conquered the Sumerians, and later by the Persians. In adopting cuneiform to their own languages, the borrowers used them to represent the *sounds* of the *syllables* in their words. In this way cuneiform evolved into a **syllabic writing system.**

Each syllable in the language is represented by its own symbol in a syllabic writing system. Words are written by juxtaposing the symbols of their individual syllables. Cuneiform writing was never purely syllabic; that is, there was always a large residue of symbols which stood for whole words. The Assyrians retained a large number of word symbols, even though every word in their language could be written out syllabically if it were desired.   Thus one could write  mātu "country" as:

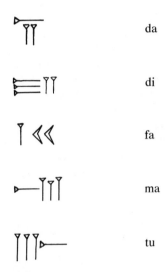

The Persians (ca. 600–400 B.C.) devised a greatly simplified syllabic alphabet for their language. They had little recourse to word symbols. By the reign of Darius I (522–468 B.C.) the writing system was in wide use. Here are a few characters of the syllabary:

da

di

fa

ma

tu

From Hieroglyphs to the Alphabet

At the time that Sumerian pictography was flourishing (around 4000 B.C.), a similar system was being used by the Egyptians, later called by the Greeks **hieroglyphics** (*hiero* "sacred," *glyphikos* "carvings"). That the early "sacred carvings" were originally pictography is shown by the following hieroglyphics:

"eye"   "giraffe"   "to rule"[3]   "fresh" or "cool"[4]

[3] The symbol is the Pharaoh's staff.
[4] Water trickling out of a vase.

Like the Sumerian pictographs, the hieroglyphs began to represent the sounds of the words they symbolized. This **phonetization** of the pictography made hieroglyphics a word-writing system, which paralleled the Sumerian cuneiform development. Possibly influenced by the Sumerians, the Egyptian system also became a word-syllabic writing.

In this advanced "syllabic" stage, hieroglyphics were borrowed by many people, including the Phoenicians, a Semitic people who lived on the eastern shores of the Mediterranean. By 1500 B.C. a system involving twenty-two syllables, The West Semitic Syllabary, was in use. In this system a single symbol represents both a consonant and a following vowel (CV).

This was the system first borrowed by the Greeks in the tenth century B.C. The syllabic system proved to be very inefficient, especially for a language like Greek with a complex syllable structure. In the Semitic languages there are many monosyllabic words, and in polysyllabic words the syllables are simple and regular.

Even in a language with a "simple" and regular syllable structure the number of syllables which would have to be used is enormous. Suppose, for example, a language sound system includes twenty consonants and five vowels. Suppose further that the typical syllable was composed of a consonant plus a vowel plus a consonant: C + V + C. This would permit 2,000 separate syllables: 20C × 5V × 20C.

Consider now a language like English. While there are constraints on which consonants can cluster, we still get syllables like:

I	[ay]	V	*an*	[æn]	VC
key	[ki]	CV	*ant*	[ænt]	VCC
ski	[ski]	CCV	*ants*	[ænts]	VCCC
spree	[spri]	CCCV	*pant*	[pænt]	CVCC
seek	[sik]	CVC	*pants*	[pænts]	CVCCC
speak	[spik]	CCVC	*splints*	[splɪnts]	CCCVCCC
scram	[skræm]	CCCVC	*stamp*	[stæmp]	CCVCC
striped	[straypt]	CCCVCC			

When you think of all the vowels and all the consonants that can occur in syllable structures of this kind it is evident that the number of syllables needed would be enormous. This kind of problem motivated the Greeks to use the symbols of the Phoenician writing system, but to represent the individual sounds—consonants and vowels. The Phoenicians had taken the first step by letting certain symbols stand for consonants alone. The language spoken by the Phoenicians, however, had more consonants than Greek, so when the Greeks borrowed the system they had symbols left over. These they allowed to represent vowel sounds, and thus they invented the **alphabetic writing system**. (The word *alphabet* is derived from *alpha* and *beta*, the first two letters of the Greek alphabet.)

Alphabetic systems are those in which each symbol represents one phoneme. It is clear that such systems are primarily *phonemic* rather than *phonetic,* as is illustrated by the fact that the *l* in both *feel* and *leaf* in the English alphabet system is represented by one rather than two "letters" even though the sounds are phonetically distinct.

There are arguments as to whether this event—the development of an alphabetic writing system—occurred more than once in history. Most scholars believe that all alphabetic systems in use today derive from the Greek system. This alphabet became known to the pre-Latin people of Italy, the Etruscans, who in turn passed it on to the Romans. The Roman Empire spread it throughout the world. Later, Christian missionaries used alphabetic systems to develop writing systems for many preliterate people. (Parts of the Bible have been translated into more than 1600 languages.)

It is a surprising fact that the alphabet, as we know it, did not have many beginnings. According to one linguist, the alphabet was not invented, it was *discovered.*[5] If language did not include discrete individual sounds, one could not have invented alphabetic letters to represent such sounds. When man started to use one symbol for one phoneme he had merely brought his intuitive knowledge of the language sound system to consciousness; he discovered what he already knew. Furthermore, children (and adults) can learn an alphabetic system only if each separate sound has some psychological reality. Since this is true of all languages, however, it is strange that this "discovery" was not made by many people in many parts of the world.

MODERN TYPES OF WRITING SYSTEMS

> . . . *but their manner of writing is very peculiar, being neither from the left to the right, like the Europeans; nor from the right to the left, like the Arabians; nor from up to down, like the Chinese; nor from down to up, like the Cascagians, but aslant from one corner of the paper to the other, like ladies in England.*
>
> —JONATHAN SWIFT, *Gulliver's Travels*

We have already discussed the three types of writing systems used in the world: *word writing, syllable writing,* and *alphabetic writing.*

In a word-writing system the written symbol represents a whole word. The awkwardness of such a system is obvious. For example, the editors of *Webster's Unabridged 3rd International Dictionary* claim more than 450,000 entries. When we consider that all these are written using only

---

[5] Dr. Sven Ohman, Professor of Phonetics, University of Uppsala, Sweden; paper presented at International Speech Symposium, Kyoto, Japan, 1969.

twenty-six alphabetic symbols, a dot, a hyphen, an apostrophe, and a space, it is understandable why, historically, word writing has given way to alphabetic systems in most places in the world.

The major exception is the writing system used in China. This system has an uninterrupted history that reaches back more than 3500 years. For the most part it is a word-writing system, each character representing an individual word or morpheme. A morpheme-writing system would be a more appropriate name, since most words are monomorphemic. Longer words may be formed by combining two morphemes, as shown by the word meaning "business" *măimài,* which was formed by combining the words meaning "buy" and "sell," but this is rare.

Chinese writing utilizes a system of **characters,** each of which represents the "meaning" of a word, rather than its sounds. Chinese dictionaries and rhyme books contain tens of thousands of these characters, but to read a newspaper one need know "only" about five thousand. It is not easy to become a scholar in China! In 1956, the difficulties prompted the government of the People's Republic of China to simplify the characters. They also adopted a spelling system using the Roman alphabet, to be used along with the regular ancient system. It is doubtful whether it will replace the traditional writing, which is an integral part of Chinese culture. In China, writing is an art — calligraphy — and thousands of years of poetry and literature and history are preserved in the old system.

There is an additional reason for keeping the traditional system. Chinese is composed of a number of dialects (at least seven) which are all mutually unintelligible in spoken form. But each dialect uses the one writing system; through writing all the Chinese can communicate. A common sight in a city like Hong Kong is for two Chinese to be talking and at the same time furiously drawing characters in the air with a forefinger to overcome their dialectal differences.

The use of written Chinese characters in this way is parallel to the use of Arabic numerals, which mean the same in all European countries. Though the word for "eight" is very different in English, Greek, and Finnish, by writing *8* you can be understood. Similarly, the word for "rice" is different in many Chinese dialects, but the written character is the same. If the writing system in China were ever to become alphabetic, each dialect would be as different in writing as in speaking, and communication would break down completely between the dialect groups.

Every writing system has some traces of word writing. In addition to numerals in which a single symbol represents a whole word, other symbols, such as $, %, &, ¢, H_2O, +, −, =, are used.

Syllabic-writing systems are more efficient than word-writing systems. They are certainly less taxing on our memory. But as discussed above, they still present serious difficulties for recording the sentences of a language.

Japanese is the only major language in the world that uses a syllabic alphabet. They borrowed and modified fifty Chinese characters to stand for each of the fifty syllables that Japanese words are composed of. This system is not purely syllabic, there being a number of word signs borrowed from Chinese, and many words are represented by a mixture of a word sign and a syllable sign. In theory, all of Japanese could be written in the fifty-character syllabary, but the large number of homophones (*ka* has over two hundred meanings, each indicated by a separate character) provides incentive for retaining the word-syllabic system.

In 1821, Sequoyah, often called the "Cherokee Cadmus," invented a syllabic writing system for his native language. Sequoyah's script proved very useful to the Cherokee people for a number of years, and was justifiably a point of great pride for them. The syllabary contains eighty-five symbols, many of them derived from Latin characters, and efficiently transcribes spoken Cherokee. A few symbols are shown here;

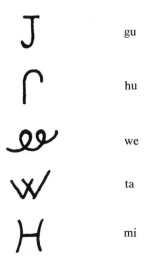

J	gu
ſ	hu
𝓮𝓮	we
W	ta
H	mi

English occasionally uses syllabic symbols. In words such as *OK* and *bar-b-q,* the single letters represent syllables (*b* for [bə], *q* for [kyu]).

Alphabetic writing systems are one of the major achievements of civilization. They are easy to learn and convenient to use, and are maximally efficient for transcribing any human language.

The term **sound-writing** is sometimes used in place of alphabetic writing, but this does not truly represent the principle involved in the use of alphabets. One-sound-one-letter would be inefficient, since we do not need to represent the [pʰ] in *pit* and the [p] in *spit* by two different letters. It would also be confusing, because the nonphonemic differences between sounds are seldom perceptible to speakers. Except for the phonetic alphabets whose function is to record the sounds of all languages for descriptive purposes, most, if not all, alphabets have been devised on the **phonemic principle.**

In the twelfth century, an Icelandic scholar developed an orthography derived from the Latin alphabet for the writing of the Icelandic language of his day. Other scholars in this period were also interested in orthographic reform, including the German, Notker, and the Englishman, Orm. But the Icelander, who came to be known as "The First Grammarian" (because his anonymous paper was the first entry in a collection of grammatical essays), was the only one of the time who left a record of his principles. The orthography which he developed was clearly based on the phonemic principle. He used minimal pairs to show the distinctive contrasts; he did not suggest different symbols for voiced and unvoiced [θ] and [ð], nor for [f] or [v], nor for velar [k] and palatal [č], since these pairs, according to him, represented allophones of the phonemes /θ/, /f/, and /k/, respectively. He, of course, did not use these modern technical terms, but the letters of his alphabet represent the distinctive phonemes of Icelandic of that century.

King Seijong of Korea (1417–1450) realized that the same held true for Korean when he designed a phonemic alphabet. The king was an avid reader (so avid that his eyes suffered greatly), and he realized that the more than 30,000 Chinese characters that were being used to write the Korean language discouraged literacy among the people.

The alphabet was not reinvented by Seijong. Indian scholars had visited Korea, and the erudite monarch undoubtedly knew of the Hindu grammarians. Still, his alphabet, called *hankul,* was conceived with remarkable insight. Originally hankul had eleven vowels and seventeen consonants (it is down to fourteen consonants and ten vowels at present). The characters representing consonants were drawn according to the place and manner of articulation. For example, $\wedge$ is meant to represent the teeth, and it is a part of each consonant character in which the tongue is placed behind the teeth (that is, alveolar or alveopalatal sounds). Thus $\wedge$ alone stands for /s/ ([s] or [š]). Cross it to get $\wedge$ and you have the character for [ts] (the initial sound of German *Zeit*) and [tš] (= [č]). A bar above the character means aspiration, so $\overline{\wedge}$ stands for [tsʰ] and [tšʰ] (= [čʰ]). Hundreds of years later, Francis Lodwick, Cave Beck, and Henry Sweet used a similar principle to design their phonetic alphabets.

King Seijong's vowels were conceived somewhat more philosophically. "King Seijong made the eleven vowels represent heaven, earth and man...."[6] Each vowel character was constructed by using one or more of three "atomic" characters: · | and —. For example, | was /i/,

---

[6] *King Seijong the Great,* prepared by the King Seijong Memorial Society of the Republic of Korea.

— was /u/ and |· was /a/. Although Korean has the sounds [l] and [r], only a single "letter" was used by Seijong because these sounds are in "complementary distribution" in Korean—allophonic variants of the same phoneme. The same is true for the sounds [s] and [š]. Seijong knew that a narrow phonetic alphabet would be unintuitive to a Korean speaker.

Seijong's contribution to the Korean people has been recorded in a delightful legend. It is said that after he designed the alphabet he was afraid it would not be accepted, and so he concocted a scheme to convince the people that it was a gift from heaven. To do this he wrote each one of his new letters in honey on individual leaves which had fallen from a tree in the palace garden. When the king walked with his soothsayer in the garden the next day, the insects had eaten the honey and the leaf fiber underneath, just as he had hoped, and the leaves were etched with the alphabetic letters. The soothsayer and the Korean people were convinced that these represented a message from the gods. It is essentially this alphabet which is used in Korea today.

Many languages have their own alphabet, and each has developed certain conventions for converting strings of alphabetic characters into sequences of sound (that is, reading), and converting sequences of sounds into strings of alphabetic characters (that is, writing). As we have illustrated with English, Icelandic, and Korean, the rules governing the sound system of the language play an important role in the relation between sound and character.

Most European alphabets make use of Latin (Roman) characters, minor adjustments being made to accommodate individual characteristics of a particular language. For instance, Spanish uses /ñ/ (an /n/ with a "tilde") to represent the palatilized nasal of señor, and German has added an "umlaut" for certain of its vowel sounds that didn't exist in Latin (for example, über.) Such "extra" marks are called **diacritics**. Often languages resort to using two letters together to represent a single sound for which there is no corresponding single letter. English includes **digraphs** such as sh [š], ch [č], ng [ŋ], and so on.

Some languages that have more recently acquired a writing system use some of the IPA phonetic symbols in their alphabet. Twi, for example uses ŋ, ɔ, and ɛ.

Besides the European languages, such languages as Turkish, Indonesian, Swahili, and Vietnamese have adopted the Latin alphabet.

The **Cyrillic** alphabet, named for St. Cyril, who brought Christianity to the Slavs, is used by many Slavic languages, including Russian. It is derived directly from the Greek alphabet without Latin mediation.

The contemporary Semitic alphabets, and those used for Persian and Urdu writing, are derived from the West Semitic Syllabary.

Figure 11.2 shows a greatly abbreviated "family tree" of alphabetic writing systems.

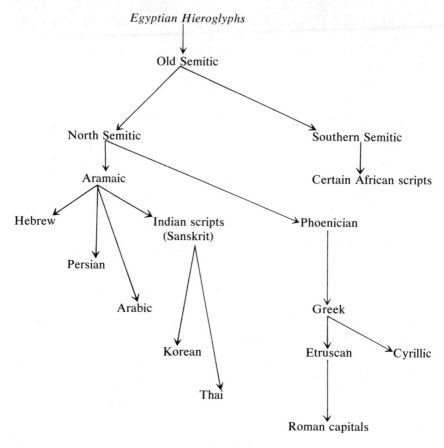

Figure 11.2 Family tree of alphabetic writing systems. (Adapted from Ernst Doblhofer, *Voices in Stone,* Viking, 1961)

WRITING AND SPEECH

> *... Ther is so great diversite*
> *In English, and in wryting of oure tonge,*
> *So prey I god that non myswrite thee ...*
>
> —GEOFFREY CHAUCER

The development of writing freed man from his earthbound status and took him to the stars, but it is language that makes man what he is. The primacy of the spoken language over the written is revealed in the short history of writing in the preceding pages. To understand language one cannot depend on its written form. A linguist would no more investigate a language via its orthography than a doctor would examine a patient via a photograph. Writing is of interest to the linguist, but only as an indirect means of learning about a language.

The written language reflects, to a certain extent, the elements and rules which together constitute the grammar of the language. The system of phonemes is represented by the letters of the alphabet, although not necessarily in a direct way. Were there no discrete sound units in language, there could be no alphabetic writing. The independence of words in a language is revealed by the spaces in the written string. But in languages where words are composed of more than one morpheme, the writing does not show the individual morphemes, even though speakers know what these are. The sentences of a language are represented in the written form by capitals and periods. Other puctuation, such as question marks, italics, commas, exclamation marks, is used to reveal syntactic structure.

The possible ambiguity in the meanings of some sentences can be prevented by the use of commas:

1. The Greeks, who were philosophers, loved to talk a lot.
2. The Greeks who were philosophers loved to talk a lot.

The difference in meaning between the two sentences is specified by the use of commas in the first and not in the second. Sentence 1, with the commas, clearly means:

1'. The Greeks were philosophers and they loved to talk a lot.

The meaning of the second sentence, without the commas, can be paraphrased as:

2'. Among the Greeks it was the philosophers who loved to talk a lot.

Similarly, by using an exclamation point or a question mark, the intention of the writer can be revealed.

3. The children are going to bed at eight o'clock. *(simple statement)*
4. The children are going to bed at eight o'clock! *(an order)*
5. The children are going to bed at eight o'clock? *(a query)*

These punctuation marks reflect the pauses and the intonations which would be used in the spoken language.

In sentence 6 the *he* can refer to either John or someone else, but in sentence 7 the pronoun must refer to someone other than John:

6. John said he's going.
7. John said, "He's going."

The apostrophe used in contractions and possessives also provides syntactic information:

8. My cousin's friends *(one cousin)*
9. My cousins' friends *(two or more cousins)*

Writing, then, does reflect the spoken language, but it does so imperfectly. Ordinary punctuation marks may be unable to distinguish between two possible meanings:

> 10. John whispered the message to Bill and then he whispered it to Mary.

In the normal written version of sentence 10, *he* can refer to either John or Bill. In the spoken sentence, if *he* receives extra stress (called **contrastive stress**), it must refer to Bill; if *he* receives normal stress, it refers to John. In speaking one can usually emphasize any word in a sentence by using contrastive stress. One sometimes attempts to show this in writing by using all capital letters or underlining the emphasized word:

> 11. <u>John</u> kissed Bill's wife.   (Bill didn't)
> 12. John <u>kissed</u> Bill's wife.   (rather than hitting her)
> 13. John kissed <u>Bill</u>'s wife.   (not Dick's or his own)
> 14. John kissed Bill's <u>wife</u>.   (not Bill's mother)

While such "visual" devices can help in English, it is not clear that this can be done in a language such as Chinese.

The written language is also more conservative than the spoken language. When we write something—particularly in formal writing—we are more apt to obey the "prescriptive rules" taught in school, or use a more formal style, than we are to use the rules of our "everyday" grammar. "Dangling participles" (for example, *While studying in the library, the fire alarm rang*) and "sentences ending with a preposition" (for example, *I know what to end a sentence with*) abound in spoken language, but may be "corrected" by copy editors, diligent English teachers, and careful writers. A linguist wishing to describe the language that people regularly use therefore cannot depend on written records alone.

SPELLING

> *"Do you spell it with a 'v' or a 'w'?" inquired the judge.*
> *"That depends upon the taste and fancy of the speller, my Lord," replied Sam.*
>
> —CHARLES DICKENS, *The Pickwick Papers*

If writing represented the spoken language perfectly, spelling reformers would never have arisen. In Chapter 3 we discussed some of the problems in the English orthographic (spelling) system. These problems prompted George Bernard Shaw to write:

> . . . it was as a reading and writing animal that Man achieved his human eminence above those who are called beasts. Well, it is I and my like who

have to do the writing. I have done it professionally for the last sixty years as well as it can be done with a hopelessly inadequate alphabet devised centuries before the English language existed to record another and very different language. Even this alphabet is reduced to absurdity by a foolish orthography based on the notion that the business of spelling is to represent the origin and history of a word instead of its sound and meaning. Thus an intelligent child who is bidden to spell debt, and very properly spells it d-e-t, is caned for not spelling it with a b because Julius Caesar spelt the Latin word for it with a b.[7]

The irregularities between **graphemes** (letters) and phonemes have been cited as one reason "why Johnny can't read." Different spellings for the same sound, the same spellings for different sounds, "silent letters," and "missing letters"—all provide fuel for the flames of spelling-reform movements. This was illustrated earlier, but merits further examples:

SAME SOUND, DIFFERENT SPELLING	DIFFERENT SOUND, SAME SPELLING	SILENT LETTERS	MISSING LETTERS
/ay/	*th*ought [θ]	lis*t*en	use /yuz/
	*th*ough [ð]	de*b*t	fuse /fyuz/
aye	*Th*omas [t]	*g*nosis	
buy		*k*now	
by	*a*te [e]	*p*sychology	
die	*a*t [æ]	ri*gh*t	
hi	f*a*ther [a]	thou*gh*	
Thai	m*a*ny [ɛ]	ar*c*tic	
		ca*l*m	
		*h*onest	
		s*w*ord	
		bom*b*	
		clu*e*	

Chapter 3 and Chapter 8 discuss some of the reasons for the non-phonemic spelling system which exists in our spelling system. "Spelling is the written trace of a word. Pronunciation is its linguistic form."[8] The spelling of most of the words in English today is based on the Late Middle English pronunciation (that used by Chaucer) and on the early forms of Modern English (used by Shakespeare). As was noted, the many changes which have occurred in the sound system of English, like the Great Vowel Shift, were not always reflected in changes in the spelling of the words which were affected.

When the printing press was introduced in the fifteenth century, not

---

[7] George Bernard Shaw, Preface to R. A. Wilson, *The Miraculous Birth of Language* (New York: Philosophical Library, 1948).

[8] D. Bollinger, *Aspects of Language* (New York: Harcourt, Brace & World, 1968).

only were archaic pronunciations "frozen" but the spelling did not always represent even those pronunciations, since many of the early printers were Dutch and were unsure of English pronunciation.

During the Renaissance, in the fifteenth and sixteenth centuries, many scholars who revered Classical Greek and Latin became "spelling reformers." Unlike the later reformers who wished to change the spelling to conform with pronunciation, these scholars changed the spelling of English words to conform to their etymologies—the "original" Latin, or Greek, or French spellings. Where Latin had a *b,* they added a *b* even if it was not pronounced; and where the original spelling had a *c* or *p* or *h,* these letters were added, as is shown by these few examples:

MIDDLE ENGLISH SPELLING		"REFORMED" SPELLING
indite	→	indi*c*t
dette	→	de*b*t
receit	→	recei*p*t
iland	→	i*s*land
oure	→	*h*our

These, then, are the reasons why modern English orthography does not represent, in all cases, what we know about the phonology of the language. In at least one respect this is a good thing. It allows us to read and understand what people wrote hundreds of years ago without the need for translations. If there were a one-to-one correspondence between our spelling and the sounds of our language, we would have difficulty reading even the Constitution or the Declaration of Independence. Constant spellings help our ever-dynamic language to span gaps of time.

Today's language is no more static than was yesterday's; it would be impossible to maintain a perfect correspondence between pronunciation and spelling. This is not to say that certain reforms would not be helpful. Some "respelling" is already taking place; newspapers often spell *though* as *tho, through* as *thru,* and *night* as *nite.*

In the case of homophones it is very helpful at times to have different spellings for the same sounds, as in the following:

The book was red.   The book was read.

Lewis Carroll once more makes the point with his own inimitable humor:

"And how many hours a day did you do lessons?" said Alice.
"Ten hours the first day," said the Mock Turtle, "nine the next, and so on."
"What a curious plan!" exclaimed Alice.
"That's the reason they're called *lessons*," the Gryphon remarked, "because they *lessen* from day to day."

There are also reasons for using the same spelling for different pronunciations. In Chapter 4 it was shown that a morpheme may be pronounced differently when it occurs in different contexts, and that in most cases the pronunciation is "regular"; that is, it is determined by rules which apply throughout the language. The identical spelling reflects the fact that the different pronunciations represent the same morpheme.

Suppose, for example, *bomb* were spelled *bom* and a child came across the word *bombardier* for the first time. He would have no way of knowing that a *bombardier* has anything to do with *bombs*. It is possible that with the present spelling of *bomb* he could figure it out. The spelling *bomb* does not create any problems. Every speaker of English knows that a *b* is not pronounced when it follows an *m* in final position of a word.

Similarly, the phonetic realizations of the vowels in the following forms are "regular":

I	E	A
div*i*ne/div*i*nity	ser*e*ne/ser*e*nity	s*a*ne/s*a*nity
subl*i*me/subl*i*mate	obsc*e*ne/obsc*e*nity	prof*a*ne/prof*a*nity
s*i*gn/s*i*gnature	hygi*e*ne/hygi*e*nic	hum*a*ne/hum*a*nity

The spelling of such pairs thus reflects our knowledge of the sound pattern of the language and the semantic relations between the words.

It is doubtful that anyone would suggest that the plural morpheme should be spelled *s* in *cats* and *z* in *dogs*. The sound of the morpheme is determined by rules, and this is just as true in other cases like those given above.

There are also different spellings which represent the different pronunciations of a morpheme when confusion would arise using the same spelling. For example, there is a rule in English phonology which changes a /t/ to an /s/ in certain cases: *democrat* → *democracy*. The different spellings are due to the fact that this rule does not apply to all morphemes, as was shown by some of the words listed above, such as *sanity*. There are many regular phoneme-to-grapheme rules which determine when a morpheme is to be spelled identically and when it is changed. Notice, also, that a *c* always represents the /s/ sound when it is followed by a *y* or *i* or *e*, as in *cynic* and *citizen* and *censure*. Since it is always pronounced [k] when it is the final letter in a word or when it is followed by any other vowel (*coat, cat, cut,* and so on), no confusion results.

Such rules of orthography can be taught to children learning to read, which would lessen the difficulties they have with the spelling system.

There is another important reason why spelling should not be tied to the phonetic pronunciation of words. Professor David Abercrombie of the University of Edinburgh tells a story about a conversation between an American and an Englishman. The American asks the Englishman what his job is and the Englishman replies: "I'm a clerk." The astonished American shakes his head and asks: "You mean you go 'tick-tock, tick-tock'?"

The common spelling *clerk* is pronounced [klərk] by Americans and [klɑːk] by the British. A popular song of the 1930s illustrates the difference between American and British English (there were Americans who thought it was "upper-class" to use British pronunciations):

> You say tomato,   and I say tomato,
>   [təmeto]   [təmato]
> You say potato,   and I say potato,
>   [pəteto]   [pətato]
> Tomato, tomato, potato, potato, let's call the whole thing off.[9]
>   [təmeto] [təmato] [pəteto] [pətato]

Other English dialects also have divergent pronunciations. Cockneys drop their "haitches" and Bostonians and Southerners drop their "r's"; *neither* is pronounced [niðər] and [niðə] by Americans, [nayðə] by the British, and [neðər] by the Irish; the Scots pronounce *night* as [nɪxt]; one hears "Chicago" and "Chicawgo," "hog" and "hawg," "bird" and "boyd"; *four* is pronounced [fɔː] by the British, [fɔr] in the Midwest, and [foə] in the South; *orange* is pronounced in two ways in the United States: [aranǰ] and [ɔrənǰ].

While dialectal pronunciations differ, the common spellings represent the fact that we can all understand each other. It is necessary for the written language to transcend local dialects. With a uniform spelling system, a native of Atlanta and a native of Glasgow can communicate through writing. If each dialect were spelled according to its own pronunciation, written communication among the English-speaking peoples of the world would suffer more than the spoken communication does today.

An Irish friend of ours has suggested that since the Irish originally taught the English to write (between 600 and 700 A.D.), spelling reforms ought to be made in Ireland. Then, says our friend, the Irish will simply teach the English to write once again. We have no idea what he has in mind for North America, should such a spelling reform movement win out.

SPELLING PRONUNCIATIONS

For pronunciation, the best general rule is to consider those as the most elegant speakers who deviate least from written words.

—SAMUEL JOHNSON (1755)

[9] Copyright © 1937 by Gershwin Publishing Corporation. Copyright renewed. Reprinted by permission of Chappell & Co., Inc.

Despite the primacy of the spoken over the written language, the written word is often regarded with excessive reverence. Undoubtedly the stability, permanency, and graphic nature of writing cause some people to favor it over ephemeral and elusive speech. Humpty Dumpty expressed a rather typical attitude: "I'd rather see that done on paper," he announced.

Writing has, however, affected speech only marginally, and most notably in the phenomenon of **spelling pronunciation.** Since the sixteenth century, we find that spelling has influenced standard pronunciation to some extent. The most important of such changes stem from the eighteenth century under the influence and "decrees" of the dictionary-makers and the schoolteachers. The struggle between those who demanded that words be pronounced according to the spelling and those who demanded that words be spelled according to their pronunciation generated great heat in that century. The "preferred" pronunciations were given in the many dictionaries printed in the eighteenth century, and the "supreme authority" of the dictionaries influenced pronunciation in this way.

Spelling also has influenced pronunciation in words that are infrequently used in normal daily speech. Many words which were spelled with an initial *h* were not pronounced with any /h/ sound as late as the eighteenth century. Thus, at that time no /h/ was pronounced in *honest, hour, habit, heretic, hotel, hospital, herb.* Frequently used words like *honest* and *hour* continued to be pronounced without the /h/, despite the spelling. But all those other words were given a "spelling pronunciation." Since people did not hear them very often, when they saw them written they concluded that they must begin with an /h/.

Similarly, many words now spelled with a *th* were once pronounced /t/ as in *Thomas;* later most of these words underwent a change in pronunciation from /t/ to /θ/, as in *anthem, author, theater.* It is interesting that "nicknames" often reflect the earlier pronunciations: "Ka*t*e" for "Ca*t*herine," "Be*tt*y" for "Elizabe*th*," "Ar*t*" for "Ar*t*hur." The words *often* and *soften,* which are usually pronounced without a /t/ sound, are pronounced with the /t/ by some people because of the spelling. At one time, however, the /t/ was never pronounced in *often* and *soften.*

The clear influence of spelling on pronunciation is observable in the way place-names are pronounced. *Berkeley* is pronounced [bɔrkli] in California, although it stems from the British [ba:kli]; *Worcester* [wustər] or [wustə] in Massachusetts is often pronounced [wərčɛstər] in other parts of the country.

While the written language thus has some influence on the spoken, it never changes the basic system—the grammar—of the language. The writing system, conversely, reflects, in a more or less direct way, the grammar that every speaker knows.

GRAFFITI

> *Banish the use of the four-letter words*
> *Whose meaning is never obscure;*
> *The Anglos, the Saxons, those bawdy old birds*
> *Were vulgar, obscene, and impure.*
> *But cherish the use of the weasling phrase*
> *That never quite says what it means;*
> *You'd better be known for your hypocrite ways*
> *Than vulgar, impure, and obscene.*
>
> — OGDEN NASH, "Ode to the Four-Letter Words"

Graffiti means different things to different people. To a lexicographer, it is the plural of *graffito;* to a philologist it is an Italian borrowing that means "scribbling" or "scratching"; to the timid, it is something shocking, and to the insolent a chance to shock; to the radical it is "mass propaganda"; to the city of Philadelphia it is a million dollars a year spent in a losing battle to scrape paint off the walls of its subway platforms; to most of us it is what we see, and perhaps what we scrawl, on the walls of public places, such as toilets.

Graffito was adopted by archeologists as a general term for the casual writings, rude drawings, and markings found on ancient buildings and monuments. It contrasted with the term *inscription,* which was reserved for more deliberate, more conventional writing or drawing. The word has undergone semantic shifting, and for many younger people it now has only a vulgar or obscene connotation, though this was not always so, nor is it so for all speakers.

The graffiti which covered the buildings in Paris during the student demonstrations of May 1948 were far from obscene. They were the written testimonials to the emotional feelings of the students. The painted words of the youth were later whitewashed out, but photographs of the graffiti record a historical moment. LA SOCIÉTÉ EST UNE FLEUR CARNIVORE" ("Society is a carnivorous flower") one sign proclaimed; another, "PRENDS MES DÉSIRS POUR LA RÉALITÉ CAR JE CROIS EN LA RÉALITÉ DE MES DÉSIRS" ("Accept my desires as real, for I believe in the reality of my desires"). By such graffiti the thoughts of the young people of the time are revealed.

Similar graffiti have been found in great abundance on monuments of ancient Egypt, usually scratched into the stone or plaster. The subjects of these scribblings include rude caricatures, obscenities, election addresses, and lines of poetry. The present-day urban crisis over graffiti has had its counterparts in history. Archeologists have found ancient Roman ruins with inscriptions begging passersby not to scribble on the walls, and in Thera, Greece, rock inscriptions have been found "consisting of . . . the perverse scribblings of street urchins"[10] which date back to the seventh century B.C.

Such graffiti are important historical clues. While "Kilroy was here" (a common "scribble" of a few years ago) may confuse future historians as to who the famous "Kilroy" was, the graffiti proclaiming "Yankee go home" will tell them that the American presence was not always welcomed in other countries.

Linguists do not consider graffiti a nuisance by any means — at least not old graffiti. Graffiti can furnish useful information about the spoken language of a particular period and place, and in the case of graffiti left by foreign "tourists," about the language of another place in the same period. They also provide information about the kind of writing system the "man in the street" was using, and hence provide valuable clues in the saga of evolving writing systems.

SUMMARY

Writing is one of the basic tools of civilization. Without it, the world as we know it could not exist.

The first writing was "picture writing," which used **pictograms** to represent objects directly. Pictograms became stylized and people came to associate them with the *word sounds* that represented the object in their language. The Sumerians first developed a pictographic writing system to keep track of commercial transactions. It was later expanded for other uses and eventually evolved into the highly stylized **cuneiform** writing. Cuneiform was borrowed by several nations and was adapted for use in a syllabic writing system by application of the **rebus principle,** which used the symbol of one word to represent any word or syllable with the same sounds.

The Egyptians also developed a pictographic system that became known as **hieroglyphics.** This system was borrowed by many peoples including the Phoenicians, who improved on it, using it as a **syllabary.** In a syllabic writing system one symbol is used for each syllable. The Greeks borrowed this Phoenician system and in adapting it to their own language used the symbols to represent individual sound segments, thus inventing the first **alphabet.**

There are three types of writing systems still being used in the world: word writing, where every symbol or character represents a word or morpheme (as in Chinese); syllable writing, where each symbol represents a syllable (as in Japanese); and alphabetic writing, where each symbol represents (for the most part) one phoneme (as in English).

[10] F. N. H. Pederson, *The Discovery of Language: Linguistic Science in the Nineteenth Century,* trans. by John Webster Spargo (Bloomington: Indiana University Press, 1962).

Many of the world's languages do not have a written form, but this does not mean the languages are any less developed. We learn to speak before we learn to write, and historically tens of thousands of years went by during which men spoke before there was any writing.

The writing system may have some small effect on the spoken language. Languages change in time, but writing systems tend to be more conservative. As the spoken and written forms of the language become divergent, some words came to be pronounced as they were spelled, sometimes due to the efforts of "pronunciation reformers."

There are advantages to a conservative spelling system. A common spelling permits speakers whose dialects have diverged to communicate through writing, as is best exemplified in China, where the "dialects" are mutually unintelligible. We are also able to read and understand the language as it was written centuries ago. In addition, besides some gross lack of correspondences between sounds and spelling, the spelling often reflects speakers' morphological and phonological knowledge.

EXERCISES

1. a. "Write" the following words and phrases using pictograms which you invent:

1. eye	5. tree	9. ugly
2. a boy	6. forest	10. run
3. two boys	7. war	11. scotch tape
4. library	8. honesty	12. smoke

   b. Which words are most difficult to symbolize in this way? Why?
   c. How does the following sentence reveal the problems in pictographic writing? "A grammar represents the unconscious, internalized linguistic competence of a native speaker."

2. A *rebus* is a written representation of words or syllables using pictures of objects whose names resemble the sounds of the intended words or syllables. For example, ◁⊙▷ might be the symbol for "eye" or "I" or the first syllable in "idea." Using this rebus principle, "write" the following:

   1. tearing   2. icicle   3. bareback   4. cookies

   Why would such a system be a difficult system in which to represent all words in English? Illustrate with an example.

3. Construct non-Roman alphabetic letters to replace the letters used to represent the following sounds in English:

   t r s k w č i æ f ŋ

Use these symbols plus the regular alphabet symbols for the other sounds to write the following words in your "new orthography."

1. character
2. guest
3. cough
4. photo

5. cheat
6. rang
7. psychotic
8. tree

4. Suppose the English writing system were a *syllabic* system instead of an *alphabetic* system. Use capital letters to symbolize the necessary syllabic units for the words listed below and list your "syllabary." Example, given the words *mate, inmate, intake,* and *elfin,* one might use: A = mate, B = in, C = take, and D = elf. In addition, write the words using your syllabary. Example: *inmate:* BA, *elfin:* DB; *intake:* BC; *mate:* A. (Do not use any more syllable symbols than you absolutely need.)

1. childishness
2. childlike
3. Jesuit

4. lifelessness
5. likely
6. zoo

7. witness
8. lethal
9. jealous

10. witless
11. lesson

5. In the following pairs of English words the italicized portions are pronounced the same but spelled differently. Can you think of any reason why the spelling should remain distinct? (Hint: *reel* and *real* are pronounced the same, but *reality* shows the presence of a phonemic /æ/ in *real*.)

1. I a*m*
2. goo*se*
3. fa*sh*ion
4. New*ton*
5. *mn*emonic
6. *n*o

ia*mb*
produ*ce*
complica*t*ion
org*an*
*N*eptune
know

6. In the following pairs of words the italicized portions in the second column are pronounced differently from those in the first column. Try to state some reasons why the spelling of the words in column B should not be changed.

A	B
1. mi*ng*le	lo*ng*
2. l*i*ne	ch*i*ldren
3. *s*onar	re*s*ound
4. *c*ent	mysti*c*
5. cru*mb*le	bo*mb*
6. cat*s*	dog*s*
7. sta*g*nant	desi*g*n
8. ser*e*ne	obs*ce*nity

7. Each of the following sentences is ambiguous (can have more than

one meaning) in the written form. How can these sentences be made unambiguous when they are spoken?

    1. John punched Bill and then he kicked him.
    2. What are we having for dinner, Mother?
    3. She's a German language teacher.
    4. They formed a student grievance committee.
    5. Charles kissed his wife and George kissed his wife, too.

8. In the written form, the following sentences are not ambiguous, but they would be if spoken. State the devices used in writing which make the meanings explicit.

    1. They're my brothers' keepers.
    2. He said, "He will take the garbage out."
    3. The red book was read.
    4. The flower was on the table.

9. If you were given the task of making changes in the present spelling system of English, what are some of the changes you would propose? Are there any "silent" letters that should be dropped from the orthography? Should some sounds always have the same letters to represent them? Should some letters with different sounds be given additional symbols? Justify your proposals.

10. Discuss the statement quoted in the chapter that "alphabetic writing was not invented, it was discovered." That is, how does the existence of alphabets reflect a linguistic universal?

References

DIRINGER, D. *The Alphabet*. New York: Philosophical Library, 1948.

DIRINGER, D. *Writing*. New York: Praeger, 1962.

DOBLHOFER, E. *Voices in Stone: The Decipherment of Ancient Scripts and Writings*. New York: The Viking Press, 1961.

GELB, I. J. *A Study of Writing*. Chicago: University of Chicago Press, 1952.

PULGRAM, ERNST. "Phone and Grapheme: A Parallel." *Words*, 7.1, 15–20 (1951).

PYLES, THOMAS. *Words and Ways of American English*. New York: Random House, 1952.

ROBERTSON, S., and CASSIDY, F. G. *The Development of Modern English*. Englewood Cliffs, N.J.: Prentice-Hall, 1954. Pp. 353–374 on spelling and spelling reform.

WANG, WILLIAM S-Y. "The Chinese Language." *Scientific American*, Vol. 228, No. 2, 50–63 (Feb. 1973).

12
The Gray Matter
of Language:
Language and the Brain

Brain, *n. An apparatus with which we think that we think.*
— AMBROSE BIERCE, *The Devil's Dictionary*

What good are brains to a ~~man?~~ They only unsettle him.
— P. G. WODEHOUSE, *The Adventures of Sally*

Every aspect of language is enormously complex. Yet, we have already noted (in Chapter 7) that as Descartes pointed out: "There are none so depraved and stupid, without even excepting idiots, that they cannot arrange different words together, forming of them a statement by which they make known their thoughts." Perhaps even more remarkable is the fact that children—before the age of five—learn this intricate system. Before they can add two plus two they are conjoining sentences, asking questions, selecting appropriate pronouns, forming negations, using the syntactic, phonological, and semantic rules of the grammar. Children are not taught language as they are taught arithmetic. They learn it by themselves as long as it is used around them.

The study of *what* children learn—the grammar—is the study of linguistic competence. The study of *how* children acquire this knowledge and how we use language to speak and understand is the study of linguistic performance (or language **behavior**). This area of linguistics is called **psycholinguistics**, since it deals with the psychological, behavioral aspects of language.

Even if we completely understood the acquisition process and the production and perception of speech (and we are just at the beginning of such knowledge), this would not tell us how man is able to accomplish these feats. Why is man the only animal that learns and uses language? What aspects of man's neurological makeup explain this ability? The study concerned with such questions—with the biological foundations

of language and the brain mechanisms underlying its acquisition and use—
is called **neurolinguistics.**

In this chapter we shall look at some of what is known in these two
areas.

LANGUAGE AND THE LEFT HEMISPHERE

It only takes one hemisphere to have a mind.

—A. L. WIGAN (1844)

In September, 1848, a foreman of a road construction gang named
Phineas Gage became a famous figure in medical history. He achieved
his "immortality" when a four-foot-long iron rod was blown through
his head. Despite the gaping tunnel in his brain, Gage lived for twelve
more years and, except for some personality changes (he became
"cranky" and "inconsiderate"), Gage seemed to be little affected by this
terrible accident. This seemed miraculous. How could so much damage
to the brain have so little effect? Both Gage and science benefited from
this explosion. Phineas gained monetarily by becoming a one-man tour-
ing circus; he traveled all over the country charging money to those
curious enough to see him and the iron rod. Science benefited because
brain researchers were stimulated to learn why his intelligence seemed
to be intact.

Since that time we have learned a great deal about the brain—the most
complicated organ of the body. It lies under the skull and consists of approximately 10 billion nerve cells (neurons) and all the billions of fibers
which connect these cells. The nerve cells or **gray matter** form the surface of the brain, which is called the **cortex.** Under the cortex is the **white
matter,** which consists primarily of the connecting fibers. The cerebral
cortex is the decision-making organ of the body. It receives messages
from all the sensory organs, and it initiates all voluntary actions. It is
"the seat of all which is exclusively human in the mind." It is the store-
house of "memory" as well. Obviously, somewhere in this gray matter
the grammar which represents our knowledge of language must reside.

The brain is divided into two parts (called **cerebral hemispheres**), one
on the right and one on the left. These hemispheres are connected like
Siamese twins right down the middle by the **corpus callosum,** which is a
pathway leading from one side to the other, permitting the "two brains"
to communicate with each other.

An interesting fact about these two hemispheres is that the left hemisphere controls the movements of the right side of the body and the right
hemisphere the movements of the left side. That is, if you scratch your

nose with your right hand, it is the left hemisphere which has "directed" your actions. If someone whispers into your left ear, the sound signal will go most directly to the right hemisphere before crossing over the pathway to get to the left.

The **cerebellum**, also divided into two halves, is located underneath the cerebral hemispheres and is responsible for controlling equilibrium. At the bottom of the brain is found the **brain stem,** which connects the brain to the spinal cord.

You might be wondering, at this point, why in a book on language we are going into all this anatomy. The details are not important, but, as Wallace Chafe pointed out: "The description of a language cannot be divorced from considerations of what is 'in people's heads.' "[1] We can't look into people's heads very easily, and even if we could we would not find any morphemes, or NP's, or S → NP VP rules. "We can only hypothesize what goes on there on the basis of indirect evidence," says Chafe. It is on the basis of such evidence that brain researchers have found that different parts of the brain are responsible for different activities and functions.

Accidents, disease, and surgery provided a great deal of information about the specific functions of different areas of the cortex. Damage (lesions) to one part of the brain causes certain malfunctions, and damage to other parts causes other kinds of pathological behavior.

In 1870, experiments on dogs were conducted by two German doctors who stimulated the cortex with electrodes. Later, the noted Montreal brain surgeon Dr. Wilder Penfield and his associates stimulated different parts of the cortex of patients who required brain surgery. They found that if a particular point in the cortex is electrically stimulated the little finger will twitch, if different neurons are stimulated the foot will move, and so on.

In these ways, the human cortex was "mapped," showing the areas responsible for motor activities of different parts of the body, sensations of touch, visual perception, and so on. Figure 12.1 shows some of these areas.

One result of such studies is the realization that lesions in certain areas of the brain produce language disorders (called **aphasia**), while lesions in other areas do not. Patients with aphasia do not seem to have any impairment of general intelligence; they can produce sounds and the motor coordination of the vocal organs remains intact, but they have difficulties with language. There are many different kinds of language impairments found in aphasia patients; some produce long strings of "jargon" which "sound like" language but which are uninterpretable by anyone listening to them; others speak perfectly well but can't under-

---

[1] Wallace Chafe, *Meaning and the Structure of Language* (Chicago: University of Chicago Press, 1970).

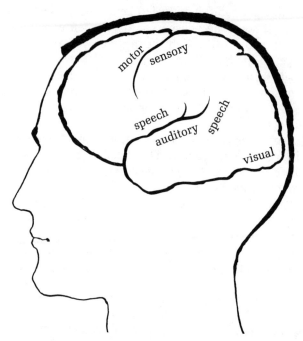

Figure 12.1 Specialized areas of the brain.

stand what is said to them; some find it difficult to "find the right word" or form "grammatical sentences"; some aphasiacs will substitute words in the same semantic class for the words they are asked to read (for example, they will read "liberty" for *democracy,* "chair" for *table*), while others substitute phonologically similar words ("pool" for *tool,* or "crucial" for *crucible*). All aphasics show some kind of language disorder.

Most of us have experienced some "aphasic symptoms," as did Alice when she said:

> "And now, who am I? I *will* remember, if I can. I'm determined to do it!" But being determined didn't help her much, and all she could say, after a great deal of puzzling, was "L, I *know* it begins with L."

This "tip-of-the-tongue" phenomenon is not uncommon. But if you *never* could find the word you wanted, you can imagine how serious a problem it would be. One aphasia patient appeared able to speak and understand perfectly well, but could not answer a direct question like "What is your wife's name?" After tremendous effort, he would grab a piece of paper and a pencil and write the answer to the question, but he could not speak the answer when a question was asked. This kind of problem is found in many aphasia patients.

The interest in aphasia goes far back in time. In the New Testament, St. Luke reports that Zacharias could not speak but could write. And in

30 A.D. the Roman writer Valerius Maximus describes an Athenian who was unable to remember his "letters" after being hit in the head with a stone.

But it was not until April 1861 that language disorders were specifically related to damage to the *left side of the brain*. At a scientific meeting in Paris, Dr. Paul Broca stated uniquivocally that we speak with the left hemisphere.[2]   Since Broca's time, the extensive research which has been conducted on language and the brain supports the view that for most normal right-handed people the left side of the brain is the language side.

This immediately sets man off from all other animals.   Generally the nervous system is symmetrical; what exists on the left exists on the right. This is equally true for man *except for the two sides of the brain*.   As a child develops, the two sides of the brain become specialized for different functions; **lateralization** (one-sidedness) takes place.   This has not been demonstrated in other animals.

There is much evidence to support the claim that language is a left-hemisphere function.[3]   As pointed out above, aphasia studies provide good evidence.   In the overwhelming number of cases, injuries to the left hemisphere result in aphasia but injuries to the right hemisphere do not. If both hemispheres were equally involved with language this could not be the case.

Other evidence is provided by patients who for various medical reasons have one of the hemispheres removed.   If the right hemisphere is cut out, language remains intact.   Because of the language impairments which would result from the removal of the left hemisphere, such surgery is performed only in dire cases.

"Split-brain" patients provide some of the most dramatic evidence. In recent years it was found that persons suffering from serious epilepsy could be treated by cutting this pathway, with little effect on their lives. We mentioned above that the two cerebral hemispheres are connected by a membrane called the corpus callosum.   This "freeway" between the two halves of the brain consists of tens of millions of nerve fibers connecting the cells of the left and right hemispheres.   If this pathway is split there is no "communication" between the "two brains."   The psychologist Michael Gazzaniga states:

> With [the corpus callosum] intact, the two halves of the body have no secrets from one another.   With it sectioned, the two halves become two different conscious mental spheres, each with its own experienced base and control system for behavioral operations. . . . Unbelievable as this

[2] In 1836, in a paper unknown to Broca, Dr. Mark Dax had made a similar claim, but little attention had been paid to it.

[3] For some people — about a third of all left-handers — there is still lateralization, but it is the right side which is specialized for language.   In other words, the special functions are switched but asymmetry still exists.

may seem, this is the flavor of a long series of experimental studies first carried out in the cat and monkey.[4]

When the brain is split surgically, certain information from the left side of the body is received *only* by the right side of the brain and vice versa (because of the "split-brain" phenomenon discussed above). For example, suppose a monkey is trained to respond with his hands to a certain visual stimulus (a flashing light, say). If the brain is split after the training period, and the stimulus is shown only to the left visual field (the right brain), the monkey will perform only with the left hand, and vice versa. Many such experiments have been done on animals. These all show the distinctness of the two sides of the brain, as well as the fact that each side of the animal's brain is capable of performing the same tasks.

Persons with split brains have been tested by psychologists. Unlike the results of experiments conducted with animals, tests with these subjects showed that messages sent to the two sides of the brain resulted in different responses. Monkeys and cats respond to the same stimuli whether they are received by the right or left hemispheres. But this is not so for man. (Many animals, however, like man, appear to be "right-handed," so the symmetry is not perfect.) If an apple is put in the left hand of a split-brain human and his vision is cut off, he cannot describe the object. The right brain senses the apple, and is able to distinguish the apple from other objects, but the information cannot be relayed to the left brain for linguistic description. But if the same experiment is repeated and in addition a banana is placed in the right hand, the subject is able to describe the banana verbally, though he is still unable to describe the apple (see Figure 12.2).

Various tests of this sort have been performed, all providing information as to the different capabilities of the "two brains." The right brain does much better than the left in "pattern-matching" tasks, or in recognizing faces, or in other kinds of spacial-perceptual tasks. The left hemisphere is superior for language, for rhythmic perception, for temporal-order judgments, for mathematical thinking. According to Gazzaniga, ". . . the right hemisphere as well as the left hemisphere can emote and while the left can tell you why, the right cannot."[5]

The evidence is overwhelming; man's brain is asymmetrical. The left brain is the language brain. But since all these cases involve "non-normal" humans (in one way or the other), other experimental techniques to explore the specialized capabilities of the two hemispheres were developed which could be used with all human subjects. One such method, called **dichotic listening,** uses auditory signals. Subjects hear two different sound signals simultaneously through earphones. For example, a subject may hear "boy" in one ear and "girl" in the other, or

---

[4] Michael Gazzaniga, *The Bisected Brain* (New York: Appleton, Century-Crofts, 1970).
[5] Ibid.

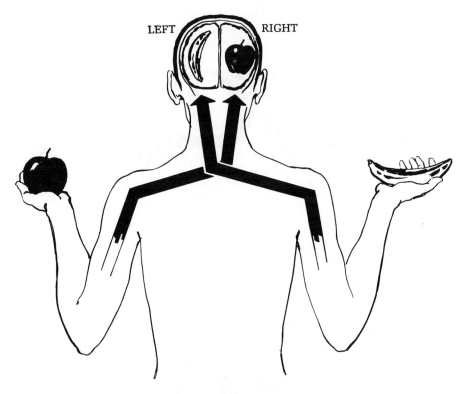

Figure 12.2

"crocodile" in one ear and "alligator" in the other. Or the subject may hear a horn tooting in one ear and a toilet flushing in the other. When asked to state what he heard in each ear, the responses to the right-ear (left-brain) stimuli are more correct when the stimuli are linguistic in nature (words, nonsense syllables, and so on), but the left ear (right brain) does better with certain nonverbal sounds (musical chords, environmental sounds, and so on). That is, if the subject hears "boy" in the right ear and "girl" in the left ear, he is more likely to report the sound heard in the right ear correctly. But if he hears coughing in the right ear and laughing in the left, he is more apt to report the laughing stimulus correctly.

Notice that if the left hemisphere is "processing" the incoming verbal stimuli, any sounds going to the right hemisphere have to cross over the pathway (the corpus callosum) to get to the left side of the brain. These messages have longer to travel and so are weakened. If the right hemisphere was equally capable of processing (as well as receiving) the signal from the left ear no differences between ears would show up.

Figure 12.3 illustrates what is going on in a highly oversimplified fashion. (The situation is actually much more complex. The signals entering

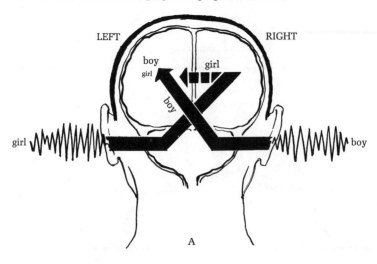

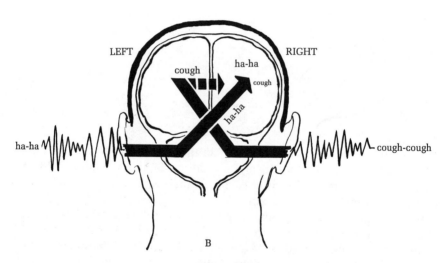

Figure 12.3

the right and left ears do have a path which goes to the right and left brains, respectively, but these are suppressed when there is another sound coming in from the crossed pathway.)   In drawing A of Figure 12.3, "boy" coming in through the *right* ear goes directly to the *left* hemisphere, where it can be processed, since this is the language-processing side of the brain; "girl" coming in through the *left* ear goes directly to the *right* hemisphere and then has to cross over to the left in order to be "understood." By the time it gets to the "language processor" it has been weakened, and so the subject makes more errors in reporting what he hears through this ear. In drawing B the reverse is true for non-linguistic sounds—the laughing coming in through the *left* ear is heard more strongly.

The superior performance of the right ear for linguistic stimuli in such dichotic-listening tasks further reflects the left-hemispheric specialization for language.

These experiments were very important in that they showed that the left hemisphere is not superior for processing *all* sounds, but only for those which are linguistic in nature. That is, the left side of the brain is specialized for *language,* not sounds.

This asymmetry of the human brain is one of man's unique characteristics. It has been argued that this "division of labor" explains man's intellectual and language abilities. In all other animals each side of the brain is equally responsible for all "mental" activities. But in man each side has developed its own "talents" and this specialization may permit increased mental powers, one of which, perhaps the most important, is the ability to learn language.

The brain mechanisms underlying human linguistic ability are just beginning to be understood. The asymmetry of the human brain may be a precondition for language development.

The lateralization of the brain is certainly connected with the language-learning abilities of children. It has long been noted that it is much more difficult to learn a language after a certain age. This "critical age" for first language acquisition seems to coincide with the period when lateralization is complete.[6] At birth the two sides of the brain do not seem to be specialized, although there is some evidence that even anatomically there are differences between the two hemispheres in humans (not found in other animals). Lateralization proceeds and is more or less complete by the age of five.[7] If you have ever listened to a five-year-old child, you know that the basic grammar of the language is also learned by this age. Language learning and lateralization seem to go hand in hand, but the relationship between the two is not clearly understood.

We are not certain whether language "input" conditions lateralization or whether lateralization precedes language acquisition. Nor are we sure of the extent to which man's linguistic ability is distinct from other cognitive or intellectual abilities. Since children are capable of learning language (the most complex of all phenomena) before they are able to learn simpler logical operations, our language-learning ability may be "preprogrammed" in special ways. These are fascinating questions which may be answered in time.

---

[6] Eric H. Lenneberg, *Biological Foundations of Language* (New York: Wiley, 1967).
[7] Stephen Krashen and Richard Harshman, "Lateralization and the Critical Period," *Journal of the Acoustical Society of America,* 52 (1972), 174.

THE ACQUISITION OF LANGUAGE

> *From this golden egg a man, Prajapati, was born. . . .*
> *A year having passed, he wanted to speak. He said* bhur
> *and the earth was created. He said* bhuvar *and the space*
> *of the air was created. He said* suvar *and the sky was*
> *created. That is why a child wants to speak after a year.*
> *. . . When Prajapati spoke for the first time, he uttered one*
> *or two syllables. That is why a child utters one or two*
> *syllables when he speaks for the first time.*
>
> — Hindu myth

From what we know about the brain we can assume that a child is
uniquely equipped with the necessary neural prerequisites for language
learning and language use. But how does he actually learn a language?

Our knowledge of the nature of human language tells us something
about what he does and does not do when learning a language. The
earlier chapters provide us with some of this information:

1. A child does not learn a language by storing all the words and all the
   sentences in some giant dictionary. The list of words is finite, but no
   dictionary can hold all the sentences, which are infinite in number.
2. A child learns to construct sentences, most of which he has never
   produced before.
3. A child learns to understand sentences he has never heard before.
   He cannot do this by matching the "heard utterance" with some stored
   sentence.
4. A child must therefore learn "rules" which permit him to use language
   creatively.
5. No one teaches him these rules. His parents are no more aware of
   the phonological, syntactic, and semantic rules than is the child. The
   child then seems to act like a very efficient linguist equipped with a
   perfect theory of language, who uses this theory to construct the grammar of the language he hears.

If you can remember your early years, you will not remember anyone
telling you to form a sentence by adding a verb phrase to a noun phrase,
or the class of sounds which are followed by an [s] to form plurals. In
St. Augustine's *Confessions,* written around 400 A.D., he writes of how he
learned to speak:

> . . . for I was no longer a speechless infant; but a speaking boy. This I
> remember; and have since observed how I learned to speak. It was not
> that my elders taught me words . . . in any set method; but I . . . did myself
> . . . practice the sounds in my memory . . . And thus by constantly hearing

DENNIS THE MENACE   **BY HANK KETCHAM**

"JOEY'S BABY SISTER SAID HER FIRST WORD TODAY,
BUT NOBODY KNOWS WHAT IT MEANS."

Courtesy Publishers-Hall Syndicate

words, as they occurred in various sentences . . . I thereby gave utterance to my will.

The child does not wake up one morning with a fully formed grammar
in his head. The language is acquired by stages, each one more closely
approximating the grammar of the adult language. Observations of children in different language areas of the world reveal that the stages are
very similar, probably universal.

When the infant first starts to babble, the sounds he produces have no
linguistic significance. He seems to be getting his vocal organs under
control, possibly learning to produce any sound which can be found in
a human language. He will have to learn which of these sounds are part
of his language and which are not; which to keep and which to suppress.

During this "babbling" stage the pitch contours of infant's utterances begin to resemble the intonation contours of sentences spoken by adults. He seems attuned to the pitch variations he hears.

Sometime after one year (it varies from child to child and has nothing to do with how intelligent the child is) the child begins to use the same string of sounds repeatedly to "mean" the same thing. At this point he has learned that sounds are related to meanings and is producing his first "words." Most children seem to go through the "one word = one sentence" stage. These one-word sentences are called **holophrastic** sentences (from *holo* "complete" or "undivided" plus *phrase* "phrase" or "sentence").

When the child puts two words together to form one sentence we can begin to talk of the child's grammar. Even at this stage the two words show definite syntactic and semantic relations. There are patterns which are evident, as the following "sentences" illustrate:[8]

allgone sock
hi Mommy
byebye boat
allgone sticky
more wet
beepbeep bang
it ball
Katherine sock
dirty sock
here pretty

There doesn't seem to be any "three-word" sentence stage. When a child starts stringing more than two words together the utterances may be two, three, four, or five words or longer. But these first complex sentences have a special characteristic. Usually the small "function" words such as *to, the, can, is,* and so on, are missing; only the words which carry the main message—the "content" words—occur. The child often sounds as if he were reading a Western Union message, which is why such utterances are called **telegraphic speech:**

Cat stand up table
What that?
He play little tune
Andrew want that
Cathy build house
No sit there

Eventually the child's utterances sound like those spoken by adults. The child has mastered the language.

Various theories have been proposed to explain how children manage

---

[8] All the examples given in this chapter are taken from actually observed utterances produced by children as reported in the literature. The various sources are listed under the subhead "Child Language" in the Reference section at the end of the chapter.

to acquire the adult language. There are those who think that children merely imitate what they hear. Imitation is involved to some extent, of course, but the sentences given above show that a child is *not* imitating adult speech. From whom would a child hear *Cat stand up table* or any of the sentences he produces like these?

> a my pencil
> other one pants
> two foot
> Mommy get it my ladder
> what the boy hit?
> cowboy did fighting me.

Even when a child is deliberately trying to imitate what he hears, he is unable to produce sentences which cannot be generated by *his* grammar.

> *Adult:* He's going out   *Child:* He go out
> *Adult:* That's an old-time train   *Child:* Old-time train
> *Adult:* Adam, say what I say: *Child:* Where I can put them?
> Where can I put them?

Neither can the "imitation" theory account for another important phenomenon. There are children who are unable to speak for neurological or physiological reasons. Yet these children learn the language spoken to them and understand what is said. When they over-come their speech impairment they immediately become able to use the language for speaking.

Another equally untenable theory of language acquisition suggests that a child learns to produce "correct" sentences because he is positively reinforced when he says something right and negatively reinforced when he says something wrong. This view assumes that the child is being constantly corrected for using "bad grammar" and patted on the head when he uses "good grammar." Even if this happened (and it seldom does), how does the child learn from such adult responses what it is he is doing right or wrong? This view does not tell us how the child constructs the correct rules. Whatever "correction" takes place is based more on the content of the message than on its *form.* That is, if a child says "Nobody don't like me," the mother may say "Everybody likes you."

Besides, all attempts to "correct" a child's language are doomed to failure. The child doesn't know what he is doing wrong and is even unable to make the corrections when they are pointed out to him, as is shown in the following examples:

> 1. *Child:*   Nobody don't like me.
>   *Mother:* No, say "Nobody likes me."
>   *Child:*   Nobody don't like me.
>   (*dialogue repeated eight times*)
>   *Mother:* Now, listen carefully, say "*Nobody likes me.*"
>   *Child:*   Oh, nobody don't likes me.

  2. *Child:*   Want other one spoon, Daddy.
    Father: You mean, you want "*the other spoon.*"
    Child: Yes, I want other one spoon, please, Daddy.
    Father: Can you say "the other spoon"?
    Child: Other . . . one . . . spoon.
    Father: Say . . . "other."
    Child: Other.
    Father: Spoon.
    Child: Spoon.
    Father: Other . . . spoon.
    Child: Other . . . spoon.   Now give me other one spoon?

Such conversations between parents and children do not take place very often. Mothers and fathers (unless they are linguists) are too busy to correct their children's speech. Besides, they are usually delighted that their young children are talking at all and consider every utterance to be a gem. The "mistakes" children make are "cute" and repeated endlessly to anyone who will listen.

The "reinforcement" theory fails along with the "imitation" theory. Neither of these views accounts for the fact that the child is constructing his own rules. Different rules govern the construction of sentences as the grammar is learned. Consider, for example, the increasing complexity of children's negative sentences. At first the child simply adds a *no* (or some negative morpheme) at the beginning or at the end of a sentence:

> no heavy
> no singing song
> no want stand head
> no Fraser drink all tea
> no the sun shining.

He doesn't hear such sentences. This seems to be the simplest way to *transform* a declarative into a negative. At some point he begins to insert a *not* or *can't* or *don't* inside the sentence.

> He no bite you
> I no taste them
> That no fish school
> I can't catch you.

The child progresses from simple rules to more complex rules; as is shown below:

Declarative: I want some food.

Negative (i): No want some food.   (*no* added to beginning of sentence)

Negative (ii): I $\begin{Bmatrix} \text{no} \\ \text{don't} \end{Bmatrix}$ want some food.   (negative element inserted; no other change)

Negative (iii): I don't want no food.   (negative element inserted; negation 'spread'; i.e. *some* becomes *no*)

Negative (iv): I don't want any food. (negative element correctly inserted, *some* changed to *any*)

The same increasing complexity is found in the learning of question constructions. At first, the child forms a question by using a "question intonation" (a rise of pitch at the end of the sentence):

> Fraser water?
> I ride train?
> Sit chair?

At the next stage the child merely "tacks on" a question word in front of the sentence; he doesn't change the word order, or insert *do:*

> What he wants?
> What he can ride in?[9]
> Where I should put it?
> Where Ann pencil?
> Why you smiling?

Such sentences are perfectly regular. They are not "mistakes" in the child's language; they reflect his grammar at a certain stage of development.

The child seems to form the simplest and most general rule he can from the language input he receives, and is so "pleased" with his "theory" that he uses the rule wherever he can. The most obvious example of this "overgeneralization" is shown when children treat irregular verbs and nouns as if they were regular. We have probably all heard children say *bringed, goed, doed, singed,* or *foots, mouses, sheeps, childs.*

These mistakes tell us more about how children learn language than the "correct" forms they use. The child couldn't be imitating; children use such forms in families where the parents would never utter such "bad English." In fact, the child may say *brought* instead of *bringed,* or *broke* instead of *breaked,* before he begins to use these incorrect forms. At the earlier stage he never uses any regular past-tense forms like *kissed, walked,* or *helped.* Thus he probably doesn't know that *brought* is a "past" at all. When he begins to say *played* and *hugged* and *helped* as well as *play, hug,* and *help* he has "figured out" how to form a past tense — *he has constructed the rule.* At that point he forms _all past tenses by this rule — he overgeneralizes_ — and he no longer says *brought* but *bring* and *bringed.* Notice that the "correct forms" were already learned (reinforced?), but the acquisition of the rule is more important than any previous or "practice" reinforcement. At some time later the child will learn that there are "exceptions" to the rule. Only then will he once more say *brought.* The child seems to look for general patterns, for systematic occurrences.

[9] These first two sentences may, of course, represent a "movement transformation," e.g., *He wants what? ⇒ What he wants?*

Such overgeneralizations have also been observed in a child's acquisition of the semantic system.   He may learn a word such as *papa* or *daddy* which he first uses only for his own father.   This word may then be extended to apply to all men.   As he acquires new words, the "overgeneralized" meaning becomes narrowed down until once more it has a single referent.   The linguist Eve Clark has found this to be true of many other words and semantic features.   She has observed that children make overgeneralizations which are based on shape, size, sound, taste, and texture.   One child's word for "moon" /mooi/ became the name for cakes, round marks on windows, writing on a window, round shapes in books, tooling on leather book covers, round postmarks, and the letter *O*.   Similarly, the word for "watch," *tick tock,* was used for all objects shaped like a watch: clocks, gas meters, a fire hose wound on a spool, a bath scale.   The word for *fly* /flai/ was used for other small-sized objects like specks of dirt, dust, all small insects, his own toes, crumbs; and /dani/ was first used for the sound of a bell, and then for a clock, a telephone, a door bell.   As more words are added, and semantic features become more specified, the meaning of these words becomes narrowed.   But again the child's ability to find general systematic patterns is observed.

The child's ability to generalize patterns and construct rules is also shown in phonological development.   In early language the child may not distinguish between voiced and voiceless consonants, for example.   But when he first begins to contrast one set—that is, when he learns that /p/ and /b/ are distinct phonemes—he also begins to distinguish between /t/ and /d/, /s/ and /z/, and so on.

Such regular stages and patterns support the notion that language acquisition is grammar construction.   The Russian linguist Kornei Chukovsky writes: "It seems to me that, beginning with the age of two, every child becomes for a short period of time a linguistic genius.   Later, beginning with the age of five or six, this talent begins to fade."[10]

The child has to construct all the phonological, syntactic, and semantic rules of the grammar.   This is a difficult task indeed, especially since all he ever hears are the "surface structures" of sentences.   The learning of negative and question rules shows he is forming transformational rules, and at some stage he, like the adult, will know that *It is too hot to eat* has three meanings.

The child seems to be equipped with special abilities, residing principally in the left side of the brain, to know just what generalizations to look for, to know what he can ignore, to find all the regularities in the language.   Chomsky explains this in the following way:

> It seems plain that language acquisition is based on the child's discovery
> of what from a formal point of view is a deep and abstract theory—a

---

[10] Kornei Chukovsky, *From Two to Five,* trans. and ed. by M. Morton (Berkeley: University of Calif. Press, 1968).

generative grammar of his language . . . A consideration of the character of the grammar that is acquired, the degenerate quality and narrowly limited extent of the available data, the striking uniformity of the resulting grammars, and their independence of intelligence, motivation, and emotional state, over wide ranges of variation, leave little hope that much of the structure of the language can be learned by an organism initially uninformed as to its general character . . . it may well be that the general features of language structure reflect, not so much the course of one's experience, but rather the general character of one's capacity to acquire knowledge. . . .[11]

The details of the "innate" language-acquisition device are far from understood. As we gain more information about brain functions and the preconditions for language acquisition, we will learn more about the nature of human language.

SUMMARY

Since man *people* is the only animal which learns language, there is considerable interest in the brain mechanisms which underlie linguistic competence and performance. This has given rise to a special area of study called **neurolinguistics,** which is concerned with the representation of language in the brain and the processing of speech.

The brain is the most complicated organ of the body, controlling motor activities and thought processes. Different parts of the brain control different body functions. The brain in all higher animals is divided into two hemispheres, but only in man is each side functionally distinct. Evidence from **aphasia,** surgical removal of parts of the brain, and **split-brain** patients shows that the "left brain" is the language hemisphere. **Dichotic listening** experiments on normal subjects confirm these findings. Thus, in the human animal, each brain is specialized for different tasks. This **lateralization** of functions develops from birth and is usually complete by five years of age. Developing lateralization coincides with the first language-learning years. It appears, then, that hemispheric specialization may be a precondition for human language.

While neurolinguistics is concerned with underlying anatomical and physiological prerequisites for language, **psycholinguistics** is the study of language in use — linguistic behavior. A major concern in this field is child language acquisition and development.

When a child learns a language he learns the grammar of that language — the phonological, syntactic, and semantic rules. No one teaches him these rules; the child just "picks them up," and in so efficient a manner as to suggest that his brain is preprogrammed for language learning.

[11] Noam Chomsky, *Aspects of a Theory of Syntax* (Cambridge: M.I.T. Press, 1965).

A child does not learn the language "all at once." Children's first utterances are one-word "sentences" (**holophrastic** speech). After a few months, two-word sentences appear which are not random combinations of words; the words have definite patterns and express grammatical and semantic relationships. Still later, more complex sentences are used. At first the child's grammar lacks many of the rules of the adult grammar, but eventually the child's grammar mirrors the language used in the community.

A number of theories have been suggested to explain the acquisition process. Neither the **imitation theory**, which claims that a child learns his language by imitating adult speech, nor the **reinforcement theory**, which hypothesizes that a child is conditioned into speaking correctly by being negatively reinforced for "errors" and positively reinforced for "correct" usage, is supported by observational and experimental studies. Neither can explain how the child forms the *rules* which he then uses to produce new sentences.

The child acquires the rules of the grammar in stages of increasing complexity. He seems to have a propensity for making broad, simple linguistic generalizations and "overgeneralizations." As he is exposed to more data, he narrows down and revises his "rules" until they match those of the adult grammar.

All normal children everywhere learn the language of their society. Genetically the "left brain" is "set" for acquiring this highly complex system.

EXERCISES

1. It has been shown that the "left hemisphere" is specialized (or lateralized) for the following: mathematical problem solving, judgments on the temporal order of events, analysis of a complex pattern into its component parts, determination of the sequencing of events, and, of course, language processing. Discuss what common factors "unite" these different tasks.

2. a. Some aphasic patients, when asked to read a list of words, substitute other words for those printed. In many cases there are similarities between the printed words and the substituted words that are read. The data given below are from actual aphasic patients. In each case state what the two words have in common and how they differ:

PRINTED WORD	WORD SPOKEN BY APHASIC
1. a. liberty	freedom
b. canary	parrot
c. abroad	overseas

d.	large	long
e.	short	small
f.	tall	long

2.
a.	decide	decision
b.	conceal	concealment
c.	portray	portrait
d.	bathe	bath
e.	speak	discussion
f.	remember	memory

   b. What do the words in groups 1 and 2 reveal about how words are likely to be stored in the brain?

3. The following are some sentences spoken by aphasic patients collected and analyzed by Dr. Harry Whitaker of the University of Rochester. In each case state how the sentence deviates from normal nonaphasic language.

    1. There is under a horse a new sidesaddle.
    2. In girls we see many happy days.
    3. I'll challenge a new bike.
    4. I surprise no new glamour.
    5. Is there three chairs in this room?
    6. Mike and Peter is happy.
    7. Bill and John likes hot dogs.
    8. Proliferate is a complete time about a word that is correct.
    9. Went came in better than it did before.

4. In this chapter the way a child learns "negation" of sentences and "question formation" was discussed. Can these be considered examples of a process of overgeneralization in syntax acquisition? If so, for each stage indicate *what* is being overgeneralized.

5. Suppose a friend of yours has a son, Tommy, who is three years old. Your friend has been explaining to you that Tommy has a problem in his speech in that he does not form "past tenses" of verbs. That is, Tommy says "Yesterday I go to park" and "Last week I swim in pool." But your friend has a plan: He is going to spend one hour each day with Tommy having the child imitate the past-tense forms of the verbs and he will give Tommy a piece of candy for each correct imitation. Explain to your friend (and to us) why his plan won't work.

6. *Baby talk* is a term used to label the word-forms which many adults use when speaking to children. Examples in English are words like *choo-choo* for "train" and *bow-wow* for "dog." Baby talk seems to exist in every language and culture. At least two things seem to be universal about baby talk: The words which have baby-talk forms fall into certain semantic categories, for example food; and the

words are "phonetically simpler" than the adult forms, for example *tummy* for "stomach." List all the baby-talk words you can think of in your native language, then (1) separate them into semantic categories, and (2) try to state general rules for the kinds of phonological "reductions" or "simplifications" that occur.

7. Find a two-year-old child and play with her/him for about thirty minutes. Keep a list of all words which are used inappropriately. Can you describe what the child's meanings for these words probably are?

References

Lateralization of Brain Functions

GAZZANIGA, MICHAEL S. *The Bisected Brain.* New York: Appleton-Century-Crofts, 1970.

KIMURA, DORREN. "The Asymmetry of the Human Brain." *Scientific American,* Vol. 228, No. 3, pp. 70–80 (1973).

LENNEBERG, ERIC H. *Biological Foundations of Language.* New York: Wiley, 1967.

PENFIELD, W., and ROBERTS L. *Speech and Brain-Mechanisms.* Princeton: Princeton University Press, 1959.

Child Language

BELLUGI-KLIMA, U. "Linguistic Mechanisms Underlying Child Speech," in E. M. Zale, ed., *Proceedings of the Conference on Language and Language Behavior.* New York: Appleton-Century-Crofts, 1968.

BLOOM, L. M. *Language Development.* Cambridge: M.I.T. Press, 1972.

BROWN, R., CAZDEN, C. B., and BELLUGI, U. "The Child's Grammar from I to III," in R. Brown, *Psycholinguistics.* New York: Free Press, 1970.

CLARK, E. "What's in a Word? On the Child's Acquisition of Semantics in His First Language," in T. E. Moore, ed., *Cognitive Development and the Acquisition of Language.* New York: Academic Press, 1973.

DALE, P. S. *Language Development: Structure and Function.* Hinsdale, Ill.: Dryden, 1972.

ERVIN, S. M. "Imitation and Structural Change in Children's Language," in E. H. Lenneberg, ed., *New Directions in the Study of Language.* Cambridge: M.I.T. Press, 1964.

MCNEILL, D. *The Acquisition of Language: The Study of Developmental Psycholinguistics.* New York: Harper & Row, 1970.

MENYUK, P. *Sentences Children Use.* Cambridge: M.I.T. Press, 1969.

SLOBIN, DAN I. *Psycholinguistics.* Glenview, Ill.: Scott, Foresman, and Co. 1971.

13
Language in the Computer Age

There once was a man who said, "Damn!"
It is borne in upon me I am
An engine that moves
In predestinate grooves,
I'm not even a bus, I'm a tram.

— MAURICE EVAN HARE

Men have become the tools of their tools.

— HENRY DAVID THOREAU

The computer is, by now, a commonplace of daily life. It is used routinely to perform such functions as the keeping of inventories, the preparation of financial accounts, the control of complex machinery in factories and refineries, the recording of ticket reservations at many events, the assigning of students to college classes, and the guidance of vehicles for space explorations.

These activities (and others) have in common the need to examine quickly large amounts of data and, based on this examination, to select one of many possible courses of action. The speed of operation is intrinsic to the machine; a computer can examine a number (even a very large number) in less than a millionth of a second. However, the machine must be instructed as to the kinds of tasks we wish it to carry out. As a result, it has been necessary to develop techniques for supplying these instructions. This has led to the development of "programming languages" with names such as Fortran, Cobol, Algol, Lisp, Focal, and Basic. These languages use words and sentences drawn from languages such as English, but they are sharply limited in their meanings and have to be "translated" by the computer into a set of instructions suitable for a machine.

The development of these languages has spurred new inquiries into the nature of language and of communication. How much easier it would be if we could just talk to a computer in natural language and have the machine carry out our instructions and even answer us in ordinary language.

In addition, the speed of the computer and the huge storage memory makes it a useful device for "processing" all kinds of language data. As a result, there has arisen a branch of linguistics called **computational linguistics.**

Computational linguistics is a term which has covered such areas as automatic syntactic analysis, sentence generation, grammar testing, concordance construction, automatic abstracting, information retrieval, stylistic studies, content processing, semantic classification studies, and other forms of text analysis. Linguists who are concerned with linguistic performance—the actual use of language by a speaker or listener—also use the computer in investigations of speech production and recognition. Some of these computer applications to linguistic problems will be examined in this chapter.

AUTOMATIC MACHINE TRANSLATION

Bless thee! Thou art translated.

—SHAKESPEARE, *A Midsummer Night's Dream*

When computers became available to assist scientific research, soon after World War II, several scientists suggested that the computer should be used to translate one language into another. The rising intensity of the "Cold War" at that time led many people to believe that the rapid translation of Russian books and journals into English would be useful to the country. The government responded with aid in the form of research grants, and serious investigation into the problems of automatic machine translation was begun.

At first there was much optimism. During World War II, American scientists, without the assistance of a computer, deciphered coded Japanese military communications and proved their skill in coping with difficult language problems. The idea of using deciphering techniques to translate from one language into another was expressed in a letter written to Norbert Wiener by Warren Weaver, a pioneer in the field of computational linguistics: "When I look at any article in Russian, I say: 'This is really written in English, but it has been coded in some strange symbols. I will now proceed to decode.' "[1]

When a human translator "decodes" a text in a **source language,** he is likely first to read long passages to get an idea of the overall context.

---

[1] W. N. Locke and A. D. Boothe, ed., *Machine Translation of Languages* (New York: Wiley, 1955).

He then chooses shorter passages, comprehends the specific meaning of each, and puts each shorter passage into sentences of the **target language,** preserving the meaning as best he can. The human relies on his knowledge of the context of the passage, his general intelligence, and his linguistic abilities in translating from source language into target language.

A human translator substitutes for one string of symbols (morphemes or words in the source language) another corresponding string (morphemes and words in the target language), possibly with some rearrangement of their order, with deletions of some symbols which occur in the source language, and/or with the addition of symbols in the target language. Suppose the source language is French and the target language is English; the process would work as follows:

SOURCE LANGUAGE	TARGET LANGUAGE
Je vous aime	→ I love you
I you love	

The idea behind automatic computer translation is for the computer to play the role of the human translator. The aim was to "feed" into the computer sentences in the source language (the input) and to receive the sentences in the target language (the output). The computer seemed ideally suited to this task. Unfortunately, what often happened was a process called by early machine translators "Language in, garbage out."

The problems arose from the fact that computers are *not* "thinking machines." They are inherently weak devices, capable of only the simplest operations. Before a computer can perform any task, the computer programmer must define each step of that task and must then write a program which consists of an instruction for each of these elementary steps. It is the ingenuity of the programmer, combined with the huge "memory" and great speed of the computer, that makes the computer a valuable and productive machine.

In the early days of machine translation it was believed that a computer program could be written to put in its memory the tens of thousands of morphemes of a source language, along with a dictionary of the corresponding morphemes in the target language, and that programs could be written with little difficulty which would permit the computer to "match" the morphemes, do the necessary reordering, deletion, and addition, and do this rapidly.

The earlier chapters of this book, which discussed the great complexity of natural language, have revealed why this approach to translation was very naïve. Just the "simple" substitution of one morpheme for another led to grave difficulties. Imagine a Russian computer trying to translate an English text in which the word *light* occurs. This word, in isolation, can mean many things and can function syntactically in many ways. Each possible use of *light* would correspond to a different Russian word.

Light may function as a noun, adjective, verb infinitive, verb imperative, verb in first person plural indicative, and so on. Even if the syntactic function of the word is determined, there is still the semantic problem. A *light* color would call for one Russian word; a *light* weight for another; a *light* job for a third; and a *light* meal for a fourth. A human translator reads these sentences:

    a. The light flooded the room.
    b. A light car is economical.
    c. Arsonists light fires for fun.

He knows immediately, because he knows the rules of grammar, the syntactic class of the word *light* in each sentence. But this knowledge has to be made very explicit in the computer program and might include "instructions" of the following sort:

1. If *light* is preceded by a determiner (*a, some, the,* and so on), and if it is *not* followed by a noun, it is a noun. (See sentence a.)
2. If *light* is preceded by a determiner and followed by a noun (or an adjective — for example, *The light blond hair*), it is an adjective. (See sentence b.)
3. If *light* is preceded by a noun, and followed by a noun phrase, it is a verb. (See sentence c.)

Instructing a computer to sort out semantic ambiguity is even more difficult. The Russian programmer would have to program his computer to do at least the following:

4. If *light* is an adjective and if it modifies a noun that has color, it means "not dark."
5. If *light* is an adjective and modifies a noun that has weight, it means "not heavy."

When these problems are compounded by thousands of similarly ambiguous words, the enormous difficulty of automatic machine translation becomes apparent.

The problem of reordering morphemes may be quite complex. In English we say *The boy kissed the girl,* but in Japanese they say *The boy the girl kissed,* and in Hebrew *Kissed the boy the girl.* The computer-translator must be programmed to recognize when reordering of elements is necessary.

The computer must also "know" when to delete a morpheme. If English is the source language and French the target language, the sentence *John wants to leave* must be translated as *Jean désire partir,* with the *to* "deleted."

The problem of adding morphemes is no easier. Suppose Thai is the "input" language and English the "output" language, and the following sentence from Thai is to be translated into English:

kɔ: lû:gcha:j   lúg   khŷn ma: chûaj mɔ:ng hǎ:
then   boy   stand up arise come help look see
Then *the* boy got up *and* came *to* help look *for* it.

The word-for-word translation is not grammatical English.

The problems of computer translation become apparent when we realize how difficult it is to get good translations even when humans do them. Some of the English signs appearing in non-English-speaking countries as "aids" to tourists show that translation can never be a simple word-by-word operation. A newspaperman, reports the following signs:

> Hen fried with butter (restaurant in France)
> Utmost of chicken with smashed pot (Greece)
> Nervous meatballs (Bulgaria)
> The nuns harbor all diseases and have no respect for religion (Swiss nunnery hospital)
> All the water has been passed by the manager (German hotel)
> Certified midwife: entrance sideways (Jerusalem)[2]

Such "translations" represent the difficulties of just finding the equivalent "words." But this is actually a minor problem in automatic translation. The syntactic problems are the "hairiest" (and how would a machine translate that?).

Early research scientists underestimated the role of syntactic analysis in automatic machine translation. Two pioneers in the field, R. H. Richens and A. D. Boothe, wrote a paper in which they presented examples of word-for-word translations that a computer was programmed to produce.[3] In their prefacing remarks the authors state that they are attempting "to illustrate the relative *unimportance* of syntax . . ." Here is an example of a computer translation from Finnish given by them:

> *Finnish:*   muut neljä ulkomaista kantaa ovat osoittautuneet viljely-sarvoltaan kovin epävarmoiksi
>
> *English (?):* other (*plural*) four foreign country [out of] standpoint (*partitive*) bear (*partitive*) are show oneself (*past plural*) cultivation value (*genitive accusative*) very insecure [become]

As the Irish playright R. B. Sheridan once said: "Egad, I think the interpreter is the hardest to be understood of the two!" To interpret the computer-interpreter of the Finnish example, we have:

> The other four standard varieties from abroad have proved very unreliable as regards cultivation value.

[2] Tom Lambert, Los Angeles *Times,* Feb. 7, 1973.
[3] R. H. Richens and A. D. Boothe in W. N. Locke and A. D. Boothe, eds., *Machine Translation of Languages* (New York: Wiley, 1955).

This example actually illustrates the relative *importance* rather than un-importance of syntax.

High-quality, efficient automatic machine translation is a goal that has never been achieved. Nonetheless, computers are being used to some small extent today to do preliminary translations of foreign texts into English. The computer gives rough outputs, similar to the translation of the Finnish passage in the previous paragraph. In addition, if there are ambiguities that the computer cannot resolve (for a word such as *light*), each possible translation is printed out. At that point a human who does not need to know the source language can take over and resolve the ambiguities and complete the translation into grammatical English. He does, of course, have to know the subject matter of what is being translated.

The more we learn about language, the better the "rough" machine translations will be, and the less work will have to be done by human assistants to get acceptable output. The last twenty years has seen many advances in our linguistic knowledge and some improvement in machine translations. The next twenty years may see even more.

DICTIONARY APPLICATIONS

Dictionaries are like watches; the worst is better than none, and the best cannot be expected to go quite true.

— SAMUEL JOHNSON (1786)

While the initial predictions for "high-quality fully automatic trans-lation" proved to be highly exaggerated, other applications of the computer for language data processing have been more successful, and have proved to be a great help for the linguist and the speech-com-munication researcher. The computer may, for example, act as an "assistant" to a human translator. In this role it generally functions as a bilingual dictionary, responding to requests for translations of words or idioms by searching its memory for the appropriate item and printing out all possible translations of it.

At present it is economically impractical to utilize a computer as a word and /or idiom dictionary, unless many translators use the computer simultaneously. A relatively complete dictionary might easily require one million entries (English would need 400,000 lexical entries with an average of two to three "derivatives" per entry). This leads to serious problems of information retrieval—that is, how to get the required information to the human translator in less time than he could have looked it up in the first place.   Any computer that is to function as a bilingual dictionary will need to be large and fast and, hence expensive.

Nevertheless, many computerized dictionaries have been compiled. At Georgetown University a Russian-English dictionary of 50,000 entries of terms used in chemistry, physics, biology, and social sciences has been put on computer tape.   A bilingual Russian-English dictionary has also been compiled by the IBM corporation with more than 150,000 entries.   A word list of English with over 350,000 entries has been put on computer tape by A. F. Brown of the University of Pennsylvania, and 240,000 items forming a Chinese-English dictionary have been put into a form which can be used by a computer by the McGraw-Hill Company.

These dictionaries can be constantly up-dated, and the advent of the multilith computer with hundreds of remote terminals may make the dictionary function of a computer feasible in the future.

TEXT PROCESSING

> [*The professor had written*] *all the words of their language in their several moods, tenses and declensions* [*on tiny blocks of wood, and had*] *emptied the whole vocabulary into his frame, and made the strictest computation of the general proportion there is in books between the numbers of particles, nouns, and verbs, and other parts of speech.*
>
> —JONATHAN SWIFT, *Gulliver's Travels*

Jonathan Swift hinted at a potentially practical way of putting the computer to work in linguistics, by applying its powers to the analysis of textual material.   A linguist interested in working on a language may record a large number of utterances, never before analyzed.   If a computer is available, the text can be put onto magnetic tape, read into the computer which has been appropriately programmed, and analyzed with respect to such properties as the distribution of sounds, allowable word orders, allowable combinations of morphemes, and so on.

Frequency studies (that is, the "general proportion" of different sounds, words, phrases, and so on), if of interest, are also easily and rapidly carried out on a computer.   In addition, the computer can be used to compare different properties of different languages either for historical-genetic classification of language families or for "typological" classification.

At the University of California at Berkeley and at the University of

Illinois, William S-Y Wang and Chin-Chuan Cheng have compiled a dialect dictionary called DOC which includes the phonetic pronunciations of over two thousand morphemes in twenty Chinese dialects. Using the computer to process this large collection of data, they are able to study aspects of linguistic sound change. They can quickly ascertain all the differences in the pronunciation of any single morpheme in the different dialects. In these ways, the computer has proved to be an important tool in linguistic investigations.

GRAMMAR TESTING

> *I have experimented and experimented until now I know that* [water] *never does run up-hill, except in the dark. I know it does in the dark, because the pool never goes dry; which it would, of course, if the water didn't come back in the night. It is best to prove things by experiment; then you* know; *whereas if you depend on guessing and supposing and conjecturing, you will never get educated.*
>
> — MARK TWAIN, *Eve's Diary*

A generative grammar of any language, constructed by a linguist, must be tested to see that it does generate the sentences in the language and does not generate anything that is not a sentence. If it does not generate all the sentences that a speaker can produce it is obviously not a good model of what he knows about the language. Similarly, if it produces sentences that a speaker considers to be "ungrammatical," it also fails. Since generative grammars are capable of producing an infinite set of sentences, a comprehensive testing procedure is a very complex task.

Computers seem ideally suited for the task of grammar testing. Since grammars consist of explicit formal rules which are to be applied automatically, such rules can be considered as the instructions to the computer. However, even a computer cannot produce an infinite number of sentences. To test whether a grammar is capable of producing all the sentences, the computer can be programmed to accept as input any sentence in the language (dreamed up by a linguist) and to determine if the stored grammar can generate this sentence. A single negative response indicates an inadequacy in the grammar.

To test whether a grammar generates *only* the sentences in the language and no "non-sentences," the computer is programmed to "generate" sentences and speakers examine these to determine whether the strings are indeed sentences in the language. Again, the generation of ungrammatical strings indicates errors and reveals that the grammar needs to be changed.

Programming a computer for these tasks is very difficult. In one case, a fairly comprehensive generative grammar of English written by a group of professors and students at UCLA[4] was tested in part by a computer program.

Our knowledge of a language includes more than merely determining what sentences are in the language. The grammar also accounts for our knowledge of sentence structures. Computers therefore are also programmed to generate structures of sentences, the trees discussed in Chapter 6.

SENTENCE PARSING

The syntactic analysis of sentences is necessary for both grammar testing and for the work that is entailed in what is now known as "speech understanding." We saw above that the possibility of automatic translation depends on correct syntactic analysis. To program a computer to "understand" an instruction in a natural language also requires such analysis.

Many **parsing** programs have been developed. Such a program analyzes a sentence into its syntactic parts which are hierarchical in nature. Computers have been programmed to take a one-dimensional string of words such as *John is easy to please* as input, and to produce a two-dimensional **structure** such as Figure 13.1 as output. Sentence parsing is a highly studied technique of computational linguistics, since linguists know that humans comprehend the sentences of their language by assigning structures such as that in Figure 13.1, and computers must also do so if they are to be useful in processing languages.

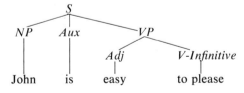

Figure 13.1

[4] Robert Stockwell, Paul Schachter, and Barbara Partee. *The Major Syntactic Structures of English.* New York: Holt, Rinehart and Winston, 1973. The computer program was developed by Joyce Friedman. See Joyce Friedman, *A Computer Model of Transformational Grammar.* New York: American Elsevier, 1971.

TRANSFORMATIONAL PARSING

We know from Chapter 6 that surface-structure grammatical relations do not provide enough information about all sentences to enable us to determine the meanings. A step toward the goal of programing a computer to "understand" sentences must then include programs which can reconstruct the deep-structure grammatical relations from surface structures. Such programs perform **transformational parsing**—"transformational" because deep structures and surface structures are related by the transformational rules of the grammar.

   In understanding the sentence *John is easy to please,* we know that it is "John" who is "pleased"; that is, *John* is the object of *please.* This grammatical relationship is concealed by the surface structure tree in Figure 13.1, where *John* is the surface subject of *is easy.* A computer program that performs transformational parsing would take Figure 13.1 as input, and give Figure 13.2 as output.

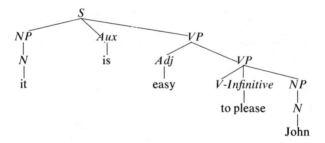

Figure 13.2

   The details of the parsing programs that have been developed are beyond the scope of this book. One would need a great deal of knowledge about computer programing to understand them. They depend on proper linguistic analysis as well as computer-programing experience, and in this task computer scientists and linguists work together.

TALKING MACHINES

Machines which, with more or less success, imitate human speech, are the most difficult to construct, so many are the agencies engaged in uttering even a single word—lungs, larynx, tongue, palate, teeth, lips—so many are the in-

flections and variations of tone and articulation, that the mechanician finds his ingenuity taxed to the utmost to imitate them.

— *Scientific American* (Jan. 14, 1871)

In 1950, the English mathematician Alan M. Turing published a paper entitled "Computing Machinery and Intelligence." Turing began his paper: "I propose to consider the question, 'Can machines think?'" To answer this question one must decide the criteria to be considered. Turing decided that a machine can think if it can pass itself off as a human being to a real human being, not counting physical characteristics such as appearance, voice, mobility, and so on. Turing assumed that his thinking machine would understand and produce language.

The difficulties in automatic speech recognition and production are as great as, if not greater than, those in automatic translation. Yet there are hundreds of scientists, including communication engineers, phoneticians, linguists, psychologists, and philosophers, who are now working in this research area.

The earliest efforts toward building "talking machines" were more concerned with machines that could produce sounds which sounded like human speech than with machines that could "think" of what to say. In 1779, Christian Gottlieb Kratzenstein won a prize for building such a machine ("an instrument constructed like the *vox humana* pipes of an organ which . . . accurately express the sounds of the vowels") and for answering a question posed by the Imperial Academy of St. Petersburg: "What is the nature and character of the sounds of the vowels *a, e, i, o, u* [which make them] different from one another?" Kratzenstein constructed a set of "acoustic resonators" similar to the shapes of the mouth when these vowels are articulated and set them resonating by a vibrating reed which produced puffs of air similar to those coming from the lungs through the vibrating vocal cords.

Twelve years later, Wolfgang von Kempelen of Vienna constructed a more elaborate machine with bellows to produce a stream of air, such as is produced by the lungs, and with other mechanical devices to "simulate" the different parts of the vocal tract. Von Kempelen's machine so impressed the young Alexander Graham Bell, who saw a replica of the machine in Edinburgh in 1850, that he, together with his brother Melville, attempted to construct a "talking head," making a cast from a human skull. They used various materials to form the velum, palate, teeth, lips, tongue, and so on, and constructed cheeks out of rubber and a metal larynx. The vocal cords were made by stretching a slotted piece of rubber over a structure. They used a keyboard control system to manipulate all the parts with an intricate set of levers. This ingenious machine produced vowel sounds and some nasal sounds and even a few short combinations of sounds.

With the advances in the acoustic theory of speech production and the technological developments in electronics, machine production of speech sounds has made great progress. We no longer have to build actual physical models of the speech-producing mechanism; we can now imitate the process by producing the physical signals by electronic means.

The research on speech has shown that all speech sounds can be reduced to a small number of acoustic components. One way to produce artificial or synthetic speech is to mix these important parts together in the proper proportions depending on the speech sounds one wishes to imitate. It is rather like following a recipe for making soup which might read: "Take two quarts of water, add one onion, three carrots, a potato, a teaspoon of salt, a pinch of pepper, and stir it all together."

This method of producing synthetic speech would include a recipe which might read: "Start with a buzzing noise corresponding to the puffs of air like those coming through the vibrating vocal cords, add different ingredients which correspond to the different vowel qualities (these being the 'overtones' resulting from the different vocal tract shapes), add the 'hissing' noise produced when fricatives occur, add nasal 'resonances' for any nasal sounds, cut off the 'buzz' to produce 'stops,' " and so on. This highly oversimplified "recipe" may be more confusing than enlightening. A more exact description would require technical knowledge of acoustic phonetics.

Although acoustic theory of speech production is very advanced, much of the speech which is synthesized still has a "machine quality." Some of it is highly intelligible despite this, and in a few cases it is hard to distinguish it from human speech. But it must be remembered that the machine only "talks" when we tell it *what* to say and *how* to say it and so is only imitating human speech on a phonetic level. This does, nevertheless, require a high level of knowledge about the important acoustic cues which listeners pay attention to in their "decoding" of spoken speech.

An important tool in acoustic research was provided by the invention of a machine called a **sound spectrograph.** When you speak into a microphone connected to this machine (or when a tape recording is plugged in), a "picture" is made of the speech signal. The patterns produced are called **spectrograms** or, more vividly, "visible speech." In the last few years these pictures have been referred to as *voiceprints*. A spectrogram of the words *heed, head, had,* and *who'd* is shown in Figure 13.3. Time in milliseconds moves horizontally from left to right; vertically, the "graph" represents pitch (or, more technically, frequency). Notice that for each vowel there are a number of very dark bands which differ in their placement according to their pitch. These represent the **overtones** produced by the shapes of the vocal tract and are called the **formants** of the vowels. Since the tongue is in a different position for each vowel, the formant frequencies or overtone pitches for each vowel differ.   It is the different frequencies of these formants which account for the different vowel qualities you hear.   The pitch of the entire utterance (intonation contour) is shown by the "voicing bar" marked *P* on the spectrogram. When the striations are far apart the vocal cords are vibrating slowly and the pitch is low; when the striations are close together the vocal cords are vibrating rapidly and the pitch is high.

By studying spectrograms of all speech sounds and many different utterances, acoustic phoneticians have learned a great deal about the basic components which are used to synthesize speech.

A new interest in these "voiceprints" has recently arisen.   Spectro-grams are being used in law courts as "evidence" to identify speakers. Spectrograms have been made from taped phone conversations, for example, and compared with spectrograms of the speech of individuals accused of making these phone calls.   The claim that voiceprints are as conclusive as fingerprints has been challenged.   A person cannot change his fingerprints, but a speaker may pronounce a word or a sentence very differently on two occasions and, in addition, his speech may be very similar to another speaker's.   Because of such factors the opinion on the reliability of voiceprint identification is far from unanimous.   In fact, a large section of the scientific community involved in speech re-search is concerned that popular opinion will accept voiceprints as infallible (influenced by Dick Tracy comic strips and various TV "who-done-it" programs). In March 1966, a meeting of the Speech Communi-cation Committee of the Acoustical Society of America unanimously passed the following resolution: "The Technical Committee on Speech Communication is concerned that 'voiceprints' have been admitted as

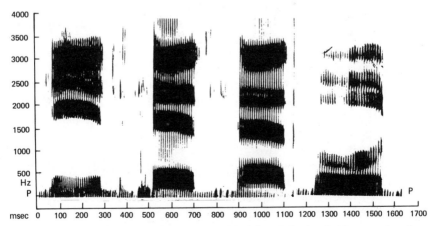

Figure 13.3 A spectrogram of the words *heed, head, had, who'd,* as spoken in a British accent (speaker: Peter Ladefoged, February 16, 1973).

legal evidence on the basis of claims which have not yet been evaluated scientifically."

There have been attempts to make more definite judgments on the reliability of voiceprint identification, but scientific opinion remains divided, with the majority opinion still skeptical. Further research, improvement of methods, and more careful training of the "analysts" may in time make spectrograms a valuable aid in legal cases. It is too early to be overly optimistic.

Spectrographic analysis, however, is an important aspect of speech research. Much of the work aimed at achieving automatic computer recognition of speech depends on our understanding of the acoustics of speech. To produce machines that can recognize speech is much more difficult than to produce machines that can synthesize speech. The problem was summed up by J. R. Pierce of Bell Telephone Laboratories:

> It is hard to gauge the success of an attempt at speech recognition even when statistics are given. In general, it appears that recognition around 95% correct can be achieved for clearly pronounced, isolated words from a chosen small vocabulary (the digits, for instance) spoken by a few chosen talkers. Better results have been attained for one talker. Performance has gone down drastically as the vocabulary was expanded, and appreciably as the number and variety of talkers were increased. . . . performance will continue to be very limited unless the recognizing device understands what is being said with something of the facility of a native speaker (that is, better than a foreigner who is fluent in the language).[5]

This sounds very bleak. By now you should have some idea of why it does sound bleak—why there are so many difficulties. Actually, it is difficult for a human to "read" a spectrogram if he doesn't know the language, the speaker, and even what was said. Language is filled with redundancies which enable a human to "decode" a very noisy or distorted utterance. We understand what is said to us because of our linguistic knowledge. The difficulty of programing a computer with the same linguistic competence speakers possess and the ability to use this knowledge in comprehending the message is enormous.

The speech signal is not physically divided into phonemes. Our ability to "segment" the signal arises from our knowledge of the grammar, knowing what to consider important, what to ignore, how to pair certain sounds with certain meanings, what sounds or words may be "deleted" or "pushed together," when two different speech signals are linguistically "the same" and when two similar signals are linguistically "different." The difficulty may be illustrated by recalling how hard it is for a nonspeaker of French even to divide an incoming French speech signal into separate words, let alone separate phonemic segments.

[5] J. R. Pierce, "Whither Speech Recognition?" *Journal of the Acoustical Society of America,* Vol. 46, pp. 1049–1050 (1969).

Yet, despite these problems, research on both automatic speech recognition and speech synthesis proceeds for practical and for "pure-research" motives. We use synthetic speech in many "controlled" perception experiments to find out what features of the speech signal are important for perception. This knowledge then helps us to write "recognition" programs. A machine can only be programed to do what we tell it and can only "know" what we know. Thus we are pushed to learn more, to fill in all our gaps in our knowledge of the communication process. As we gain more knowledge, recognition programs will be improved. "Recognition" research is proceeding along many lines – automatic speech analysis, automatic parsing, semantic programing, and so on. One cannot predict what the year will be – 1984, 2000, 3000? – but one day we may be able to go up to a computer, ask it a question, and get an answer back in what sounds like human speech.

Whether Turing's dream of a thinking-machine ever materializes or not, computers have a place in the field of linguistics, and the limitations of their usefulness will always be proportional to our as yet limited understanding of human language.

If language could just be put into a "mathematical" form, computers would be ideally suited for solving almost any kind of language problem. Mathematicians and linguists have attempted to discover the mathematical properties of language, and this subject will be discussed in the next section.

MATHEMATICAL LINGUISTICS

I admit that mathematical science is a good thing. But excessive devotion to it is a bad thing.

— ALDOUS HUXLEY

. . . mathematics may be defined as the subject in which we never know what we are talking about, nor whether what we are saying is true.

— BERTRAND RUSSELL (1901)

In his book *One, Two, Three . . . Infinity*, George Gamow entertained the following method of producing sentences of English. Let a team of monkeys be trained to peck out strings of letters on typewriters. Gamow predicted that while most of the strings they produced would be nonsense (nonsentences), eventually they would type out such strings as *Humpty Dumpty sat on a wall* and *Linguistics is the scientific study of language.* Given enough monkeys, typewriters, and time, Gamow speculated that all the great works of English literature, past, present and future, all the great (and not-so-great) speeches in English, all the textbooks, personal letters, and messages scrawled on building walls would eventually be produced.

Gamow was correct in thinking of a sentence of a language as a string of symbols, although that is not all that a sentence is. Still, it is not an unreasonable oversimplification to suppose that there is some set of symbols — phonetic symbols, or letters of the alphabet — and that a sentence in a language is just a particular linear combination of these symbols. A language is in this sense the collection of all such special strings of symbols.

When you know a language you know which strings of symbols belong to the language (the sentences) and which do not. Part of what a grammar must do, then, is generate just the correct strings, reflecting the speakers' linguistic knowledge.

Mathematics deals with the manipulation of symbols, and in the 1950s linguists and mathematicians joined forces to see if they could devise a mathematical method of producing (or *generating*) just those strings that belong to a language. The outcome of this endeavor was the formation of a subfield of linguistics called **mathematical linguistics.**

These linguists hoped that research on the mathematical properties of *formal* languages might lead to a greater understanding of the properties of *natural* languages. Formally, they defined a language as a set of "well-formed" sentences and defined a sentence as a string of symbols. Different languages, then, would consist of different sets of sentences, with certain characteristics.

Consider a formal language, for example, in which the sentences consist of strings of any number of *a*'s or any number of *b*'s. This language would have a vocabulary of two items: *a* and *b*. Among the grammatical sentences in this language would be:

> a, aa, aaa, aaaa, aaaaa, aaaaaa, . . .
> b, bb, bbb, bbbb, bbbbb, bbbbbb, . . .

The following strings would be "ungrammatical" in this language:

> *ab, *aab, *aaaaab, *bababa, . . .

Consider another language in which the strings also consist of *a*'s and *b*'s, but in which the "grammatical" or "well-formed" strings always contain an even number of *a*'s and *b*'s, and in which the first half of the string is the same as the second half taken in reverse order. The following would be sentences in this language:

> aa
> bb
> abba
> baab
> abbbba
>
> . . .

Notice that each sentence is composed of an even number of symbols: 2, 4, 6, . . . In a "sentence" like *abba,* the first half (*ab*) is the same as the second half (*ba*), but the symbols are reversed. Similarly, *bbbaaaaaabbb* is a grammatical string in this language with twelve symbols, whose first half (*bbbaaa*) equals its second half (*aaabbb*), but the second half is the *mirror image* of the first. For obvious reasons a language whose sentences consist of this special property is called a *mirror-image* language.

Mathematical linguists constructed "grammars" to generate all and only the sentences of such languages. To do this, they worked with a mathematical device called a **rewriting system.** A rewriting system consists of a set of symbols (called an **alphabet**) and rules by means of which one can start with a single symbol and produce successively larger strings, finally terminating with some finite string of symbols of the alphabet. Such a rewriting system can be thought of as a grammar, and may be illustrated by the **rewrite rules** necessary to generate the mirror-image language described above. (You will notice that the rules look like those discussed in previous chapters.)

This grammar requires three symbols, *a, b,* and *S,* a special symbol called the *start* symbol. The rules are constructed such that by starting with S, strings consisting of *a*'s and *b*'s can be derived. Let one rule be:

Rule 1. S → aSa.

This rule means that the symbol S may be replaced by the three symbols aSa. Let another rule be:

Rule 2. S → bSb.

This rule means that S can be replaced by the string bSb. The grammar requires two more rules:

Rule 3. S → aa.
Rule 4. S → bb.

The sentences of this language are generated as follows:

Start with the start symbol S:	S	
Apply any rule, say Rule 2:	bSb	
Keep applying rules as long as you can.	baSab	(Rule 1)
	baaaab	(Rule 3)

STOP (no rule can be applied).

Thus the rewriting system consisting of the alphabet {a, b, S}, with S as start symbol, and Rules 1–4, is capable of generating the string *baaaab.* Here are several other **derivations:**

S	
bSb	Rule (2)
bbbb	Rule (4)
	STOP

```
        S
       aSa              Rule (1)
       abba             Rule (4)
                        STOP


        S
       bSb              Rule (2)
      bbSbb             Rule (2)
     bbbSbbb            Rule (2)
    bbbaSabbb           Rule (1)
   bbbaaSaabbb          Rule (1)
  bbbaaaaaabbb          Rule (3)
                        STOP
```

The strings *bbbb, abba,* and *bbbaaaaaabbb* all belong to the *language* generated by the rewriting system.

If we continue to generate strings by using this rewriting system, we will see that the terminal strings (the sentences) always contain an even number of *a*'s and *b*'s and that the second half of the string is a mirror image of the first.

It can be proved mathematically that any string that is composed of any combination of *a*'s and *b*'s, juxtaposed (or *concatenated* — strung together) with the identical string in reverse order can be generated by this grammar, or rewriting system. Any such string will be a sentence in this language. For example, a random string of *a*'s and *b*'s might be *aabab*. In reverse order, we have *babaa*. Concatenating these two, we get *aababbabaa*. Here is a derivation of that string:

```
        S
       aSa              Rule (1)
      aaSaa             Rule (1)
     aabSbaa            Rule (2)
    aabaSabaa           Rule (1)
   aababbabaa           Rule (4)
                        STOP
```

It can also be proved that no other kind of string can be generated by this system. Column A gives a list of some of the strings that belong to the language, and Column B a list of strings that cannot be generated and therefore are not sentences in the language.

A	B
abba	abb
aabbaa	baba
abaaba	aaa
bb	abbaa
baaaaaaaaaaaab	baaabb

We see then that the grammar which we have constructed is the correct grammar to generate the sentences of a mirror-image language of this kind: it generates *all* the strings of the mirror-image language, and it generates *only* the strings of the mirror-image language.

The alphabet of a rewriting system may consist of the phonetic symbols necessary to describe the surface strings of a natural language. It may also be the totality of words or morphemes of a language. In Chapter 6 the phrase-structure rules were a rewriting system whose alphabet contained grammatical categories.

Mathematical linguists thought that by studying the intricacies of rewriting systems (we have seen an exceedingly simple example) and learning much about natural language, it would be possible to develop a rewriting system that could generate all and only the sentences of a natural language.

The immensity of this task can be seen by returning to Gamow and his monkeys. He realized that all the monkeys and typewriters in the world would be far too slow to accomplish anything useful in the life-span of the universe. He therefore decided to replace each of the monkeys and its typewriter with a printing press capable of producing 1 quadrillion (10^{15}) symbols per second. This was still too slow, so he decided to let every atom in the universe be such a printing press! Even so, it would still take billions of years merely to produce the known literature in one language, English.

The problem, of course, is that too much nonsense would be produced. Mathematical linguists faced the same problem in working with rewriting systems. Any system that would produce a large number of sentences in a natural language also produced an ungodly number of strings that were not sentences, and any system which produced only sentences did not produce all the sentences. No rewriting system has ever come close to being able to generate a natural language.

Even if this endeavor were successful, linguists would still be dissatisfied. They want a grammar to reflect what a speaker knows about sentences of his language. Besides the ability to distinguish sentences from nonsentences, he knows how the parts of a sentence are interrelated, how different surface strings are related to each other, which sentences are ambiguous and why, and all the things which have been discussed in the previous chapters. A rewriting system can only reflect a fraction of this knowledge.

Whatever mathematical properties languages have, they have not been revealed in any depth by the study of formal languages. Apparently the mathematical properties of natural language are vastly more complex than those of any formal language man has invented and studied. However, one of the mathematical devices for describing formal languages has been "borrowed" by linguists in the writing of phrase-structure rules.

Transformational grammars are basically mathematical systems, but they are much more complex than rewriting systems, which they incorporate as a subpart (phrase-structure rules are such, as we have already pointed out above). The goal of transformational grammarians is to develop a grammar rich enough not only to generate all the sentences of a language and only the sentences, but also to capture the significant relationships between sentences and between elements of a sentence and to "explain" how speakers are able to produce and understand sentences. This goal has not been achieved, though much progress has been made in the past fifteen years. Whether it will be achieved in this century, or in two centuries, is a question that is held open because of the vast complexity, richness, and subtlety of natural language.

SUMMARY

Computers have had some effect on all scientific disciplines. Linguistics is no exception. The field of **computational linguistics** includes the use of these machines for analysis and synthesis of language competence and performance data.

The first major efforts in the new field were aimed at the **automatic machine translation** of languages. Because of the complexities of all languages, and the gaps in our knowledge, efficient, high-quality machine translation has not been achieved to date.

The large memory and high processing speed of the computer make it a useful tool in other linguistic tasks, however. Computers can be used as automatic dictionaries, to process textual materials, and to test grammars that linguists write.

To make computers more useful for dealing with natural languages, programs have been developed by which the deep structure of sentences is recovered from the surface structure. Such programs include **sentence parsing**—the assigning of structures to surface strings—and **transformational parsing**—the recovery of deep structures from such surface structures.

As a step toward Turing's goal of constructing a "thinking machine," linguists and engineers are attempting to "teach" computers to speak and to understand spoken language. Attempts to produce **synthetic speech** by mechanical means—to produce noises which sound like human speech—go back at least two hundred years. The advances in electronic technology and in the understanding of the acoustics of speech production have brought us close to our goal of synthesizing speech sounds. Our knowledge of the important acoustic properties of speech was aided greatly by the development of an instrument called a **sound spectrograph,** which produces a visual display of the physical acoustic signal called a

spectrogram. Acoustic analysis of speech sounds can also be performed by computers.

Automatic **speech recognition** (or "understanding") is a much more difficult task. Humans use their linguistic knowledge to comprehend a spoken message. The physical signal alone is not enough to account for our ability to understand speech. At present, no machine can be programed to contain even a fraction of the knowledge that every speaker has about his language. There is, however, serious ongoing research in this field, which should also help to contribute to our understanding of speech production and perception.

Computers are ideal for working with mathematical systems, since such systems are specified down to the finest detail. Linguists and mathematicians have attempted to discover the mathematical properties of natural languages by studying the mathematical properties of **formal languages.** One basic mathematical device for describing formal languages — **rewriting systems** — has been incorporated into grammars of natural languages as the phrase-structure rules. In addition to such rules it has been shown that the grammars of natural languages require transformational rules. All the formal properties of such rules are not as yet known.

Technological developments are providing linguists with more sophisticated instruments and tools for the study of the properties of natural language and its use. If computers at some future date will be programed to analyze language data, to "understand" human speech, and to answer in spoken language, it will be because men understand more about the complexities of language and language use.

EXERCISES

1. Suppose that the following list of words was to be put into a computer as part of the English entries in a bilingual dictionary. State what information would have to accompany each entry. Example: if one entry were *light,* the following information would be necessary: noun; adjective; verb; adverb; as a noun it can mean illumination in general, or it may be a specific apparatus for illumination; as an adjective it can modify "weight," "color," "degree of difficulty"; as a verb it can mean "ignite," "make bright."

1. pervert	5. scream
2. command	6. you
3. bank	7. trip
4. fight	8. fall

2. Indicate a step-by-step procedure for translating the given sentences (from Chapter 9, Exercise 5). Make each step as simple and concise as possible and thus appropriate as an outline of a computer program for translating the sentences. Example:

Thai:

dèg	khon	níi	kamlang	kin
boy	*classifier*	this	*progressive aspect*	eat

This boy is eating.

Step 1: Delete the "classifier."
Step 2: Translate "progressive aspect" as "is".
Step 3: Add the progressive ending *ing* to the verb that follows *kamlang.*
Step 4: Put the demonstrative "this" before the noun it comes after.

1. French:

cet	homme	intelligent	arrivera
this	man	intelligent	will arrive

This intelligent man will arrive.

2. Japanese:

watasi	ga	sakana	o	tabete	iru
I	*subject marker*	fish	*object marker*	eat	*progressive aspect, first person singular*

I am eating fish.

3. Swahili:

mtoto		alivunja		kikombe		
m-	toto	a-	li-	vunja	ki-	kombe
the	child	he	*past*	break	the	cup

The child broke the cup.

4. Korean:

kɨ	sonyɔn-nɨn		wɨyu-lɨl		masi-ass-ta		
kɨ	sonyɔn-	nɨn	wɨyu-	lɨl	masi-	ass-	ta
the	boy	*subject marker*	milk	*object marker*	drink	*past*	*assertion*

The boy drank milk.

3. Describe the "language" of each of the following grammars (the "language" is the set of grammatical sentences):

1. S → aSa
   S → b

2. S → aSb
   S → ab

3. S → old S
   S → old men snore

4. S → he knows that T
   S → he knows that old men snore
   T → I know that S
   The "start symbol" is S.

4. Write a grammar that generates the following sentences:

1. ab	2. ba
abab	baa
ababab	baaa
abababab	baaaa
. . .	baaaaa
	. . .

3. The children ran.
   The children ran and ran.
   The children ran and ran and ran.
   The children ran and ran and ran and ran.

   . . .

5. The use of "voiceprints" for speaker identification is based on the fact that no two speakers ever talk *exactly* alike. List some of the differences you have observed in the speech of different individuals. What are some of the possible reasons why such differences exist?

6. Can you think of any practical uses for automatic speech recognition and synthesis? For example, one possible use would be in the postal service. Imagine a machine which would sort letters for individual states by being given verbal instructions. The mail clerk could put a letter on a conveyer belt and say "New Jersey," "Nevada," and so on, or "10028," "94619," and so on, and the computer would automatically send the letter to the correct bin. Another example would be in a library where someone could walk up to the computer and say, "Where will I find such and such a book?" and receive the answer "Section P. 3." Think up as many such uses as you can.

References

COOPER, F. S. "Speech Synthesizers." *Proceedings of the 4th International Congress of Phonetic Sciences.* s' Gravenhage, 1962.

DENES, P. B., and PINSON, E. N. *The Speech Chain.* New York: Anchor Books, 1973.

FLANAGAN, J. L. "The Synthesis of Speech." *Scientific American,* Vol. 226, No. 2, pp. 48–58 (Feb. 1972).

FROMKIN, V. A. *The Computer as a Research Tool in the Construction of Models of Linguistic Performance.* Information Processing 68. North-Holland Publishing Co., 1969.

GARVIN, P. L., ed. *Natural Language and the Computer.* New York: McGraw-Hill, 1963.

GHIZZETTI, A., ed. *Automatic Translation of Languages.* Papers presented at NATO Summer School held in Venice, July 1962. Symposium Publications Division, Pergamon Press, 1966.

HAYS, D. G. *Introduction to Computational Linguistics.* New York: American Elsevier Co., 1967.

HAYS, D. G. *Research Procedures in Machine Translation.* Memorandum RM-2916-PR of the RAND Corporation. Prepared for *United States Air Force Project Rand,* 1961.

LADEFOGED, P. "Some Possibilities in Speech Synthesis." *Language and Speech,* VII, 205–214 (1964).

LINDGREN, NILO. "Machine Recognition of Human Language." *IEEE Spectrum,* Part I (March 1965) 114–36; Part II (April 1965) 45–59.

LOCKE, W. N., and BOOTHE, A. D., eds. *Machine Translation of Languages.* Cambridge: The Technology Press of the Massachusetts Institute of Technology; New York: John Wiley, 1955.

PIERCE, J. R., and DAVID, E. E. *Man's World of Sound.* New York: Doubleday, 1958.

Index